BEYOND THE REPUBLICAN REVIVAL

This is the first book-length treatment of both the non-positive and the positive-liberty strands of the republican revival in political and constitutional theory. The republican revival, pursued especially over the last few decades, has presented republicanism as an exciting alternative to the dominant tradition of liberalism.

The book provides a sharply different interpretation of liberty from that found in the republican revival. It argues that this different interpretation is not only historically more faithful to some prominent writers identified with the republican tradition, but is also normatively more attractive. The normative advantages are revealed through discussion of some central concerns relating to democracy and constitutionalism, including the justification for democracy and the interpretation of constitutional rights.

The book also looks beyond republican liberty by drawing on the republican device of sortition (selection by lot). It proposes the use of large juries to decide bill-of-rights matters. This novel proposal indicates how democracy might be reconciled with constitutional review based on a bill of rights. Republicanism is not pitted against liberalism: the favoured values and institutions fit with liberal commitments.

Beyond the Republican Revival

Non-Domination, Positive Liberty and Sortition

Eric Ghosh

·HART·

OXFORD · LONDON · NEW YORK · NEW DELHI · SYDNEY

HART PUBLISHING

Bloomsbury Publishing Plc

Kemp House, Chawley Park, Cumnor Hill, Oxford, OX2 9PH, UK

1385 Broadway, New York, NY 10018, USA

29 Earlsfort Terrace, Dublin 2, Ireland

HART PUBLISHING, the Hart/Stag logo, BLOOMSBURY and the Diana logo are
trademarks of Bloomsbury Publishing Plc

First published in Great Britain 2020

First published in hardback, 2020
Paperback edition, 2022

A catalogue record for this book is available from the British Library.

Library of Congress Cataloging-in-Publication Data

Names: Ghosh, Eric, author.

Title: Beyond the republican revival : non-domination, positive liberty and sortition / Eric Ghosh.

Description: Oxford, UK ; New York, NY : Hart Publishing, an imprint of Bloomsbury Publishing,
2020. | Includes bibliographical references and index.

Identifiers: LCCN 2020024466 (print) | LCCN 2020024467 (ebook) | ISBN 9781509925469
(hardback) | ISBN 9781509925476 (ePDF) | ISBN 9781509925483 (Epub)

Subjects: LCSH: Republicanism. | Liberty.

Classification: LCC JC423 .G439 2020 (print) | LCC JC423 (ebook) | DDC 321.8/6--dc23

LC record available at https://lccn.loc.gov/2020024466

LC ebook record available at https://lccn.loc.gov/2020024467

ISBN: HB: 978-1-50992-546-9
PB: 978-1-50994-466-8
ePDF: 978-1-50992-547-6
ePub: 978-1-50992-548-3

Typeset by Compuscript Ltd, Shannon

To find out more about our authors and books visit www.hartpublishing.co.uk. Here you will find
extracts, author information, details of forthcoming events and the option to sign up for our newsletters.

PREFACE

With Richard Price being a central figure especially in the first two parts of the book, it was difficult to resist for the cover a cartoon by the preeminent eighteenth-century caricaturist James Gillray. A description follows:

> Dr. Price (right), seated in an armchair at a small writing-desk, turns in horror towards a vision emerging from clouds (left): Burke is represented by an enormous spectacled nose … The spectacles support …: 'Reflections on the Revolution in France …' Prices pen drops from his hand; the paper before him is headed 'On the Benifits of Anarchy Regicide Atheism'. … Against his chair leans an open book: 'Treatise on the ill effects of Order & Government in Society, and on the absurdity of serving God, & honoring the King'. Beside it lies a pamphlet: 'Sermon preached Novr 4 1789. by Dr R. Price, before the Revolution Society'. On the wall above Price's head is a picture: 'Death of Charles Ist or, the Glory of Great Britain'; a headsman raises his axe to smite the King whose head is on the block; men with pikes are indicated in the background. After the title is etched 'Vide. A troubled – conscience.' 3 December 1790[1]

The caricature points to the fierce critical reaction to Price's work. This reaction included what David Thomas appropriately characterises as Edmund Burke's bitter and unfair critique of Price's comments on the French Revolution.[2]

While Burke influenced understanding of Price into the nineteenth century, Price has obtained prominence much more recently through the sympathetic treatment he receives in the republican revival, especially within its non-positive-liberty strand. This strand also offers an interpretation of the critical reaction to Price's support for American colonists seeking independence from British rule. Price offered that support 13 years before his comments on the French Revolution. I reveal, however, some misunderstanding of what alarmed these critics. I also provide an alternative reading of Pricean liberty, and suggest that it avoids some of the normative difficulties of the interpretations of liberty favoured in the republican revival. Pricean liberty, I argue, can offer us attractive guidance on political and constitutional matters.

---

[1] The print 'Smelling out a Rat; – or – The Atheistical Revolutionist disturbed in his Midnight "Calculations"' is held by the British Museum (and available in its online collection), and the quotation is from M. Dorothy George, 'Catalogue of Political and Personal Satires in the British Museum', VI, 1938. The title satirises the calculations published by Price on the population of England, etc.

[2] E Burke, 'Reflections on the Revolution in France' [1790] in *Revolutionary Writings*, ed, I Hampsher-Monk (Cambridge, Cambridge University Press, 2014) 1–250; R Price, 'A Discourse on the Love of Our Country' [1789] in *Political Writings*, ed, DO Thomas (Cambridge, Cambridge University Press, 1991) 176–96; DO Thomas, *The Honest Mind: The Thought and Work of Richard Price* (Oxford, Clarendon Press, 1977) ch XV.

Turning to more personal matters, my interest in the republican tradition was sparked by John Braithwaite's republican model of judicial decision-making, which came to my attention when Wojciech Sadurski taught some weeks into Chris Birch's LLM jurisprudence unit at Sydney Law School, a little more than 20 years ago. Wojciech became one of my doctoral supervisors. I very much valued his advice throughout the doctoral thesis and afterwards. His gentle jibe that he hopes I finish the book while he is still alive so he can read the acknowledgment page may not have quickened the process, but I am glad to say: 'Here it is!'

I also thank Margaret Allars, my other doctoral supervisor, for her helpful comments and attention to detail. I have also appreciated advice as to what changes would be helpful for turning the thesis into a monograph that one examiner, Tom Campbell, who unfortunately died last year, provided me. I am also grateful for the comments by my other examiner, Martin Krygier.

The University of New England's Law School has provided a supportive environment for working on the monograph. I especially thank Mark Lunney for his advice and support. More generally, I thank my friends at the university for their encouragement and feedback on draft chapters. At the institutional level, the support entailed through obtaining some periods of research leave was essential for completing work that has fed into the book. I very much appreciate those who have accepted me as a visitor during those periods: Stephen Guest, at University College London, Neil McCormick at Edinburgh University, Adam Tomkins at Glasgow University, Martin van Gelderen at the European University Institute and at the Lichtenberg-Kolleg, and Chris Zurn at the University of Massachusetts. I also appreciate the feedback I've received over the years from academics at those institutions and elsewhere, including at conferences of the Australian Society of Legal Philosophy, for work that has made its way into the monograph. Most recently, that has included Kevin Walton's helpful comments on chapter one. I also thank those working for Hart for being so helpful and efficient, including the commissioning editor Bill Asquith. I also thank the anonymous referees for their helpful comments on the proposal and sample chapter.

Finally, my father, Sailesh Ghosh, a political scientist, had a profound influence on my intellectual development and in shaping my interests while he was alive during my school years. The advice, encouragement and love he provided have not been forgotten. My greatest debt, though, is to my mother, Lucie Ghosh-van de Leur, for her love and support over all these years. I dedicate this book to her.

CONTENTS

1

Introduction

I. Introduction

The revival of the republican political tradition has been a significant development in political and constitutional theory in the last few decades. Some of the world's top intellectual historians have provided provocative interpretations of the republican tradition, while some of the world's top political and constitutional theorists have provided a conceptual framework within which to understand the tradition and its contemporary implications.[1] These writers have especially focused on the tradition's interpretation of liberty.

This book aims to engage with the republican revival critically and constructively. It reveals new flaws in major historical and normative claims made by republican revivers, but also attempts reconstruction. I suggest that historical writers the revivers point to and practices found in some regimes associated with the republican tradition can illuminate important contemporary questions, including questions relating to democracy and constitutionalism. I devote particular attention to insights relevant to constitutionalism.

Elaborating further on the critical and constructive aims of the book, the critical aim is furthered in two main ways. First, the book provides a historical and normative critique of the non-positive-liberty strand of the republican revival. This strand refers to a tradition spanning from ancient Rome to at least eighteenth-century Britain. The value most closely associated with this strand is a non-domination conception of liberty. Liberty as non-domination is diminished by mere vulnerability to arbitrary power. In *Republicanism* (1997), moral and political philosopher Philip Pettit articulated this conception, describing it as the central value of the republican tradition. Through a comprehensive work of political philosophy, he argued that it should be our central value too. In *Liberty before Liberalism* (1998), Quentin Skinner defended a similar interpretation of

---

[1] In relation to intellectual history, see, eg, JGA Pocock, *The Machiavellian Moment: Florentine Political Thought and the Atlantic Republican Tradition* [1975], with a new introduction by Richard Whatmore (Princeton, NJ, Princeton University Press, 2016) and Q Skinner, *Liberty before Liberalism* (Cambridge, Cambridge University Press, 1998). In relation to political and constitutional theory, see, eg, P Pettit, *Republicanism: A Theory of Freedom and Government* (Oxford, Clarendon Press, 1997) and F Michelman, 'The Supreme Court, 1985 Term – Foreword: Traces of Self-Government' (1986) 100 *Harvard Law Review* 4–77.

republican liberty and, through doing so, lent his authority as an intellectual historian to some of Pettit's main historical claims. In articulating a conception of liberty diminished by mere vulnerability to arbitrary power, they both raised important questions about the appropriate approach that should be taken to arbitrary power. Liberty as non-domination has become perhaps the most discussed conception of liberty in the academic literature in the last few decades.

The second main way in which the critical aim of the book is furthered is through a historical and normative critique of the positive-liberty strand of the republican revival. This is the older strand of the revival, which Pettit and Skinner were challenging. With this strand, positive liberty is identified with an active political life, involving virtuous participation. In *The Machiavellian Moment* (1975), intellectual historian John Pocock described a republican tradition spanning from ancient Athens to eighteenth-century Britain and America. This tradition was drawn upon by constitutional scholar Frank Michelman in defending left-of-centre activist interpretations of the US Bill of Rights. It is particularly Michelman's work that I will critique. At the normative level, what is partly at stake here is the neutrality the state should demonstrate towards different conceptions of the good life (or, in short, 'the good'). Should the state promote an active political life on the ground that that life is the most valuable one for individuals to pursue?

The constructive aim of the book is also furthered in two main ways. First, I defend an alternative interpretation of liberty, which is derived from eighteenth-century dissenting minister Richard Price, a central historical figure in the republican revival.[2] Price provided a complex account of liberty, part of which involved a non-domination conception of liberty. I argue that Price's interpretation of liberty as non-domination may provide more attractive guidance on democracy and constitutionalism than Pettit's and Skinner's interpretations. I also draw attention to some aspects of Priceian liberty that have strong affinities with positive liberty. I suggest that some of these 'positive-liberty dimensions' may be more appealing than Michelman's preferred interpretation.

The second way in which I further the constructive aim of the book is by drawing attention to sortition (selection by lot) as a republican device that can be applied to constitutionalism. I defend the possibility of constitutional review based on a bill of rights being undertaken by large juries (described as constitutional juries) rather than by judges. This exploration of constitutional juries is intended to illuminate a central concern relating to constitutionalism. The concern is that democratic values are troublingly compromised by judicial review based on a bill of rights. I argue that constitutional juries offer the promise of reconciling democracy with constitutionalism.

---

[2] R Price, 'Observations on the Nature of Civil Liberty, the Principles of Government, and the Justice and Policy of the War with America' [1776] in *Political Writings*, ed, DO Thomas (Cambridge, Cambridge University Press, 1991) 20–75.

The critical and constructive aims of the book support each other. Most substantially, the alternative interpretation of liberty as non-domination I present emerges through the critiques of Pettit and Skinner. This alternative interpretation does, at the same time, illuminate the interpretations provided by Pettit and Skinner. My defence of constitutional juries also throws critical light upon the republican revival. It leads, for instance, to further reflection on some of the conceptions of liberty discussed in the book.

The book is distinctive in that it discusses the two main strands of the republican revival and historical as well as normative claims made by exponents of each strand. This enables an overview of some of the most important contributions to the republican revival. There is also here a pattern of mutual illumination. To mention a few examples of this, discussing the two strands together throws light on each.[3] Both strands define themselves partly through contrasts between negative and positive liberty. Secondly, the historical and normative claims have close connections. Most importantly, the historical claims of the revivers support the plausibility of their normative claims.

With the book closely engaging with work in the republican revival, it is helpful before describing my arguments further to say more about the revival and also about political and constitutional theory. I will describe the two main strands of the revival in Sections II and III. However, for those familiar with these strands, and who may therefore wish to skip these sections, the accompanying note mentions the main distinction I will refer to.[4] Section IV explains how the three parts of this book relate to political and constitutional theory. With this background, Section V explains, through a chapter outline, the broad arguments of this book. Section VI concludes with some general points about my approach to the republican and liberal traditions.

II. Positive-Liberty Republicanism

I begin this description of the positive-liberty strand by first referring to the distinction between negative and positive liberty made by the liberal philosopher and historian of ideas Isaiah Berlin in the late 1950s.[5] He in fact favoured negative liberty, which he identified with a zone of non-interference. Within positive liberty, he

---

[3] For a different way of characterising strands within the republican revival, see, eg, Y Elazar and G Rousselière, 'Introduction' in Y Elazar and G Rousselière (eds), *Republicanism and the Future of Democracy* (Cambridge, Cambridge University Press, 2019) 1–10.

[4] Sections II and III distinguish between non-positive and positive liberty. Within non-positive liberty, I include negative liberty and liberty as non-domination (which I describe as non-negative to highlight it being undiminished by constraints). I also describe the positive liberty associated with the republican tradition as full-blown positive liberty. This identifies liberty with virtuous political participation.

[5] I Berlin, 'Two Concepts of Liberty' [1958] in *Four Essays on Liberty* (Oxford, Oxford University Press, 1969) 118–72.

accommodated several conceptions of liberty. One conception identifies liberty with political participation. Berlin was concerned that identifying liberty with political participation, or at least the opportunity to share in government, can divert attention from the negative impact political regimes can have on individual liberties. He suggested that the Athenian polis had a highly democratic system of government, but there was little recognition of the importance of protecting individuals against the exercise of state power.

Another conception Berlin accommodated within positive liberty was liberty as rational self-direction. Superstition and ignorance, for instance, could be understood as constraints that prevent individuals from being governed by reason. He was concerned, however, that this identification of liberty with rational self-direction could take a sinister turn. Those with values deemed to be unreasonable could be declared to be suffering from internal constraints. Coercion of those individuals could then be justified in the name of liberty.

Berlin also associated positive liberty with a monistic approach to normative questions. This approach assumes that there can only be one correct answer to moral questions. The monistic approach also assumes that we have an essential nature that we should seek to realise. Most darkly, he associated fascism and communism with this approach.[6] By contrast, the pluralistic approach Berlin favoured suggests that there are a range of reasonable responses to moral questions and it also points to our diversity. This pluralistic approach, Berlin claimed, highlights the importance of negative liberty.

However, around the same time as Berlin, the political theorist Hannah Arendt suggested that experience with fascism and communism pointed to the importance of positive liberty, where this is identified with political participation. She depicted the Athenian polis as one in which citizens participated with diverse others in open discussion and debate on political questions.[7] Through participation, citizens recognise that politics involves conflict between diverse and legitimate interests. By contrast, in political systems where citizens lack the experience of participation, citizens' capacity to form appropriate political judgements is damaged. Isolated, apolitical individuals can be vulnerable to ideologies such as fascism and communism that appear to satisfy a yearning for a sense of belonging and identification with something larger, but which also crush individuals.[8]

Arendt's understanding of the liberty available in the Athenian polis privileges a virtuous political life. In other words, this conception of liberty is so closely tied to the claim that the best life is one of active political participation aimed at the

---

[6] See C Galipeau, *Isaiah Berlin's Liberalism* (Oxford, Clarendon Press, 1994) 108–12.

[7] H Arendt, *The Human Condition* [1958], with an introduction by Margaret Canovan, 2nd edn (Chicago, University of Chicago Press, 1998).

[8] See, eg, M Canovan, *Hannah Arendt: A Reinterpretation of Her Political Thought* (Cambridge, Cambridge University Press, 1992) 54; C Volk, *Arendtian Constitutionalism: Law, Politics and the Order of Freedom* (Oxford, Hart Publishing, 2015) 155–72.

public good that one does not count as free unless one leads this life. I will describe this conception as full-blown positive liberty. It is this conception that is identified with the positive-liberty strand of the republican revival.

Arendt saw a republican tradition based on positive liberty spanning from the Athenian polis to the Italian Renaissance. Pocock, on the other hand, presented a republican tradition based on positive liberty that extended to seventeenth- and eighteenth-century England and to eighteenth-century America.[9] It is a tradition, then, that includes ancient writing that provided justifications for Athenian democracy or republican Rome, Renaissance Italian defences of non-monarchical regimes, seventeenth-century defences of the English common-wealth, eighteenth-century British literature that expressed democratic ideas, and American revolutionary pamphlets. Pocock challenged the assumption that certain prominent seventeenth- and eighteenth-century writing could be associated with liberalism. Instead, the ideal of positive liberty retained its hold on the imagination of political thinkers despite the disappearance of city-states.

The work of intellectual historians that suggested a republican presence in eighteenth-century American thought interested some US constitutional scholars, such as Michelman and Cass Sunstein, for this work raised the possibility of a republican influence in the period when the US Constitution and the subsequent bill of rights were drafted and adopted.[10] Their aim was not to invoke republicanism in constitutional interpretation in an originalist fashion. In other words, the scholars were not claiming that constitutional interpretation by the US Supreme Court should strictly follow the framers' intentions and those intentions reflected a republican ideology. Instead, in articles written in the 1980s, they attempted to bolster left-of-centre ideas, ideas that contrasted with the classical liberalism that originalists found in the Constitution. Republicanism had the advantage that it could be argued that it formed part of America's tradition.[11]

---

[9] See Pocock, *Machiavellian Moment* at 550 for Arendt's influence. For a summary of some of Pocock's ideas, see P Craig, *Public Law and Democracy in the United Kingdom and the United States of America* (Oxford, Clarendon Press, 1990) 318–34. For an overview of republicanism, see R Hammersley, 'Introduction: The Historiography of Republicanism and Republican Exchanges' (2012) 38 *History of European Ideas* 323–37.

[10] Michelman and Sunstein are most strongly associated with this republican revival in constitutional theory, with Mark Tushnet and Bruce Ackerman employing republicanism less extensively: M Tushnet, *Red, White, and Blue: A Critical Analysis of Constitutional Law* (Cambridge, Mass., Harvard University Press, 1988); B Ackerman, *We the People*, vol 1: Foundations (Cambridge, Mass., Belknap Press of Harvard University Press, 1991). See also S Sherry, 'Civic Virtue and the Feminine Voice in Constitutional Adjudication' (1986) 72 *Virginia Law Review* 543–616. Republicanism was also urged by prominent legal scholars who would not be classified as constitutional scholars, eg, M Horwitz, 'Republicanism and Liberalism in American Constitutional Thought' (1987) 29 *William and Mary Law Review* 57–74. Some writers are described as republican although they do not relate their favoured conclusions in a detailed way to republicanism. See, eg, the reference to Tushnet, Perry and Levinson in R Kahn, *The Supreme Court and Constitutional Theory: 1953–1993* (Lawrence, Kan., University Press of Kansas, 1994) ch 7.

[11] On the relationship of republicanism to originalism, see B Friedman, 'The Turn to History' (1997) 72 *New York University Law Review* 928–65, 944. For more general discussion of the American revival,

Michelman suggested that the republicanism found in America may have been based predominantly on negative rather than positive liberty.[12] With the negative-liberty strand, political participation and virtue are associated with liberty not because it is through virtuous political participation that citizens achieve the freedom that comes from greater rationality, but because such participation protects citizens against their government. Nevertheless, it was especially the positive-liberty strand of republicanism that interested scholars such as Michelman and Sunstein.[13] They contrasted the republican insistence upon political participation and dedication to the public good with pluralist politics. The latter is marked by citizen disengagement from politics, with decisions being made through deals between powerful sectional interests.

Michelman and Sunstein sought to defend and guide judicial activism. Focusing here on Michelman, he suggested that rather than being overly deferential to the elected branches of government, Supreme Court judges, due to their insulation from pluralist politics, can represent to the community the conscientious deliberation on the common good that republican liberty is associated with. Judges can also declare rights which protect marginalised groups. Michelman provided a republican slant upon those rights through highlighting their role in enabling those groups to participate more fully in community life. Such participation can prompt and inform moral reflection, and thereby promote rational self-direction. Liberalism, by contrast, fails to emphasise the importance of citizens deliberating together on moral questions.

Political philosophers also revived the republican tradition for contemporary guidance. In *Democracy's Discontent* (1996), Michael Sandel defended republican positive liberty, suggesting that active participation in the community can address a range of contemporary problems such as feelings of alienation and disempowerment.[14] He criticised the liberal ideal of state neutrality between conceptions of the good, arguing that this can only lead to a thin toleration of those conceptions. By contrast, public debate about conceptions of the good can lead to community endorsement of a range of diverse ways of living, including an active political life. Sandel argued that recognising that an active political life is individually beneficial, and does not only have a collective benefit, could also motivate the level of participation that negative-liberty republican revivers

---

see GE White, 'Reflections on the "Republican Revival": Interdisciplinary Scholarship in the Legal Academy' (1994) 6 *Yale Journal of Law & the Humanities* 1–35.

[12] Michelman, 'Traces of Self-Government' 47–8.

[13] See, eg, C Sunstein, 'Beyond the Republican Revival' (1988) 97 *Yale Law Journal* 1539–90, 1548.

[14] M Sandel, *Democracy's Discontent: America in Search of a Public Philosophy* (Cambridge, Mass., Belknap Press of Harvard University Press, 1996). See also M Sandel, 'Reply to Critics' in A Allen and M Regan (eds), *Debating Democracy's Discontent: Essays on American Politics, Law, and Public Philosophy* (Oxford, Oxford University Press, 1998) 319–35. In relation to other political theorists reviving republicanism, see, eg, A Oldfield, *Citizenship and Community: Civic Republicanism and the Modern World* (London, Routledge, 1990) and for further references, W Kymlicka, *Contemporary Political Philosophy: An Introduction*, 2nd edn (New York, Oxford University Press, 2002) 294–99.

favour in order to achieve the collective benefit of security from arbitrary state interference.[15] I turn, then, to negative republican liberty, which I place within the non-positive-liberty strand.

III. Non-Positive-Liberty Republicanism

From the late 1970s, Skinner suggested that republicanism and liberalism both endorsed negative liberty.[16] Drawing especially upon Machiavelli, Skinner argued that the major aim of the republic, expressed through the value of liberty, was to ensure that citizens were free from constraints.[17] Skinner nevertheless argued that republicans attached greater importance than liberals to political participation. They did not do so for the positive-liberty reason that participation represents the essence of liberty, providing citizens with the opportunity to realise their potential as moral, rational beings. Instead, republicans believed that citizens would only be free from constraints – they would only enjoy negative liberty – if a substantial number of them participated in the political life of the community and contributed militarily as well, thereby protecting the community against domestic tyranny and foreign domination. Skinner argued that the republican approach raises for us the question of whether liberalism has focused too much upon individual rights and not enough on the duties that citizens must perform to secure those rights.[18]

Pettit initially followed Skinner in viewing republican liberty as negative.[19] However, in *Republicanism*, he described republican liberty as a non-domination conception of liberty. He argued that it did not fit within Berlin's positive or negative liberty.[20] It was not positive because it was not defined in terms of self-rule. It was also not negative because it was not diminished by interference. Instead, it was diminished by mere vulnerability to arbitrary power. Vulnerability to arbitrary power occurs when others can, without suffering a significant penalty, interfere

---

[15] Sandel, 'Debating Democracy's Discontent' 325.

[16] See, eg, Q Skinner, *Foundations of Modern Political Thought*, vol 1: The Renaissance (Cambridge, Cambridge University Press, 1978) ch 6; Q Skinner, 'Machiavelli on *Virtù* and the Maintenance of Liberty' in *Visions of Politics*, vol II: Renaissance Virtues (Cambridge, Cambridge University Press, 2002) 160–85; Q Skinner, 'The Idea of Negative Liberty: Machiavellian and Modern Perspectives' in *Visions of Politics*, vol II: Renaissance Virtues (Cambridge, Cambridge University Press, 2002) 186–212. The last two are revised versions of essays published in 1983 and 1984 respectively.

[17] For one discussion of Pocock's and Skinner's contrasting interpretations, see D Castiglione, 'Republicanism and Its Legacy' (2005) 4 *European Journal of Political Theory* 453–65. For a critique of Pocock's interpretation of Machiavelli, see V Sullivan, 'Machiavelli's Momentary "Machiavellian Moment": A Reconsideration of Pocock's Treatment of the *Discourses*' (1992) 20 *Political Theory* 309–18.

[18] For a suggestion that this concern especially resonated with an interest in citizenship in political theory in the 1990s, see Kymlicka, *Contemporary Political Philosophy* 284–5.

[19] See, eg, P Pettit, 'Liberalism and Republicanism' (1993) 28 (Special Issue on Australia's Republican Question) *Australian Journal of Political Science* 162–89.

[20] Pettit, *Republicanism* 21–2.

with you on an arbitrary basis (ie, without having to take proper account of your interests). Pettit argued that liberalism's dominant conception of liberty is only diminished by actual interference. Liberal liberty therefore suggests that arbitrary power need only be minimised where there is a significant probability of interference. Consequently, republicanism provides a more stringent ideal when addressing relationships involving subordination. The slave of a benevolent, non-interfering master is simply unfree, from a republican perspective. From a liberal perspective, though, the slave does enjoy some liberty.

Pettit claimed that republican liberty is not only different from the liberal conception of liberty as non-interference. It also contrasts with positive liberty. Republican liberty does not focus on citizens ruling themselves because active participation prompts the normative reflection that enables individuals to achieve rational self-direction.[21] Instead, republican liberty suggests a focus on how the people can constrain the arbitrary power of their rulers. Pettit claims that this value thereby provides a distinctive and attractive approach to democracy and constitutionalism.

In *Liberty before Liberalism*, Skinner accepted Pettit's contention that republicanism favoured a different conception of liberty from liberalism.[22] Skinner actually referred to 'neo-roman' rather than 'republican' thought, but later reverted to 'republican' in deference to terminology used by others.[23] He agreed that republican liberty was diminished by arbitrary power, but he also argued that it was diminished by interference. While Pettit suggested that republican liberty does not fit within the established categories of negative and positive liberty, Skinner described his interpretation as negative. I will use the term 'non-positive' to include Pettit's and Skinner's interpretations of republican liberty.

While positive-liberty republicanism traces to ancient Athens, the non-positive-liberty strand traces to ancient Rome, especially Roman law with its distinction between citizen and slave.[24] Skinner also agreed with Pettit on the contemporary implications of republican liberty, in that republican liberty prompts us to consider whether we are doing enough to address arbitrary power possessed by the state and by private agents.

After the publication of these books, Pettit and Skinner continued to develop their ideas.[25] There have also been other historical and theoretical contributions to this strand of the revival.[26] However, Pettit and Skinner have been the most prominent writers within this strand, with Pettit being especially conspicuous. While

---

[21] ibid 18–19.

[22] Skinner, *Liberty before Liberalism*.

[23] See, eg, Q Skinner, 'Freedom as the Absence of Arbitrary Power' in C Laborde and J Maynor (eds), *Republicanism and Political Theory* (Malden, MA, Blackwell, 2008) 83–101, 84.

[24] *cf* M Edge, 'Athens and the Spectrum of Liberty' (2009) 30 *History of Political Thought* 1–45 for an argument that Athenian liberty was largely negative.

[25] See, eg, P Pettit, *On the People's Terms: A Republican Theory and Model of Democracy* (New York, Cambridge University Press, 2012); Skinner, 'Freedom as the Absence of Arbitrary Power'.

[26] For theoretical work, see F Lovett, *A General Theory of Domination and Justice* (New York, Oxford University Press, 2010) and J Maynor, *Republicanism in the Modern World* (Cambridge, Polity Press,

Skinner has focused mostly on historical claims, Pettit embedded his historical claims within a substantial discussion of political philosophy. Pettit's interpretation has not only received the most attention from political philosophers and constitutional scholars.[27] It also crossed over to practical politics when it was adopted by José Zapatero, who was the Spanish Prime Minister from 2004 to 2011.[28] It provided a new way to challenge inequality, for instance. Pettit had pointed to the grievance of living at the mercy of another, a circumstance plagued by uncertainty and an inability to look the other in the eye.[29]

IV. Political and Constitutional Theory

With this book seeking to contribute to political and constitutional theory, I elaborate here upon these bodies of thought and how they relate to the three parts of the book. The book focuses on constitutional theory when possible in considering the implications of the republican tradition, and I begin with this here.

Constitutional theory is substantially concerned with constitutionalism, where rules and principles enjoying a fundamental status confer and constrain political power. Those rules and principles may be entrenched in a written constitution or found in statute, common law, or custom.[30] A central concern of constitutional theory lies in the potential for such rules and principles to constrain democracy. One aspect of that concern lies in the legitimacy of constraining democracy to a certain institutional form. Sheldon Wolin, for instance, conceived of democracy as rebellious, as tending towards anarchy, while constitutionalism attempts to domesticate democracy through law.[31] While Wolin suggested that constitutionalism is

2003). For a work that is historical as well, see M Viroli, *Republicanism*, trans, A Shugaar (New York, Hill and Wang, 2002).

[27] For applications of liberty as non-domination to judicial review, see H Spector, 'Judicial Review, Rights, and Democracy' (2003) 22 *Law and Philosophy* 285–334; in the UK, A Tomkins, *Our Republican Constitution* (Oxford, Hart Publishing, 2005) and R Bellamy, 'Democracy as Public Law: The Case of Constitutional Rights' (2013) 14 *German Law Journal* 1017–37; and in Australia, G Williams and D Hume, *Human Rights under the Australian Constitution*, 2nd edn (Melbourne, Oxford University Press, 2013). For further references, see P Pettit, 'The General Will, the Common Good, and a Democracy of Standards' in Y Elazar and G Rousselière (eds), *Republicanism and the Future of Democracy* (Cambridge, Cambridge University Press, 2019) 13–40, 14 fn 2.

[28] J Martí and P Pettit, *A Political Philosophy in Public Life: Civic Republicanism in Zapatero's Spain* (Princeton, Princeton University Press, 2010).

[29] Pettit, *Republicanism* 5.

[30] For a broad interpretation of constitutions, see L Kramer, 'The Supreme Court 2000 Term Foreword: We the Court' (2001–2002) 115 *Harvard Law Review* 5–169, 16. See also P Pettit, 'Republican Liberty and Its Constitutional Significance' (2000) 25 *Australian Journal of Legal Philosophy* 237–56, 237–8. For discussion of the historical meaning of 'constitution', see G Maddox, 'Constitution' in T Ball, J Farr and R Hanson (eds), *Political Innovation and Conceptual Change* (Cambridge, Cambridge University Press, 1989); H Pitkin, 'The Idea of a Constitution' (1987) 37 *Journal of Legal Education* 167–9. For the application of a broad meaning in the Australian context, see B Lim, *Australia's Constitution after Whitlam* (Cambridge, Cambridge University Press, 2017) ch 2.

[31] S Wolin, 'Norm and Form: The Constitutionalizing of Democracy' in J Euben, J Wallach and J Ober (eds), *Athenian Political Thought and the Reconstruction of American Democracy* (Ithaca, NY,

inherently undemocratic, a quite different concern is that a particular process for making and amending constitutional rules might be undemocratic.[32]

The most substantial literature in constitutional theory, however, has been prompted by anxiety about the democratic legitimacy of judges interpreting constitutional constraints, especially those found in a bill of rights. These rights are expressed in general language and appear to give judges substantial discretion. The anxiety is most acute where judges exercise strong-form judicial review based on a bill of rights. Decisions delivered in the course of strong-form judicial review cannot be abrogated by ordinary parliamentary legislation, in contrast to decisions made through weak-form judicial review.[33] Instead, a more stringent procedure must be followed, generally because constitutional amendment is necessary. This is not to imply, though, that questions of democratic legitimacy are insignificant when considering weak-form judicial review or, indeed, constitutional law proceedings involving the interpretation of provisions other than those contained in a bill of rights, or administrative law proceedings where a party seeks a declaration that a decision by the executive lacked legislative authority. Nevertheless, my references to 'judicial review' will largely be to judges applying a bill of rights, especially where they exercise strong-form judicial review.

Concern about the democratic legitimacy of strong-form judicial review is often described as the counter-majoritarian difficulty. The counter-majoritarian difficulty has implications for whether judges should have authority to interpret a bill of rights and, if so, whether they should enjoy powers of strong- or weak-form judicial review. How one responds to the counter-majoritarian difficulty also has implications for the desirable scope of judicial review in terms of what rights should be included or found in a bill of rights, how deferential judges should be to the elected branches of government, and how those deciding these cases should be selected. Furthermore, there is a link between the democratic legitimacy of judges interpreting constitutional rules and the broad values that should guide the interpretation of those rules, for some constitutional theorists (including Michelman) seek to vindicate judicial review partly through indicating what values should guide judges in their decisions.[34]

Questions about the democratic legitimacy of judicial review and the values that should inform its exercise also fall, however, within general political theory.

Cornell University Press, 1994) 29–58. The relationship between constitutionalism and democracy at this general level is also discussed in the republican revival. See, eg, M Vatter, 'Political Ontology, Constituent Power, and Representation' (2015) 18 *Critical Review of International Social and Political Philosophy* 679–86. For a discussion of Arendt's approach, see Volk, *Arendtian Constitutionalism* ch 5, s III.

[32] See, eg, C Zurn, *Deliberative Democracy and the Institutions of Judicial Review* (New York, Cambridge University Press, 2006).

[33] See S Gardbaum, *The New Commonwealth Model of Constitutionalism: Theory and Practice* (Cambridge, Cambridge University Press, 2013).

[34] K Whittington, 'Constitutionalism' in K Whittington, R Kelemen and G Caldeira (eds), *Oxford Handbook of Law and Politics* (Oxford, Oxford University Press, 2008) 281–99, 283.

Political theory is partly concerned about legitimate forms of government and the values that the state should pursue. The judicialisation of politics – the reliance on courts to address core public policy questions – is a significant phenomenon of late twentieth- and early twenty-first-century government.[35] The waves of democratisation that occurred since World War II were often accompanied by strong-form judicial review. Furthermore, in the last four decades, weak-form judicial review has been introduced in some Commonwealth countries.[36]

While the next section provides a chapter outline, it is possible here to indicate briefly how this book seeks to contribute to political and constitutional theory. This book's emphasis on constitutional theory is manifest in several ways. Part I's exploration of the attractiveness of liberty as non-domination especially highlights implications for constitutionalism. The constitutional matters considered range from the broad question of what approach should be taken to the dispersion of power associated with constitutionalism, to the more particular question of how to interpret a constitutional right to liberty. Part II's examination of the positive-liberty republican revival focuses on Michelman's attempt to draw from positive liberty implications for US judicial review. Part III considers what insights sortition can generate into the counter-majoritarian difficulty.

In relation to political theory, Parts I and II focus substantially on the major political ideal of liberty. Part I devotes greater attention to Pettit rather than Skinner, since Pettit embeds his account of liberty in a substantial work of political theory. Part II especially focuses on Michelman. Of the constitutional scholars who attempted to revive republicanism, he provided the deepest exploration of liberty both as a historical conception and as a contemporary guiding value. Part III focuses on sortition. There has been increased interest in this over the last few decades, interest that has been tied, for instance, to deliberative democratic theory.

V. Chapter Outline

I will now explain more fully the three parts of the book and what each chapter seeks to do. Part I explores the non-positive-liberty strand of the revival, focusing on liberty as non-domination. This strand of the revival has attracted the most attention in the last few decades, and it is also the strand that I most substantially discuss.

This Part first critiques historical claims about republican and liberal liberty made by Pettit and Skinner (chapters two and three). It devotes significant attention to the period that Pettit and Skinner see as the transition from republican to liberal liberty. This occurred in late eighteenth-century Britain. On the republican

---

[35] R Hirschl, 'The Judicialization of Politics' in K Whittington, R Kelemen and G Caldeira (eds), *Oxford Handbook of Law and Politics* (Oxford, Oxford University Press, 2008) 119–41, 119.
[36] Gardbaum, *The New Commonwealth Model of Constitutionalism*.

side, the most prominent work considered is Price's *Observations*.[37] This was a radical and popular work published in England in 1776. The contrasting conception of liberty, which Pettit and Skinner associate with liberalism, is liberty as non-interference. This, they suggest, was championed by some prominent critics of Price: John Lind, Jeremy Bentham, and William Paley. I argue that Pettit and Skinner have misinterpreted the conceptions of liberty favoured by the historical writers and thereby provide a misleading contrast between liberty as non-domination and liberty as non-interference and between republicanism and liberalism.

The historical critique raises doubts about some normative claims made by Pettit and Skinner. Some of those normative claims are directly addressed in chapters four and five. Chapter four argues that Pettit and Skinner have failed to successfully challenge a liberal approach involving liberty as non-interference. Chapter five presents an alternative interpretation of liberty as non-domination. It is based on Price, and draws on the historical discussion of earlier chapters. I suggest Priceian liberty as non-domination can be a helpful value to consult.

Part II explores positive-liberty dimensions found in the non-positive-liberty and positive-liberty strands of the revival. The conception of positive liberty associated with the positive-liberty republican revival is a narrow one: it concentrates together several ideas that Berlin associated with positive liberty. I described it earlier as full-blown positive liberty. It identifies liberty with virtuous political participation. Accounts of liberty, though, can involve ideas associated with positive liberty without amounting to full-blown positive liberty. Those ideas provide an account of liberty with what I describe as positive-liberty dimensions. Chapter six reveals such dimensions in some historical works relied on by Pettit and Skinner and in Pettit's and Skinner's own interpretations of republican liberty that they present for contemporary guidance. This undermines the sharp contrast they draw between republican liberty and positive liberty.

Chapter seven turns to the positive-liberty strand of the republican revival, through examining Michelman's use of republican positive liberty to defend US judicial review. It first questions his historical claims about republican liberty, focusing on seventeenth-century English writer James Harrington. I then turn to Michelman's adaptation of republican liberty to render it suitable for contemporary guidance. Through considering Michelman's application of his favoured value to judicial review, I point to normative difficulties with it. I suggest that some positive-liberty dimensions found in Price, on the other hand, may be more attractive.

While Michelman's defence of judicial review is unpersuasive, he presented an intriguing vision of a constitutional court understood as virtually representative of the community. Virtual representation works through similarity with the

---

[37] Price, 'Observations' [1776].

community rather than through electoral selection. Michelman failed, however, to persuasively indicate how judges could be viewed as virtual representatives.

Part III explains how Michelman's vision could be realised. This Part shifts from conceptions of liberty to institutional devices associated with republicanism, namely, sortition and the mixed constitution. I attempt to use these devices to throw light upon constitutionalism. This attempt involves defending the idea of constitutional juries interpreting a bill of rights. Constitutional juries could realise Michelman's hope that a constitutional court could be perceived as involving virtual representatives of the people.

Chapter eight lays the historical foundation for my defence of constitutional juries as a republican device. I connect constitutional juries to the Athenian People's Court, and point to the republican association of sortition with democracy. I then turn to normative foundations, through considering values that should inform the assessment of institutional arrangements. I consider, for instance, the tension between sortition and liberty as non-domination. I finally turn to empirical foundations, with reference to experience with deliberative polls.

Chapter nine makes the case for constitutional juries. It does so by proposing and defending an Australian Citizens' Court involving such juries. If it is accepted that such a proposal may well be feasible, this raises a new concern about the democratic legitimacy of judicial review, and also throws light on some arguments used in supporting and opposing judicial review. My defence also draws on ideas and values considered earlier in the book. For instance, the chapter explains how having constitutional interpreters as virtual representatives connects to positive liberty. The connection is not to Michelman's interpretation of positive liberty, where liberty is identified with participation. The connection instead lies in affirming Price's positive-liberty dimension of democratic status. Constitutional juries would provide a powerful affirmation of the capacity of citizens to determine questions of justice when provided with appropriate incentives and opportunities to do so.

The final (and tenth) chapter concludes with some general observations about the republican revival and what I have sought to achieve.

VI. Conclusion

It will become apparent that the republican revival has leached out diversity in the writers it associates with republicanism and liberalism. This book does not attempt to confirm a republican tradition spanning from ancient Greece to eighteenth-century Britain and America that unites over a commitment to a core value or institutional feature. It does not, then, attempt to resolve disputes over whether republicanism should be identified with certain core values found in ancient Greek or Roman thought or practice and which influenced later writers defending somewhat democratic ideas. There is dispute over what these core values are. Eric

Nelson, for instance, has suggested that the division between Greek and Roman republican thought is best understood in terms of justice rather than liberty.[38] Iseult Honohan points to a range of conceptions of liberty within the republican tradition.[39] Bernard Manin identifies the republican tradition not with a core value but with the institutional practice of sortition.[40]

Furthermore, there is disagreement over whether republicanism should be associated with Athens, with Rome, or with both, and whether it extends to Renaissance Italy including Machiavelli, or with Machiavelli representing a rupture to the tradition so that one should sharply distinguish ancient from modern republicanism.[41] There is disagreement over whether the tradition extends to seventeenth- and eighteenth-century Britain, for instance, and to America.[42] There is also disagreement that stems from whether 'the republic' that the tradition defends should be restricted to non-monarchical regimes or regimes with a mixed constitution that includes monarchical and popular components.[43] Rachel Hammersley has suggested that republicanism should be treated 'not as a tradition with fixed characteristics, but rather as analogous to a living language containing distinct varieties sharing only family resemblances, albeit no more accidentally than members of a real family'.[44]

Liberalism is squarely in focus in this book as well. The republican revivers I discuss contrast republicanism with liberalism. The liberal tradition too is contested. While liberalism is associated with giving primacy to individual liberty, there is dispute over how liberty should be defined and, indeed, over its primacy at a theoretical level, with alternatives including utility and equality.[45]

This book focuses on certain claims by republican revivers as well as drawing on Manin's discussion of republicanism and sortition. It discusses only a few historical writers. The republican revival looks to writing articulating ideas supportive of, for instance, ancient Athenian democracy, republican Rome,

---

[38] E Nelson, *The Greek Tradition in Republican Thought* (Cambridge, Cambridge University Press, 2004).

[39] I Honohan, *Civic Republicanism* (New York, Routledge, 2002).

[40] B Manin, *The Principles of Representative Government* (Cambridge, Cambridge University Press, 1997) 42.

[41] See, eg, P Rahe, 'Situating Machiavelli' in J Hankins (ed), *Renaissance Civic Humanism: Reappraisals and Reflections* (Cambridge, Cambridge University Press, 2000) 270–308. For the claim that Machiavelli does not fit at all within republicanism, see J McCormick, *Machiavellian Democracy* (New York, Cambridge University Press, 2011).

[42] For discussion of the republican influence in seventeenth- and eighteenth-century Britain, see, respectively, V Sullivan, *Machiavelli, Hobbes, and the Formation of a Liberal Republicanism in England* (Cambridge, Cambridge University Press, 2004) and M Philp, 'English Republicanism in the 1790s' (1998) 6 *Journal of Political Philosophy* 235–62. On America, see D Rodgers, 'Republicanism: The Career of a Concept' (1992) 79 *Journal of American History* 11–38.

[43] See, eg, D Wootton, Review of *Republicanism: A Shared European Heritage* edited by M van Gelderen and Q Skinner (2005) 120 *English Historical Review* 135–39.

[44] Hammersley, 'Introduction' 336–7.

[45] On the latter, see, eg, R Dworkin, *Sovereign Virtue: The Theory and Practice of Equality* (Cambridge, Mass., Harvard University Press, 2000) ch 3.

somewhat democratic regimes in Renaissance Italy, and the English republic.[46] However, with this capacious approach, the sheer diversity of regimes and writing supporting such regimes makes it difficult to identify fixed characteristics, to use Hammersley's term. That task is easier with liberalism. Liberalism is understood here as a tradition with a commitment, for instance, to certain freedoms such as of conscience, religion and speech, extending to tolerance towards a diverse range of conceptions of the good, and a commitment to limited and representative government, the rule of law and a significant place for the free market.

This book endorses republican and liberal ideas. My attempt to draw on the Athenian People's Court can be described as an attempt to draw on a republican institution. The constitutional juries I propose are envisaged to promote liberal rights. My engagement with Price derives from an examination of the republican revival. However, I suggest that Priceian liberty as non-domination fits well with Shklar's liberalism of fear, and Priceian moral liberty fits well with a perfectionist strand of liberalism. The title of the book, *Beyond the Republican Revival*, is partly intended to indicate that the claims pursued arise from engagement with republicanism but are consistent with liberalism.[47]

---

[46] For an attempt to redress lack of attention to continental republican writers, see M van Gelderen and Q Skinner (eds), *Republicanism: A Shared European Heritage*, vol. 1: Republicanism and Constitutionalism in Early Modern Europe (Cambridge, Cambridge University Press, 2002).

[47] There is a similarity here with Sunstein, 'Beyond the Republican Revival'.

PART I

Liberty as Non-Domination

2

Pettit's Narrative of the Eclipse of Republican Liberty

I. Introduction

Philip Pettit's book, *Republicanism*, is the most influential work of the non-positive-liberty strand of the republican revival.[1] Pettit provided here a new interpretation of two political traditions, republicanism and liberalism, and argued that his new interpretation of republican liberty offers more attractive political guidance than the dominant liberal conception of liberty. Pettit subsequently defended his interpretation of republicanism in a series of books and articles, with the most substantial being *On the People's Terms*.[2]

He describes republican liberty as a non-domination conception of liberty. It is only diminished by arbitrary power, not by interference. It thereby contrasts with liberty as non-interference, which he describes as the main liberal conception of liberty. Pettit argues that republican liberty was so thoroughly eclipsed by liberal liberty that it largely disappeared from view. Furthermore, it may have been eclipsed partly because it targeted more sharply the evil of arbitrary power. Pettit argues that liberal liberty only attained currency through its assertion in late eighteenth-century Britain by John Lind, Jeremy Bentham and William Paley. They used the non-interference conception of liberty to oppose radical democratic demands that invoked republican liberty. The most prominent writer making such demands was Richard Price. Republican liberty also sat uncomfortably with other relationships of subordination, such as in employment, and this could also have contributed to its demise.

Pettit's account of the eclipse of republican liberty is presented in *Republicanism* and reiterated in *On the People's Terms*.[3] The narrative supports his case for equating liberty as non-domination with republicanism and liberty as non-interference

---

[1] P Pettit, *Republicanism: A Theory of Freedom and Government* (Oxford, Clarendon Press, 1997).

[2] P Pettit, *On the People's Terms: A Republican Theory and Model of Democracy* (New York, Cambridge University Press, 2012).

[3] This narrative is also reiterated in F Lovett, 'Non-Domination' in D Schmidtz and C Pavel (eds), *The Oxford Handbook of Freedom* (Oxford, Oxford University Press, 2018) 106–20, 117 and in discussion aimed at a more popular audience: P Pettit, *Just Freedom: A Moral Compass for a Complex World* (New York, WW Norton & Co, 2014) 13–16.

with liberalism. It also supports his argument that liberty as non-domination is significantly more radical than liberty as non-interference. Indeed, it suggests that liberty as non-interference is tainted by the possibility that it may well have been adopted partly to avert attention from important forms of subordination. The narrative suggests that Pettit has indeed uncovered a significant interpretation of liberty, one that unsettles established understandings of republicanism and liberalism, and which may provide us with a challenging and attractive ideal.

This chapter argues, however, that Pettit's narrative is flawed.[4] The rival conceptions of liberty that were urged at that time cannot be captured satisfactorily through non-domination and non-interference conceptions of liberty. The writers Pettit identifies as opponents of Price's non-domination conception of liberty were instead reacting substantially to a positive-liberty dimension found in Price: Price identified liberty with the franchise. Furthermore, Price's opponents did not focus upon liberty as non-interference.

Pettit's narrative is embedded in an account that makes other historical claims, including the existence of a republican tradition that spans from ancient Rome to at least eighteenth-century Britain and which shared liberty as non-domination as its core value. Some of Pettit's claims have been challenged. For instance, the helpfulness of his characterisation of republicanism has been questioned. Should the republican tradition be associated with a different conception of liberty or several conceptions?[5] Instead of focusing on conceptions of liberty in understanding the tradition, should the focus instead be on arguments about liberty, such as how liberty is best secured?[6] Or should republicanism be treated as a language through which diverse concerns were expressed?[7] Pettit's characterisation of liberalism as substantially centred on liberty as non-interference, in contrast to liberty as non-domination, has also been questioned. It has been argued, for instance, that the non-domination conception of liberty is found in the work of important liberals.[8]

The critiques, however, have not focused on Pettit's narrative of the eclipse of republican by liberal liberty. Focusing on this narrative is not only helpful in casting critical light on Pettit's historical account. It also provides helpful material for

---

[4] This chapter is a significantly revised and extended version of E Ghosh, 'From Republican to Liberal Liberty' (2008) 29 *History of Political Thought* 132–67.

[5] For reference to autonomy instead, see R Dagger, '*Republicanism* Refashioned: Comments on Pettit's Theory of Freedom and Government' (2000) 9(3) *The Good Society* 50–3, 52; R Dagger, *Civic Virtues: Rights, Citizenship, and Republican Liberalism* (New York, Oxford University Press, 1997). For reference to several conceptions, see I Honohan, *Civic Republicanism* (New York, Routledge, 2002). See also JGA Pocock, 'Afterword' [2003] in *The Machiavellian Moment: Florentine Political Thought and the Atlantic Republican Tradition*, 2nd edn (Princeton, NJ, Princeton University Press, 2016) 553–83.

[6] P Mouritsen, 'Four Models of Republican Liberty and Self-Government' in I Honohan and J Jennings (eds), *Republicanism in Theory and Practice* (London, Routledge, 2006) 17–38. See also M Canovan, 'Two Concepts of Liberty – Eighteenth-Century Style' (1978) 2 *The Price–Priestley Newsletter* 27–43.

[7] See, eg, M Philp, 'English Republicanism in the 1790s' (1998) 6 *Journal of Political Philosophy* 235–62.

[8] C Larmore, 'Liberal and Republican Conceptions of Freedom' (2003) 6 *Critical Review of International Social and Political Philosophy* 96–119. See below ch 3, s IVC.

chapter three's critique of Skinner, chapter four's normative critique of liberty as non-domination and chapter five's reconstruction of liberty as non-domination, based on Price.

I begin in the next section with a description of Pettit's interpretation of republican liberty and his account of its eclipse by liberal liberty. My examination of the approaches to liberty adopted by the protagonists in Pettit's narrative starts in Section III, with Price. Price is the main republican figure in Pettit's narrative. Sections IV–VI discuss, respectively, Lind, Bentham and Paley: they are the writers Pettit associates with the rejection of republican liberty in favour of liberal liberty in the 1770s and 1780s. Section VII extends the discussion to the last decade of the eighteenth century and into the nineteenth century, and also from constitutional to social questions, in particular, employment relations. The final section sums up conclusions reached and indicates their implications for understanding republican and liberal liberty more generally.

II. Pettit's Account

I start, then, with a description of Pettit's account of republican liberty and its eclipse in late eighteenth-century Britain. I draw mostly on Pettit's *Republicanism*, but I also refer to *On the People's Terms*.

Republicanism takes the republican tradition to have originated in classical Rome and to have been resurrected in the Renaissance, especially in the northern Italian republics, featuring powerfully in the writing of Machiavelli.[9] The tradition also 'had a particular salience in the Dutch Republic, during the English Civil War, and in the period leading up to the American and French Revolutions'.[10] The tradition was unified partly by support for an empire of law rather than an empire of men, a mixed constitution, in which different powers serve to check and balance each other, and a regime of civic virtue, under which people are disposed to serve, and serve honestly, in public office.[11]

Pettit claims, however, that the most important unifier of the tradition lay in its espousal of a non-domination conception of liberty. With this conception, the mere existence of arbitrary power diminishes liberty. Arbitrary power exists to the extent to which someone has a capacity to interfere with an agent without being forced to track those interests of the agent that are consistent with the common interest.[12] Interference involves worsening the agent's choice situation.[13]

Pettit suggested in *Republicanism* that where an agent with arbitrary power interferes, the act of interference can be described as procedurally arbitrary even

---

[9] Pettit, *Republicanism* 19.
[10] ibid.
[11] ibid 20.
[12] ibid 55. Ch 4, s II below elaborates on Pettit's analytical understanding of republican liberty.
[13] ibid 53.

if the interference reflects those interests of the agent that are consistent with the common interest. If the interference actually fails to properly reflect these interests, the interference is also substantively arbitrary. However, Pettit now avoids referring to arbitrariness at least partly because of its multiple meanings.[14] He now refers to 'uncontrolled interference' for procedurally arbitrary interference. I will follow this terminology. However, I will describe substantively arbitrary interference as 'unjustified interference'. I will also continue to refer to 'arbitrary power' even though Pettit now refers to 'alien control': the term 'arbitrary power' is well established in the literature. 'Alien control' is also a little different. In *Republicanism*, there is no arbitrary power where the power-holder is forced to track the agent's interests that are consistent with the common interest. In *On the People's Terms*, there is no alien control when the power-holder is forced *by the agent* to track the agent's interests. Admittedly, the practical implications of this difference do not seem large, since the goal of no alien control is qualified to the extent necessary to give other agents a share in controlling decisions that affect them as well.[15]

In summary, interference by an agent with arbitrary power is 'uncontrolled interference'. Where that interference goes against the interests of the person affected that are consistent with the common interest, there is 'unjustified interference'. However, liberty as non-domination is only diminished by vulnerability to arbitrary power; it is not additionally diminished by actual interference. While I generally describe liberty as non-domination as diminished by arbitrary power, a nuance can be added: this conception can also be diminished by alien control. Liberty as non-domination can accommodate different understandings of the power that diminishes it.

Pettit contrasts liberty as non-domination with positive and negative liberty. He refers to Berlin's association of positive liberty with conceptions that identify liberty with individuals being ruled by their own reason, or identify liberty with political participation due to the fulfilment and/or sense of belonging that such participation allegedly brings.[16] Liberty as non-domination does not require the self-mastery obtained when the individual is ruled by reason, nor is it identified with political participation. The primary focus of republicans in relation to political participation was on avoiding evils associated with interference.[17]

Pettit argues, though, that the republican emphasis on avoiding interference came out of a belief not in liberty as non-interference but in liberty as non-domination.[18] He provided two supporting reasons. First, liberty is cast in terms of an opposition between citizen and slave. Republicans understood this primarily as a difference in status: the citizen enjoys the status of not being subject to

---

[14] Pettit, *On the People's Terms* 58.
[15] ibid 167. This is discussed further in ch 4, s VIA.
[16] Pettit, *Republicanism* 17–19.
[17] ibid 27.
[18] ibid 31.

the arbitrary power of another. The citizen–slave distinction did not turn on whether one was interfered with: a slave could have a non-interfering master. The second reason for supporting a republican belief in liberty as non-domination rather than as non-interference is that republicans viewed properly constituted law (ie, law passed by a regime that was appropriately democratic) as constitutive of liberty.[19] While the law does interfere with citizens, it does not diminish their liberty at all.

Liberty as non-interference, however, became dominant within nineteenth-century British liberalism. This liberal conception of liberty is only diminished by actual interference. Adherents of liberal liberty can also be concerned about arbitrary power, since arbitrary power can make actual interference more likely. It is, though, only the non-domination conception of liberty that is directly diminished by arbitrary power.[20] It is diminished even when there is very little prospect of interference. Pettit suggests that republicans recognised that arbitrary power is damaging even in the absence of interference.[21]

I will describe the damage caused by arbitrary power in the absence of actual interference as 'power damage', in contrast to 'interference damage', which is the damage caused by actual unjustified interference. The power damage that Pettit points to includes uncertainty, the need to be deferential towards those who possess arbitrary power, and having an inferior social status.[22] I will also describe Pettit's liberty as non-domination as power-centred: it focuses on arbitrary power. By contrast, liberty as non-interference is probabilistic: it focuses on the probability of interference. Adherents of this value were especially concerned about unjustified interference.

Thus, while Pettit points in relation to political participation to a republican emphasis on interference damage in distinguishing liberty as non-domination from positive liberty, he points to power damage when distinguishing liberty as non-domination from liberty as non-interference. It would seem, then, that when republicans emphasised interference damage, they were focusing on what for them was a secondary evil; they were not endorsing liberty as non-interference.[23] The primary evil was vulnerability to arbitrary power. The main contrast, it seems, between the two conceptions is that liberty as non-domination recognises power damage while liberal liberty only recognises interference damage.

One implication of republican liberty, according to Pettit, is that this value conveys a deeper concern to secure people from arbitrary power. The liberty of a person is inversely related to the arbitrary power that others enjoy over that person. This sensitivity to arbitrary power provides additional support for democracy.

---

[19] ibid 35.
[20] ibid 34.
[21] ibid 85.
[22] ibid 86–7.
[23] See also P Pettit, 'Keeping Republican Freedom Simple: On a Difference with Quentin Skinner' (2002) 30 *Political Theory* 339–56.

While benevolent rule might do well in minimising unjustified state interference, it does not diminish the state's arbitrary power.[24]

A second implication of republican liberty is lesser scepticism of state intervention. Under liberal liberty, any constraint imposed by the state necessarily involves some diminution of liberty even if that diminution is offset by the positive consequences of that intervention.[25] By contrast, constraints imposed by a state whose power is properly checked do not diminish republican liberty at all.

Pettit claims that these contrasts between republican and liberal liberty were reflected in actual debate. Republican liberty was adhered to by supporters of republican government, ie, government that, at that time, would have been relatively democratic. By contrast, the non-interference conception was employed in seventeenth-century England by Thomas Hobbes and Robert Filmer in supporting authoritarian rule.[26] Pettit says, though, that the non-interference conception of liberty only attained popular currency after it was reiterated in the 1770s and 80s by writers opposed to American independence.[27]

It is Pettit's claims about the use of liberty in late eighteenth-century debates that are the focus of this chapter.[28] Price was the major figure on the republican side. Pettit mentions that Price employed republican liberty in claiming that the British political system rendered American colonists and the disenfranchised in Britain unfree.

According to Pettit, one writer on the side of the non-interference conception of liberty was Lind. Lind denied Price's claim that the American colonists were in a state of slavery.[29] Instead, the colonists were in a similar position to people in Britain. Lind argued that the legitimacy of British rule over America should be determined by considering its impact on the security or happiness of the colonists.[30] Lind was particularly influenced by the interpretation of liberty favoured by Bentham, who also opposed American independence. Bentham understood liberty as the absence of interference.[31] Indeed, Pettit suggests that perhaps Bentham did the most to establish this conception of liberty.[32]

Pettit says that it was Paley, though, who articulated most clearly the case for liberty as non-interference. Paley made three criticisms of republican liberty.[33] First, republican liberty confused liberty with security: it made liberty to consist not merely in the exemption from constraints but in being free from the danger

---

[24] See Pettit, *Republicanism* 31–5.
[25] ibid 148–9.
[26] ibid 37–8.
[27] ibid 41–5.
[28] Hobbes is discussed below in ch 3, s IVB.
[29] J Lind, *Three Letters to Dr Price* (London, T Payne, J Sewell, and P Elmsly, 1776) referred to in Pettit, *Republicanism* 42.
[30] Pettit, *Republicanism* 43.
[31] ibid 44.
[32] ibid 45.
[33] See W Paley, *The Principles of Moral and Political Philosophy* [1785], Forward by DL Le Mahieu (Indianapolis, Ind., Liberty Fund, 2002). Paley is discussed in Pettit, *Republicanism* 45–9.

of having constraints imposed. Secondly, its hyperbolic talk of liberty and slavery was scientifically less satisfying: such talk was not conducive to recognising that there are degrees of liberty. Thirdly, republican liberty was overly demanding.

Pettit suggests that the liberal ideal of equality may have made republican liberty appear overly demanding. Premodern republican thought had assumed that only a small elite of males could enjoy liberty.[34] However, if everyone was entitled to republican liberty, this would have sat uneasily with the subjection experienced by employees (who were seen as servants under the will of their masters) and women (who were subject to the will of their husbands).

Pettit says that the demanding nature of republican liberty when it was combined with equality might partly explain why republican liberty 'lost its place in the work of Bentham and Paley and, later, in the work of those who would have claimed the new name of liberal'.[35] The idea of securing a non-dominated status for every adult might well have seemed a fantasy to thinkers who took for granted the subordinate status of employees and women. Bentham and Paley's goal of utility, on the other hand, required the reduction of many forms of interference, but it would not necessarily have required that everyone should be free from the arbitrary will of others. Pettit says, 'The considerations which weighed with Paley in embracing liberty as non-interference must have weighed also with others of his ilk in the years that followed.'[36] This notion of liberty rapidly took hold among those who described themselves as liberal, but it did so with little discussion.[37]

Pettit says that the liberal tradition emerged towards the end of the eighteenth century and became established in the nineteenth century. It shares with republicanism the presumption that it is possible to organise a viable state and civil society on a basis that transcends many religious and related divides.[38] However, in most of its influential varieties, liberalism is associated with the non-interference conception of liberty and, consequently, with the assumption that:

> there is nothing inherently oppressive about some people having dominating power over others, provided they do not exercise that power and are not likely to exercise it. This relative indifference to power or domination has made liberalism tolerant of relationships in the home, in the workplace, in the electorate, and elsewhere, that the republican must denounce as paradigms of domination and unfreedom.[39]

On the People's Terms maintains this narrative.[40] Like in the earlier book, Pettit mentions some qualifications to his historical claims. While *Republicanism* notes that there may be objection to his distinction between republicanism and liberalism, *On the People's Terms* mentions in a footnote that there may be some merit in

[34] Pettit, *Republicanism* 48.
[35] ibid 49.
[36] ibid.
[37] ibid 49–50.
[38] ibid 8.
[39] ibid 9.
[40] See Pettit, *On the People's Terms* 9. See generally at 8–10.

describing his approach as republican liberalism or liberal republicanism.[41] Both books also suggest that if the historical claims are not accepted, the philosophical claims remain.[42] Nevertheless, the later book recognises that the historical claims support the 'intellectual plausibility' of the philosophical claims.[43] The later book does contain the qualification that some of those he describes as adherents of liberty as non-interference might support liberty as non-domination or positive liberty, but this qualification is largely relegated to footnotes.[44]

In summary, Pettit's narrative of the eclipse of republican by liberal liberty points to the demandingness of republican liberty when applied to relationships of subordination. This supports his contrast between these conceptions of liberty. That contrast can be captured in a few points:

1. republican liberty is only diminished by vulnerability to arbitrary power, with interference being only a secondary affront to liberty;
2. liberal liberty is only diminished by interference;
3. republican liberty is a more radical value: it targets arbitrary power even where there is little prospect of interference; and
4. republican liberty's targeting of arbitrary power involves a recognition of power damage, while liberal liberty only captures interference damage.

III. Price

My examination of the historical writers commences with Price. He was the major foil for Lind, Bentham and Paley. Price is also one of the writers Pettit relies most upon in articulating republican liberty.[45]

In understanding Price, some background is helpful. John Reid says, 'In the eighteenth century vocabulary of Anglo-American politics and law, no term invoked more emotions than liberty ... It was a term on everyone's lips, flowing from everyone's pen, and appealed to by supporters of every political position.'[46] In the first half of the century, disgruntled politicians and a small core of writers argued that the principles of the Glorious Revolution of 1688 had been betrayed by the government.[47] They argued that liberty and the common good were threatened

---

[41] Pettit, *Republicanism* 10, Pettit, *On the People's Terms* 11, fn 8.

[42] Pettit, *Republicanism* 10–11. See also Pettit, *On the People's Terms* 19.

[43] Pettit, *On the People's Terms* 19.

[44] See ibid 16, including fn 17 and 17 fn 18.

[45] Pettit, *Republicanism* 27, fn 2.

[46] J Reid, *The Concept of Liberty in the Age of the American Revolution* (Chicago, University of Chicago Press, 1988) 11 referring to the passage that appears in R Price, 'Observations on the Nature of Civil Liberty, the Principles of Government, and the Justice and Policy of the War with America' [1776] in *Political Writings*, ed, DO Thomas (Cambridge, Cambridge University Press, 1991) 20–75, 23.

[47] See, eg, P Miller, 'Introduction' in J Priestley, *Political Writings* ed, P Miller (Cambridge, Cambridge University Press, 1993) xi–xxviii, xi–xii and M Goldie, 'The English System of Liberty' in M Goldie and R Wokler (eds), *The Cambridge History of Eighteenth-Century Political Thought* (Cambridge, Cambridge University Press, 2006) 40–78, 64.

by political corruption, partly due to the existence of parliamentary representatives dependent on the crown. While the Glorious Revolution appeared to represent the triumph of an independent parliament constraining the crown, they argued that the executive was now insufficiently constrained by parliament.

In the second half of the century, friction with the colonies introduced a new element to the debate. The American colonists' complaint of being taxed without adequate representation resonated with the belief of some opponents of the British government that lack of adequate representation was a problem within Britain itself. Only 10 per cent of the male population were enfranchised, for instance, and there were additional distortions in the electoral system.[48] The American colonists' emphasis on individual consent also resonated with the demand for legislative change to achieve greater religious tolerance in Britain. The Test and Corporation Acts excluded from public office those unwilling to take the sacrament according to the rites of the Church of England. Concerns about religious toleration and representation were powerfully expressed by Price, a dissenting minister. Bentham noted that Price's *Observations* was a work of the greatest popularity, reckoning by its sales in 1776.[49] It was also one of the most controversial, going on the number of pamphlets critiquing it.[50]

Price commenced Part I section I of his *Observations* by distinguishing physical, moral, religious and civil liberty.[51] Physical liberty involves the power to command our own actions, so that we are governed by our own will rather than an external will. Moral liberty 'is the power of following, in all circumstances, our sense of right and wrong', so that we are not controlled by our passions.[52] Religious liberty requires the power of exercising that mode of religion that accords with our own conscience. Civil liberty is the power of a state 'to govern itself by its own discretion'.[53]

He said that the one general idea that runs through them all is self-government. Where the power of self-government is restrained, slavery is introduced.[54] These four types of liberty are 'the foundation of all honour, and the chief privilege and glory of our natures'.[55] For example, where there is no religious and civil liberty, man 'is a poor and abject animal, without rights, without property, and without a conscience, bending his neck to the yoke, and crouching to the will of every silly creature who has the insolence to pretend to authority over him'.[56]

---

[48] J Cannon, *Parliamentary Reform 1640–1832* (Cambridge, Cambridge University Press, 1973) 30.

[49] See D Long, *Bentham on Liberty: Jeremy Bentham's Idea of Liberty in Relation to His Utilitarianism* (Toronto, University of Toronto Press, 1977) 55.

[50] R Frame, *Liberty's Apostle: Richard Price, His Life and Times* (Cardiff, University of Wales Press, 2015) 111–13. See also Y Elazar, 'The Liberty Debates: Richard Price and His Critics on Civil Liberty, Free Government, and Democratic Participation' (PhD thesis, Princeton University, 2012).

[51] Price, 'Observations' [1776] 21–2.

[52] ibid 22.

[53] ibid. *Cf* Pettit, *Republicanism* 29, where Pettit states that Price did not define liberty 'by participatory access to democratic controls'.

[54] Price, 'Observations' [1776] 22.

[55] ibid 23.

[56] ibid.

In Section II, Price focused on civil liberty, and mentioned that in 'every free state every man is his own Legislator'.[57] A state is 'free or self-governed ... in proportion as it is more or less fairly and adequately represented'.[58] In such a state, 'Every member ... having his property secure and knowing himself his own governor, possesses a consciousness of dignity in himself and feels incitements to emulation and improvement'.[59]

In Section III, Price turned to foreign domination. He said that the tyranny that occurs where one state is subject to another is worse than the tyranny a domestic population is subject to when there is an internal despot: with a foreign despot, there is none of the fellow-feeling that can be prompted when despots witness the suffering they perpetrate.[60]

In Part II, Price turned more sharply to prosecuting his case against British military attempts to squash the demands of American colonists. It suffices to note here that Price argued that the absolute discretion that the British claimed over the American colonies, in the absence of those colonists enjoying representation in the British Parliament, reduced the colonists to slavery.[61]

It seems, then, that Price's conception of civil liberty requires liberty as non-domination. Price was suggesting that the British claim to be able to make laws binding the colonies involved the assertion of a power that reduced the colonists to slavery. Thus, the mere presence of arbitrary power removes liberty. This seems consistent with Pettit's account.

However, Priceian liberty also requires the power of self-government. Price identified civil liberty with democratic government in his definition of civil liberty. Civil liberty exists where 'every man is his own Legislator'. Priceian liberty does not, though, conform to the republican revivers' understanding of positive liberty, which I also describe as 'full-blown positive liberty'. Focusing on Pettit here, he associates republican positive liberty with valuing democratic government very largely for its role in enabling citizens, through political participation, to develop their moral faculties and perhaps their sense of belonging to a community.[62] Price's emphasis, by contrast, was on the avoidance of unjustified interference. This emphasis on the protective role of the franchise fits well with negative liberty. Price claimed that the end of free government is 'that it secures the liberty of the public against foreign injury ... [and] private injury'.[63] The importance of citizens exercising this right also lies in the avoidance of unjustified interference. Price warned about complacency in the face of arbitrary power.[64] Where there is arbitrary

[57] ibid 23–4.
[58] ibid 25.
[59] ibid 29.
[60] ibid 30–1.
[61] ibid 37–8.
[62] See, eg, Pettit, *Republicanism* 17–19.
[63] Price, 'Observations' [1776] 27.
[64] ibid 30.

power, there is likely interference. Where a state is not free, it is ruled by 'rapacious individuals'.[65]

Price's focus on avoiding unjustified interference as a major advantage of liberty sits uneasily with Pettit's emphasis on power damage when considering republican liberty. Admittedly, Pettit states that republicans emphasised the evil of interference when asserting the importance of a right of political participation. However, this republican emphasis on interference seems in tension with Pettit's claim that the evil of interference was, for republicans, merely a secondary affront to liberty. There is no such tension in Price's account. For him, the primary evil of arbitrary power was the likely unjustified interference that would follow. Price did not emphasise power damage in the absence of unjustified interference, for his emphasis was on likely unjustified interference.

Pettit points to two attributes of liberty as non-domination to support his claim that domination was the primary concern for republicans, not interference. The first attribute is that liberty is cast in terms of an opposition between citizen and slave, and this distinction did not turn on whether one is being interfered with. The second attribute is that interference imposed by a democratic regime does not diminish liberty. These attributes fit perfectly with Price. It is also true that Price did not endorse liberty as non-interference. However, Pettit jumps from not adhering to liberty as non-interference to a concern about power damage. However, Price's concern about unjustified interference resulting from arbitrary power is consistent with an interpretation of liberty that accepts that justified law does not diminish liberty at all. To reiterate, endorsing liberty as non-domination does not indicate that the primary concern was domination rather than interference, be it justified or unjustified. Instead, endorsing liberty as non-domination is consistent with a primary concern with unjustified interference. Sections IV to VI will suggest that the critics of Price were not seeking to shift attention from power to interference damage. Price was emphasising interference damage.

Apart from Price's emphasis on likely unjustified interference, another feature of Price's approach that sits uneasily with Pettit's interpretation is that while Priceian liberty is not full-blown positive liberty, it does have an affinity with positive liberty through its incorporation of a right of democratic participation. I describe this affinity as giving Priceian liberty a positive-liberty dimension. Sections IV to VI suggest that it was Price's identification of liberty with the franchise that caused the greatest concern for Lind, Bentham and Paley. Pettit instead claims that Lind, Bentham and Paley were rejecting a non-domination conception of liberty, in other words, a conception of liberty that is diminished where there is arbitrary power. Pettit also claims they rejected this conception in favour of liberty as non-interference. I will also demonstrate, though, that Pettit has overstated their reliance upon liberty as non-interference.

---

[65] ibid 27.

IV. Lind

Price viewed Lind as his most capable critic.[66] Lind was a pamphleteer whose family had known Bentham's since the 1750s.[67] After significant political experience abroad, Lind returned to London in 1773 and became a pamphleteer for Prime Minister Lord North. Bentham was a largely unacknowledged co-author of some of Lind's pamphlets. Lind began his critique of Price in collaboration with Bentham, but he finished it alone.[68] It is a spirited attack from the outset, describing Price's *Observations* as including 'intemperate ebullitions of misguided zeal' and 'gloomy pictures of a disturbed imagination'.[69] It is also a lengthy critique, but I will focus on points relevant to Pettit's account of the eclipse of republican liberty.

The first two of Lind's *Three Letters to Dr Price* are the most relevant.[70] Beginning with the first letter, one of its principal criticisms is that Price took liberty as a positive idea: it involves 'the power of self-direction or self-government'.[71] Lind suggested, though, that terms such as liberty and self-government were best understood as conveying only negative ideas. He credited an unidentified person for suggesting that liberty is not positive.[72] It was, in fact, Bentham.[73] Lind explained:

> With respect to any particular act, when you say a man is *free*, that he enjoys the power of *Self-direction* or *Self-government*, what is it you mean? Clearly no more than this; that no other agent whatever has, or means to *exercise* the power of constraining him to do, or to forbear that act.[74]

Lind was not challenging here liberty as non-domination and proposing instead liberty as non-interference. Instead, he was challenging what he described as the positive notion of liberty as self-government and proposing instead a conception of liberty diminished by a power of interference where that power constrains self-government. Lind's proposed conception of liberty is similar to Pettit's current interpretation of liberty as non-domination! Lind's suggested conception is diminished by alien control, which occurs where someone has the power to constrain an agent from directing himself or herself.[75]

---

[66] R Price, *Additional Observations on the Nature and Value of Civil Liberty, and the War with America* (London, T Cadell, 1777) xiv–xv. This is from the introduction, which is omitted from the Thomas edition.

[67] Long, *Bentham on Liberty* 51.

[68] P Miller, *Defining the Common Good: Empire, Religion, and Philosophy in Eighteenth-Century Britain* (Cambridge, Cambridge University Press, 1994) 393.

[69] Lind, *Three Letters to Dr Price* i.

[70] In his third letter, Lind did not explicitly refer to liberty. Instead, he challenged Price's claim that American colonists were significantly less secure than the inhabitants of Britain.

[71] Lind, *Three Letters to Dr Price* 15.

[72] ibid 16 fn*.

[73] Long, *Bentham on Liberty* 54.

[74] Lind, *Three Letters to Dr Price* 16.

[75] 'Alien control' was referred to above in s II.

There are, though, two important differences with Pettit's liberty as non-domination. First, Pettit's liberty as non-domination is undiminished where people have the control over decisions that is consistent with the equality of others who are also affected by those decisions.[76] A democratic state, then, may not possess arbitrary power. By contrast, for Lind, arbitrary power will be possessed by any state, since an individual veto is not feasible.

Secondly, Pettit's liberty as non-domination is undiminished by interference. By contrast, Lind was not distinguishing his conception from liberty as non-interference. This is hinted at by Lind not only saying that liberty is diminished by another agent having power, but by an agent meaning to exercise that power. It is confirmed in Lind's elaboration upon his conception, where he says that liberty involves the absence of coercion.[77]

Lind can be understood as favouring a mixed conception that combined liberty as non-domination, involving the absence of alien control, and liberty as non-interference. This mixed conception's attribute of being diminished by justified as well as by unjustified interference was helpful in supporting three criticisms Lind made of Price's approach to liberty. First, he criticised Price's assertion of an inalienable right to liberty. Such a right was not possible since even justified laws that constrain people diminish their liberty.[78]

Secondly, he criticised what he viewed as Price's black-and-white approach to liberty, where one is either free or a slave.[79] This failed to recognise 'intermediate gradations'. Lind attributes this difficulty to Price viewing liberty as 'something positive'. I can add here that with Lind's mixed conception being inevitably constrained by law, it fits well with recognising degrees of liberty: full liberty is unattainable under any regime.

Thirdly, he criticised Price's idea that liberty is the highest value. Lind suggested that this excludes values such as utility.[80] Furthermore, while Price described liberty as 'the chief privilege and glory of our natures', Lind suggested that liberty is also enjoyed by 'the lion that ranges in the wilds of Africa'.[81] This example points to another distinction between Lind's mixed conception and Pettit's liberty as non-domination and liberty as non-interference. For Pettit, liberty can only be enjoyed by people and can only be diminished by human action.

Nevertheless, either of these interpretations of liberty by Lind and Pettit is helpful in challenging Price's understanding of liberty as intrinsically linked to our dignity as humans. That link to dignity is at least a major reason why Price regarded liberty as the highest value. For Price, that dignity is attributable to our capacity for moral liberty, a crucial component in his overall conception of liberty

---

[76] Pettit, *On the People's Terms* 167.
[77] Lind, *Three Letters to Dr Price* 16.
[78] ibid 24.
[79] ibid 25.
[80] ibid 26.
[81] ibid 26–7.

as self-government. Moral liberty is fostered, Price thought, by civil liberty, for this provides security. Civil liberty, through the franchise, also recognises our capacity to govern ourselves.[82] This recognition can itself motivate people to exercise moral liberty. Lind's and Pettit's interpretations of liberty do not require individuals to enjoy Price's moral liberty; they do not require individuals to exercise their moral capacities, the capacities that bring them closest to God.

In his first letter, Lind was discussing liberty in general. In his second letter, Lind suggested definitions of civil or political liberty and civil or political security. These appear to be conceptions that it is appropriate for the state to aim at. While Lind provided definitions of liberty and security, I will describe them as both involving different levels of security. Lind's civil/political *liberty* involves the absence of coercion that citizens enjoy against each other that is secured by ordinary law.[83] I will describe this as 'legal security'. Lind's civil/political *security* is achieved where constitutional arrangements best conduce to enacting laws that maximise utility.[84] I will describe this as 'constitutional security'. Lind says that Montesquieu had this idea in mind when he referred to that 'tranquillity of spirit which comes from the opinion each one has of his security'.[85]

These definitions contrasted with Price's conception of civil liberty. Lind argued that Price's conception was so demanding that it was unachievable. For example, Price's idea of every man being his own legislator suggested a rule of unanimity: if legislation is imposed upon a man who does not consent to it, he is in a state of slavery. Lind pointed out that a rule of unanimity would lead to the dissolution of even very small states.[86]

Lind also claimed that Price's idea of every man being his own legislator had other odd implications. Lind asked whether Price intended to include women. If not, women must be slaves: all those who do not enjoy the franchise are slaves.[87] Pettit points to Lind's query to suggest that Lind was aware of the demanding nature of republican liberty: republican liberty suggested that all who lacked the franchise were in a state of slavery.[88] Pettit suggests that Lind believed that the quality of Priceian liberty which made it too demanding was it being diminished by arbitrary power. Pettit's suggestion is incorrect: Lind understood Priceian liberty in terms of self-government, and it was *this idea* that he thought was overly demanding. Lind said that Price failed to recognise Montesquieu's point that we should not confuse the power of the people with their liberty.[89] Price simply asserted that liberty and security require that power be distributed to the people at large, but he offered no proof of this. However, Lind continued, if we look to experience, such as

---

[82] See quote to above n 59.

[83] Lind, *Three Letters to Dr Price* 67.

[84] ibid 72–3.

[85] ibid 72 fn †. See C Montesquieu, *The Spirit of the Laws* [1748], trans and eds, A Cohler, B Miller and H Stone (Cambridge, Cambridge University Press, 1989) 157 (Book XI, ch VI).

[86] Lind, *Three Letters to Dr Price* 44.

[87] ibid 40.

[88] Pettit, *Republicanism* 48–9.

[89] Lind, *Three Letters to Dr Price* 75. See Montesquieu, *Spirit of the Laws* 155 (Book XI, ch II).

ancient Rome, we see that in no country 'have the people at large had discernment to perceive … any effectual means of guarding against the power and artifices of the few'.[90] Lind suggested, though, that to achieve what I describe as constitutional security, there should be a legislature which is elected for a limited time by a competent number of the people: this is the '*most*, perhaps the *only*, effectual means' of inseparably blending the interests of govern*ors* and the govern*ed*'.[91]

I can now sum up the main differences between Pettit's and my own understanding of Lind's critique of Price. Pettit's account of the eclipse of republican liberty points to demanding features of liberty as non-domination. Pettit mentions that Lind resisted the idea that the American colonists were in a state of slavery due to them being merely vulnerable to the arbitrary power of the Imperial Parliament. Instead of this demanding approach, the focus should be on the impact of British rule. This is suggested by Lind's interest in liberty as non-interference. More generally, the demandingness of republican liberty lay in suggesting that mere vulnerability to arbitrary power, quite apart from any consideration of the likelihood of interference, is damaging – I referred to this as power damage.

Turning to my understanding, Lind did not challenge liberty as non-domination but, instead, liberty as self-government. He favoured a mixed conception involving liberty as non-domination and liberty as non-interference, seemingly unaware that he had combined two distinct conceptions of liberty. He claimed that his favoured conception of liberty is superior to liberty as self-government, but his main interest lay in urging a focus on what I describe as legal and constitutional security: these are the values the state should aim at. Instead of identifying liberty with the franchise, one should consider under what regime legal and constitutional security is best promoted. These forms of security not only safeguard against unjustified interference, but ensure that people do not suffer from feeling insecure (a form of power damage). If Lind had addressed Price's conception of liberty as non-domination, he may first have said that liberty as non-domination is a superior conception of liberty to liberty as self-government. It is, at least, a negative conception of liberty. Secondly, he may have said that liberty as non-domination is an unattainable ideal because individuals cannot be given a veto over legislation. Thirdly, if Lind had addressed Pettit's claim that liberty as non-domination is democratically demanding in the sense of requiring a broad franchise, Lind would have denied this. He would have claimed that the enfranchised masses would be unable to check the power of those they elect.

V. Bentham

Pettit argues that Bentham was perhaps most influential in his assertion of liberty as non-interference. Bentham can be discussed more briefly than Lind

---

[90] Lind, *Three Letters to Dr Price* 84.
[91] ibid 90.

since Bentham did not himself publish a critique of Price. Instead, he contributed to Lind's. Nevertheless, Bentham's manuscripts of the 1780s indicate his likely approach to Price, which differs in some respects from Lind's.

In these manuscripts, Bentham referred to two understandings of constitutional liberty.[92] It can mean constitutional security, that is, security from abuse of governmental power. However, in the 'party sense', it asserts that the measure of security 'is exactly in the proportion as the share which the whole body of the people to be governed possess in the exercise of the powers of government'.[93] Bentham probably had Price in mind here.[94] Bentham, however, doubted the existence of a neat correlation between political participation and security. He thought it a question of probability to be calculated from experience.[95] Extending the right of political participation extends power, and we need to consider whether that power will be used to coerce others.[96]

While Lind was responding to Price's *Observations*, Bentham was writing after Price's *Additional Observations*, in which Price responded to his critics. Price indicated here that his statement in *Observations* that every man is his own legislator, a statement that had 'occasioned no small part of the opposition which has been made to the principles advanced in the *Observations*', simply meant that every independent agent should have a share in government.[97] However, this may not have reassured readers, since there were elitist and egalitarian interpretations of what was necessary to be an 'independent agent'. Indeed, Price referred approvingly in a footnote to John Cartwright's *Take your Choice* (1777), which recommended universal male suffrage and annual elections.[98]

Like Lind, Bentham was troubled by the assertion that liberty requires the broadest franchise. In other words, he too would have been most concerned about the positive-liberty dimension to Pricean liberty, where liberty is defined partly by reference to the right of political participation. However, Bentham was more anxious than Lind to avoid the term 'liberty'. He felt it was commonly used in two incompatible ways.[99] It could mean the absence of any constraint upon doing as one pleases. On the other hand, it could mean the security for one's person and possessions brought about by government. The latter ties liberty to governmental

---

[92] Long in fact notes some development in Bentham's idea of liberty as he moved from a focus on criminal law to civil law, but they are not relevant here: Long, *Bentham on Liberty*, ch 10.

[93] ibid 173–4.

[94] See text to above n 58.

[95] Long, *Bentham on Liberty* 172.

[96] ibid 174.

[97] R Price, 'Additional Observations on the Nature and Value of Civil Liberty, and the War with America' [1777] in *Political Writings*, ed, DO Thomas (Cambridge, Cambridge University Press, 1991) 76–100, 80.

[98] ibid 93 fn 8. See also DO Thomas, *The Honest Mind: The Thought and Work of Richard Price* (Oxford, Clarendon Press, 1977) 201–4.

[99] F Rosen, 'Introduction' in J Bentham, *An Introduction to the Principles of Morals and Legislation*, eds, JH Burns and HLA Hart (Oxford, Clarendon Press, 1996) xxxi–lxix, xxxv. For other reasons why Bentham preferred liberty as non-interference, see Long, *Bentham on Liberty* 18–24.

constraints that create security.[100] To achieve clarity, Bentham restricted 'liberty' to the absence of any constraint, while 'security' referred to that security brought about by government. He mentioned that 'security depends on the care taken to save from disturbance the current of expectation'.[101] This understanding, articulated in the 1780s, was affirmed in the 1820s, when he wrote that security was the principal object of the law.[102]

Returning to Bentham's manuscripts of the 1780s, he also thought that the term 'liberty' was inflammatory: 'At the mention of liberty every man conceives it to be his right, and many a man conceives it to be his duty to fall into a passion'.[103] Bentham was also probably concerned that 'slavery', the antonym for liberty often employed by Price, was an emotive term. A suggestion that the disenfranchised were slaves could imply that they have a right to resist government. Instead, any decision to resist government should be based on a careful assessment of the likely consequences for security and utility.[104] Clear language and rigorous terminology were 'the only effectual antidote against the fascinations of political enthusiasm'.[105] The narrowness of his definition of 'liberty' directed attention towards the less emotive term, 'security'.

Bentham, then, opposed emotive references to a right to liberty, in contrast to rational calculation aimed at promoting security of expectations and, thereby, the ultimate value of utility. From Bentham's perspective, perhaps the most troubling feature of Priceian liberty was its incorporation of a right to political participation. Bentham was not responding to liberty as non-domination, nor was he seeking to shift attention only to interference damage, which is what a focus on liberty as non-interference might suggest. Instead, he was concerned that people should feel secure.

VI. Paley

Pettit mentions that while Bentham was perhaps most influential in establishing liberty as non-interference, Paley was also influential.[106] Paley's *Principles of Moral and Political Philosophy* (1785) became a leading textbook for the teaching

---

[100] Lind described this as civil or political liberty. See text to above n 83.

[101] See PJ Kelly, *Utilitarianism and Distributive Justice: Jeremy Bentham and the Civil Law* (Oxford, Clarendon Press, 1990) 77.

[102] ibid.

[103] Long, *Bentham on Liberty* 173.

[104] See, eg, Bentham's argument that there is no 'sign', such as the violation of a particular natural right, which grounds a right to resist government: J Bentham, 'A Fragment on Government' [1776] in *A Comment on the Commentaries and a Fragment on Government* eds, JH Burns and HLA Hart (London, University of London Athlone Press, 1977) 393–551, 484 (ch IV, para 22).

[105] Long, *Bentham on Liberty* 60.

[106] Pettit, *Republicanism* 45.

of political theory throughout the nineteenth century.[107] Pettit also mentions that Paley recognised most clearly the shift from liberty as non-domination to liberty as non-interference.[108]

Paley described civil liberty as consisting in 'not being restrained by any law, but what conduces in a greater degree to the public welfare'.[109] For Paley, public welfare was to be assessed against utility. Thus, laws justifiable on utilitarian grounds would not diminish civil liberty.

Paley in fact contrasted his conception of civil liberty with liberty as non-interference, which he called 'natural liberty'.[110] Natural liberty is the liberty to do as one pleases. In elaborating upon the contrast between natural and civil liberty, Paley said: 'Natural liberty is the right of common upon a waste; civil liberty is the safe, exclusive, unmolested enjoyment of a cultivated enclosure'.[111] Paley envisaged here that civil liberty requires law – presumably, the safe, exclusive enjoyment of a cultivated enclosure is the product of law. While Paley's formal definition of civil liberty identifies liberty with the absence of unjustified law, it is clear that he also identifies civil liberty with the presence of justifiable law. It requires laws that protect people from unjustified interference. Paley's civil liberty, then, is what I have described as 'legal security' when examining Lind – it requires the protection of ordinary laws.[112] Paley's preferred conception of civil liberty is not, then, the non-interference conception that Pettit in *Republicanism* identified Paley with.[113]

However, Pettit's discussion is most misleading on how Paley supported his preferred conception of civil liberty. Pettit claims that Paley regarded republican liberty as too demanding. In fact, Paley, in criticising certain definitions of liberty as too demanding, was not referring to liberty as non-domination. I will demonstrate this by pointing to the passages surrounding Paley's comment about overly demanding conceptions of liberty.

Paley noted that apart from his preferred conception of civil liberty, there was 'a common understanding of civil liberty'. This is equivalent to what I described as constitutional security when considering Lind.[114] Constitutional security requires a political system that is most likely to enact laws that maximise utility. In discussing this 'common understanding of civil liberty', Paley said:

> Were it probable that the welfare and accommodation of the people would be as studiously, and as providently, consulted in the edicts of a despotic prince, as by the

---

[107] Q Skinner, *Liberty before Liberalism* (Cambridge, Cambridge University Press, 1998) 78, referring to DL LeMahieu, *The Mind of William Paley: A Philosopher and His Age* (Lincoln, University of Nebraska Press, 1976) 155–6.

[108] Pettit, *Republicanism* 45.

[109] Paley, *Principles* 311 (Book VI, ch 5).

[110] ibid.

[111] ibid 312.

[112] This is Lind's civil or political liberty: see text to above n 83.

[113] P Pettit, *A Theory of Freedom: From the Psychology to the Politics of Agency* (Cambridge, Polity, 2001) 147–8, fn 1 acknowledges that Paley's civil liberty is not the non-interference conception, but then discounts the significance of this.

[114] See text to above n 84.

resolutions of a popular assembly, then would an absolute form of government be no less free than the purest democracy.[115]

Paley is confirming a probabilistic approach to constitutional security: security is obtained where interference is unlikely, rather than focusing on whether others lack a power of interference.[116] After suggesting that constitutional security may vary depending upon the form and composition of the legislature, he said: 'The definitions which have been framed of civil liberty, and which have become the subject of much unnecessary altercation, are most of them adapted to this idea.'[117] In other words, they are adapted to the idea of security. He then continued:

> Thus one political writer makes the very essence of the subject's liberty to consist in his being governed by no laws but those to which he hath actually consented; another is satisfied with an indirect and virtual consent; another, again, places civil liberty in the separation of the legislative and executive offices of government; another, in the being governed by *law*, that is, by known, preconstituted, inflexible rules of action and adjudication ... Concerning which, and some other similar accounts of civil liberty, it may be observed, that they all labour under one inaccuracy, *viz.* that they describe not so much liberty itself, as the safeguards and preservatives of liberty: for example, a man's being governed by no laws but those to which he has given his consent, were it practicable, is no otherwise necessary to the enjoyment of civil liberty, than as it affords a probable security against the dictation of laws imposing superfluous restrictions upon his private will.[118]

After some further elaboration, he then suggested that (and it is this passage that Pettit quotes):

> ... those definitions of liberty ought to be rejected, which, by making that essential to civil freedom which is unattainable in experience, inflame expectations that can never be gratified, and disturb the public content with complaints, which no wisdom or benevolence of government can remove.[119]

Commenting on this passage, Pettit says:

> It is difficult to know exactly what Paley had in mind in putting freedom as non-domination in the 'too hard' basket ... I agree with Paley that the republican ideal of freedom as non-domination is indeed a very dense and demanding goal around which

---

[115] Paley, *Principles* 314.

[116] ibid. Pettit agrees that Paley understood security in a probabilistic sense: Pettit, *Republicanism* 74. In an earlier statement, Paley describes constitutional security as requiring 'not merely in an actual exemption from the constraint of useless and noxious laws and acts of dominion, but in being free from the *danger* of having such hereafter imposed or exercised': Paley, *Principles* 313. However, the quote to above n 115 suggests a probabilistic approach rather than aiming to render the imposition of unjustified laws an actual impossibility.

[117] Paley, *Principles* 314.

[118] ibid 314–15. Paley seems to be suggesting here that the requirement of 'being governed by *law*' should be separated from a definition of liberty. He is dealing here with a rule-of-law culture, such as the norms that the state must be constrained by its laws and that laws should be highly stable. This contrasts with the protection provided by ordinary law that is contemplated by his preferred conception of civil liberty.

[119] ibid 315 referred to in Pettit, *Republicanism* 47.

to orient our social and political institutions; it would support radical changes in traditional social life ...[120]

Pettit refers to the republican goal being inconsistent with the position of employees and women at that time.[121]

It is clear, though, that the definitions of liberty that Paley said ought to be
rejected are definitions of liberty that identify liberty with *conditions* that were
too demanding. Paley was not saying that constitutional security itself is too
demanding.[122] Also, we need not speculate on whether Paley had the subordination of employees and women in mind when referring to inflaming expectations.
Paley's focus was clearly on constitutional matters. To take the first definition Paley
listed in the substantial quotation above, he undoubtedly would have regarded
the view that individual consent is necessary to preserve liberty as unrealistic and
inflammatory.[123] Paley probably had Price in mind here.

While Paley did not regard constitutional security as overly demanding, he
did, nevertheless, suggest that identifying liberty with constitutional security
is somewhat problematic: it had led to definitions that are 'the subject of much
unnecessary altercation'. Recall that his preferred definition of civil liberty involves
legal, not constitutional, security. It seems that Paley was concerned that if liberty
is defined as constitutional security, one can more easily slide into identifying
liberty with preferred constitutional arrangements. That identification obscures
the contingent nature of the relationship between those constitutional arrangements and constitutional security.

From Paley's perspective, Priceian liberty was primarily objectionable because
it identified liberty with a right of political participation. Paley undoubtedly
believed that we should coolly evaluate individual consent in terms of its role in
promoting what I describe as constitutional security.[124] Indeed, while he stated
that 'the irregularity of the popular representation' was 'the most flagrant incon-
gruity' in the British constitution, he said that closer examination suggested that
this irregularity in fact led to representatives who were more likely to promote the
public interest than those who would be appointed by a purely popular franchise.[125]
Security of property would be diminished by a popular franchise.

The restricted franchise, in Paley's view, better achieved constitutional security. Paley favoured constitutional security; he was only suggesting that there are
risks in defining liberty in terms of constitutional security. It is hardly surprising,

---

[120] Pettit, *Republicanism* 47.

[121] ibid 48.

[122] This error is also made in Pettit, *A Theory of Freedom* 147–8 and Pettit, *On the People's Terms* 9.

[123] See quote to above n 118.

[124] See Paley's statement that the right to representation should only be extended so far as this
conduces to public utility: Paley, *Principles* 344 (bk VI, ch 7). Interestingly, Paley denied that there was
a natural, inalienable right to representation. If there were, Paley continued at 344 fn*, it should extend
to women, yet all plans for reform seem to exclude women. This seems similar to Lind's statements
about whether Price's approach suggested that women were slaves: see text to above n 87.

[125] ibid 342–6.

then, that he did not firmly reject what he described as the common under-standing of liberty. Instead, he said that this common understanding (which is constitutional security) and his preferred definition of liberty (which is legal security) lead to the same requirements: 'Of the two ideas that have been stated of civil liberty ... this is the conclusion – that *that* people, government, and consti-tution, is the *freest*, which makes the best provision for the enacting of expedient and salutary laws.'[126]

Pettit has badly misinterpreted Paley's comment about demanding conceptions of liberty. Paley was not discussing liberty as non-domination. Paley's concerns in general seem close to Lind's and Bentham's. Like Lind, Paley was concerned that terms such as 'liberty' and 'slavery' were sometimes used in an absolute sense rather than in a way which recognised that there are degrees of liberty.[127] Like Bentham, Paley was concerned that the idea of liberty was attended with 'uncer-tainty and confusion'.[128] Bentham would probably have felt that Paley added to the confusion by conflating liberty with utility and by continuing with a term which aroused so much passion.[129] Nevertheless, they both sought to define liberty so that it was more likely that various constitutional arrangements suggested by political activists or writers would be coolly assessed in terms of their role in promoting security and utility, rather than simply being favoured because political activists or writers happened to identify them with 'liberty'. They did not challenge liberty as non-domination. If Paley had addressed liberty as non-domination, he would likely have suggested, like Lind, that a broad franchise would increase arbitrary power. While Lind referred to the arbitrary power that the rulers would enjoy over the masses, Paley referred to the arbitrary power that the propertied would be vulnerable to.[130]

VII. Tracking Liberty as Non-Domination After 1785

Pettit's claim that liberal liberty may have been asserted partly to avoid the radical qualities of liberty as non-domination is based upon Lind's, Bentham's and Paley's writing in the 1770s and 1780s. However, Pettit also claims that nineteenth-century liberals may have preferred liberty as non-interference for the same reason. The demanding implications related not just to the relationship between state and

---

[126] ibid 316.

[127] ibid 312.

[128] ibid 315.

[129] The conflation of liberty and utility lies in Paley's assertion that civil liberty is not diminished by law that promotes utility. See F Rosen, *Bentham, Byron, and Greece: Constitutionalism, Nationalism, and Early Liberal Political Thought* (Oxford, Clarendon Press, 1992) 32–3.

[130] In relation to Lind, see text to above n 90. Paley's concern was, in fact, expressed by some other critics of Price as well: see A de Dijn, 'Republicanism and Democracy: The Tyranny of the Majority in Eighteenth-Century Political Debate' in Y Elazar and G Rousselière (eds), *Republicanism and the Future of Democracy* (Cambridge, Cambridge University Press, 2019) 59–74, 65.

citizen, but between employers and employees, and men and women.[131] Pettit states that later liberals who adopted the non-interference conception of liberty did so with little or no discussion of the republican alternative. Pettit suggests, though, that they were influenced by Bentham and Paley.

In understanding the early nineteenth-century use of liberty in dealing with arbitrary state power, it is worth tracking debate that applied liberty to constitutional matters during the few decades following the publication of Paley's *Principles* in 1785. Subsection A attempts this task. Subsection B turns to Pettit's claims concerning social relations. This involves going back to the seventeenth century, with Locke, to establish what Pettit views as the republican approach to employment relations. I then return to the eighteenth and nineteenth centuries.

A. Constitutional Questions

The French Revolution dominated debate in the decade after Paley's *Principles*. In *A Discourse on the Love of Our Country*, Price excitedly supported the Revolution, suggesting it contained lessons for the partial and corrupt English system of representation.[132] Indeed, the Revolution spurred Bentham to recommend reform more radical than Price: Bentham recommended a franchise including all males and females divided into equal electoral districts and voting in annual elections for a unicameral legislature.[133] Price had only directed his criticisms at the House of Commons. He thereby accepted a substantial role for the House of Lords.[134] Furthermore, Price's position towards the franchise was not quite as radical as it sometimes appeared. David Thomas points to a letter, for instance, that Price wrote in 1783 indicating that it was important to have regard to the circumstances in any particular country when considering how far the franchise should extend.[135] Thomas sums up Price's position as one where ideally, there should be a universal male franchise but, as Price mentioned in his *Additional Observations*, there are values other than liberty that need to be considered, such as wisdom in deliberating and resolving political matters.[136]

Nevertheless, his public position suggested greater radicalism, and this was exploited by Edmund Burke, the most prominent critic of Price's *Discourse*.[137]

---

[131] Pettit, *Republicanism* 48.

[132] R Price, 'A Discourse on the Love of Our Country' [1789] in *Political Writings*, ed, DO Thomas (Cambridge, Cambridge University Press, 1991) 176–96, 195. For discussion of English support of 'French liberty' and Burke's *Reflections*, see A Goodwin, *The Friends of Liberty: The English Democratic Movement in the Age of the French Revolution* (London, Hutchinson, 1979) ch 4.

[133] Rosen, *Bentham, Byron, and Greece* 50–2.

[134] Price, 'Observations' [1776] 26–7.

[135] Thomas, *The Honest Mind* 151–2. See also at 201–4.

[136] ibid 152 referring to Price, 'Additional Observations' 79–80. See also Thomas, *The Honest Mind* ch XIV.

[137] Thomas, *The Honest Mind* 308, 332.

Burke delivered a bitter attack, accusing Price, amongst other things, of ignoring experience and embracing abstract reasoning.[138] Burke did not, however, challenge a non-domination conception of liberty. Instead, he argued that since the liberty produced by the Revolution conferred power upon the people, it was important to consider how that power would be used.[139] Again, it was the identification of liberty with popular participation that created consternation.

Dismay with the French Revolution intensified throughout 1792 and into 1793, with the execution of Louis XVI.[140] Indeed, Bentham was so shocked by French developments that he turned against reform of the British constitution.[141] Mark Philp mentions that in this more conservative climate, the language of republicanism, natural rights and even utilitarianism became yoked to 'French principles'.[142] The safest course, and one which dominated the reform movement for the first third of the nineteenth century, was to adopt a Burkean reverence for the constitution and to focus on less abstract justifications and less threatening targets within that framework.[143] Reform was supported by invoking rights or freedoms supposedly conferred by the British constitution.

The discourse of common-law constitutionalism in fact contrasted liberty with arbitrary power. Since the common law did not conceive of liberty as opposed to arbitrary power in general but, instead, tied liberty to particular rights the common law recognised, I regard it as a qualified form of liberty as non-domination.[144] While the climate for reform in Britain improved after the Napoleonic Wars, the Priceian approach to liberty did not revive. The opposition between liberty and slavery and the identification of liberty with popular participation perhaps continued to evoke revolutionary excess. While Philp mentions that utilitarianism was also yoked to French principles, it was not so strongly associated with revolutionary excess, and perhaps could therefore revive more easily. Utility was not defined as that happiness achieved when each person is a legislator.

---

[138] See, eg, ibid ch XV.

[139] E Burke, 'Reflections on the Revolution in France' [1790] in *Revolutionary Writings*, ed, I Hampsher-Monk (Cambridge, Cambridge University Press, 2014) 1–250, 9.

[140] E Macleod, 'British Spectators of the French Revolution: The View from across the Channel' (2013) 197 *Groeniek* 377–92, 381.

[141] Rosen, *Bentham, Byron, and Greece* 57–8. See also JH Burns, 'Bentham and the French Revolution' (1966) 16 *Transactions of the Royal Historical Society* 95–114, 112.

[142] Philp, 'English Republicanism in the 1790s' 259.

[143] J Epstein, *Radical Expression: Political Language, Ritual, and Symbol in England, 1790–1850* (Oxford, Oxford University Press, 1994) 23–8. See also P Harling, 'Leigh Hunt's *Examiner* and the Language of Patriotism' (1996) 111 *English Historical Review* 1159–81. Whether the use of the constitutionalist idiom should be seen more as an adaptive response to government repression rather than as a continuation of eighteenth-century vocabulary is unclear: J Belchem, 'Republicanism, Popular Constitutionalism and the Radical Platform in Early Nineteenth-Century England' (1981) 6 *Social History* 1–32.

[144] Pettit also does not equate common law constitutionalism with liberty as non-domination, although he views them as consistent. See Pettit, *Republicanism* 20–1 and also his reference at 50, fn 9 to the French juridical tradition where public liberty is equated with liberty assured under law. He says this is not a non-interference conception, but he does not state that it is a non-domination conception. See also Reid, *Liberty in the Age of the American Revolution*.

Utilitarianism may have seemed a more rational and soothing language through which to pursue reform. It was a discourse, though, which still enabled concern about arbitrary power to be expressed. Bentham said in the 1820s: 'The greater a man's power, the stronger his propensity in all possible ways to abuse it. Of this fact, all history is one continued proof.'[145] Bentham attacked the power enjoyed by elites and argued that democratisation was necessary to constrain this. James Mill, another contributor to liberal democratic theory in the first part of the nineteenth century, agreed that people have a propensity to abuse power and he also suggested that the main goal in designing a constitution should be curbing arbitrary power.[146] Avoiding Price's incorporation within liberty of a right of political participation was consistent with still challenging arbitrary power and supporting a broader franchise.

B. Social Questions

Pettit also contends that liberty as non-interference may have been partly motivated by the demanding implications of liberty as non-domination when applied to social questions, in particular, employment and gender relations. An examination of Pettit's claims with respect to gender relations would reveal difficulties with Pettit's account.[147] This subsection will demonstrate that even with employment relations, an issue that attracted greater attention in the period under consideration, Pettit's claim is implausible.

Pettit suggests that the doctrine of freedom of contract was invoked in eighteenth- and nineteenth-century Britain to defend some appalling contractual arrangements. Pettit claims that this development could never have materialised, in all likelihood, if people had continued to think that freedom required the absence of domination, not just the absence of interference.[148] Traditional republicans were consistently hostile towards the slave contract. Pettit refers here to Locke. Liberty as non-interference, Pettit continues, may have been partly motivated by a desire for an interpretation of liberty more consistent with freedom of contract.

---

[145] J Bentham, *Constitutional Code*, eds, F Rosen and JH Burns, vol 1 (Oxford, Clarendon Press, 1983) 122 (ch VI, s 31, art 22).

[146] J Mill, 'Essay on Government' [1820] in *Utilitarian Logic and Politics: James Mill's 'Essay on Government', Macauley's Critique and the Ensuing Debate*, eds, J Lively and J Rees (Oxford, Clarendon Press, 1978) 53–95, 58 (on the main constitutional goal) and at 67 (on the propensity to abuse power).

[147] For a discussion of some of Pettit's claims relating to gender relations, see P Springborg, *Mary Astell: Theorist of Freedom from Domination* (Cambridge, Cambridge University Press, 2005); P Springborg, 'Republicanism, Freedom from Domination, and the Cambridge Contextual Historians' (2001) 49 *Political Studies* 851–76, 863–8. In relation to Bentham's discussion of women, and his use of the analogue of slavery, see L Campos Boralevi, *Bentham and the Oppressed* (Berlin, W de Gruyter, 1984) ch 2.

[148] Pettit, *Republicanism* 62.

There seem to be three propositions that would be helpful in supporting Pettit's claim that a motivation behind liberty as non-interference may have been the overly demanding implications of liberty as non-domination for employment relations. The first is that adherents of liberty as non-domination opposed freedom of contract. The second is that adherents of liberty as non-interference recognised that unlike their preferred value, liberty as non-domination opposed freedom of contract. The third is that adherents of liberty as non-interference applied this value rather than liberty as non-domination to employment relations.

The first proposition is helpful because it supports the plausibility of the second proposition. If adherents of liberty as non-domination did not themselves oppose freedom of contract, it makes it less likely that liberals would have recognised that liberty as non-domination is associated with opposition to freedom of contract. The relevance of the second and third propositions to Pettit's claim is self-evident.

I will first focus on writing in the seventeenth and eighteenth centuries. This has to carry the burden in supporting Pettit's claim, since he does not refer to nineteenth-century writing that explicitly considered the demandingness of republican liberty in the context of employment relations. Instead, the conjecture must be that the earlier debate clearly indicated the demanding quality of republican liberty for employment relations. I then extend into the nineteenth century, with Bentham.

I turn, then, to the first proposition: that adherents of liberty as non-domination opposed freedom of contract. Pettit states that republicans were consistently hostile towards the slave contract. I will look at Locke and Price. Price is the second of the historical republicans Pettit mentions as having a position inconsistent with the subordinate position of employees at that time.[149]

Locke understood liberty in society as existing where there is a legislative power established by consent and where individuals are not subject to the 'Arbitrary Will of another Man'.[150] Locke also said that a man cannot by his own consent enslave himself to anyone.[151] This supports Pettit's claim about Locke's hostility to the slave contract. However, Locke's narrow definition of a slave contract should be acknowledged. Locke was referring to a man putting himself under the power of a slave-master, ie, a master who has the power of life and death over his slaves.

Locke, in fact, accepted contractual arrangements that gave substantial, although not absolute, power to one party. He said:

> I confess, we find among the *Jews*, as well as other Nations, that Men did sell themselves; but, 'tis plain, this was only to *Drudgery, not to Slavery*. For, it is evident, the Person sold was not under an Absolute, Arbitrary, Despotical Power.[152]

---

[149] ibid 49.
[150] J Locke, 'Second Treatise of Government' [1689] in *Two Treatises of Government*, ed, P Laslett, 2nd edn (Cambridge, Cambridge University Press, 1967) 285–446, 302 (para 22).
[151] ibid (para 23).
[152] ibid (para 24).

Locke referred here to the Book of Exodus, which mentions that bought servants must not to be killed, must be freed if maimed by their master, and must be freed in their seventh year. Locke, then, drew the line between contract and slavery in a way which rendered drudgery consistent with liberty.

Price's position was similar to Locke's. In his *Additional Observations*, he referred to 'servitudes founded on voluntary compacts', where servants can agree to the conditions of employment and can terminate the contracts when they choose to.[153] Entering such compacts was consistent with liberty. Locke and Price, then, do not support the first proposition, which is that adherents of liberty as non-domination opposed the doctrine of freedom of contract.

I turn now to the second proposition: that adherents of liberty as non-interference recognised that, unlike their favoured value, liberty as non-domination opposed freedom of contract. Pettit gives the example of Lind: he points out that Lind claimed that Price's principle that to be guided by another is the characteristic of servitude suggests that servants are, in fact, slaves.[154] While Lind's claim does suggest that contracts for service involve servitude, this provides limited support for the second proposition. First, Lind understood Priceian liberty in terms of self-government, not liberty as non-domination. Secondly, Lind was not here directly addressing employment relations but, instead, making a passing comment relating to the conduct of the American War of Independence.[155]

I turn finally to the third proposition: that adherents of liberty as non-interference applied this value, rather than liberty as non-domination, to employment contracts. Out of Lind, Bentham and Paley, Bentham most consistently adhered to liberty as non-interference. Nevertheless, he approached freedom of contract in a similar way to Locke. In distinguishing slavery from contract labour, Bentham said that an important difference is that the master of a slave is entitled to the services of the slave in perpetuity.[156] Due to this, it is extremely difficult to limit the power of masters. Even if there are laws that purport to limit the power of masters, slaves will not dare to irritate their master by asserting their entitlements: 'they will be driven to captivate … [their master] by an unlimited submission'. They know that 'an insolent subject' will be tormented.

Like Locke, Bentham distinguished slavery by referring to the indefinite time of service of a slave and the consequent impossibility of constraining the master's power. If Bentham was concerned that a republican focus upon arbitrary power could challenge freedom of contract, one would have expected him to have avoided this focus in his own discussion of slaves and servants.[157]

---

[153] Price, 'Additional Observations' 85–6. Price's approach to employment relations will be discussed further in ch 3, s IIIB.

[154] Pettit, *Republicanism* 49; Lind, *Three Letters to Dr Price* 156–7 referring to Price, 'Observations' [1776] 67.

[155] See the references to Lind and Price in above n 154.

[156] See J Bentham, *The Theory of Legislation* [1840], ed, C Ogden (London, Morrison & Gibbs, 1931) 201–2 ('Principles of the Civil Code' Pt 3, ch II).

[157] Bentham also referred to other considerations in distinguishing slaves from servants, such as slaves' lack of productivity. See, eg, his comparison between slaves and free day-labourers in ibid 205–6.

There is little support for Pettit's claim that there was a strong association between liberty as non-domination and hostility to wage slavery by the late eighteenth and early nineteenth centuries that could have featured in a liberal preference for liberty as non-interference, to the extent that such a preference was expressed. I will also argue, in chapter three, that there are analytical difficulties in using Pettit's or Price's interpretation of liberty as non-domination to challenge freedom of contract.[158]

VIII. Conclusion

Pettit has constructed a beguiling tale of historical excavation. A long-lost and forgotten political ideal is discovered, painstakingly restored, and commended to us. This ideal, of liberty as non-domination, was too subversive in late eighteenth-century Britain when combined with the value of equality. It was partly for that reason that it may have been eclipsed by the more modest ideal of liberty as non-interference. However, the older ideal, Pettit argues, is more attractive. While no longer subversive, when applied to contemporary Western democracies, it is still challenging. It directs attention towards combating remaining forms of subordination by prompting us to consider how damaging vulnerability to arbitrary power is, even in the absence of actual interference.

Pettit suggests that major protagonists in this contest over ideals were Price, a radical espousing the republican non-domination conception of liberty, and Lind, Bentham and Paley, asserting the more modest ideal of liberty as non-interference. For Pettit, this contest was over approaches to arbitrary power. Price used republican liberty's feature of being diminished by mere vulnerability to arbitrary power to argue that American colonists and even the disenfranchised in Britain were unfree. The suggestion was that mere vulnerability to arbitrary power is itself damaging – I described this as power damage. However, Pettit continues, Lind, Bentham and Paley opposed the radicalism of Price and others espousing this conception of liberty. They did so by asserting that liberty is only diminished by actual interference; they thereby focused upon interference damage. This non-interference conception of liberty, Pettit continues, was not only convenient in avoiding radical proposals in relation to the franchise or the status of the American colonies, but it may have been regarded as convenient by later liberals, given the arbitrary power suffered by groups including employees and women.

There is enough truth in Pettit's narrative to give it some plausibility. Price did assert that liberty is diminished by mere vulnerability to arbitrary power and

---

For a discussion of this comparison, including left-wing criticism of referring to slavery due to the problem of day-labourers, see Campos Boralevi, *Bentham and the Oppressed* ch 7. Paley's approach will not be discussed here. His understanding of civil liberty requires security against interference by other citizens in the form of legal protection. Also, his discussion of labour contracts largely deals with issues not relevant here: Paley, *Principles* 100–2.

[158] See ch 3, s III B, including n 75.

that liberty therefore required independence for American colonists. Bentham proposed liberty as non-interference and appeared to challenge Price. Lind referred to liberty as non-interference approvingly in his conservative critique of Price. And Paley, in favouring a conception of liberty that was not diminished by arbitrary state power, argued that certain other conceptions of liberty were overly demanding.

However, Pettit's suggestion that liberty as non-domination may have been avoided because of the radical implications of its focus upon arbitrary power, a focus suggesting a keen appreciation of power damage, lacks support. Price did not emphasise power damage with his conception of liberty as non-domination. He emphasised interference damage. It is also not evident that Lind, Bentham and Paley sought to ignore power damage: they recognised the importance of feeling secure.

Lind, Bentham and Paley did not target liberty as non-domination. What they did oppose, or express concern about, were approaches to liberty that:

1. prized liberty as the supreme value – such approaches matched popu-lar discourse on liberty, with its excited references to liberty, and thereby impeded rational discussion;
2. equated constraints upon liberty with slavery – such approaches tended to produce a black-and-white approach to issues, which also impeded rational discussion;
3. identified liberty with favoured constitutional arrangements – these approaches did not promote rational discussion of the precise role that those arrangements played in promoting security, and were particularly unfortunate when the arrangement stipulated (such as a right of political participation) was inflammatory and had an uncertain empirical relationship to security; and
4. could easily slide into equating liberty with favoured constitutional arrange-ments – an example of such an approach is employing what I have described as constitutional security.

If Lind, Bentham and Paley had addressed liberty as non-domination, it seems likely that they would have questioned its feasibility: any state will enjoy some arbitrary power over its citizens; individual citizens cannot enjoy a veto over legis-lation. Most likely, they would not have accepted that the value is democratically demanding in the sense of requiring a broad franchise. What was radical in Price's work was the assumption that distributing power from the existing elite to the people in general would reduce arbitrary power overall.

The debate between these writers also focused on constitutional matters. Pettit's claim that liberty as non-domination may have been rejected partly due to its radical implications for employment relations is implausible. Locke and Price had no difficulty in reconciling freedom of contrast with understanding liberty as diminished by mere vulnerability to arbitrary power. Interestingly, Bentham himself, despite his preference for liberty as non-interference, approached freedom of contract in a similar way to Locke and Price.

The deep flaws in the interpretation of the writers so centrally relied upon in contrasting republican and liberal negative liberty cast doubt on Pettit's historical interpretation of these values. To give one example, Pettit's acknowledgement that republicans' primary focus in relation to political participation was avoiding interference sits oddly with then regarding interference as a secondary affront to liberty, with mere vulnerability to arbitrary power being the primary evil. That tension is avoided by Price. Further difficulties with Pettit's historical interpretation will also be revealed in the next chapter, since there are commonalities in the accounts of Pettit and Skinner.

The difficulties with Pettit's historical account also cast doubt on his normative case for liberty as non-domination. As he indicates, his historical claims about the two conceptions of liberty provide his broad analytical and normative arguments about these conceptions with 'intellectual plausibility'.[159] The plausibility of his claims about the radical implications of liberty as non-domination, in contrast to liberty as non-interference, gain credence from the suggestion that these implications were recognised in the late eighteenth century and into the nineteenth century. Major normative claims that Pettit makes about these two conceptions of liberty will be challenged in chapters four and five.

---

[159] Pettit, *On the People's Terms* 19.

3

Skinner's Republican
and Liberal Liberty

I. Introduction

Quentin Skinner has been the most prominent intellectual historian to have challenged the positive-liberty interpretation of the republican political tradition articulated by Pocock. Pocock had understood the tradition as resting ultimately on what I have described as full-blown positive liberty, where virtuous political participation enables citizens to achieve their rational potential and thereby become free.[1] In work from the late 1970s to early 1990s, Skinner agreed that the tradition did emphasise political participation by citizens. However, he argued that the tradition nevertheless endorsed a negative conception of liberty, just like liberalism. It is just that republicans focused upon the duties citizens must perform in order to safeguard their liberties. One duty was to participate in politics. This approach, Skinner suggested, was eclipsed by liberalism, which tends to focus on the individual rights that are necessary to achieve protection against the state.[2] Skinner suggested that the republican approach might prompt us to consider whether we should focus more on the duties that citizens should perform in order to safeguard their rights.

However, in *Liberty before Liberalism* (1998), Skinner argued that the republican tradition did endorse a conception of liberty that was distinct from the negative conception associated with liberalism. While Skinner's initial interpretation was largely based on Machiavelli, his later interpretation looked at writing in seventeenth- and eighteenth-century Britain. Skinner's book came soon after Pettit's *Republicanism* (1997), with both writers influencing each other. Skinner had pointed Pettit to historical sources, and Pettit had pointed Skinner towards

---

[1] JGA Pocock, *The Machiavellian Moment: Florentine Political Thought and the Atlantic Republican Tradition* [1975], with a new introduction by Richard Whatmore (Princeton, NJ, Princeton University Press, 2016).

[2] See, eg, Q Skinner, 'The Idea of Negative Liberty: Machiavellian and Modern Perspectives' in *Visions of Politics, vol II: Renaissance Virtues* (Cambridge, Cambridge University Press, 2002) 186–212 (this is a revised version of a chapter published in 1984) and Q Skinner, 'The Republican Ideal of Political Liberty' in G Bock, Q Skinner and M Viroli (eds), *Machiavelli and Republicanism* (Cambridge, Cambridge University Press, 1990) 293–309.

a new way of conceptualising republican liberty.[3] Both writers drew significantly on Richard Price, although Skinner's main focus was on seventeenth-century interregnum writers, including Marchamont Nedham, John Milton, James Harrington, Henry Neville and Algernon Sidney.[4]

Skinner followed Pettit in seeing the distinctive aspect of the republican conception as lying in it being diminished by mere vulnerability to arbitrary power. He also agreed that republican liberty can helpfully prompt us to consider whether we should do more to minimise arbitrary power. Nevertheless, Skinner made distinct historical claims about republican liberty. He embedded his conception of republican liberty in a wider account about liberty that refers to self-government. He also claimed that republican liberty is diminished not only by an arbitrary power to interfere, but also by dependency upon an arbitrary power to offer benefits. Skinner's interpretation of the contrasting liberal conception of liberty also diverges from Pettit's: Skinner associates this value with a different historical criticism of republican liberty. On the other hand, they both associate liberal liberty with anti-democratic thought.

The chapter has three objectives: first, to clarify Skinner's approach to republican liberty as a conception diminished by dependency on arbitrary power; secondly, to expose some difficulties with Skinner's interpretation of republican and liberal liberty; and thirdly, to further illuminate Pettit's interpretation. The third objective is achieved most obviously through exploring the anti-democratic associations of liberal liberty, since both Pettit and Skinner make similar claims.

While the last chapter discussed Pettit's narrative of the eclipse of republican liberty, this chapter covers wider ground. The last chapter facilitates this coverage since it discussed historical writers who also feature in this chapter. Overall, Skinner makes more cautious claims than Pettit. Nevertheless, significant doubts about Skinner's approach are raised in this chapter.

This chapter proceeds in the following way. Section II describes Skinner's evolving conception of republican liberty. Three interpretations are isolated. The first two have been referred to, and the third was provided in 2008.[5] Section III examines Skinner's interpretation of republican liberty by exploring Price and Harrington. Both writers feature prominently in Skinner's account. Section IV turns to Skinner's (and Pettit's) interpretation of liberal liberty. Pettit made some similar claims to Skinner about liberal liberty. The chapter concludes by referring to Skinner's well-known writing on the appropriate methodology to employ in intellectual history. I suggest that Skinner appears to have fallen into the trap that

---

[3] P Pettit, *Republicanism: A Theory of Freedom and Government* (Oxford, Clarendon Press, 1997) ix, R Prokhovnik, 'An Interview with Quentin Skinner' (2011) 10 *Contemporary Political Theory* 273–85, 278–9.

[4] Q Skinner, *Liberty before Liberalism* (Cambridge, Cambridge University Press, 1998) 12–16.

[5] Q Skinner, "Freedom as the Absence of Arbitrary Power" in C Laborde and J Maynor (eds), *Republicanism and Political Theory* (Malden, MA, Blackwell, 2008) 83–101.

he warned against in this methodological writing.[6] Present-day concerns appear to have distorted Skinner's understanding of the historical material.

Before commencing, I should note that Skinner referred in *Liberty before Liberalism* to neo-roman, rather than republican, liberty to indicate that the writers he has in mind were not necessarily anti-monarchical.[7] However, in deference to continuing usage, he later reverted to the term 'republican'.[8] I too will refer to 'republican liberty'.

II. Skinner's Account of Republican Liberty

A. The Initial Interpretation and Some Introductory Remarks

This subsection sketches Skinner's initial interpretation. While the focus of this chapter is on the last two interpretations, where republican liberty is interpreted as diminished by dependency, the first interpretation provides a helpful context. Subsection B describes his interpretation in *Liberty before Liberalism*, and subsection C describes his most recent interpretation.

Skinner's initial interpretation drew primarily on Machiavelli. Skinner argued that republicanism shared with liberalism a negative conception of liberty. Republican liberty was also diminished by constraints, although it emphasised those 'which arise from personal dependence and servitude'.[9] However, while liberals might focus directly on what rights to liberty should be recognised by the state, so that individuals can enjoy maximum liberty without encroaching unduly on the rights of others, republicans emphasised the duties that citizens must perform in order to reduce the risk of interference by an ambitious aristocracy or a foreign power.[10] Republicans believed that citizens' liberty would be at risk if citizens placed their trust in princes, ie, those with arbitrary power. Because arbitrary power is likely to be abused, citizens had to be willing to engage in political action aimed at limiting or forestalling it. Furthermore, citizens must be prepared to bear arms to defend their republic against foreign encroachment. The state should encourage (and perhaps coerce to some extent) the necessary participation.

When considering the contemporary implications of republican liberty, the lesson Skinner drew was that instead of adopting the liberal focus on rights,

---

[6] Q Skinner, 'Meaning and Understanding in the History of Ideas' (1969) 8 *History and Theory* 3–53; Q Skinner, 'A Reply to My Critics' in J Tully (ed), *Meaning and Context: Quentin Skinner and His Critics* (Cambridge, Polity Press, 1988) 231–88.

[7] Skinner, *Liberty before Liberalism* 55, fn 176.

[8] See, eg, Skinner, 'Freedom as the Absence of Arbitrary Power' 84.

[9] Skinner, 'The Republican Ideal of Political Liberty' 302.

[10] See, eg, Skinner, 'The Idea of Negative Liberty' 200–5.

we should consider more seriously the duties of citizens. The tradition warns us that 'unless we place our duties before our rights, we must expect to find our rights themselves undermined'.[11] Skinner thereby carved out a republican approach that provided a different contrast with liberalism from Pocock's interpretation. The positive-liberty republican revival had contrasted liberal individualism, with its focus on self-interest and individual rights, to positive liberty, with its claim that an active, virtuous political life is the best conception of the good.[12] Skinner's interpretation distanced republicanism from the liberal focus on rights, but it did not privilege an active, virtuous political life as the best conception of the good. On the other hand, Alan Patten argued that Skinner had thereby failed to provide a distinctive alternative to liberalism. Patten argued that liberals 'agree that liberty cannot be maintained unless individuals ... recognize a duty to support just institutions'.[13] Skinner's interpretation of Machiavelli was also challenged.[14]

In any case, Skinner influenced Pettit's initial interpretation of republican liberty. Pettit, too, understood republican liberty as negative.[15] However, while Skinner suggested that republicans and liberals had different approaches to promoting the same conception of liberty, Pettit claimed that there were different conceptions at work. Pettit suggested that liberal liberty only requires the absence of interference. For republican liberty, 'the absence of interference is not enough; what is also necessary is that the agent be protected against interference'.[16] It requires, then, resilient non-interference. Furthermore, Pettit clearly had unjustified interference in mind: he saw a well-conceived rule of law as constitutive of liberty, despite it imposing some constraints.[17]

In *Republicanism*, Pettit sharpened the distinction between liberal and republican liberty by claiming that republican liberty was only diminished by arbitrary power, not by interference.[18] The next subsection indicates that while

---

[11] Q Skinner, 'The Paradoxes of Political Liberty' in S McMurrin (ed), *The Tanner Lectures on Human Values*, vol VII (Cambridge, Cambridge University Press, 1986) 225–50, 249–50. Skinner recommends this within the constraints imposed by a system of representative rather than direct democracy.

[12] ibid 249.

[13] A Patten, 'The Republican Critique of Liberalism' (1996) 26 *British Journal of Political Science* 25–44, 36. *Cf* J-F Spitz, 'The Concept of Liberty in "A Theory of Justice" and Its Republican Version' (1994) 7 *Ratio Juris* 331–47 and A Swift, 'Response to Spitz' at 349–52.

[14] See, eg, P Rahe, 'Situating Machiavelli' in J Hankins (ed), *Renaissance Civic Humanism: Reappraisals and Reflections* (Cambridge, Cambridge University Press, 2000) 270–308; CK Shaw, 'Quentin Skinner on the Proper Meaning of Republican Liberty' (2003) 23 *Politics* 46–56 and J Charvet, 'Quentin Skinner on the Idea of Freedom' (1993) 2 *Studies in Political Thought* 5–16. For an approach with similarities to Skinner's, see M Canovan, 'Two Concepts of Liberty – Eighteenth-Century Style' (1978) 2 *The Price-Priestley Newsletter* 27–43.

[15] P Pettit, 'Liberalism and Republicanism' (1993) 28 (Special Issue on Australia's Republican Question) *Australian Journal of Political Science* 162–89, 164–5.

[16] ibid 165.

[17] ibid 167.

[18] Pettit, *Republicanism* 21–2. This sharp distinction was, however, somewhat obscured by continued reference to 'resilient non-interference': see ibid 69 including fn 6. He mentioned at 69 that liberty as non-domination requires being possessed 'not just of non-interference by arbitrary powers but of a

Skinner continued to claim in *Liberty before Liberalism* that republican liberty *was* diminished by interference, he did follow Pettit in suggesting that republican liberty was a distinct conception of liberty, for it was also diminished by arbitrary power.

B. Liberty before Liberalism

Liberty before Liberalism suggests some assumptions and analogies that inform republican liberty. One assumption is that 'any understanding of what it means for an individual citizen to possess or lose their liberty must be embedded within an account of what it means for a civil association to be free'.[19] In understanding a free civil association, republican writers relied on the ancient metaphor of the body politic, which suggests an analogy between human and political bodies. A human body was understood to be free if it could act at will. This suggested that for a state to be free, it too must be governed by its own will. That meant that a state must be governed by its citizens as a whole. Few republican writers, however, exhibited any enthusiasm for giving the masses a direct share in government. Instead, the right solution was for 'the mass of the people to be represented by a national assembly of the more virtuous and considering'.[20]

Skinner then says that when republicans turn to discuss civil associations that are not free, they refer to what it means for a person to be made a slave.[21] Under Roman law, a slave is not only the property of someone else, but lies within someone else's jurisdiction or power.[22] When this idea was applied to the state, it suggested that a state is unfree not only when its actions are actually directed by the will of anyone other than the representatives of the body politic as a whole. A state is also unfree when its actions are subject to the exercise of discretionary power by someone other than the representatives of the body politic as a whole.[23] Members of such a state, republicans thought, lack civil liberty. The conception of republican liberty that Skinner settles on is diminished by interference but also dependency upon the arbitrary power of another.

Skinner argued that this conception of liberty was adopted by republican writers during the interregnum, such as Nedham, Milton and Harrington. It was opposed by writers employing a contrasting conception of liberty that has become associated with liberalism. Under this contrasting conception, liberty is

---

secure or resilient variety of such non-interference'. See also at 51 and 148 (these additional references are mentioned in Skinner, *Liberty before Liberalism* 83–4 fn 55).

[19] Skinner, *Liberty before Liberalism* 23.

[20] ibid 32.

[21] ibid 36.

[22] ibid 40–1. For a critique of Skinner focusing on Rome, see C Ando, '"A Dwelling Beyond Violence": On the Uses and Disadvantages of History for Contemporary Republicans' (2010) 31 *History of Political Thought* 183–217.

[23] Skinner, *Liberty before Liberalism* 49–50.

only diminished by interference. Skinner mentions that this idea can be found in the law of Rome and was adopted by some Royalists after the outbreak of the English civil war.[24] The clearest formulation of it, though, was provided by Hobbes. Hobbes suggested that the subject is free so long as there is an absence of physical or legal coercion.[25] Hobbes denied the republican association between free states and civil liberty. Instead, freedom is to be assessed by the extent to which one is uncoerced by law.[26]

In distinguishing republican from liberal liberty, Skinner also provided an account of the eclipse of republican by liberal liberty in late eighteenth-century Britain. Skinner focuses on Paley's criticism that the neo-roman interpretation confused liberty with security.[27] Skinner mentions that his discussion of Paley's criticism clarifies his differences with Pettit, since Pettit provided a different explanation for why Paley's criticism is unconvincing.[28]

As the last chapter indicated, Pettit claimed that Paley articulated most clearly the case in favour of liberty as non-interference, and one criticism that Paley made of republican liberty is that it confused liberty with security: it made liberty to consist not merely in the absence of interference but in being free from the danger of having constraints imposed. According to Pettit, Paley thought that when republicans spoke of wanting to safeguard or secure non-interference, they wanted to increase the probability of non-interference.[29] In fact, Pettit continued, republicans wanted to protect people from an arbitrary power to interfere.

Skinner, on the other hand, suggests that the distinctive republican claim not recognised by Paley was that to live in a condition of dependence was itself a form of constraint: 'As soon as you recognise that you are living in such a condition, this will serve in itself to constrain you from exercising a number of your civil rights.'[30] Thus, advisers to arbitrary rulers were unable to speak freely in the interests of the public good. The disgusted reactions of British neo-roman writers to the servility of such advisers helps to explain why these writers so often championed the figure of the independent country gentleman as the repository of moral dignity and worth.[31]

Skinner says that neo-roman writers recognised the liberal tenet, expressed by Bentham, that liberty is a negative concept: it should be measured by the extent to which you are not constrained from acting at will in pursuit of your chosen ends.[32] Skinner says, contrary to Pettit, that republicans were 'far from merely

[24] ibid 5–6.
[25] ibid 6–10.
[26] Q Skinner, *Hobbes and Republican Liberty* (Cambridge, Cambridge University Press, 2008) 154ff.
[27] Skinner, *Liberty before Liberalism* 79–82, 97. For a recent iteration of Bentham's and Paley's complaint, see R Goodin, 'Folie Républicaine' (2003) 6 *Annual Review of Political Science* 55–76, 60–1.
[28] Skinner, *Liberty before Liberalism* 78 fn 43.
[29] Pettit, *Republicanism* 73–4. See also ch 2 n 116.
[30] Skinner, *Liberty before Liberalism* 84.
[31] ibid 95.
[32] ibid 82–3.

wishing to put forward an alternative account of unfreedom according to which it is held to be the product' only of dependence upon arbitrary power rather than actual interference.[33] It is just that republicans recognised an additional constraint. The problem with Paley's argument, Skinner says, is that he assumed that security simply consists in the secure enjoyment of the same absence of constraints that one may happen to enjoy in a regime where that absence of constraints is precarious. However, security actually removes a constraint otherwise suffered: the constraint of having to avoid actions that, while not expressly forbidden, incur the displeasure of the person who enjoys arbitrary power.

Skinner suggests that the neo-roman approach slipped almost wholly out of sight in the nineteenth century, with Paley's criticism prevailing. It was a criticism also made by Lind, it was reinforced by Bentham's and John Austin's jurisprudence, and it was affirmed at the end of the nineteenth century by Henry Sidgwick.[34] Neo-roman liberty may also have fallen from favour because the social assumptions underpinning the theory appeared outdated: the virtues of the independent gentleman began to look irrelevant.[35] The ideological triumph of liberalism left the neo-roman theory discredited.[36]

Lack of awareness of the neo-roman approach is evident, Skinner says, in Berlin's influential discussion of negative and positive liberty. By equating negative liberty with the classical liberal understanding of liberty as non-interference, and then contrasting this with the positive conception of liberty as self-realisation, the neo-roman interpretation of negative liberty is overlooked.[37] A state does not promote neo-roman liberty merely by ensuring its citizens do not suffer unjust interference. It must also ensure that 'its citizens do not fall into a condition of avoidable dependence on the goodwill of others'.[38] Uncovering neo-roman liberty can prompt us today to question whether we have done enough to reduce such dependence.[39]

Skinner's second formulation, then, involves a wider conception of negative liberty than his conception of liberal liberty as non-interference. The latter recognises that A interferes with B when A prevents B from doing what B could otherwise have done.[40] A can achieve this by physically preventing B from acting or through issuing a threat that renders the constrained action ineligible. Liberty as non-interference, however, is not diminished where B is constrained to behave, say, deferentially towards A in order to reduce the likelihood of A imposing a

---

[33] ibid 83.
[34] ibid 97–8.
[35] ibid 96–7.
[36] ibid x.
[37] ibid 112–14.
[38] ibid 119.
[39] For contemporary implications, see Prokhovnik, 'An Interview with Quentin Skinner' 279–80, Q Skinner, 'Freedom of Inclination: On the Republican Theory of Liberty' (2014) 21 *Juncture* 131–35, 133–5.
[40] Q Skinner, 'A Third Concept of Liberty' (2002) *Proceedings of the British Academy* 237–65, 244.

sanction, even though A has not threatened any such sanction if A fails to behave deferentially. By contrast, republican liberty is diminished by this constraint.[41]

Skinner's second formulation did not, however, involve a radical departure from his previous understanding. He had understood that republican liberty was diminished by interference and republicans had emphasised the constraints arising from dependence upon the will of another. His main concern had been to distinguish republican liberty from positive liberty. With his second formulation, he distinguished republican liberty from liberal negative liberty. Through his defence of republican liberty against Paley's criticism that republican liberty was confused, Skinner associated liberal liberty with overlooking the constraint of deference. Under his initial interpretation, he associated liberal liberty with overlooking citizens' duties.

C. Freedom as the Absence of Arbitrary Power

In a 2008 chapter, Skinner revised his interpretation.[42] The revision appears to have been prompted by Pettit's criticism of *Liberty before Liberalism* and also criticisms made by some contemporary champions of liberty as non-interference.[43] I will mention Pettit's criticism here; other criticisms are discussed in the next chapter.[44]

Pettit questioned Skinner's claim that republican liberty was not only diminished by arbitrary power but also by interference. Pettit thought that Skinner's approach suggested that republicans were equally concerned about arbitrary power and about interference. Instead, republicans were primarily concerned about arbitrary power. Republican writers contrasted the civil liberty enjoyed under the rule of law with licentiousness (the freedom available when the proper legal restraints are absent). The scorn they poured on licentiousness shows that they did not think the restrictions imposed by the rule of law were a serious infringement of liberty. Pettit suggested, nevertheless, that those restrictions can be viewed as relevant not to formal liberty, but to its effective realisation.[45]

---

[41] Carter refers to this as a case of anticipated reaction, in contrast to coercion: I Carter, 'How Are Power and Unfreedom Related?' in C Laborde and J Maynor (eds), *Republicanism and Political Theory* (Malden, MA, Blackwell, 2008) 58–82, 60.

[42] Q Skinner, 'Freedom as the Absence of Arbitrary Power' in C Laborde and J Maynor (eds), *Republicanism and Political Theory* (Malden, MA, Blackwell, 2008) 83–101. By contrast, Skinner, *Hobbes and Republican Liberty* continued earlier themes. It elaborated upon Hobbes's support for liberty as non-interference and affirmed that republicans were concerned about the constraint of deference.

[43] P Pettit, 'Keeping Republican Freedom Simple: On a Difference with Quentin Skinner' (2002) 30 *Political Theory* 339–56; Carter, 'How Are Power and Unfreedom Related?'; M Kramer, 'Liberty and Domination' in C Laborde and J Maynor (eds), *Republicanism and Political Theory* (Malden, MA, Blackwell, 2008) 31–57.

[44] See ch 4, s VB and C, including n 68. The main criticism is that the constraint of deference that Skinner envisages as only diminishing republican liberty should instead be understood as diminishing liberty as non-interference.

[45] Pettit, 'Keeping Republican Freedom Simple' 343.

In other words, the extent to which people can enjoy non-dominated choice will depend upon the range of choices effectively available to them.[46]

Pettit did not address the possibility that republican liberty is diminished by arbitrary power and by *unjustified* interference.[47] This possibility is consistent with disapproval of licentiousness and equating liberty with the rule of law. In any case, Skinner mentioned that he accepted Pettit's correction that the primary affront to republican liberty is the existence of arbitrary power rather than interference.[48] He said that republican writers prior to the outbreak of the English civil wars in 1642 complained about state interference with specific liberties and rights. Skinner continued:

> But they argued at the same time that these infringements amounted to mere surface manifestations of a deeper affront to liberty. What basically troubled them was that, by emphasizing its prerogative rights, the crown was laying claim to a form of discretionary and hence arbitrary power that gave it the means to undermine specific rights and liberties with impunity.[49]

Skinner also agreed with Pettit that 'the capacity to engage in acts of arbitrary interference depends upon the prior possession of arbitrary power, and thus that the underlying presence of such power must constitute the fundamental affront to liberty'.[50]

Skinner did not, however, state that he accepts Pettit's suggestion that republican liberty is only diminished by arbitrary power and not by interference. Indeed, he later said in an interview that the 'republican agrees, of course, that if you are coerced then you are not free'.[51] In other words, Skinner's position remains that republican liberty is diminished by arbitrary power and by interference. The first target of republicans was, though, arbitrary power.

The critical revision that Skinner made was no longer conceptualising vulnerability to arbitrary power in terms of constraints. He mentions that while Roman moralists and historians were concerned about the constraint of deference, not all republicans were: he refers to Locke.[52] Indeed, Skinner suggests that both he and Pettit had perhaps unduly focused on the constraint of deference.[53] Vulnerability to arbitrary power changes the character of one's actions: those actions are at the

---

[46] Pettit's distinction between formal and effective liberty is discussed further in ch 4, s II.

[47] Indeed, Skinner mentions in 'Freedom as the Absence of Arbitrary Power' 84 that his position was that republican liberty could be diminished by arbitrary power or by arbitrary interference. He recognises that early-modern theorists of republican liberty embraced a moralized conception, ie, a conception only diminished by unjustified interference. However, in *Liberty before Liberalism* 82–3, he stated that republican liberty was diminished by any form of interference.

[48] Skinner, 'Freedom as the Absence of Arbitrary Power' 84.

[49] ibid.

[50] ibid.

[51] Q Skinner and R Marshall, 'Liberty, Liberalism and Surveillance: A Historic Overview' *OpenDemocracy* (26 July 2013) at www.opendemocracy.net/en/opendemocracyuk/.

[52] Skinner, 'Freedom as the Absence of Arbitrary Power' 91.

[53] ibid 93.

pleasure of the possessor of arbitrary power. That vulnerability impacts upon one's status.

The principal remaining difference with Pettit lies in Skinner referring to dependency on arbitrary power. Skinner referred in *Liberty before Liberalism* to being in a condition of dependence, such as the advisers to rulers.[54] Skinner seems to envisage the arbitrary power that can diminish liberty as either a capacity to interfere or to offer benefits that are depended on, while Pettit envisages only the former as diminishing republican liberty.

It is perhaps primarily to emphasise this divergence from Pettit that Skinner does not describe republican liberty as a non-domination conception.[55] For Skinner, domination appears to involve only an arbitrary power to interfere. However, the wider definition of non-domination that I adopt is diminished by vulnerability to an arbitrary power of interference or dependency on an arbitrary power to confer benefits or both.[56] On the other hand, I understand liberty as non-domination as a conception that is undiminished by constraints. I therefore describe it as a non-negative conception of liberty.[57] I characterise Skinner's third formulation of republican liberty as a mixed conception: it consists in liberty as non-domination (which is diminished by arbitrary power and not by constraints) and liberty as non-interference (which is diminished by constraints).

III. Examining Skinner's Republican Liberty

A. Introductory Comments

In examining Skinner's account of republican liberty, the focus will be on his interpretation in *Liberty before Liberalism*. For the purposes of this section, the revisions brought about by his third formulation are not material; they are, however, referred to in Section IVA. Of the historical writers Skinner relied on for his interpretation of republican liberty, Price and Harrington will be discussed here.[58] While Skinner particularly focuses on some seventeenth-century writers, he notes that Price expressed certain republican themes with greater clarity.[59]

---

[54] See, eg, Skinner, *Liberty before Liberalism* 87–91.

[55] Skinner's lack of clarity on this is reflected in Pettit's assumption that dependency and domination *are* synonymous: Pettit, 'Keeping Republican Freedom Simple' 341–2.

[56] This is consistent with Lovett's description of his own interpretation of liberty as non-domination. Lovett's conception is diminished by a power to offer benefits as well as to interfere: F Lovett, *A General Theory of Domination and Justice* (New York, Oxford University Press, 2010) 49–52. See also Skinner, 'A Third Concept of Liberty' 255 fn 99.

[57] This is further discussed in ch 5, s IIB.

[58] Skinner also refers to other writers during and after the interregnum, including Sidney, Nedham and Milton. See, eg, A Sidney, *Discourses Concerning Government* [1698], ed, T West (Indianapolis, Liberty Fund, 1996) ch 1, ss 2 and 5 for, respectively, positive-liberty dimensions and liberty as non-domination.

[59] Skinner, *Liberty before Liberalism* 26 fn 80.

The seventeenth-century writer discussed is Harrington. His *Commonwealth of Oceana* (1656) is described by Skinner as the most original and influential of all English treatises on free states.[60] Its influence lay on other thinkers rather than in practice. Henry Neville, a member of the Rump Parliament, presented Harrington's ideas for establishing a new government to Parliament in 1659, but his effort was rebuffed.[61] Skinner is, of course, attempting to generalise across writers, so a precise fit with any particular writer may not be expected. My discussion will, though, raise doubt about Skinner's interpretation. Price and Harrington are significant figures in Skinner's account.

In relation to these historical writers, three arguments will be pursued. It will first be argued that Skinner's conception of republican liberty does not fully recognise some positive-liberty dimensions in the accounts of the historical writers. As in previous chapters, I am referring here to accounts of liberty that have an affinity with positive liberty through connecting liberty, for instance, with the exercise of reason or with political participation; they do not, however, go further by identifying liberty with virtuous political participation. It is only necessary to point here to a few positive-liberty dimensions in order to support my concern that Skinner draws an overly sharp contrast between the historical conceptions and positive liberty. That overly sharp contrast also connects to a difficulty with Skinner's narrative of the eclipse of republican liberty, discussed in Section IVA. Chapter six pursues the positive-liberty dimensions in Price and Harrington more fully.

My second argument is that Skinner's account understates the importance the writers attributed to reducing the likelihood of being interfered with. This can give an exaggerated impression of the significance of power damage in the form of deference or lower status. This is, again, significant. It is the focus on power damage that provides the main point of distinction, for Skinner, between republican liberty and liberty as non-interference. Power damage is caused by mere vulnerability to arbitrary power, while interference damage is that caused by actual unjustified interference.

Thirdly, it will be argued that Skinner may overstate historical support for the view that the arbitrary power that diminishes republican liberty is not only an arbitrary power of interference but also an arbitrary power to offer benefits that are depended upon. This impacts upon how well republican liberty can challenge subordination.

B. Price

The last chapter suggested that Price did endorse a non-domination conception of liberty. However, Price also emphasised self-government and drew an analogy

---

[60] ibid 15.

[61] V Sullivan, *Machiavelli, Hobbes, and the Formation of a Liberal Republicanism in England* (Cambridge, Cambridge University Press, 2004) 144.

between a free individual and a free state: just as an individual is only free when directed by his or her own will, a state is not free unless governed by its own will.[62]

Skinner captures this well in his broad account of republican liberty. Skinner also indicated that the state's will was generally understood in terms of the will of its more virtuous citizens: few republicans were keen on giving the masses a direct share in government. I can add here that Price appeared to be one of those few.[63] He appeared to define liberty in terms of a broad franchise.

My main concern is that the notion of self-government, in terms of the individual being ruled by their own reason, or in terms of the franchise, recedes from view when focusing on Skinner's conception of republican liberty as dependency upon arbitrary power. For Skinner, individual self-government merely provided an analogy for a free state. This does not, however, capture the importance of self-government for Price. Indeed, from the perspective of his critics, perhaps the most prominent feature of his approach was that he tied civil liberty to a seemingly broad franchise, as the last chapter demonstrated. Section IVA will show that this feature is not highlighted in Skinner's discussion of the critics.

Skinner also does not convey Price's main rationale for opposing arbitrary power. Skinner refers, for instance, to Price's discussion of the plight of American colonists, where Price said that freedom is lost from the moment a state becomes liable to interference by another power.[64] The implication could be that the mere existence of arbitrary power is damaging. Instead, the principal reason Price offered for opposing arbitrary power is that it leads to likely interference.[65] Price's references to power damage were thereby generally in the context of situations where interference is occurring or very likely.

The remainder of this subsection will demonstrate that Skinner's view that republican liberty is diminished by dependency on an arbitrary power to confer benefits as well as by an arbitrary power to interfere is not found in Price. Exploring this is helpful in explaining the conceptual basis for the finding in the last chapter that Price did not challenge freedom of contract's legitimation of relationships involving subordination.[66] I will begin by amplifying on that finding.

Price said that in a state of nature, there is no right to abridge anyone of their liberty.[67] However: 'The superiorities and distinctions arising from the relation of parents to their children, from the differences in the personal qualities and abilities of men, and from servitudes founded on voluntary compacts, must have existed

---

[62] R Price, 'Observations on the Nature of Civil Liberty, the Principles of Government, and the Justice and Policy of the War with America' [1776] in *Political Writings*, ed, DO Thomas (Cambridge, Cambridge University Press, 1991) 20–75, 26. See also above ch 2, s II.

[63] See ch 2, ss V and VIIA.

[64] Skinner, *Liberty before Liberalism* 50.

[65] Above ch 2, s III.

[66] See ch 2, s VIIB.

[67] R Price, 'Additional Observations on the Nature and Value of Civil Liberty, and the War with America' [1777] in *Political Writings*, ed, DO Thomas (Cambridge, Cambridge University Press, 1991) 76–100, 86.

in a state of nature'.[68] Price describes these as natural subordinations. They involve being under the direction of another. The subordinate is subject to power of an arbitrary or non-arbitrary character. The parent–child relationship involves power of a non-arbitrary character because, he felt, parental love provided a dependable constraint upon oppression.[69]

I will focus, here, though, on the employment relationship. In relation to voluntary servitudes, Price said:

> A person ... in a state of nature, might let out his labour or give up to another, on certain stipulated terms, the direction of his conduct, and this would so far bring him into that station of a servant, but being done by himself, and on such terms only as he chuses to consent to, it is an instance of his liberty, and he will always have it in his power to quit the service he has chosen or to enter into another.[70]

Price said that a free state does not add to these natural subordinations. The natural equality respected by a free state is the equality amongst independent agents, ie, those 'grown up to maturity' who are capable of acquiring property and directing their own conduct.[71] Thus, the subordination of servants to their masters is not compounded by political subordination. For political purposes, servants can be independent agents.[72]

The above quotation indicates, then, that Price regarded the subordination that can occur in employment as compatible with liberty. A definition of liberty that suggested subordination in employment was inconsistent with liberty would suggest exclusion from the franchise. The equality of a free state, Price mentioned, was an equality amongst independent agents.

As indicated earlier in this subsection, Price emphasised interference damage. This was sufficient to critique arbitrary state power, since the state clearly enjoys a power of interference.[73] However, a focus on interference damage does not seem adequate in addressing subordination in employment. Here, a notion of dependency is helpful. As Carole Pateman has argued, the key to understanding the subordination that can underlie employment relations is the vulnerability of the applicant facing poor options.[74] It is difficult to view exploitative job offers as involving interference. Rather than worsening an agent's choice situation, an

---

[68] ibid 85.

[69] R Price, *Additional Observations on the Nature and Value of Civil Liberty, and the War with America* (London, T Cadell, 1777) 24 fn (a). This footnote does not appear in the DO Thomas edition of Price, 'Additional Observations' 87.

[70] Price, 'Additional Observations' 86.

[71] ibid 85–6.

[72] Price's position towards the enfranchisement of servants was actually more ambivalent than is suggested here by his discussion of liberty. Other considerations can support a more restricted franchise. See ch 2, s VIIA.

[73] Skinner, *Liberty before Liberalism* 119 also refers to interference in the context of the state–citizen relationship, and dependency in the context of the relationship between citizens.

[74] C Pateman, *The Sexual Contract* (Cambridge, Polity, 1988) 149.

exploitative offer adds to the choices available.[75] Furthermore, once an offer has been accepted, the employer does not appear to enjoy arbitrary power, but only that power that the employee has agreed to.

While a focus on an arbitrary power of interference may have assisted Price in viewing liberty and subordination as compatible, he recognised that some relationships of subordination were problematic. He referred to the Crown under-mining the independence of the House of Commons by making offices available to members of the House.[76] While he regarded servants as independent agents for the purpose of eligibility for the franchise, Price clearly thought a higher stand-ard of independence was appropriate for parliamentarians. Entering voluntary servitude may be an instance of liberty, but for parliamentarians, it could be an instance of corruption. Furthermore, Price did not regard voluntary servitude in general, outside natural subordination, as ideal. Recall that for Price, liberty as non-domination is part of a broader conception of liberty that includes self-government. In a later piece on America, he indicated a preference for a society of independent yeomen.[77] He regarded independence as better than voluntary servitude.

Price's approach contrasts with Skinner's interpretation of republican liberty. Skinner's republican liberty is diminished by dependency on an arbitrary power to confer benefits. This would cover the benefits of an employment contract. With Price being a prominent writer relied upon in the republican revival, it may come as a surprise to the reader of Skinner to discover that Price did not follow Skinner's conception of republican liberty in this respect. While it might seem unfortu-nate that Price did not treat subordination in employment as diminishing liberty, Skinner's conception can be used to justify a narrow franchise.[78] Price avoided that implication.

Conclusions drawn from the three arguments that were pursued can now be indicated. First, with Price, the positive-liberty dimension of self-government is highly prominent: Price described this as his underlying idea. However, this

---

[75] P Pettit, 'A Definition of Negative Liberty' (1989) II *Ratio* 153–68, 163. On the other hand, Pettit later claimed that an offer of employment *could* constitute interference if the offer is inferior to custom-ary expectations: Pettit, *Republicanism* 53–4. He retracted this claim, claiming that exploitative offers involve domination but do not reduce freedom, in P Pettit, *On the People's Terms: A Republican Theory and Model of Democracy* (New York, Cambridge University Press, 2012) 54 fn 31. Pettit is interpreting 'domination' here more broadly than he had previously. He had equated domination with the absence of republican liberty: see Pettit, *Republicanism* 52.

[76] Price, 'Additional Observations' 97.

[77] R Price, 'Observations on the Importance of the American Revolution' [1785] in *Political Writings*, ed, DO Thomas (Cambridge, Cambridge University Press, 1991) 116–51, 145.

[78] Interestingly, two implications for employment of a dependency conception of liberty were drawn in the US in the nineteenth century. One was that freedom of contract was consistent with liberty, for otherwise the conclusion must be that workers lack full citizenship. The other was that workers' unfreedom could be remedied through, for instance, the application of democratic principles to the work environment. See A Gourevitch, 'Labor and Republican Liberty' (2011) 18 *Constellations* 431–54, 439–42 and, more generally, A Gourevitch, *From Slavery to the Cooperative Commonwealth: Labor and Republican Liberty in the Nineteenth Century* (New York, Cambridge University Press, 2015).

idea drops from view with Skinner's conception of republican liberty. Secondly, Skinner points to Priceian liberty being diminished by mere vulnerability to arbitrary power, but does not provide Price's main rationale for this, which lay in likely unjustified interference. Skinner's account thereby seems to point to power rather than interference damage. Thirdly, Priceian liberty is not diminished by dependency upon an arbitrary power to confer benefits. This has implications for the treatment of subordination in politics and employment.

C. Harrington

As with Price, some key features in Skinner's account are present in Harrington, although not as clearly. In Harrington, there is a contrast between being vulnerable to the lust of tyrants versus the freedom of being in a state consisting in an empire of laws and governed by its people.[79] I accept that Harrington did favour a non-domination conception of liberty. This subsection will consider whether the three arguments just applied to Price also apply to Harrington.

The first argument related to positive-liberty dimensions not being recognised. Like Price, Harrington equated individual freedom with being guided by reason. He associated being ruled by passion with bondage.[80] Harrington also suggested, analogously with individual freedom, that a state is free when it is governed by the people and ruled by rational laws.[81] I simply note here that this notion of self-government is important in Harrington's approach, although it is ultimately missing from Skinner's conception of republican liberty. However, that importance will be demonstrated in chapter six.[82] It is *Price's* identification of liberty with the broad franchise which is most important for this chapter, as the next section will indicate.

My second argument is that Skinner's account does not reflect the importance historical writers attributed to avoiding unjustified interference. Skinner says that of all the writers he has considered, Harrington offered one of the most challenging responses to the liberal approach to liberty, which, in the seventeenth century, was most prominently articulated by Hobbes. Skinner says:

> Hobbes speaks with scorn of the self-governing republic of Lucca and the illusions fostered by its citizens about their allegedly free way of life. They have written, he tells us, 'on the Turrets of the city of *Luca* in greater characters at this day, the word LIBERTAS'. But they have no reason to believe that, as ordinary citizens, they have any more liberty than they would have had under the sultan in Constantinople. For they fail to realise that what matters for individual liberty is not the source of the law but its

---

[79] J Harrington, 'The Commonwealth of Oceana' [1656] in *The Commonwealth of Oceana and A System of Politics*, ed, JGA Pocock (Cambridge, Cambridge University Press, 1992) 1–266, 19–20.
[80] ibid 19.
[81] ibid 19–20.
[82] See ch 6, s IVA.

extent, and thus 'whether a Common-wealth be Monarchical, or Popular, the Freedome is still the same'.[83]

Lucca enjoyed a republican form of government in Renaissance Italy, while Turkey was often used as an exemplar of despotism.[84] Harrington argued that in Constantinople, 'the greatest bashaw is a tenant, as well of his head as of his estate, at the will of his lord'.[85] By contrast, 'the meanest Lucchese that hath land is a free-holder of both, and not to be controlled but by the law; and that framed by every private man unto no other end (or they may thank themselves) than to protect the liberty of every private man'.[86]

Skinner says that Harrington was suggesting that in Constantinople, people were constrained from speaking or acting in such a way as to cause the sultan offence.[87] However, Harrington did not refer to this constraint. He was simply noting that the Lucchese enjoy security with respect to their person and property: this form of liberty is achieved through freehold title to land and the control over the law achieved by a republican form of government. Harrington was affirm-ing the conventional Western understanding of oriental despotism. Patricia Springborg has argued that the idea of oriental despotism, first arising in ancient Greece and then revived after Venice's defeat of the Ottoman Empire in the sixteenth century, was linked to the system of land tenure there, where the land was owned by the monarch and leased to subjects.[88] For Harrington, security in property was linked closely to liberty.[89] Power follows from property ownership. The system of tenure in Turkey suggested in the West that Turkish subjects were entirely beholden to their king. Harrington suggested elsewhere a concern with interference damage: he said that it is a mistake '[w]here a people that can live upon their own imagine that they can be governed by others, and not lived upon by such governors'.[90] Where a state is not free, people are exposed to the 'lusts of tyrants'.[91]

Skinner conceded in 'Freedom from Arbitrary Power' that he had previ-ously emphasised unduly the constraint of deference in his conceptual account of republican liberty. We can note here that this emphasis seems to have also affected

---

[83] Skinner, *Liberty before Liberalism* 85, referring to Hobbes's *Leviathan*.

[84] On Turkey, see, eg, J Priestley, 'An Essay on the First Principles of Government' [2nd ed, 1771] in *Political Writings*, ed, P Miller (Cambridge, Cambridge University Press, 1993) 1–127, 33.

[85] Harrington, 'The Commonwealth of Oceana' 20.

[86] ibid.

[87] Skinner, *Liberty before Liberalism* 86.

[88] P Springborg, *Western Republicanism and the Oriental Prince* (Cambridge, Polity Press, 1992) 281. For a discussion, see A Kamugisha, 'Orientalism, Western Republicanism, and the Ancient *Polis*: Patricia Springborg's *Western Republicanism and the Oriental Prince* and the Canon of Political Thought' (2007) *The Philosophical Forum* 173–98.

[89] L Campos Boralevi, 'James Harrington's "Machiavellian" Anti-Machiavellism' (2011) 37 *History of European Ideas* 113–19, 118–19.

[90] J Harrington, 'A System of Politics' [1770] in *The Commonwealth of Oceana and A System of Politics*, ed, JGA Pocock (Cambridge, Cambridge University Press, 1992) 267–93, 270.

[91] Harrington, 'The Commonwealth of Oceana' 19–20.

his interpretation of Harrington.[92] In 'Freedom from Arbitrary Power', Skinner instead highlighted lower status as the distinctive harm republicans focused upon. However, Harrington's main concern seems to have been interference damage, not power damage in the form of deference or lower status.

Finally, the third argument to consider is that Skinner may overstate historical support for the view that the arbitrary power that diminishes republican liberty is not only an arbitrary power of interference but also an arbitrary power to offer benefits that are depended upon. Harrington stated that 'The man that cannot live upon his own must be a servant; but he that can live upon his own may be a freeman.'[93] In the same way, only when a people can live on their own can there be a democracy.[94] Free government is befitting a people capable of independence. Harrington does link independence to liberty: the franchise does not extend to servants.[95]

With Harrington, then, there is support for Skinner's claim that republican liberty is diminished by dependency upon an arbitrary power to confer benefits.[96] Harrington's approach suggests that this dependency should be interpreted broadly. A narrow interpretation of dependency would suggest that a vulnerable job applicant with a number of poor job offers does not lack liberty: that applicant is not dependent on any particular employer. However, Harrington refers to those who cannot live upon their own. The vulnerable job applicant would fall into this category. The breadth of Harringtonian dependency is also indicated in his statement that a man who can live upon his own, *may* be a freeman. Parliamentarians who accept offices from the Crown, to take Price's concern, may lack Harringtonian liberty. While they are capable of independence, they may have placed themselves in a relationship of dependence. They may be 'bound by golden fetters', as Lovett puts it.[97] Harrington does, then, offer support for Skinner's position on dependency, and suggests as well a broad interpretation of dependency.

To conclude, this discussion of the two most prominent seventeenth- and eighteenth-century writers associated with republicanism raises three questions

---

[92] Another example of downplaying likely interference in characterising the evil of arbitrary power is in Q Skinner, 'Classical Liberty and the Coming of the English Civil War' in M van Gelderen and Q Skinner (eds), *Republicanism: A Shared European Heritage*, vol II: The Values of Republicanism in Early Modern Europe (Cambridge, Cambridge University Press, 2002) 9–28, 27. Skinner cites a passage from an anonymous pamphlet *The Vindication of the Parliament and their Proceedings* (15 October 1642) suggesting that it is better for a crane to keep his head out of a wolf's mouth rather than stand at his mercy as to whether the wolf will bite off his neck. Skinner cites this in support of the proposition that 'it is all too easy to live in servitude without suffering actual oppression or constraint'.

[93] Harrington, 'A System of Politics' 269 (ch I aphorism 13).

[94] ibid 270 (ch I aphorism 14).

[95] Harrington, 'The Commonwealth of Oceana' 75.

[96] See also R Sparling, 'Political Corruption and the Concept of Dependence in Republican Thought' (2013) 41 *Political Theory* 618–47, 629–33.

[97] Lovett, *A General Theory of Domination and Justice* 40. He also indicates in ch 2 that a vulnerable job applicant lacks liberty under his interpretation of liberty as non-domination: they suffer 'decentralized domination'.

about Skinner's interpretation of republican liberty. First, the notion of self-government, including a connection between this and reason, does not feature in Skinner's conception of republican liberty, but only in his broader account of republican liberty. Skinner thereby downplays this positive-liberty dimension at least in Price's account. I mentioned this concern in relation to Harrington, but I only support it in chapter six. Secondly, both these writers emphasised interference rather than power damage. Thirdly, relationships of subordination not involving an arbitrary power of interference do not diminish the conception of liberty proposed by Price, but do diminish Harringtonian liberty. While Skinner's claim that dependency diminishes liberty assists in recognising subordination in employment, this claim can also be used to justify subordination in politics.

Subsection A indicated why the three questions I posed were significant. They go to the contrast drawn between republican liberty and positive liberty as well as liberty as non-interference, and also to how well republican liberty can perform in challenging relationships of subordination. Skinner has been the most prominent intellectual historian to distinguish republican liberty from positive liberty, the main conception he distinguishes liberty as non-domination from is liberty as non-interference, and the main attraction he sees in liberty as non-domination is its targeting of subordination.

IV. Skinner's (and Pettit's) Interpretation of Liberal Liberty

A. Liberal Liberty's Oversight

This section turns to Skinner's interpretation of liberal liberty. Skinner favourably contrasts republican liberty to liberty as non-interference. Three of Skinner's claims about liberty as non-interference will be examined. This subsection begins with Skinner's association of liberty as non-interference with a failure to recognise the constraint of deference. The second and third claims are shared by Skinner and Pettit, and are considered in subsections B and C. The second claim is that there is an association between liberty as non-interference and anti-democratic arguments. The third claim is that liberty as non-interference is the conception of liberty that should be identified with liberalism.

I turn, then, to the first of Skinner's claims. The association between liberty as non-interference and not recognising deference as a constraint is based on this lack of recognition being a factor underlying the assertion of liberty as non-interference in the late eighteenth century and beyond. Section III already cast some doubt on this claim: I argued that Skinner's highlighting of deference does not seem to be reflected in Price and Harrington. If the historical writers were not highlighting deference, that diminishes the significance of the claim that liberty as non-interference failed to recognise deference. It does not enable as stark a contrast between the two conceptions. Here, though, I discuss those writers Skinner identifies with liberty as non-interference.

Skinner, like Pettit, focuses on Paley.[98] Skinner mentions that of the adherents of liberty as non-interference, Paley offered the fullest critique of republican liberty. However, Pettit and Skinner concentrate on different criticisms that Paley made. Pettit is most interested in Paley's concern that certain conceptions of liberty were too demanding.[99] Skinner, on the other hand, discusses Paley's concern that certain conceptions of liberty were confused.[100] Paley argued that certain conceptions of liberty confused liberty with 'the safeguards and preservatives of liberty'.[101]

Skinner assumes that this criticism was directed at republican liberty, and he suggests a major factor behind the eclipse of republican liberty may be that it was seen as confusing liberty with security. In *Liberty before Liberalism*, Skinner defended republican liberty against this charge. Skinner said that republican liberty was not simply the secure enjoyment of the same absence of constraints enjoyed where there is liberal liberty. Republican liberty removes an additional constraint resulting from the existence of arbitrary power, which is the constraint of having to be deferential. Skinner's argument suggested that the crucial difference between liberal and republican liberty lies in the latter's recognition of the constraint of deference.

On the other hand, in 'Freedom as the Absence of Arbitrary Power', the crucial difference between republican and liberal liberty appears to be that the former recognises that arbitrary power imposes harm that is distinct from the imposition of constraints. That harm lies especially in a loss of status. With this revision in mind, Skinner might suggest the following defence against Paley's criticism that republican liberty involves a confusion. He might argue that this criticism failed to recognise that republican liberty is not simply the secure enjoyment of the same absence of constraints enjoyed where there is liberal liberty. Instead, republican liberty recognised harm that cannot be attributed purely to constraints. A failure to recognise the loss of status resulting from arbitrary power should, then, be associated with liberal liberty.

The last chapter showed, however, that Paley did not in fact favour liberty as non-interference. Paley's preferred conception of liberty requires the security achieved by the presence of justified law. Paley expressed reservations about conceptions of liberty which, in addition, require the security achieved by constitutional arrangements. Constitutional arrangements can promote security if they reduce the likelihood of unjustified laws being enacted. Paley was not,

---

[98] Skinner had in fact pointed Paley out to Pettit: Pettit, *Republicanism* 27 fn 2.
[99] Ch 2, s VI discussed Paley.
[100] Skinner, *Liberty before Liberalism* 80–4.
[101] W Paley, *The Principles of Moral and Political Philosophy* [1785], forward by DL Le Mahieu (Indianapolis, Ind., Liberty Fund, 2002) 315. The fuller quote is provided above in text to ch 2 fn 118.

then, simply comparing non-interference and secure non-interference. He was, instead, comparing different levels of security, which I described as legal and constitutional security. His main objection to equating liberty with constitutional security was that with this interpretation, liberty was more susceptible, in careless hands, of becoming identified with the favoured constitutional mechanisms of particular writers. Liberty is thereby confused with those favoured constitutional mechanisms.

One of the writers Paley probably had in mind was Price. He would have been concerned that by identifying liberty with the franchise, Price confused liberty with the franchise. This confusion would have been avoided even if Price had defined liberty in terms of constitutional security, but then have made his case for why he believed constitutional security would be promoted by a broad franchise. Better still, if Price had defined liberty in terms of legal security, there may have been less chance that he would have identified liberty with the franchise.

Skinner's defence of republican liberty on the ground that it does not confuse liberty with security clearly misses the mark, since Paley never alleged that republican liberty was necessarily muddled. Paley simply did not discuss a conception of liberty diminished by arbitrary power. Skinner, however, says that it was not only Paley who argued that neo-roman liberty is confused, but also Lind, Bentham and, later, Austin.[102] He mentions that by the end of the nineteenth century, Sidgwick could declare in his summation of classical liberalism that it was a confusion to think of the freedom of citizens as possible only within free states.

Again, though, Skinner mistakes what confusion was alleged. The last chapter discussed Lind and Bentham.[103] Lind's main concern was the identification of liberty with a broad franchise. Lind mentioned that Price failed to recognise that we should not confuse the power of the people with their liberty. Bentham expressed the same concern. So too did Sidgwick. He said that to identify liberty with the franchise is to overlook the lack of individual freedom, understood as restraint upon following one's preferences, that a minority may suffer.[104]

In the last section, I indicated that self-government falls from view in Skinner's definition of republican liberty. Overlooking this positive-liberty dimension appears to have played a part in his misinterpretation of the criticism of various writers that certain other conceptions of liberty were confused. Part of the confusion that was being alleged by these writers lay in identifying the liberty of the people with the extent to which they shared in government. This comes from identifying liberty with self-government at the political level. While Skinner and Pettit provide different accounts of the eclipse of republican liberty, they both fail

---

[102] Skinner, *Liberty before Liberalism* 97–8.

[103] Ch 2, ss IV and V.

[104] H Sidgwick, *The Elements of Politics*, 2nd edn (London, Macmillan, 1897) 46. Austin also offers no support for Skinner's claim. Indeed, he objected to the moralized nature of Paley's conception of liberty, suggesting that this involved a confusion: see John Austin, *The Province of Jurisprudence Determined* (London, John Murray, 1832) 276 fn * (at 279–80).

to recognise that Price's critics were responding to a positive-liberty dimension in Price's account. Returning to the claim being contested here, though, Skinner has not established that liberty as non-interference should be especially associated with overlooking deference or a loss of status.

B. The Association of Liberty as Non-Interference with Anti-Democratic Arguments

I now turn to some claims made not only by Skinner but also by Pettit. This subsection examines the association of liberty as non-interference with anti-democratic arguments that emerges from their accounts. I am referring here to arguments not only in favour of authoritarian rule but also arguments that oppose, for instance, a broader franchise. Skinner and Pettit contrast liberty as non-interference with republican liberty, which they associate with democratic arguments.

Beginning with Skinner, he suggests that one implication of republican liberty is that the state must not only aim to avoid interfering unjustly with its citizens, an aim that can be expressed through liberty as non-interference. It must also ensure that citizens are not unnecessarily dependent upon the goodwill of state officials. Republican liberty thereby more strongly supports democracy. A benevolent dictatorship might permit significant liberty as non-interference, but it cannot provide its subjects with republican liberty. The historical record appears to resonate with this, for liberty as non-interference, in Skinner's account, was asserted for conservative purposes against adherents of republican liberty. Apart from Paley, Lind, and Bentham in the eighteenth century, there was Hobbes and Filmer in the seventeenth century.[105]

Skinner's point about benevolent dictators not providing their subjects with republican liberty is consistent with Pettit. Pettit's account of the eclipse of republican liberty refers to this value's demandingness – arbitrary power is intolerable even where it is claimed that unjustified interference is unlikely. Pettit also refers to Hobbes and Filmer as employing liberty as non-interference for anti-democratic purposes. However, Pettit also makes a distinct claim. He argues that only republican, not liberal, liberty 'holds out any hope of sustaining the claim that democratization can make the government freedom-friendly'.[106] Pettit says that laws that impose constraints necessarily diminish liberty as non-interference, but such laws do not diminish republican liberty if they are enacted under constitutional arrangements that suitably remove arbitrary power. He refers to Hobbes and Filmer as providing historical support for his claim here about liberty as non-interference.

---

[105] Skinner, *Liberty before Liberalism* 6–10, 97–8.
[106] P Pettit, 'Republican Freedom and Contestatory Democratization' in I Shapiro and C Hacker-Cordón (eds), *Democracy's Value* (Cambridge, Cambridge University Press, 1999) 163–90, 163.

This last claim is not as easily available to Skinner, since he views republican liberty as diminished by interference. In any case, it is the broad historical association of liberty as non-interference with anti-democratic arguments that is of interest here. Both writers contrast this value with liberty as non-domination, which they associate with democratic arguments. The last chapter raised some doubts about this contrast. The critics of Price were responding to his identification of liberty with the franchise; they were not responding to liberty as non-domination. If they had been, they probably would have denied that liberty as non-domination suggests a wide franchise. Furthermore, out of Lind, Bentham and Paley, only Bentham adhered to liberty as non-interference, and he did so partly to divert attention to security, which Lind and Paley also focused on. Their main challenge to a broad franchise rested upon the value of security.

It is true, though, that Hobbes directly employed liberty as non-interference to make anti-democratic arguments. I already referred to Hobbes when discussing Harrington.[107] In critiquing Harrington, Hobbes used the non-interference conception of liberty to suggest that since one is not free from law in either a monarchy or a democracy, the liberty of subjects in each regime is the same.[108] Hobbes was attempting to ridicule the assertion that subjects were only free in governments with a democratic component. Instead, people are subject to constraints in any regime.

However, Hobbes was not suggesting liberty as non-interference as a substantial value. Like Lind, Bentham and Paley, Hobbes highlighted security. He believed that the republican approach of dividing and dispersing power was mistaken because it would produce unstable government. Stable law backed by strong government provided the best security. Any insecurity resulting from an absolute sovereign was insignificant compared to the insecurity produced by anarchy and civil war. His argument rests ultimately upon the value of security, a value not necessarily compromised by legal constraints. Like Bentham, he justified the diminution of liberty as non-interference that accompanied security-enhancing laws:

> For the use of Lawes, (which are but Rules Authorized) is not to bind the People from all Voluntary actions; but to direct and keep them in such a motion, as not to hurt themselves by their own impetuous desires, rashnesse, or indiscretion; as Hedges are set, not to stop Travellers, but to keep them in the way.[109]

---

[107] See s IIIC above.
[108] T Hobbes, *Leviathan* [1651], ed, R Tuck (Cambridge, Cambridge University Press, 1996) 149 (ch 21). For Hobbes's attack on supporters of republican government, see Sullivan, *Machiavelli, Hobbes, and the Formation of a Liberal Republicanism in England* 101–5.
[109] Hobbes, *Leviathan* 239–40 (ch 30). There is an echo of this in Locke: 'that ill deserves the Name of Confinement which hedges us in only from Bogs and Precipices … *the end of Law* is not to abolish or restrain, but *to preserve and enlarge Freedom*': J Locke, 'Second Treatise of Government' [1689] in *Two Treatises of Government*, ed, P Laslett, 2nd edn (Cambridge, Cambridge University Press, 1967) 285–446, 323–4 (para 57). Pettit uses this passage from Locke to illustrate the contrasting republican approach to liberty and law in 'Republican Freedom and Contestatory Democratization' 171.

Since security was the substantial value, the role of liberty as non-interference in pursuing his anti-democratic ideas should not be overstated.

An examination of Filmer would confirm that liberty as non-interference (the liberty to do as one pleases unconstrained by law[110]) also played a limited role in his anti-democratic arguments; he did not propose this value as the state's target. The examination of Price's critics in the last chapter and Hobbes in this subsection, though, is sufficient to suggest that there is an association between liberty as non-interference and anti-democratic arguments. However, this discussion also points to a risk in overstating its significance. In pursuing their anti-democratic arguments, the writers discussed relied heavily upon the value of security.

C. Liberalism and the Two Conceptions of Liberty

The final association examined here is between liberty as non-interference and liberalism. Skinner and Pettit see liberty as non-interference as the dominant liberal interpretation of liberty, with liberty as non-domination overlooked.[111] Of course, if liberalism is defined largely by reference to whether there is a commitment to liberty as non-interference to the exclusion of liberty as non-domination, then liberalism must overlook liberty as non-domination. One way to avoid such circularity would be to broadly accept the conventional understanding of who are prominent liberals. Charles Larmore assumes that Pettit's and Skinner's redefinition of liberalism can be challenged by arguing that some writers centrally identified with liberalism did not espouse liberty as non-interference but, instead, recognised the role of law in constituting freedom.[112] The major writers Larmore discusses are Locke, Benjamin Constant and John Rawls. I will focus a little more sharply on whether those writers actually endorsed liberty as non-domination, but I will keep my discussion brief; I broadly agree with Larmore's conclusion that liberalism cannot be adequately understood in terms of a commitment to liberty as non-interference to the exclusion of liberty as non-domination. I will also briefly discuss Friedrich von Hayek.

I begin, then, with Locke. Larmore indicates that Locke clearly did not espouse liberty as non-interference.[113] The passage Larmore refers to shows that

---

The similarity of this passage to Hobbes indicates that despite the difference between Hobbes and Locke on the question of whether justified law diminishes liberty, both shared a positive attitude towards justified law.

[110] R Filmer, 'Observations Upon Aristotles Politiques, Touching Forms of Government, Together with Directions for Obedience to Governours in Dangerous and Doubtfull Times' [1652] in *Patriarcha and Other Writings*, ed, J Sommerville (Cambridge, Cambridge University Press, 1991) 235–86, 275.

[111] Skinner, *Liberty before Liberalism* 114 fn 22.

[112] C Larmore, 'Liberal and Republican Conceptions of Freedom' (2003) 6 *Critical Review of International Social and Political Philosophy* 96–119, 107. See also C Larmore, 'A Critique of Philip Pettit's Republicanism' (2001) 11 *Philosophical Issues* 229–43; S Ratnapala, 'Republicanism's Debt to Liberalism: Comments on Pettit' (2000) 25 *Australian Journal of Legal Philosophy* 263–71.

[113] Larmore, 'A Critique of Philip Pettit's Republicanism' 235.

Locke's conception of liberty is undiminished by justified interference. This, though, indicates a moralized version of liberty as non-interference: it requires the application of moral criteria in determining whether certain interference diminishes liberty. Skinner and Pettit, however, view Locke as endorsing liberty as non-domination.[114] I would instead describe Locke as endorsing a qualified form of liberty as non-domination. It is not diminished by arbitrary power in general. Instead, Locke contrasted liberty with 'an Absolute, Arbitrary, Despotical Power'. As chapter two indicated, Locke had in mind an extreme form of arbitrary power.[115] Locke also referred to the arbitrary power that exists where others are unconstrained by law.[116] The contrast here seems to be between arbitrary power and the rule of law.

Locke, then, identified liberty with a qualified form of liberty as non-interference and of liberty as non-domination. I agree, though, with Larmore's conclusion that 'Surely something is amiss in a definition of liberalism which accommodates Hobbes, but excludes Locke'.[117] This oddity arises from making their conceptions of liberty so central to understanding their thought and the traditions to which they belong.

Turning to Constant, he also supported a qualified form of liberty as non-domination. In this case, liberty is diminished by the absence of what can be described as particular classic liberal rights that protect against 'the arbitrary will of one or more individuals'.[118] As with Locke, it would be odd to marginalise or exclude Constant from liberalism.

Moving briskly to Rawls, in describing the liberty provided by law, Rawls does so in terms very similar to Pettit's initial formulation of republican liberty.[119] This required resilient non-interference, which consists in the absence of unjustified interference and protection from such interference.[120] This is very similar to liberty as non-domination; it primarily differs in that it is also diminished by unjustified interference. Again, it would be odd to exclude Rawls from liberalism.

While Rawls was a left-of-centre liberal, the conception of liberty employed by one of the twentieth century's most prominent right-wing liberals, Hayek, recommended returning to what he described as the original meaning of freedom, where it was contrasted with slavery. It means 'independence of the arbitrary will

---

[114] Skinner, *Liberty before Liberalism* 55 fn 177, Pettit, *Republicanism* 40.

[115] See ch 2, s VIIB.

[116] Locke, 'Second Treatise of Government' 323–4 (para 57).

[117] Larmore, 'A Critique of Philip Pettit's Republicanism' 235–6. A similar point is made in M Rogers, 'Republican Confusion and Liberal Clarification' (2008) 34 *Philosophy & Social Criticism* 799–824, 805–12. Interestingly, Hobbes is described as 'no liberal' and Locke as a liberal influenced by republican themes in Pettit, 'Liberalism and Republicanism' 166, 167–8.

[118] Larmore, 'A Critique of Philip Pettit's Republicanism' 236 referring to and translating B Constant, 'De la liberté des Anciens compareée à celle des Modernes' in *De la liberté chez les Modernes* (Paris, Pluriel, 1980).

[119] Larmore, 'Liberal and Republican Conceptions of Freedom' 238 referring to J Rawls, *A Theory of Justice* (Oxford, Oxford University Press, 1972) 202.

[120] See text to above n 16.

of another'.[121] This is liberty as non-domination. He claimed that this value was promoted by the rule of law. Interestingly, Hayek provided a different narrative from Skinner's and Pettit's for the eclipse of liberty as non-domination. The value lost ground not to liberty as non-interference but to liberty identified with political participation, under the influence of the French Revolution, and, subsequently, liberty as power, with the rise of the welfare state.[122]

To understand liberalism to a substantial extent through its commitment to liberty as non-interference seems to at least marginalise major figures that are usually associated with liberalism, such as Locke, Constant, Rawls, and Hayek. To describe liberty as non-interference and as non-domination as republican and liberal conceptions is problematic. My references to 'republican' and 'liberal' liberty should generally be understood as references to what is described *by republican revivers* as the conceptions of liberty endorsed by these political traditions.

V. Conclusion

I will sum up conclusions reached in this chapter by relating them to some of Skinner's methodological claims. His 1969 article on methodology was one of the main articles articulating what became known as the Cambridge School of contextualism.[123] Skinner argued for the importance of taking into account what authors were seeking to do with their writing.[124] What debate were they seeking to contribute to? What practical issues were they responding to? He argued that an inadequate understanding of texts may be reached when this historical context is neglected, with the vacuum filled by contemporary concerns and assumptions. Indeed, the actual concerns motivating the writer being examined are likely to be so different from contemporary concerns that little contemporary guidance is likely to be obtained.[125] At the same time, though, he suggested that the contemporary value of studying past texts is that the contingency of our own beliefs may be revealed.[126]

---

[121] FA Hayek, *The Constitution of Liberty* [1960], ed, R Hamowy (Chicago, Chicago University Press, 2011) 59 (ch 1).

[122] ibid 259–60 (ch 11). Hayek refers here to Price, which involves two errors: first, not recognising that Price also had a non-domination conception of liberty and, secondly, that Price's identification of liberty with political participation preceded the French Revolution. In relation to the welfare state, see ibid 65, 354.

[123] Skinner, 'Meaning and Understanding'. See also P Koikkalainen, 'Contextualist Dilemmas: Methodology of the History of Political Theory in Two Stages' (2011) 37 *History of European Ideas* 315–24.

[124] Skinner, 'A Reply to My Critics'.

[125] Skinner, 'Meaning and Understanding' 52–3.

[126] For suggestion that there is a tension between Skinner's contextualism and his attempt at conceptual history, including of liberty, see R Lamb, 'Recent Developments in the Thought of Quentin Skinner and the Ambitions of Contextualism' (2009) 3 *Journal of the Philosophy of History* 246–65.

Skinner saw his work on republicanism as contributing to awareness of the contingency of some of our beliefs concerning liberty. With his initial interpretation of republican liberty, he mentioned that examining republicanism prompts recognition that liberty and individual rights, which are closely tied together in liberalism, can be decoupled. Machiavelli referred to liberty from interference, but emphasised civic responsibilities rather than individual rights. This can prompt us to consider whether we have failed to devote sufficient attention to the link between active citizenship and the protection of individual liberties. Skinner sharply distinguished republican liberty from positive liberty, which might value active citizenship as the best conception of the good rather than merely for its protective role.

This chapter, of course, focused on his later interpretations of republican liberty. While we might assume that the main choices are between positive liberty and liberal liberty as non-interference, the republican tradition, Skinner argues, points to a conception of liberty diminished by dependency upon arbitrary power. This can prompt us to consider whether sufficient attention is paid to dependency as an evil separate from the interference that diminishes liberal liberty as non-interference. I described that separate evil as power damage. *Liberty before Liberalism* pointed to deference and 'Freedom from Arbitrary Power' pointed to status damage.

Skinner is interested in distinguishing republican liberty from positive liberty and liberal negative liberty. This chapter raises the question of whether this interest has led to some misinterpretation of what he describes as republican and liberal liberty and has also contributed to an account that could mislead. In distinguishing republican from positive liberty, Skinner's definition of republican liberty does not seem to reflect the importance of individual self-government in the conceptions of liberty of some of the principal writers he refers to. Furthermore, the distance between liberty as non-domination and liberty as non-interference would indeed be greater if the former were motivated or justified primarily by concern with power damage. However, this chapter raises the question of whether the historical writers Skinner identifies with republicanism were instead employing republican liberty primarily to highlight interference damage. In relation to Skinner possibly overstating support for republican liberty being diminished by dependency on an arbitrary power to offer benefits, this might arise through a concern to present a republican tradition unified by a single conception of liberty, a tradition that can then be contrasted with a liberal tradition based on liberty as non-interference.

Turning to Skinner's interpretation of liberal liberty, his association of this with not recognising the need to be deferential or the loss of status consequent upon vulnerability to arbitrary power is helpful in presenting republican liberty as an attractive value quite distinctive from liberty as non-interference and from positive liberty. This association arises from the criticism of republican liberty that Skinner identifies with liberal liberty. The criticism is that republican liberty confuses liberty with security. I have argued instead that adherents of liberal liberty were troubled by identifying liberty with a broad franchise, a confusion associated with positive liberty.

The chapter then addressed two claims shared by Skinner and Pettit. First, there is the association between liberty as non-interference and anti-democratic thought. I argued that the significance of this should not be overstated, given actual reliance upon the value of security in pursuing anti-democratic ideas. Secondly, there is the association between liberty as non-interference and liberalism. I pointed, however, to the significant place of liberty as non-domination within liberalism, suggesting that to distinguish republicanism and liberalism based on liberty as non-interference and republican liberty is problematic.

Both of the claims about liberty as non-interference considered here overstate the contrast between the two conceptions of liberty and the significance of that contrast for the two traditions. Skinner mentions that he is not 'suggesting that intellectual historians should turn themselves into moralists'.[127] Nevertheless, his work on republican liberty raises the question of whether some of his claims about historical writers may have been influenced by an interest in demonstrating their contemporary relevance.

---

[127] Skinner, *Liberty before Liberalism* 117–18.

4

The Challenge of Liberty
as Non-Interference

I. Introduction

The previous two chapters examined some historical claims of Pettit and Skinner about liberty as non-domination and non-interference. However, Pettit's and Skinner's *revival* of the republican tradition lies in claiming that liberty as non-domination is a more attractive contemporary value than liberty as non-interference. This chapter challenges that claim. I argue that the implications of liberty as non-domination are not as distinct as Pettit and Skinner suggest, for liberty as non-domination is dependent upon considerations relevant to liberty as non-interference. Furthermore, liberty as non-interference, considered together with other values, is better able to target interests that are compromised by arbitrary power. It is in relation to these interests that liberty as non-domination is supposed to have an advantage.

There has been substantial discussion of Pettit's and Skinner's interpretation of liberty as non-domination in the last few decades. Limiting myself to a few examples where an alternative conception of liberty is proposed, some critics have urged a positive conception of liberty: Richard Dagger points to autonomy[1] and Sandel identifies liberty with an active political life.[2] Negative conceptions of liberty have also been employed in critiquing liberty as non-domination. Phillipe van Parijs champions real freedom, which involves the actual possibility, encompassing the means and not just the right, to do whatever one might want to do.[3]

---

[1] R Dagger, 'Autonomy, Domination, and the Republican Challenge to Liberalism' in J Christman and J Anderson (eds), *Autonomy and the Challenges to Liberalism: New Essays* (Cambridge, Cambridge University Press, 2005) 177–203. See also J Maynor, *Republicanism in the Modern World* (Cambridge, Polity Press, 2003) ch 2. *Cf* P Pettit, 'On *Republicanism*: Reply to Carter, Christman and Dagger' (2000) 9(3) *The Good Society* 54–7, 57; P Pettit, *Republicanism: A Theory of Freedom and Government* (Oxford, Clarendon Press, 1997) 81–2; P Pettit, *A Theory of Freedom: From the Psychology to the Politics of Agency* (Cambridge, Polity, 2001) ch 6. For a conception of autonomy that has affinities with liberty as non-domination, see M Garnett, 'The Autonomous Life: A Pure Social View' (2014) 92 *Australasian Journal of Philosophy* 143–58.

[2] M Sandel, 'Reply to Critics' in A Allen and M Regan (eds), *Debating Democracy's Discontent: Essays on American Politics, Law, and Public Philosophy* (Oxford, Oxford University Press, 1998) 319–35, 325–6.

[3] P van Parijs, 'Contestatory Democracy Versus Real Freedom for All' in I Shapiro and C Hacker-Cordón (eds), *Democracy's Value* (Cambridge, Cambridge University Press, 1999) 191–98,

On the other hand, others have proposed a conception much closer to Pettit's and Skinner's interpretation of liberty as non-domination. Frank Lovett argues for an alternative interpretation of liberty as non-domination, while Christian List and Laura Valentini view their conception of 'freedom as independence' as sharing with liberty as non-domination the attribute of requiring the robust absence of constraints.[4]

This chapter, though, builds on a revealing exchange in 2008 between Matthew Kramer and Ian Carter, who champion liberty as non-interference, and Pettit and Skinner.[5] This chapter reinforces Kramer's and Carter's claim that a liberal approach including liberty as non-interference seems superior to relying upon liberty as non-domination. I will focus especially on Pettit and Kramer. Pettit offers a more detailed conceptual analysis of liberty as non-domination than Skinner. While this chapter generally just refers to 'liberty as non-domination', I especially have in mind Pettit's interpretation of this value. Nevertheless, a substantial part of the discussion will be relevant to Skinner's interpretation, and Skinner will be referred to.

Turning to Kramer, his critique fits more neatly with the discussion here than Carter's, and their critiques are consistent with each other.[6] While I refer to 'liberty as non-interference', Kramer and Carter refer to modern interpretations of negative liberty. Furthermore, Kramer mentions that negative liberty is not specifically liberal, although he recognises that most exponents of negative liberty have been liberals.[7] Nevertheless, Pettit and Skinner are contrasting republican liberty as non-domination with liberal liberty as non-interference, and in understanding this contest, Kramer's and Carter's ideas can be described as favouring liberty as non-interference.

To outline how the argument proceeds, Section II describes the analytical understanding of liberty as non-domination and liberty as non-interference presented in Pettit's *Republicanism*. Section III suggests that Kramer's critique poses two challenges to liberty as non-domination. Sections IV and V provide

---

P van Parijs, *Real Freedom for All. What (If Anything) Can Justify Capitalism?* (Oxford, Clarendon Press, 1995) 32–3. *Cf* P Pettit, *On the People's Terms: A Republican Theory and Model of Democracy* (New York, Cambridge University Press, 2012) 42.

[4] F Lovett, *A General Theory of Domination and Justice* (New York, Oxford University Press, 2010), C List and L Valentini, 'Freedom as Independence' (2016) 126 *Ethics* 1043–74. *Cf* I Carter and R Shnayderman, 'The Impossibility of "Freedom as Independence"' (2019) 17 *Political Studies Review* 136–46.

[5] The exchange appears in C Laborde and J Maynor (eds), *Republicanism and Political Theory* (Malden, MA, Blackwell, 2008). See M Kramer, 'Liberty and Domination' 31–57; I Carter, 'How Are Power and Unfreedom Related?' 58–82; P Pettit, 'Republican Freedom: Three Axioms, Four Theorems' 102–30; and Q Skinner, 'Freedom as the Absence of Arbitrary Power' 83–101.

[6] Carter's critique partly engages with Pettit's interpretation of autonomy. This value links liberty with fitness to be held morally responsible. Pettit regards this as an important ideal, but liberty as non-domination is the appropriate conception for the state to aim at. See Pettit, *A Theory of Freedom*.

[7] M Kramer, *The Quality of Freedom* (Oxford, Oxford University Press, 2003) 122. *Cf* Carter, whose aim is to contribute to a liberal theory of justice: I Carter, *A Measure of Freedom* (Oxford, Oxford University Press, 1999) ch 1.

further support for these two challenges, largely in the context of private domination (citizen to citizen). Section IV also includes a discussion of Pettit's *On the People's Terms*. In Section VI, I argue that the two challenges to liberty as nondomination are also pertinent to public domination (state to citizen). Section VII concludes.

II. Pettit's Analytical Account

I commence with Pettit's analytical account of the two conceptions of liberty in *Republicanism* and in writing in the following few years that offered clarifications. Some positions adopted in *On the People's Terms* that warrant separate treatment are discussed in Section IVB.

Starting with liberty as non-interference, Pettit refers to Berlin's understanding of this: an agent is free to the extent to which the agent enjoys unimpeded and uncoerced choice.[8] Interference reduces the agent's choices by, for instance, reducing the range of available options or reducing the expected pay-offs assigned to those options.[9] The interference that diminishes liberty must be intentional in the sense that it involves conduct for which the interferer can be held responsible.[10] It extends, then, to conduct that could foreseeably cause interference. Pettit accepts that adherents of this value may also be interested in the prospect of interference: they can be concerned about the potential severity and probability of interference.[11]

By contrast, liberty as non-domination is diminished by an arbitrary power to interfere, but not by interference.[12] Explicating 'arbitrary power', A has arbitrary power over B when A can intentionally interfere with B without tracking B's interests. 'Tracking interests' requires decisions in accordance with those interests.

In terms of the interests that must be tracked, there are two points to note. First, those interests must be avowed or readily avowable by B. These are interests that B can immediately express or can recognise without great effort.[13] Suppose B's understanding of B's own interests has been distorted through A's manipulation or deception. It would be wrong to identify B's interests with these distorted interests, where that distortion can be dispelled, say, through the provision of appropriate

---

[8] Pettit, *Republicanism* 17.

[9] ibid 53.

[10] In ibid 52, Pettit refers to actions for which negligence can be sensibly alleged but it is clear that Pettit is not intending a restriction to morally culpable behaviour: see Pettit's reference at 52 to D Miller, *Market, State, and Community: Theoretical Foundations of Market Socialism* (Oxford, Clarendon Press, 1989) 35. Miller at 36 distinguishes moral responsibility from moral culpability.

[11] Pettit, *Republicanism* 46 fn 7.

[12] ibid 21–2.

[13] Pettit, *A Theory of Freedom* 156–8. For an earlier formulation of 'avowable interests', see P Pettit, 'Republican Freedom and Contestatory Democratization' in I Shapiro and C Hacker-Cordón (eds), *Democracy's Value* (Cambridge, Cambridge University Press, 1999) 163–90, 176.

information. By referring to avowable interests, Pettit seeks to avoid paternalism while, at the same time, recognising that interference can involve manipulation or deception.[14]

Secondly, only B's interests that are consistent with the common interest must be tracked. Pettit envisages a democratic process for institutionally determining the common interest, although he recognises that this can fail on occasions, for example, where the majority oppresses a minority.[15] The question of what process is appropriate to constrain the state to tracking the common interests of citizens is relevant to public domination, and that is especially considered in Section VI. Sections II to V are largely concerned with hypotheticals involving private domination where it is assumed that A has an arbitrary power to interfere with B's interests that are consistent with the common interest.

Turning now to the measurement of arbitrary power, Pettit considers A's ease of interference and the severity of that potential interference.[16] With respect to ease of interference, he has in mind A's capacity to interfere and the costs A would experience if A attempts to interfere. The costs of interference can take into account whether A adheres, or at least aspires to adhere, to a moral code. In that case, A can be exposed to effective rebuke if A interferes with B's interests.[17] Pettit mentions that the incentives of shame and glory are invoked throughout the republican tradition.[18] Presumably, a virtuous agent can be more easily shamed. Thus, the intensity of domination is less where A is virtuous. However, domination is not lessened if A just happens to be inclined not to interfere.

In explaining the protection offered by liberty as non-domination, Pettit suggests this value is modally robust: it guarantees liberty not only in this world, given existing inclinations of those with arbitrary power, but also in a world where those with arbitrary power are inclined against us. He said: 'Let the agents in question take against me ... None of this matters if I really enjoy non-domination.'[19]

It would seem that modal robustness does not extend to a world where those with arbitrary power not only have hostile inclinations but also possess significantly less virtue: the assessment of liberty as non-domination takes into account virtue but not inclinations. On the other hand, the constraint of virtue is triggered, it seems, where A is rebuked or anticipates being rebuked. The probability of such rebuke would be less in a world where A's associates who also enjoy arbitrary

---

[14] P Pettit, 'Republicanism: Once More with Hindsight' in *Republicanism: A Theory of Freedom and Government*, paperback edn (Oxford, Clarendon Press, 1999) 283–305, 290–1, Pettit, *Republicanism* 53, Pettit, *On the People's Terms* 58–9. In the case of children, Pettit suggests their liberty as non-domination would only be diminished if their guardians, etc, have a capacity to interfere with those interests that children are commonly accepted as having. There is no reference here to readily avowable interests. See Pettit, *Republicanism* 119–20.

[15] Pettit, *Republicanism* 55–6, 197–200.

[16] ibid 57.

[17] ibid 64.

[18] ibid 225–6.

[19] ibid 69.

power are inclined against B. In this way, virtue may be a weaker constraint in the counterfactual world.

Liberty as non-interference is also modally robust. This value is diminished not only by constraints upon the achievement of the preferences people have in this world. It is also diminished by constraints upon the achievement of preferences people might otherwise have had.[20] Thus, liberty as non-interference is not enlarged by individuals adapting their preferences so that they are consistent with the constraints they face.

The most prominent contrast between the values, though, is highlighted through a hypothetical involving slaves with contrasting masters.[21] One master does not interfere, while the other master frequently interferes. Pettit claims that the slave of the non-interfering master enjoys significantly greater liberty as non-interference than the slave of the interfering master, but each slave suffers the same absence of liberty as non-domination if each master possesses the same arbitrary power. In other words, each slave faces the same level of domination.

Pettit softens the contrasting implications of these conceptions by suggesting that while formal liberty as non-domination is diminished by arbitrary power, this value's effective realisation depends upon 'conditioning factors': these include interference and also natural and social limitations upon the range of choice people enjoy.[22] Pettit is drawing here on a distinction between formal and effective liberty used by some adherents of liberty as non-interference.[23] Focusing on liberty as non-interference might suggest overlooking whether people have the resources to avail themselves of the negative liberties they formally enjoy. However, an interest in freedom of choice suggests an interest in people's capacity to effectively utilise the choices available to them: it suggests an interest in effective, not just formal, liberty.[24] With this approach, the slave with the interfering master has less effective liberty as non-domination than the other slave. It is, though, formal liberty as non-domination that Pettit relies on in distinguishing liberty as non-domination from liberty as non-interference.

With formal liberty only being diminished by arbitrary power, it targets circumstances where people suffer the damage caused by mere exposure to arbitrary power even if they are not interfered with.[25] I describe this as 'power damage'. Pettit draws attention to three types of power damage. First, there is the uncertainty and consequential anxiety and inability to plan caused by the possibility of interference. Secondly, there is the need to engage in strategic conduct in order to lower the probability of interference. Thirdly, those vulnerable to arbitrary

---

[20] ibid 69 fn 6.

[21] ibid 22–3, 64.

[22] ibid 75–6. The effective realisation of liberty as non-interference includes all these factors except for intentional interference: this diminishes formal liberty as non-interference.

[23] See, eg, WL Weinstein, 'The Concept of Liberty in Nineteenth Century English Political Thought' (1965) 13 *Political Studies* 145–62.

[24] Pettit, *Republicanism* 83.

[25] ibid 85.

power suffer a loss of status.[26] I will also refer to 'interference damage', which is the damage directly caused by actual unjustified interference. Since both forms of damage can result from exposure to arbitrary power, 'power damage' has a narrow meaning here: it is the damage caused by arbitrary power excluding the direct damage caused by interference.

Pettit seems to suggest that for adherents of liberty as non-interference, power damage may or may not be focused on, depending upon what other values are consulted. Pettit claims that an advantage of liberty as non-domination is that it can be the state's single target. It is a value that does not require the supplementation by other values that is necessary if one applies liberty as non-interference and opposes a minimal state.[27] Those other values are likely to be contentious.[28] Furthermore, Pettit believes that having a single value provides clearer guidance than a pluralistic approach that does not rank values or principles.[29] If a pluralistic approach does rank values or principles, a monistic approach still has an advantage: it is likely to be especially arresting. He suggests that the influence of Rawls and Hayek is partly attributable to them presenting a unifying idea. Pettit recognises, though, that any monistic approach that is recommended must also provide attractive guidance: it must unify our significant commitments.

III. Kramer's Critique and Two Challenges to Liberty as Non-Domination

Kramer pursued his critique initially in a chapter in *The Quality of Freedom* and then, more briefly, in an exchange on this value with Pettit, Skinner and Carter.[30] It suffices here to focus mostly on the shorter piece. Kramer largely targets Skinner but also Pettit, since Pettit's and Skinner's claims are quite similar. Kramer's criticisms can be broadly captured in terms of the two challenges to liberty as non-domination that will be pursued in this chapter. I will mention the two challenges and give for each challenge an example from Kramer.

The first challenge is to the distinctiveness of its implications. The distinctive quality of liberty as non-domination is that it is diminished by power. I describe this conception of liberty as entailing a 'power-centred approach'. By contrast, liberty as non-interference is concerned about actual interference and the probability of interference: I describe this as a 'probabilistic approach'. Clearly, if adherents of both conceptions need to largely focus on the same set of probabilities, the

---

[26] ibid 87.

[27] ibid 80–1.

[28] ibid 12, 96 fn 3.

[29] P Pettit, 'In Reply to Bader and Vatter' in M Williams and S Macedo (eds), *Political Exclusion and Domination* (New York, New York University Press, 2005) 182–8, 184–5. The monistic/pluralistic distinction here is different from what Berlin had in mind: see ch 1, s II.

[30] Kramer, *The Quality of Freedom*, Kramer, 'Liberty and Domination'.

distinctiveness of a power-centred approach will be undermined. The example Kramer gives is that adherents of liberty as non-domination will need to be concerned about the probability of agents gaining access to arbitrary power, for they wish to reduce vulnerability to arbitrary power. Kramer says that adherents of liberty as non-interference should share this concern since substantial arbitrary power is likely to be abused.[31]

The second challenge to liberty as non-domination is to how well this value captures the damage caused by arbitrary power in comparison to a liberal approach involving liberty as non-interference. One way Kramer pursues this is by suggesting that liberty as non-interference does better than Pettit and Skinner realise. Kramer quotes the following passage from Skinner:

> What the [civic-republican] writers repudiate *avant la lettre* is the key assumption of classical liberalism to the effect that force or the coercive threat of it constitute the only forms of constraint that interfere with individual liberty. The writers insist, by contrast, that to live in a condition of dependence is in itself a source and a form of constraint.[32]

Kramer, however, argues that one's overall liberty as non-interference is not just diminished by force or coercive threats.[33] It is also diminished, for instance, by the need to be deferential. Kramer argues that this constraint reduces the range of options available to the person who is vulnerable to arbitrary power. If the existence of that power means that the vulnerable person cannot do X without being deferential, that power has removed the option of being able to do X without being deferential.

Kramer's critique involves a direct comparison between the two conceptions of liberty. However, while Pettit favours liberty as non-domination as a single target partly because this monistic approach can provide clearer guidance, adherents of liberty as non-interference instead supplement liberty as non-interference with other values. This supplementation is, indeed, necessary if Pettit's other forms of power damage (uncertainty and lack of status) are to be considered.

The extent to which Pettit's monistic approach provides clearer guidance has been challenged by Wojciech Sadurski in the criminal justice context. He argued that promoting republican liberty requires the same weighing and balancing job that is 'faced in a more traditional retributivism-cum-utilitarian mix'.[34] In other words, while republican liberty can unify our commitments in the sense of including them, this is not especially helpful because it does not provide clearer guidance than the traditional pluralistic approaches. I elsewhere focused on the opposite problem: that republican liberty's exclusion of desert in the criminal

---

[31] Kramer, 'Liberty and Domination' 46–7.

[32] This is part of a quote from Q Skinner, *Liberty before Liberalism* (Cambridge, Cambridge University Press, 1998) 84 (fns omitted) in Kramer, 'Liberty and Domination' 37.

[33] Kramer, 'Liberty and Domination' 37–9.

[34] W Sadurski, Review of *Not Just Deserts: A Republican Theory of Criminal Justice* by John Braithwaite and Philip Pettit (1991) 10 *Law and Philosophy* 221–34, 230.

justice context is problematic.[35] In a similar vein here, I raise the question of whether Pettit's theory excludes too much to offer a satisfying theory. In other words, does it unify enough of our significant commitments? I raise this question in the context of the second challenge: the concern is whether liberty as non-domination performs well enough, in comparison to a pluralistic approach involving liberty as non-interference, in capturing the damage caused by arbitrary power. Discussion of this, though, draws attention to other values that seem to merit separate consideration and which target concerns going beyond arbitrary power. Those other values are excluded by Pettit's approach. For Pettit, part of the advantage of liberty as non-domination is that it does not need to be supplemented by other values.

IV. The Distinctiveness of Liberty as Non-Domination

A. Introductory Remarks

The first challenge to liberty as non-domination to be explored here goes to its distinctiveness. I begin with the role that distinctiveness plays in the case for liberty as non-domination. Pettit and Skinner argue that the attractiveness of liberty as non-domination lies in how it sensitises us to arbitrary power. It draws on the plight of a slave, a paradigmatic example of an unfree person. The central feature of slavery, they suggest, is being vulnerable to the arbitrary power of a master. By contrast, liberty as non-interference only looks to actual interference or the prospect of interference. Liberty as non-interference, they claim, thereby fails to target circumstances where there is arbitrary power but there is no interference and no significant likelihood of interference. More generally, liberty as non-interference downplays the gravity of what I have described as power damage, that is, the damage caused by arbitrary power excluding that directly caused by interference. Liberty as non-interference downplays power damage by suggesting that even slaves may enjoy some liberty. In a hypothetical of two slaves, where one has a non-interfering master and the other an interfering master, liberty as non-interference suggests that the former slave enjoys greater liberty. By contrast, the two slaves suffer the same domination.

It is the claimed lack of variation of liberty of non-domination in the face of different probabilities of interference that suggests that liberty as non-domination is uncompromising in the face of arbitrary power: even those with non-interfering masters enjoy no more liberty as non-domination than those with

---

[35] E Ghosh, 'Applying Pettit's Republican Liberty to Criminal Justice and Judicial Decision-Making: The Need for Other Values Including Desert and a Suggestion That They Be Understood Consequentially' (1999) 22 *University of New South Wales Law Journal* 122–54. See also RA Duff, *Punishment, Communication, and Community* (Oxford, Oxford University Press, 2001) 10.

interfering masters. I will argue, though, that this stark contrast, where liberty as non-domination does not vary with the likelihood of interference, while liberty as non-interference does, is overdrawn. This is part of a discussion that questions the extent to which liberty as non-domination has distinct policy implications. Furthermore, it will become evident that applying liberty as non-domination is more complex than one might have supposed. In pursuing the first challenge, subsection B focuses on the interpretation of liberty as non-domination found in Pettit's *Republicanism*, as clarified in subsequent writing. Subsection C focuses on some points made in *On the People's Terms* that warrant separate discussion.

B. Pettit's Interpretation in *Republicanism*

I will build here on Kramer's critique. Section III mentioned Kramer's claim that adherents of both conceptions will often focus on the same set of probabilities. One principal reason is that since it is typically the case that substantial arbitrary power is likely to be abused, adherents of liberty as non-interference will also focus on reducing the probability of agents gaining access to the means of such arbitrary power.[36] I will illustrate this and also indicate additional ways in which both approaches may need to focus on the same set of probabilities.

Let us start with an agent's capacity to interfere. Consider where a slave can exercise a right of appeal to a magistrate before a master can engage in certain severe forms of interference. In determining the arbitrary power the master possesses, we need to recognise that the capacity to interfere will depend upon the probability of that contemplated interference being disallowed by the appellate authority. On the other hand, we would also need to consider the slave's vulnerability to the arbitrary power of the magistrate. To assess this, we need to consider the probability of the master seeking to severely interfere with the slave, since that is the precondition for the magistrate having any decision-making power here. Thus, in determining the overall power that the slave is vulnerable to, we must assess the probability of certain decisions by both the master and magistrate. The application of liberty as non-interference would also require assessment of these probabilities, but without the additional complexity of having to relate that assessment back to the measurement of power.

I turn now to ease of interference and, in doing so, return to Pettit's hypothetical concerning slaves with contrasting masters. Pettit posits two masters who both enjoy the same arbitrary power; it is just that one is inclined to interfere while the other is not. I will point to some difficulties in understanding that both masters actually have the same power.

---

[36] Kramer, 'Liberty and Domination' 46–7.

The underlying assumption seems to be that the masters have the same capacity and ease of interference. Focusing on ease of interference, both masters must, then, experience the same absence of external and internal sanctions. The absent external sanction is a legal penalty for interference. The internal sanction lies in the pangs of a guilty conscience that virtuous masters would suffer if they interfere and are rebuked. Pettit's hypothetical, then, suggests masters with the same level of virtue and under the same legal regime.

Further stipulations are, however, necessary. If the interfering master interferes more due to obtaining greater gratification from interference, that master would in fact enjoy greater arbitrary power, for ease of interference must not only take into account costs but also benefits from interference. It is surely net costs of interference that are relevant to the degree of arbitrary power enjoyed.

Another reason, however, why one master may be more inclined to interfere is not due to any greater benefit from interference, but due to less self-control. Even with this circumstance, it is still difficult to regard the power of both masters as the same. Pettit's hypothetical overlooks the fact that power is dependent partly upon the slave's assessment of the probability of interference if the slave does not act in accordance with the perceived preferences of the master. Such power can be exercised, as Carter notes, even in the absence of any threat.[37] The assessment of the probability of interference is likely to depend upon whether the master has in the past demonstrated an inclination to interfere or not. This insight was accepted by Machiavelli, a prominent figure for the republican revivers. He suggested that a ruler that punishes a few can establish a reputation that assists in maintaining order.[38] He suggested that to control an army, on the other hand, a reputation for cruelty may be necessary. He also recognised, however, that excessive interference, leading to hatred, can undermine power. A propensity to interfere, then, can affect the degree of power enjoyed, and the relationship between the two variables is not a simple one.

Pettit's hypothetical of an interfering and non-interfering master who nevertheless share the same arbitrary power is intended to illustrate the distinctiveness of liberty as non-domination. This hypothetical, however, loses some plausibility when one looks closely at it. The very low probability of interference by one of the masters suggests that this master may enjoy less ease of interference. Even if this is not the case, the lower probability of interference is likely to suggest, via the slave's awareness of this, that the non-interfering master enjoys less arbitrary power, at least until the master demonstrates a willingness to interfere. These conclusions are significant, for the attractiveness of liberty as non-domination is partly reliant upon it providing a contrasting alternative to liberty as non-interference: the former focuses on power while the latter focuses on probability. The latter thereby

---

[37] See, eg, I Carter, 'How Are Power and Unfreedom Related?' 58–82, 59–61.
[38] N Machiavelli, *The Prince* [1532], eds, Q Skinner and R Price (Cambridge, Cambridge University Press, 1988) 58–60 (ch 17).

contrasts with the strong republican message that slaves, no matter how little they are interfered with, simply lack liberty.

Interestingly, Pettit himself explicitly relies on probabilistic considerations when discussing the responsibilities of the state to protect its citizens against crime: he relies on the likely deterrent effect of different penalties in assessing what penalties would sufficiently constrain arbitrary power.[39] Furthermore, in considering how to reduce the arbitrary power of state officials, Pettit refers to what he calls deviant- and complier-centred strategies. The deviant-centred strategy focuses on those who will immediately deviate in the absence of sanctions, while the complier-centred strategy focuses on those who will tend in the first instance to comply. Pettit's preference for the complier-centred strategy is substantially based on his understanding of the probable impact of those strategies in reducing deviant behaviour by officials.[40]

While I have highlighted the importance of considering the probability of interference when assessing arbitrary power, Pettit's suggestion that liberty as non-domination is modally robust provides a way of avoiding probabilistic calculations.[41] With this approach, the adequacy of protection against arbitrary power is assessed upon the assumption that all agents who possess arbitrary power are inclined against us. This seems similar to the assumption that there is a high probability that all agents will abuse any substantial arbitrary power they possess.

Let us return to the hypothetical of a slave-master where the slave can appeal to a magistrate before severe interference is perpetrated. To assess whether the protection is modally robust, we must assume that the master and the magistrate are inclined against the slave. In that case, it seems quite likely that both would agree to interfere and, consequently, the dispersion of power achieved through the appellate mechanism would be ineffective. By contrast, an assessment of actual probabilities might suggest that the appellate mechanism would be helpful. The master may obtain significant benefits from interference that do not obtain to the magistrate. There may be a significance chance that the magistrate will disallow contemplated interference by the master, and thereby curtail the master's arbitrary power.

The conclusion that it is only by taking into account the actual probability of interference that persuasive support for dispersing power may be available sits awkwardly with Pettit's claim that liberty as non-domination supports the

---

[39] J Braithwaite and P Pettit, *Not Just Deserts: A Republican Theory of Criminal Justice* (Oxford, Clarendon Press, 1990) 139–40. While this work applied Pettit's earlier, negative conception of republican liberty, their approach to criminal-law matters is endorsed in Pettit, *Republicanism* 155.

[40] See Pettit, *Republicanism* ch 7 including 217–19. On the more general relationship between domination and interference, see also B de Bruin, 'Liberal and Republican Freedom' (2009) 17 *Journal of Political Philosophy* 418–39, 427. He argues for the epistemological priority of liberal over republican freedom. In other words, one cannot determine that an inequality of resources leads to domination without knowledge that resource inequality is often accompanied by interference.

[41] This was mentioned in text to above n 19.

dispersion of power.[42] Indeed, with the modal robustness assumption, it may be hard to envisage measures that can significantly reduce domination. Non-domination may be an unattainable ideal. Pettit, however, proposes the value as a challenging, yet attainable, ideal.[43] This characterisation of the ideal may be easier to defend if the modal robustness assumption is dropped and one assesses the actual probability of interference.

This discussion, however, also raises a question about Kramer's approach. Kramer mentions that the application of liberty as non-interference will often focus on the same set of probabilities as liberty as non-domination because substantial arbitrary power is likely to be abused. This might suggest that his approach to liberty as non-interference also counsels despair in thinking about whether institutional arrangements can ever afford significant protection against interference.

Kramer, however, was only suggesting that the autocratic power that troubled republicans should also trouble adherents of liberty as non-interference.[44] This does not undermine his general approach to assessing what liberty is possessed where arbitrary power is present. He said, 'The crucial consideration … is not the sheer fact of the domination, but the probability that that fact will result in the prevention of certain actions or combinations of actions.'[45] In other words, the crucial consideration is the probability that arbitrary power will lead to constraints.

C. Pettit's Interpretation in *On the People's Terms*

The last subsection illustrated ways in which Pettit's power-centred approach is dependent upon probabilistic calculation. This undermines the distinctiveness of liberty as non-domination. This subsection argues that Pettit's more recent interpretation of liberty as non-domination, found in *On the People's Terms*, is open to the same challenge. I first consider Pettit's treatment of interference that is perpetrated by someone with arbitrary power. Secondly, I consider how ease of interference is assessed and, thirdly, how the enjoyment of an adequate level of liberty is recognised.

In *Republicanism*, Pettit suggested that interference does not diminish liberty as non-domination, but it does condition it; it renders liberty less effective. In this way, Pettit maintained the distinctiveness of liberty as non-domination while not excluding the relevance of interference. Pettit's approach, however, was flawed, as Ronen Shnayderman pointed out. If A has the arbitrary power to prevent B doing x,

---

[42] Pettit, *Republicanism* 173.
[43] ibid 47–8.
[44] See Kramer, 'Liberty and Domination' 46–7.
[45] Q Skinner, 'Freedom as the Absence of Arbitrary Power' 50.

then B simply lacks formal liberty of non-domination in relation to x; there is no formal liberty that can be more or less effective.[46]

Pettit no longer relies on a distinction between formal and effective liberty. Instead, his inclination is to treat the damage caused by interference by a person with arbitrary power as distinct from the loss of liberty, but it could also be treated as a freedom-related harm.[47] It is unclear how this is consistent with Pettit's monistic consequentialism. Where a state has limited resources to address all domination, the probability of interference is surely relevant in determining priorities.

The second aspect of Pettit's interpretation that will be addressed here concerns ease of interference. Pettit had described both penalties and rewards as sanctions.[48] They were both relevant to ease of interference. However, in *On the People's Terms*, ease of interference only takes into account penalties and not rewards. This enables a new contrast between the conceptions of liberty. Liberty as non-interference may be promoted by offering potential interferers rewards for non-interference, while liberty as non-domination requires penalties for interference.[49] Pettit says that even if the reward route reduces the probability of interference to a greater extent than the penalty route, liberty as non-domination suggests the penalty route. The problem with the reward route is that it preserves the option of interference; it is just that it provides a further option of not interfering and collecting a reward.

Pettit is assuming, it seems, that the choice is not, say, between a relatively small penalty and foregoing a substantial and eagerly sought benefit.[50] This choice does indicate, though, that it is the felt costs for the possessor of arbitrary power that is critical, not whether those costs take the form of a penalty or reward.

In any case, Pettit provides another justification for the penalty route: only it conveys community disapproval. He mentions:

> Criminological evidence suggests that what keeps most people on the right side of the criminal law is the fact that that law communicates public disapproval of offenders and leads most people to put most offences off the menu of possibilities that they consider as genuine options.[51]

Pettit's use of this evidence is another example of how he assesses ease of interference partly through considering the probable effect of different strategies on

---

[46] R Shnarydermann, 'Liberal vs Republican Notions of Freedom' (2012) 60 *Political Studies* 44–58, 53.

[47] Pettit, *On the People's Terms* 68–9. Skinner could instead have recourse to liberty as non-interference since this, together with liberty as non-domination, constitute republican liberty. His interpretation of liberty as non-interference is inconsistent with a distinction between formal and effective liberty: Q Skinner, 'A Third Concept of Liberty' (2002) *Proceedings of the British Academy* 237–65, 244–6.

[48] Pettit, *Republicanism* 212.

[49] Pettit, *On the People's Terms* 70.

[50] See also Pettit, *A Theory of Freedom* 23.

[51] Pettit, *On the People's Terms* 118, referring to T Tyler, *Why People Obey the Law* (New Haven, Yale University Press, 1990).

reducing interference.[52] If the penalty route is more effective in reducing the probability of interference, liberty as non-interference will also favour this route.

The third aspect of Pettit's recent interpretation that will be addressed here is the test for enjoying an adequate level of liberty. He mentioned in *Republicanism* that an advantage of liberty as non-domination is being able to look others 'in the eye'.[53] He now suggests that this eyeball test provides a good index for private domination. The test involves the application of standards found in particular societies:

> The reference to the standards of their society is necessary since there is likely to be cultural variation in what counts as mere timidity rather than rational fear or deference. People are liable to vary across societies in the different levels of vulnerability to which they have become inured, in the probability that they assign to others becoming hostile, and in the level of trust that they invest in one another.[54]

The perceived probability of others interfering informs, then, the test of what level of arbitrary power is acceptable in a particular society. To the extent to which perceived probabilities track actual probabilities, Pettit confirms yet another way in which the two conceptions of liberty take into account similar probabilities.

To conclude this section, under either Pettit's older or more recent interpretation, the actual probability of interference is highly relevant to measuring liberty as non-domination. This undermines the distinctiveness of the implications of this value, in contrast to liberty as non-interference. It also suggests significant complexity in applying liberty as non-domination. In considering the same probabilities as liberty as non-interference, liberty as non-domination does so circuitously, for those probabilities are only relevant to measuring arbitrary power. An approach resistant to assessing probabilities is suggested by Pettit's modal robustness criterion. With this approach, one instead assumes that all agents with arbitrary power are likely to interfere with us. On the other hand, I suggested that it might fit better with Pettit's overall approach to reject this criterion.

Pettit's approach in his recent interpretation to assessing an acceptable level of liberty as non-domination draws on the perceived probability of interference. Where there is a close connection between perceived and actual probabilities, this provides another way in which the actual probability of interference is relevant.

Finally, Pettit concedes that interference damage may need to be considered as a distinct type of loss or as a freedom-related harm. In this way, probability again needs to be considered, say, in determining priorities in addressing subordination, but this time, directly, in the same way as it would be considered by adherents of liberty as non-interference.

---

[52] For some other examples, see text to above n 39.
[53] Pettit, *Republicanism* 87.
[54] Pettit, *On the People's Terms* 85. See also 84 and 176.

This section began by noting that the sharp exclusion of probabilistic consideration from liberty as non-domination underpins the uncompromising stance that liberty as non-domination is supposed to take to arbitrary power. While that uncompromising stance has been undermined here by pointing to the role of probabilistic analysis, it has not been denied that liberty as non-domination may be more substantially diminished than liberty as non-interference where there is arbitrary power but interference is highly unlikely. How advantageous this is, though, will depend partly upon how effectively liberty as non-domination captures power damage. This is considered in the next section.

V. The Damage Caused by Arbitrary Power and Looking Beyond Liberty

A. Introductory Remarks and Interference Damage

The second challenge to liberty as non-domination queries how well this value performs, compared to a pluralistic approach involving liberty as non-interference, in targeting the damage caused by vulnerability to arbitrary power: highlighting such damage is supposed to be the strength of liberty as non-domination. This section also considers whether liberty as non-domination unfortunately excludes values that are compromised by arbitrary power but are also compromised in other ways. This is also relevant to the attractiveness of Pettit's monistic approach.

Pettit and Skinner accept that liberals will target arbitrary power where there is a significant probability of interference. The claimed difficulty of liberty as non-interference lies in its insensitivity to power damage, that is, the damage caused by arbitrary power in the absence of interference. As Pettit says, 'on the liberal understanding, asymmetries in interpersonal power are not in themselves objectionable'.[55] Most of this section is concerned with power damage. However, interference damage is also significant; indeed, it may well be more damaging than power damage, so I begin with this.

The disadvantage of liberty as non-interference that Pettit, at least, would see, is that it is undiscriminating.[56] All laws that impose constraints diminish liberty. Liberty as non-interference thereby fails to strongly support regimes that do suitably minimise arbitrary power, since its laws also diminish liberty, just as the laws of a regime that has arbitrary power.[57] Liberty as non-interference is also unsupportive of the welfare state: the constraints imposed by such a state involve some diminution of liberty.

---

[55] Pettit, *On the People's Terms* 11.
[56] Pettit, *A Theory of Freedom* 136.
[57] Pettit, 'Republican Freedom and Contestatory Democratization'. See also above ch 3, s IVB.

In their defence, liberals can argue that it is important to recognise that all interference diminishes liberty. Liberty as non-domination suggests that a prisoner rightly or wrongly convicted of a crime retains his or her liberty if the sentence resulted from a criminal justice process that appropriately curtails arbitrary power and the crime itself was established by a state lacking arbitrary power.[58] Liberals would claim that it is appropriate that imprisonment is understood as diminishing liberty: if one considers core examples of lack of liberty, imprisonment seems to be one of them. The liberal approach highlights the need for imprisonment to be justified even if the criminal justice process did not expose the prisoner to arbitrary power. Moreover, the liberal approach does not suggest hostility towards legal regulation or the welfare state. Instead, it simply suggests that any constraints need to be justified. Indeed, Waldron has employed liberty as non-interference in challenging homelessness.[59] Having responded to the particular criticisms of Pettit's, liberals can then point out that liberty as non-interference has a decisive superiority in recognising interference damage resulting from arbitrary power. Recall that liberty as non-domination is not diminished by interference at all.

It is hardly surprising, then, that Pettit and Skinner see the particular strength of liberty as non-domination as lying in its targeting of power damage. Pettit identifies three forms of power damage: first, suffering uncertainty, which impairs planning and leads to feelings of anxiety; secondly, having to engage in strategic conduct in order to avoid or reduce interference; and thirdly, suffering lower status. Skinner focused on deference, which is a form of strategic conduct, in *Liberty before Liberalism* and on status in 'Freedom from Arbitrary Power'.[60] The next subsection focuses on deference. Subsection C looks at the damage of lower status and uncertainty.

B. Strategic Conduct

Section III mentioned Kramer's claim that liberty as non-interference is diminished by having to be deferential in order to avoid certain other constraints. This subsection starts with Kramer and then supplements his critique.

Kramer mentions that if the existence of an arbitrary power means that the vulnerable person cannot do X without being deferential, that power has removed the option of being able to do X without being deferential. This constraint is the result of human action, and human actions can diminish liberty be they intentional or unintentional.[61] The human action in these cases would seem to be the

---

[58] Pettit, *On the People's Terms* 178, Pettit, *Republicanism* 56 fn 3.

[59] J Waldron, 'Homelessness and the Issue of Freedom' (1991–92) 39 *University of California Law Review* 295–324, 304.

[60] See ch 3, s IIB and C.

[61] Kramer, 'Liberty and Domination' 37–9. Carter also views non-intentional constraints as diminishing liberty: see *A Measure of Freedom* 221.

assumption by individuals of arbitrary power over others, or the imposition or maintenance of structures that involve arbitrary power.

Pettit has a different interpretation of liberty as non-interference. Pettit views interference as diminishing the agent's choice situation. He says:

> [Interference] encompasses a wide range of possible behaviours. It includes coercion of the body, as in restraint or obstruction; coercion of the will, as in punishment or the threat of punishment; and, to add a category that was not salient in earlier centuries, manipulation ...[62]

Interference does not extend, though, to include conduct that leads to others suffering the constraint of deference.[63]

With Pettit's willingness to extend the notion of interference beyond coercion and explicit threats to manipulation, it is unclear why it cannot also extend to constraints such as deference. Being vulnerable to arbitrary power can itself lead the vulnerable to modify their behaviour to avoid a sanction that they have cause to believe, even in the absence of any threat, might otherwise materialise.

For Pettit, though, it is not mere interference that diminishes liberty; that interference must be intentional. However, he defines 'intentional constraints' broadly to include actions for which agents can be held responsible.[64] With this definition, however, deference will often be an intentional constraint. The conditions for this to obtain are where A voluntarily assumes arbitrary power over B and A should be able to foresee that this arbitrary power is likely to impose a constraint upon B to be deferential to some degree.[65] Or, where A does not voluntarily assume arbitrary power, there are agents who bear special responsibility for the circumstances that leads A to have arbitrary power over B and they should be able to foresee the constraint of deference. Under either Kramer's or Pettit's interpretation, the need to be deferential should be understood as generally diminishing liberty. Pettit cannot avoid Kramer's claim that deference should be understood as constraining

---

[62] Pettit, *Republicanism* 53.

[63] ibid 87.

[64] ibid 52. Kramer says that Pettit's requirement of intentional interference is unacceptable in a non-moralized theory of liberty: 'Liberty and Domination' 41. However, Kramer defines elsewhere moralized conceptions of liberty as requiring assessment of whether the interference is morally justified: *The Quality of Freedom* 100–4. Pettit's requirement of intentional interference enables the conclusion that liberty is diminished even though the interference was morally justified. Pettit describes his approach to liberty as unmoralized: *Republicanism* 54. To view Pettit's approach as moralized, a broader definition of 'moralized' is necessary: one requiring the formation of moral judgements as to responsibility without requiring a conclusion that a moral wrong has occurred. It is perhaps this broader interpretation Kramer has in mind in 'Liberty and Domination'.

[65] Indeed, the complaint of placing others in a situation of having to behave deferentially is found in the republican political tradition. See F Guicciardini, *Dialogue on the Government of Florence*, ed, A Brown (Cambridge, Cambridge University Press, 1994) 27–8 (in Bk 1) referring to the Medici's imposition of a system of arbitrary taxation, unconstrained by rules, 'forcing men to divine how to obey them even in the smallest matters'. The reference to 'divining how to obey' is perhaps suggestive of strategic behaviour, in contrast to being faced with a direct order.

liberty as non-interference by suggesting that his own interpretation of liberty as non-interference is preferable.

Kramer, though, points to a contrast between how liberty as non-interference and as non-domination treat the constraint of deference. He suggests that where there is a significant possibility of interference when deference is not demonstrated, liberty as non-interference is diminished. Where there is no real possibility of interference, liberty as non-interference is not diminished, and this conclusion appropriately reflects the absence of significant constraints.

Kramer gives the example of a gentle giant who grows up in a community, and soon realises that with his vastly superior strength and intelligence, he could exercise an autocratic sway over his community.[66] However, he loathes the idea of becoming a tyrant; his principal desire is to seclude himself from his community. Thus: 'He does indeed depart therefrom, in order to reside in a cave among the nearby hills where he contentedly feeds off natural fruits and wildlife and where he spends his time in solitary reflection and reading and exercise.' From the perspective of liberty as non-domination, though, the community is unfree. Kramer, however, suggests that it is not helpful to view the gentle giant as significantly reducing the liberty of anyone. There is no need for the community to be deferential.

Another example might be helpful. Consider two slave-masters. One might be disgusted by a slave's flattery and then interfere *more*. With another master, flattery may be effective in avoiding interference. Again, the probability of interference where this form of deference is not exhibited seems the key to assessing how significant the constraint of deference is in particular situations. It seems that liberty as non-interference can track the constraint of deference better than liberty as non-domination.

This provides a perspective on Pettit's comment that no theory that leads to the conclusion that ingratiation can be a means of liberation can be regarded as adequate.[67] Let us consider, though, a slave who is bound in chains most of the time but, then, through ingratiation, is successful in becoming unchained and largely unconfined, subject to performing light tasks. Is it really odd to conclude that the slave now enjoys greater liberty, although the slave's overall liberty is nevertheless severely compromised? While Pettit claims that from the perspective of liberty as non-interference, adoption of the strategy of ingratiation is unproblematic, this fails to recognise that the very need to adopt that strategy due to arbitrary power should itself be understood as reducing liberty as non-interference.

In summary, the need to be deferential in order to avoid a range of constraints should be understood to itself generally constrain liberty as non-interference. Furthermore, liberty as non-interference better tracks the constraint of deference where there is vulnerability to arbitrary power.

---

[66] Kramer, 'Liberty and Domination' 47.
[67] Pettit, *On the People's Terms* 65, including fn 36.

C. Status and Uncertainty

In his response to Kramer's and Carter's critiques in the 2008 exchange, Pettit draws attention to status.[68] Pettit says that Carter's and Kramer's central claim is that republicans should understand that liberty is affected by the probability of a master interfering, not just by the capacity of the master to interfere.[69] Pettit, however, says, 'To be subject to the power of someone with a lash is to suffer the evil of alien control, regardless of the exact probabilities of the lash being applied'.[70] He also says that having one's liberty as non-domination diminished is an inter-personal burden, while lacking liberty as non-interference may involve restrictions indiscernible from those resulting from a natural accident: 'You may be obstructed by a tree across the road in just the way I may obstruct you.'[71] By drawing attention to the relational aspect of liberty as non-domination, Pettit seems to be highlighting status.

The performance of liberty as non-domination in recognising status damage is, however, questionable. As with deference, probability of interference seems relevant to status. The contrast underlying liberty as non-domination between the free person and the slave points to the crucial role of the state in providing legal protection against interference. The loss of status resulting from vulnerability to arbitrary power may lie in the message that the vulnerable are not worthy of legal protection. The more likely interference is, the more potent that message is likely to be.

How do liberals approach status damage? Pettit says, with reference to Berlin, that freedom is usually contrasted within the liberal tradition 'with the feeling of freedom and, more generally, with subjective or intersubjective status'.[72] Berlin stated that the demand to be free from the status of political or social dependence is not a demand easily identified with liberty. Liberty as non-interference, Pettit continues, might be enjoyed even when lacking legal protection from arbitrary power, due to good fortune. By contrast, liberty as non-domination requires legal protection, and common knowledge of that protection. This confers a certain status upon those protected.

It is helpful, though, to indicate Berlin's rationale for distinguishing status from liberty. Berlin claimed that the desire for status and recognition 'is something no

---

[68] This is also true of Skinner. Skinner mentions that he and Pettit perhaps overly relied on the point that the need to be deferential is a constraint recognised by republican liberty. He says that the lack of liberty suffered by slaves is only secondarily due to a reduction in available options. See Skinner, 'Freedom as the Absence of Arbitrary Power' 93, 99.

[69] P Pettit, 'Republican Freedom: Three Axioms, Four Theorems' 102–30, 123.

[70] ibid 124–5. Pettit used the language of 'alien control' in 'The Determinacy of Republican Policy: A Reply to McMahon' (2006) 34 *Philosophy and Public Affairs* 275–83, 278. Its distinctiveness became clearer later: see above ch 2, s II.

[71] Pettit, 'Republican Freedom' 124.

[72] Pettit, *Republicanism* 72. See I Berlin, 'Two Concepts of Liberty' [1958] in *Four Essays on Liberty* (Oxford, Oxford University Press, 1969) 118–72, 158 (s VI).

less profoundly needed' than freedom.[73] He said that 'I may … prefer to be bullied and misgoverned by some member of my own race or social class, by whom I am, nevertheless, recognised as … an equal – to being well and tolerantly treated by someone from some higher and remoter group'.[74] Berlin was suggesting that when, say, a community achieves liberty from a colonial administrator, individuals within that community have not necessarily gained overall in liberty; one would need to consider how the community is now governed, in comparison to the previous regime.

Pettit's liberty as non-domination does not capture the type of status Berlin was highlighting. The status derived from being free from political or social dependence upon arbitrary power is different from the status of being ruled at least by members of one's own race or social class. The status Berlin had in mind is not covered by either conception of liberty. Berlin was distinguishing liberty from status in order to draw attention to both status and the prospect of interference.

Berlin's pluralistic approach, where liberty as non-interference is only one value, is consistent with how liberty as non-interference is generally employed. While Pettit suggests that the strength of liberty as non-domination is that it requires a certain status, this might be a weakness from Berlin's perspective: by subsuming status within liberty, liberty as non-domination will exclude important aspects of status that merit separate consideration. This raises, at least, the question of whether Pettit's monistic approach does manage to unify our main commitments or it excludes too much to be satisfying.

This subsection now turns to the final form of power damage, which is uncertainty, with its consequential impairment of a capacity to plan and its impact on anxiety. Again, a liberal pluralistic approach including liberty as non-interference is likely to track this better. First, this damage is likely to be strongly influenced by the occurrence of actual interference and the likelihood of interference.[75] Thus, applying liberty as non-interference may incidentally capture circumstances prompting uncertainty more effectively than liberty as non-domination, with its focus on arbitrary power. Secondly, as in the case with status, factors unrelated to arbitrary power or the probability of interference are relevant. Fear of crime, for instance, may be influenced by a change in media reporting rather than any change in arbitrary power enjoyed by certain agents or the probability of being a victim of crime.

On the other hand, if we turn from measuring liberty as non-domination to the question of what in a particular society is an acceptably low level of arbitrary power, perceptions of the probability of interference are relevant to applying the eye-ball test discussed in Section IVC. An ability to look others in the eye, though,

---

[73] Berlin, 'Two Concepts of Liberty' 158.

[74] ibid 157.

[75] This was recognised by Bentham. He claimed that as attacks upon property take a habitual character, insecurity increases: J Bentham, *The Theory of Legislation* [1840], ed, C Ogden (London, Morrison & Gibbs, 1931) 117 ("Principles of the Civil Code" Pt 1 ch X).

is different from whether one enjoys the certainty that enables one to plan. The former seems to relate more to what level of deference people might be inclined to demonstrate. That was not considered in the previous subsection because that was concerned with the objective need to engage in strategic conduct. The point to note here, though, is that feelings of uncertainty may best be considered directly, rather than via liberty as non-domination or liberty as non-interference.

In conclusion, this section considered forms of damage caused by arbitrary power in order to test whether liberty as non-domination has an advantage over liberty as non-interference. Pettit claims that through targeting the damage caused by arbitrary power, liberty as non-domination provides a more attractive approach than liberty as non-interference, as the latter needs to be supplemented by other values if a liberal approach is to successfully challenge arbitrary power. However, liberty as non-domination seems inferior to a liberal approach that includes liberty as non-interference in capturing interference and power damage. This at least raises doubt about the attractiveness of a monistic approach based on liberty as non-domination.

VI. Public Domination, Democracy and Constitutionalism

A. Public Domination

I have so far explored the two conceptions of liberty in hypotheticals that assume that A has arbitrary power over B. However, Pettit indicated that arbitrary power only exists where A has an arbitrary power to act against those interests of B consistent with the common interest. A democratic process seems necessary to determine the common interest and constrain decision-makers to this interest. I turn, then, to public domination. Up until now, most of my examples have dealt with private domination, especially the hypotheticals relating to slaves. This subsection explains Pettit's approach to determining public domination. The following subsections apply the two challenges to liberty as non-domination discussed so far to Pettit's approach to democracy and constitutionalism.

To elaborate a little further on Pettit's position in *Republicanism*, with arbitrary power involving a power to act against those interests of individuals consistent with the common interest, the common interest is a critical notion. Pettit said that the common interest is judged not from a privileged evaluative standpoint but from the perspective of the local culture.[76] In a later clarification, Pettit referred to a hypothetical society where there is a widely shared religious belief in favour of arrangements that subject women to domination by their husbands. He suggested

---

[76] Pettit, *Republicanism* 56–7.

that in this society, there may not be the common agreement that provides the state with authority to remove those arrangements.[77] Women would continue to face private, but not public, domination. Once the state is constrained through institutional arrangements to track interests recognised by the community to be held in common, the state does not dominate its citizens. Pettit would have been assuming in this hypothetical society that women enjoy the franchise. The common interest is determined through democratic decision-making.

In *On the People's Terms*, Pettit conceptualises arbitrary power as alien control: it is power uncontrolled by the person who can be interfered with. Arbitrary state power is minimised when each citizen has such control over the state that is consistent with the equality of others.[78] With such control in place, the imposition of a law a citizen disagrees with is not the imposition of an alien will upon that citizen. It does not indicate that the citizen is being dominated by the state. Generally, the citizen should recognise that he or she has suffered merely the tough luck of being on the losing side of an argument. It would be different, though, if the individual belongs to a minority identified, say, by creed or colour, that is persistently on the losing side.[79] While the eyeball test (being able to look fellow citizens in the eye) is the index for private domination, the tough-luck test is a good index for whether there are effective controls against public domination.[80]

B. Democracy

Pettit argues that liberty as non-domination offers attractive guidance on institutional arrangements. It provides, for instance, stronger support for democracy: the benevolence of a non-democratic regime does not provide any comfort from the perspective of whether there is public domination.[81] By contrast, a benevolent regime may not infringe significantly upon liberty as non-interference.

My first challenge to liberty as non-domination was to the distinctiveness of its implications. Section IVA argued that non-interfering masters may enjoy less arbitrary power than interfering ones. That also applies to benevolent non-democratic regimes. For example, the benevolence of the regime may be partly attributable to the rulers obtaining little benefit from unjustified interference. Given this, they face relatively high effective costs in interfering. Perceptions of the likelihood of unjustified interference also affect how much arbitrary power is possessed. Liberty as non-domination may vary with the benevolence of a non-democratic regime. Liberty as non-domination does not provide the uncompromising message that

---

[77] Pettit, 'The Determinacy of Republican Policy' 282–3.
[78] Pettit, *On the People's Terms* 167.
[79] ibid 212.
[80] ibid 176.
[81] Pettit, *Republicanism* 31–5.

no liberty is to be enjoyed where there is arbitrary state power, regardless of the likelihood of interference.

The second challenge queried how well liberty as non-domination performs in targeting the damage caused by vulnerability to arbitrary power. Liberty as non-domination does not target interference at all; only arbitrary power. This can suggest privileging regimes that have the least arbitrary power even if they lead to greater unjustified interference. This privileging can provide stronger support for democratic regimes than liberty as non-interference. Whether that is an advantage is questionable. The prospect of interference seems relevant even if it tends against democracy in a particular case. Of course, it may do the opposite: a consideration in favour of a democratic regime may be the lesser likelihood of unjustified interference.

My pursuit of the second challenge mostly focused, though, on power damage. The supposed strength of liberty as non-domination lies in targeting this. I agreed with Kramer that strategic conduct is covered by liberty as non-interference. Of the two other forms of power damage, status and uncertainty, I will focus here on status. Pettit criticised the liberal approach of considering status as a separate matter from liberty, but I suggested that this separate treatment has the advantage of recognising circumstances that impair status but which are neither captured by liberty as non-domination nor by liberty as non-interference.

That advantage is evident when considering democracy. Liberty as non-domination excludes from consideration what I describe as 'democratic status': this is the status obtained from having the opportunity to exercise political power, say, through voting and other forms of political participation. Chapter six will indicate that this is a positive-liberty dimension found in Price: it follows from understanding freedom in terms of autonomy. It appears that for Price, the franchise suggests faith in citizens' capacity to reason conscientiously on moral questions. This consideration in favour of democracy is excluded by focusing on liberty as non-domination. Liberty as non-interference, on the other hand, is associated with a pluralistic approach. Status is a value separate from liberty. Waldron, for instance, supports liberty as non-interference but also regards democratic status as a weighty interest.[82]

In summary, liberty as non-domination does not contrast as sharply with liberty as non-interference when considering the liberty possessed in non-democratic regimes as might initially appear to be the case. To the extent that the contrast is achieved by not considering the prospects of interference under an alternative democratic regime, the contrast is achieved through the exclusion of a relevant consideration. Liberty as non-domination also excludes support for democratic regimes by not taking into account democratic status. Adherents of liberty as non-interference, on the other hand, take a pluralistic approach.

---

[82] On democratic status, see J Waldron, *Law and Disagreement* (New York, Oxford University Press, 1999) ch 12. On liberty as non-interference, see text to above n 59.

C. Constitutionalism

I have so far discussed what support liberty as non-domination provides to democracy in general. However, Pettit also suggests that democracy should take a contestatory form: people should individually and collectively be able to contest what government decides.[83] That contestability can partly be promoted through deliberative democracy. In *Republicanism*, he referred to Sunstein's 'republic of reasons', which requires, for instance, transparency and decision-making aimed at identifying the common good, rather than mere bargaining aimed at promoting sectional interests.[84] Contestability is also promoted through appellate resources.[85] One appellate resource associated with constitutionalism is judicial review based on a bill of rights.[86] I will focus on this mechanism here and the protection of vulnerable minorities. Again, I apply the two challenges to liberty as non-domination.

The first challenge queries the distinctiveness of a power-centred, in contrast to a probabilistic, approach. Pettit views liberty as non-domination as helpful in recognising the plight of minority groups who are vulnerable to the majority's arbitrary power. This value does not require them to demonstrate a significant likelihood of interference. However, with the first challenge, I explained how the assessment of arbitrary power that a party is vulnerable to requires consideration of the probability of unjustified interference. What can be added here is that the very identification of who is vulnerable depends on probabilistic considerations. A slave's vulnerability is marked out by the absence of formal legal protection. By contrast, the vulnerability of minority groups is likely to be marked out by a pattern of unjustified interference. It is the present or past occurrence of such interference that indicates that the costs of interference may be insufficiently high. Pettit himself relies on the frequency with which a group loses in majority decision-making and the nature of those losses to mark out a group as vulnerable to domination rather than merely experiencing the tough luck of disagreeing with certain majority decisions.[87] In other words, the same considerations that are relevant to estimating future interference are relevant to identifying a group as vulnerable to arbitrary power.

---

[83] Pettit, *Republicanism* 185. Pettit, *On the People's Terms* 14–15 contrasts this contestatory form with the form suggested by Rousseau, where liberty is simply identified with participation and the decisions of a popular assembly. The latter form is hostile to constitutional constraints upon or avenues to contest democratic decisions.

[84] Pettit, *Republicanism* 188–9, referring, for instance, to C Sunstein, *The Partial Constitution* (Cambridge, Mass., Harvard University Press, 1993). See also Pettit, *A Theory of Freedom* 162, Pettit, *On the People's Terms* 215.

[85] Pettit, *A Theory of Freedom* 167–8.

[86] Pettit, *Republicanism* 181; P Pettit, 'Minority Claims under Two Conceptions of Democracy' in D Ivison, P Patton and W Sanders (eds), *Political Theory and the Rights of Indigenous Peoples* (Cambridge, Cambridge University Press, 2000) 199–215, 208. Cf Pettit, *A Theory of Freedom* 172; Pettit, *On the People's Terms* 284–5.

[87] See text to above n 79.

How effective might judicial review be in constraining the power of the popularly elected branches of government to interfere unjustifiably with vulnerable groups? Section IVB employed a hypothetical where a slave-master is subject to a magistrate's appellate power before the master can severely interfere with his or her slave. I pointed out how the impact of an appellate mechanism upon arbitrary power can only be appreciated by considering the probability of that appellate body disallowing unjustified decisions by the original decision-maker. Judicial review can be understood as a form of appellate power. Pettit favours such measures as assisting in the dispersion of power. He suggests that such dispersion should reduce the likelihood of any agency in the government attempting to interfere in an unjustified way where they are unlikely to obtain the agreement of any other agency whose cooperation is necessary.[88] Pettit's position here is clearly dependent upon some probabilistic claims.

Probabilistic calculations will be at the fore when assessing the efficacy of judicial review in lessening the arbitrary power of parliament and the executive to interfere with vulnerable minorities. Section IVB also pointed to the complexity of probabilistic calculation when applying liberty as non-domination, due to its relevance initially being constrained to an assessment of power and only secondarily being relevant in evaluating interference as a distinct or freedom-related harm, to use the approach suggested in *On the People's Terms*. A further difficulty is that Pettit's reluctance to explicitly recognise the importance of probabilistic factors tells against considering these properly.

Section IVB also considered Pettit's claim that domination is sufficiently checked when non-domination is modally robust. In other words, non-domination must not only be guaranteed in this world, given existing inclinations of those with arbitrary power, but also in a world where those with arbitrary power are inclined against us.[89] Again relying upon the hypothetical with the slave-master and magistrate, I suggested that this dispersion of power is unlikely to be effective where the slave-master and the magistrate are inclined against the slave. Similarly, constitutional measures such as judicial review seem undermined where the assumption is that judges as well as the original decision-maker are inclined against the applicant in the judicial review proceeding. Indeed, a general assumption of likely interference averts attention from groups that may be especially likely to be interfered with: those groups might especially benefit from constitutional protection. Furthermore, the modal robustness criterion seems to counsel despair at the possibility of constitutional measures being effective, yet Pettit regards non-domination as helpful in supporting such measures.

The second challenge to liberty as non-domination considered its performance in targeting interference and power damage. Constitutional measures might derive part of their justification from their role in reducing unjustified interference

---

[88] Pettit, *On the People's Terms* 223.
[89] Pettit, *Republicanism* 69, referred to above in s IVB.

by the state. This advantage cannot be properly appreciated using liberty as non-domination, for it is undiminished by interference.

In relation to power damage, I suggested that strategic conduct should be viewed as diminishing liberty as non-interference under Pettit's interpretation of this conception, and that uncertainty and status are worth separate consideration. I will only refer to status and will again consider judicial review. With strong-form judicial review, courts can restrict the power of parliament. This makes democratic values relevant. One such value is democratic status. Indeed, Waldron employed democratic status to oppose strong-form judicial review. He argued that judicial review suggests distrust in citizens' capacity to respect individual rights.[90] The exclusion of democratic status that results from only adhering to the single goal of liberty as non-domination can impoverish understanding of what is at stake with judicial review.

To sum up this subsection, liberty as non-domination does not offer support for constitutionalism that is as distinctive as one might have supposed. Probabilistic considerations are highly relevant. Identifying vulnerable groups depends upon probabilistic assessment, and so does an assessment of the effectiveness of constitutional mechanisms such as judicial review. With the relevance of probabilistic considerations being somewhat disguised by Pettit's approach, there is a risk that they may not be properly considered. Furthermore, liberty as non-domination excludes relevant considerations, such as democratic status.

VII. Conclusion

This chapter has revealed normative difficulties with Pettit's (and Skinner's) interpretation of liberty as non-domination through a comparison with a pluralistic approach that incorporates liberty as non-interference. Two challenges to liberty as non-domination were pursued.

The first challenge was to its distinctiveness. I argued that Pettit and Skinner overstate the difference in implications of liberty as non-domination and as non-interference. Liberty as non-domination does not provide the strong message against arbitrary power that Pettit claims. It is not a value that is simply diminished by arbitrary power regardless of the probability of interference. This value, along with liberty as non-interference, is likely to vary as the probability of interference varies. Furthermore, the circuitous way that probability is relevant points to complexity in applying liberty as non-domination. The overly sharp distinction between power-centred and probabilistic approaches drawn by Pettit also tells against probabilistic considerations being properly considered in determining arbitrary power. Indeed, his modal robustness claim, with its assumption of all

---

[90] Waldron, *Law and Disagreement* ch 12.

agents being inclined against us, excludes probabilistic assessment, but leads to implications that Pettit would himself resist.

The second challenge was to how well liberty as non-domination tracks interference and power damage, which are the two forms of damage arising from arbitrary power. Liberty as non-interference has a clear advantage in tracking interference damage, so the discussion mostly focused on the supposed strength of liberty as non-domination, which lies in its tracking of power damage. I first discussed the form of power damage constituted by deference and argued that liberty as non-interference seems to track this better. I then turned to status damage and pointed out that a probabilistic approach is helpful in understanding the status damage arising from arbitrary power, but this is excluded by liberty as non-domination. More importantly, though, a pluralistic approach that includes liberty as non-interference encourages a separate consideration of status. This enables regard to forms of status damage that do not result from arbitrary power. A similar conclusion was also reached in relation to suffering uncertainty, another form of power damage.

The last section focused on democracy and constitutionalism as two means of minimising public domination. The difficulties demonstrated in the earlier discussion of private domination are all relevant to public domination. I will recall here some distinctive points that arose from considering public domination. In relation to the first challenge, a consideration of judicial review pointed to an additional way that probabilistic analysis is necessary. While slavery is marked out so clearly by its legal status, determining the vulnerability of groups that could especially benefit from constitutional protection requires probabilistic assessment. In relation to the second challenge, liberty as non-domination excludes democratic status, an important consideration in supporting democracy, and one which also needs to be taken into account when assessing constitutional arrangements such as judicial review.

In summary, understanding liberty as non-domination as a single target, one that contrasts sharply with liberty as non-interference, leads to substantial difficulties. A way out of these difficulties is suggested in the next chapter. I will suggest that with Price's interpretation of this value, liberty as non-domination can be reconciled with liberty as non-interference.

5

Vindicating Liberty as Non-Domination

I. Introduction

This chapter proposes an alternative interpretation of liberty as non-domination from those that appear in the contemporary literature. The interpretation is based on Richard Price.[1] Of all the early writers referred to by those reviving the republican tradition, Price provided the most substantial discussion of liberty as non-domination. He is one of the writers that Pettit and Skinner rely most heavily upon in articulating the republican approach to freedom.[2]

I argue that the criticisms levelled in the last chapter at the interpretations of Pettit and Skinner do not apply to Price's interpretation.[3] Indeed, Price's interpretation provides a critical perspective on their interpretations. This alternative interpretation comes, however, with more modest ambitions. It is not proposed as a rival, but as a supplement, to liberty as non-interference. It is also not proposed in opposition to liberalism. Indeed, Judith Shklar's liberalism of fear is enlisted to support it.[4] I claim that it should be welcomed within the scheme of political values that are worth considering. It is a value that can usefully remind us of historical writing that highlighted the danger of oppression where there is substantial arbitrary state power.

This chapter explores Price's interpretation of liberty as non-domination largely through a comparison with Pettit's interpretation. Pettit provides a more substantial analytical treatment of liberty as non-domination than Skinner. However, there is much in common between their accounts, so my comparison with Pettit's interpretation applies significantly to Skinner as well. The distinctive aspects of Skinner's interpretation, though, will not be considered. The most important one

---

[1] R Price, 'Observations on the Nature of Civil Liberty, the Principles of Government, and the Justice and Policy of the War with America' [1776] in *Political Writings*, ed, DO Thomas (Cambridge, Cambridge University Press, 1991) 20–75; R Price, 'Additional Observations on the Nature and Value of Civil Liberty, and the War with America' [1777] in *Political Writings*, ed, DO Thomas (Cambridge, Cambridge University Press, 1991) 76–100.

[2] Ch 2, s II; ch 3, s IIIA.

[3] P Pettit, *Republicanism: A Theory of Freedom and Government* (Oxford, Clarendon Press, 1997); Q Skinner, *Liberty before Liberalism* (Cambridge, Cambridge University Press, 1998).

[4] J Shklar, 'The Liberalism of Fear' in N Rosenblum (ed), *Liberalism and the Moral Life* (Cambridge, Mass., Harvard University Press, 1989) 21–38.

is that it is not only diminished by vulnerability to an arbitrary power of interference, but also by dependency on an arbitrary power to confer benefits.

This feature of Skinner's interpretation is also shared by another prominent interpretation of this conception, which is by Frank Lovett.[5] Lovett's interpretation has some further features. Most importantly, it only requires rules that are commonly known and which effectively constrain discretion. There is no additional requirement that the political regime is constrained to enact rules that track the interests of those affected. With Lovett's liberty as non-domination equating with the rule of law, it is a qualified form of liberty as non-domination.[6] It is not diminished by arbitrary power in general, including the power that follows from the absence of democratic rule. Lovett offers a philosophical treatment of non-domination; he is not concerned with tying it closely to historical analysis.[7] This chapter, on the other hand, suggests that some deviations by Pettit and Skinner from what I claim is a historically sound interpretation of Priceian liberty as non-domination come at a normative cost.

I will now indicate how this chapter proceeds. Section II isolates a conception of liberty as non-domination within Price's complex account of liberty, and indicates some of its analytical features that contrast especially with Pettit's interpretation of this value. Section III argues that the challenges to Pettit's and Skinner's interpretation of liberty as non-domination made in chapter four are inapplicable to Price's interpretation. These challenges were in defence of liberty as non-interference and the pluralistic approach associated with it.

The attractiveness of Priceian liberty as non-domination, however, depends significantly on the soundness of its assumption of likely interference where there is substantial arbitrary state power. Section IV suggests that Shklar's liberalism of fear demonstrates how this assumption can be defended in a contemporary context. Priceian liberty as non-domination fits quite well with the liberalism of fear. Section V further illustrates Priceian liberty as non-domination by applying it to an Australian case where the courts restrained the arbitrary power that the government was claiming it enjoyed.

II. Priceian Liberty as Non-Domination

A. Self-Government and Liberty as Non-Domination

As chapter two mentioned, Price's *Observations* attracted great attention.[8] It was a radical work, suggesting not only that the American colonists' complaints

---

[5] F Lovett, *A General Theory of Domination and Justice* (New York, Oxford University Press, 2010).

[6] See, eg, the discussion of common-law constitutionalism in ch 2, s VIIA and Locke's conception of liberty in ch 3, s IVC.

[7] Lovett, *A General Theory of Domination and Justice* 9.

[8] Price, 'Observations' [1776]. See ch 2, s III.

were legitimate, for the colonists lacked liberty, but that the disenfranchised in Britain were also unfree: they too were in a state of slavery. Self-government, Price explained, ran through his understanding of physical, moral, religious, and civil liberty. Physical liberty involves the power to command our own actions, moral liberty is the power of following our moral conscience, religious liberty requires the ability to pursue the religion that accords with our own conscience, and civil liberty is the power of a state 'to govern itself by its own discretion'.[9]

It might be argued that the power to govern ourselves necessarily requires the absence of others having a power to govern us, so liberty as non-domination is merely a logical entailment of Priceian liberty as self-government; it is not a conception of liberty that should be separately considered. That argument is challenged in this subsection. At the same time, this subsection provides some background that will be helpful for subsection B's description of some features of Priceian liberty as non-domination that contrast with Pettit's interpretation of this value. While chapter two largely focused on Price's *Observations*, for this was the target of Lind, I will instead refer here to his *Additional Observations*.

Price mentioned in his *Additional Observations* that a 'citizen is free when the power of commanding his own conduct and the quiet possession of his life, person, property and good name are secured to him by being his own legislator'.[10] In other words, 'every independent agent in a free state ought to have a share in the government of it'.[11] Just as individuals 'in private life, while held under the power of masters, cannot be denominated free however equitably and kindly they may be treated', so too communities: if there is any human power that can encroach upon the community's capacity to govern itself, the community is in a state of slavery.[12] Individuals under the power of masters and communities ruled by despots may enjoy some freedom, but since it is 'an indulgence of a precarious nature', it is 'of little importance'.[13]

The principal reason why civil liberty is valuable is that it 'alone can give just security against oppression'.[14] Price stated:

> Were there any men on whose superior wisdom and goodness we might absolutely depend, they could not possess too much power and the love of liberty itself would engage us to fly to them and to put ourselves under their direction. But such are the principles that govern human nature, such the weakness and folly of men, such their love of domination, selfishness, and depravity, that none of them can be raised to an elevation above others without the utmost danger. The constant experience of the world has verified this and proved that nothing intoxicates the human mind so much as

---

[9] ibid 22. See also Price, 'Additional Observations' 80–1.
[10] Price, 'Additional Observations' 82.
[11] ibid 80.
[12] ibid 77. Being 'under the power of masters' does not cover employment contracts where the employee has the legal right to terminate the contract: see ch 3, s IIIB.
[13] ibid.
[14] ibid 83.

power, and that men, when they have got possession of it, have seldom failed to employ it in grinding their fellow-men and gratifying the vilest passions … [If a people in establishing government] trust the arbitrary will of any body or succession of men, they trust enemies and it may be depended on that the worst evils will follow.[15]

Price's claim that in this world, arbitrary power leads to unjustified interference is used to justify his conclusion that it is appropriate to view liberty as diminished where there are governors not constrained through a broad franchise.

The above quotation also suggests that Price did not endorse the conception of positive liberty that is identified with the positive-liberty strand of the republican revival. Chapter one indicated that this strand identifies liberty with the political participation that enables citizens to exercise and enhance their moral capacities. Since Price did not identify liberty with virtuous political participation, I have not described his conception of liberty as positive. Instead, his approach has positive-liberty dimensions: he identifies liberty with the franchise and with self-government. Its distance from positive liberty is partly indicated by Price not having the benefits of virtuous political participation uppermost in his mind when discussing the hypothetical of a totally trustworthy elite with superior wisdom and goodness. Price did not indicate that some positive liberty is lost even if we place ourselves under the direction of an elite that is absolutely trustworthy. His emphasis upon the right of political participation is based significantly on the chief justification he mentioned, which was to avoid the likely unjustified interference that occurs where there are rulers with substantial arbitrary power. His emphasis on avoiding arbitrary power so as to minimise unjustified interference and his explicit identification of liberty with the absence of arbitrary power make it appropriate to refer to a non-domination conception as part of Price's account.

B. Some Features of Priceian Liberty as Non-Domination

This subsection points to six features of Price's interpretation of liberty as non-domination that distinguish it from Pettit's interpretation. These features will be relied on in the following two sections.

The *first feature* lies in Price's emphasis on interference damage. In previous chapters, I mentioned two forms of damage resulting from vulnerability to arbitrary power: that caused by actual interference (interference damage) and that caused in the absence of interference (power damage). Power damage includes uncertainty, having to be deferential, and lower status. Price highlighted interference damage: this is the main reason why liberty as non-domination is valuable. Where there is arbitrary power but no significant chance of interference, such as with his hypothetical of an absolutely trustworthy and wise elite, Price did not apply liberty as non-domination.

---

[15] ibid.

Price did speak at several points of liberty as the absence of unjustified interference.[16] However, this liberty is so precarious that it is of little value unless liberty as non-domination is also enjoyed. It is the secure absence of unjustified interference that is valuable, and only this counts as real freedom. It can be said, then, that underlying liberty as non-domination is security from unjustified interference.

Price's discussion of power damage tended to be in the context of interference occurring. Price, for example, mentioned that in the absence of religious and civil liberty, 'man ... is a poor and abject animal ... bending his neck to the yoke, and crouching to the will of every silly creature who has the insolence to pretend to authority over him'.[17] While 'crouching' suggests power damage in the form of being deferential and fearful, his neck is also bent to the yoke.

By contrast, Pettit's liberty as non-domination highlights power damage.[18] It is this damage that is captured by liberty as non-domination, unlike liberty as non-interference. Pettit reflects the sharp contrast he draws between these conceptions by describing liberty as non-domination as falling outside 'the now established negative–positive dichotomy'.[19] While Pettit was concerned to distinguish liberty as non-domination from Berlin's liberty as non-interference, he was not necessarily precluding the possibility that liberty as non-domination could be characterised as negative under a broader understanding of negative liberty.[20] However, his exchange with Kramer and Carter sharpened the distinction with negative liberty, for it became necessary for Pettit to indicate why liberty as non-domination could not be accommodated within the more expansive interpretation of negative liberty provided by these writers.[21]

I will characterise liberty as non-domination as non-negative rather than simply negative in order to draw attention to it not being diminished by the constraints that diminish prominent theories of negative liberty.[22] I also describe it as non-positive to distinguish it from the positive liberty associated with the republican revival.

This description of the non-domination conception of liberty as non-negative and non-positive also applies to Price's interpretation. On the other hand, Price's

---

[16] See text to above n 13. See also Price, 'Observations' [1776] 26, where he refers to 'the exercise of Liberty' under a despotic government as involving the form rather than the reality of liberty. See also Price, 'Additional Observations' 77, where he distinguishes between 'a free government and a government under which freedom is enjoyed', and at 82, where he refers to 'the mere possession of liberty'.

[17] Price, 'Observations' [1776] 23. See also Price, 'Additional Observations' 85.

[18] Pettit, *Republicanism* 27, 85, discussed above in ch 2, s III.

[19] ibid 51, 21–2.

[20] P Pettit, 'Keeping Republican Freedom Simple: On a Difference with Quentin Skinner' (2002) 30 *Political Theory* 339–56, 340 describes republican liberty 'as certainly negative'. Skinner continued to describe republican liberty as negative, even after his third formulation: Q Skinner, 'On the Slogans of Republican Political Theory' (2010) 9 *European Journal of Political Theory* 95–102, 95–6.

[21] See ch 4.

[22] *Cf* E Nelson, 'One Concept Too Many?' (2005) 33 *Political Theory* 58–78, 72 and J Christman, 'Saving Positive Freedom' (2005) 33 *Political Theory* 79–88, 86.

emphasis upon interference damage connects his conception with liberty as non-interference, at least in a moralized form, where it involves the absence of unjustified interference. This affinity with negative liberty can be recognised by describing Priceian liberty as non-domination as not just non-negative, but having a negative-liberty dimension. This negative-liberty dimension sharply contrasts with Pettit's liberty as non-domination.

The *second feature* of Priceian liberty as non-domination is that it has a discontinuous feature, where one is either unfree or free. In the case of civil liberty, individuals simply lack liberty where they are denied the franchise: they are vulnerable to arbitrary power. Where people do enjoy the franchise, they are free, subject to certain conditions such as parliamentary terms being sufficiently short. By contrast, Pettit's liberty as non-domination comes in degrees: it varies inversely with the extent of arbitrary power that one is vulnerable to.[23]

There is also, though, a continuous quality to Priceian liberty as non-domination that commences where people enjoy the franchise and parliamentary terms are not overly long. Shorter parliamentary terms, for instance, can increase liberty.[24] Liberty is 'most complete and perfect' where there is direct democracy, but this was only practical in very small states.[25] In the context of private domination, however, Price only speaks of being free or unfree. As chapter three indicated, the distinction between servants and slaves depends upon whether there is a right to enter and terminate contracts of employment.[26] If there is, one is simply free.

The discontinuous feature was criticised by his contemporaries. Lind criticised Price for adopting in his *Observations* a black-and-white approach, where one is either free or a slave.[27] In his *Additional Observations*, Price maintained this discontinuous feature. He did not retreat from his stern warnings about the arbitrary power that exists in the absence of the franchise. The substantial quotation above involved the claim that the 'worst evils will follow' from vulnerability to arbitrary power.[28]

On the other hand, he said later in the same section in which the earlier quotation appears:

> I have shewn at the beginning of this section that it is free government alone that can preserve from oppression, give security to the rights of a people, and answer the ends of government. It is necessary I should here observe that I would not be understood to mean that there can be no kind or degree of security for the rights of a people under any government which cannot be denominated free. Even under an absolute monarchy or

---

[23] Pettit, *Republicanism* 57, discussed above in ch 4, s II.

[24] See Price, 'Observations' [1776] 25. At 26, Price refers to degrees of liberty from 'that which is complete and perfect, to that which is merely nominal'. However, with the franchise providing a marker between liberty and slavery, his approach does have a discontinuous feature.

[25] See ibid 77.

[26] See ch 3, s IIIB.

[27] J Lind, *Three Letters to Dr Price* (London, T Payne, J Sewell, and P Elmsly, 1776) 25 referred to above in ch 2, s IV.

[28] See quote to above n 15.

an aristocracy there may be laws and customs which, having gained sacredness by time, may restrain oppression and afford some important securities.[29]

Laws and custom restrain through diminishing power:

... it is the fear of exciting insurrections by contradicting established maxims that restrains oppression. But, as, in general, a people will bear much, and are seldom driven to resistance till grievances become intolerable, their rulers can venture far without danger, and, therefore, under such governments are very imperfectly restrained.[30]

Price recognised, however, that it is not only self-interest that restrains rulers, but also their humanity:

It deserves to be added here, that as there can be no private character so abandoned as to want all virtue, so there can be no government so slavish as to exclude every restraint upon oppression. The most slavish and, therefore, the worst governments are those under which there is nothing to set bounds to oppression besides the discretion and humanity of those who govern.[31]

He also said that self-interest and humanity would cause a master to be less oppressive to slaves under his eye than to slaves on a distant plantation.[32] Thus, American colonists were in a worse position than the disenfranchised residents of Britain. Members of the British Parliament could develop some fellow-feeling towards residents in Britain and could see the consequences of their oppression. Price, then, maintained that those vulnerable to the arbitrary power he had in mind were simply unfree. Their security, though, may vary.

The above quotations exploring the discontinuous feature of Priceian liberty as non-domination also reveal the third to fifth distinctive features of Price's approach. It is clear that the arbitrary power Price contemplates as diminishing liberty is a power of serious interference: he is contemplating a power that can lead to oppression. It seems appropriate to limit the arbitrary power of interference that diminishes liberty to an arbitrary power of serious interference. Furthermore, it is consistent with Price targeting situations that are seriously problematic to also limit the arbitrary power that diminishes liberty to situations where there are fairly low costs to the power-holder in interfering. Thus, the *third feature* of Priceian liberty as non-domination is that it is only diminished where there is significant ease of serious interference. Pettit's liberty as non-domination is not limited in this way.

This third feature enables Price to distinguish liberty from security: this is the *fourth feature* of Priceian liberty as non-domination. 'Security' involves some protection against oppression that may be less than that required for liberty.[33]

---

[29] Price, 'Additional Observations' 91–2.
[30] ibid 92.
[31] ibid 93. This was reiterating a point made in Price, 'Observations' [1776] 30–1.
[32] Price, 'Additional Observations' 93.
[33] See quote to above n 29.

In this way, Price could recognise differences in people's circumstances without abandoning the discontinuous feature of liberty. This approach is not necessary for Pettit, since he recognised degrees of liberty as non-domination.

The *fifth feature* of Price's approach is that the liberty of those vulnerable to arbitrary power is not affected by the degree of virtue that the power-holders possess. Admittedly, Price's approach is not entirely consistent. Price indicated that humanity constrains oppression; he used the terms 'virtue' and 'humanity' interchangeably.[34] On the other hand, he also stated that the 'worst evils' will inevitably follow from arbitrary government.[35] That seems to suggest that humanity does not constrain oppression. However, the reference to 'worst evils' occurs in an impassioned warning about arbitrary power and seems hyperbolic. Indeed, in the same passage, Price mentioned that men seldom fail to abuse power. This suggests that rulers sometimes do not abuse power. I think Price's intentions can be indicated more precisely in the following way: '[If a people in establishing government] trust the arbitrary will of any body or succession of men, they trust enemies and it may be depended on that the worst evils will *almost always* follow.' Price's reference here to a 'succession of men' seems to point to the possibility that once a regime of arbitrary rule is in place, that paves the way for successive despots, and having a succession of good despots is even more unlikely than having a single good despot.

Price seems to have been suggesting that arbitrary power is assessed against a profile of agents who have some empathy, empathy that is triggered by face-to-face contact, but that empathy will not prevent oppression. The bleakness of this picture of human nature is lessened by two considerations. First, he suggested that goodness is not generally found amongst the restless and ambitious people who seek political office.[36] Thus, the profile that is appropriately applied to those in power may not be a universal profile. Secondly, he acknowledged that a good individual despot will sometimes arise.[37] Those vulnerable to the arbitrary power of even a good despot are not free. Their vulnerability to arbitrary power is judged against a general profile of rulers, not those rare rulers who are benevolent. However, those ruled by a benevolent despot are less oppressed. In summary, then, Price determines the arbitrary power that diminishes liberty against a general profile of agents who have some virtue.

By contrast, Pettit's measurement of arbitrary power takes into account the particular level of virtue of those possessing arbitrary power. A virtuous agent subject to rebuke will experience greater costs, in the form of shame, if he or she interferes.[38] These greater costs reduce the agent's arbitrary power and thereby increase the liberty of non-domination enjoyed by others.

---

[34] See quote to above n 31.
[35] See quote to above n 15.
[36] Price, 'Additional Observations' 87.
[37] Price, 'Observations' [1776] 35.
[38] Pettit, *Republicanism* 64, referred to above in ch 4, s II.

The *sixth feature* of Priceian liberty as non-domination is that while Price gave examples involving masters and slaves, his focus is purely on the state, that is, on public domination. Chapter three referred to Price's treatment of subordination in the private sphere, for example, involving parents and children, and employers and employees.[39] Price did not suggest that these relationships diminish liberty. Indeed, I argued that Priceian liberty as non-domination does not capture well subordination in employment. Pettit, on the other hand, while especially focusing on the state–citizen relationship, is very much interested in applying the value to the private sphere. He criticises liberalism for its insensitivity to domination in this sphere.[40]

In summary, Priceian liberty as non-domination has the following features: it is diminished by arbitrary power involving significant ease of serious interference, that power is determined employing a profile of agents with limited empathy, and liberty has a discontinuous feature. However, unfree individuals may suffer more or less insecurity or oppression, and a constraint upon oppression can be the virtuous disposition of the agent. Furthermore, Price focuses on arbitrary state power, and his chief concern is interference damage.

By contrast, Pettit's liberty as non-domination varies according to the extent of arbitrary power one is exposed to, and one variable is the extent of virtue possessed by the power-holder. Pettit recommends applying this value to the public and private spheres, and he especially highlights power damage.

While this subsection contrasts Price with Pettit, I can note here that Skinner's account is consistent with Pettit's, but lacks the analytical detail to indicate whether on some of the differences, it sides with Pettit. However, chapter three indicated that Skinner too highlights power damage and Skinner recommended applying the value to the public and private spheres.

III. Applicability of Chapter Four's Challenges to Liberty as Non-Domination

A. First Challenge

This section considers how Price's non-domination conception fares against the two challenges to Pettit's non-domination conception pursued in the last chapter. Those were challenges in defence of liberty as non-interference. They will be discussed respectively in this and the following subsection.

The first challenge questioned the distinctiveness of liberty as non-domination. Pettit highlights its distinctiveness with the hypothetical of slaves with

---

[39] See ch 3, s IIIB.
[40] Pettit, *Republicanism* 49.

non-interfering and interfering masters. The slave with the non-interfering master might enjoy significantly greater liberty as non-interference than the slave with the interfering master, but no greater liberty as non-domination. Pettit points, then, to situations where there is a low probability of interference, but a high degree of arbitrary power, to contrast liberty as non-domination and liberty as non-interference. The strong opposition to arbitrary power conveyed by liberty as non-domination lies in liberty remaining invariably low where there is arbitrary power, regardless of the probability of interference.

I argued, though, that the distance Pettit claims between the two conceptions is achieved by not acknowledging the role of probability of interference in assessing arbitrary power. In fact, it is more plausible to suggest that the non-interfering master is likely to have less arbitrary power than the interfering master. The variability of liberty as non-domination, along with non-interference, to the probability of interference by the possessor of arbitrary power undermines the sharp distinction Pettit suggests.

Priceian liberty as non-domination avoids this criticism. The arbitrary power of both the interfering and non-interfering master is measured against a general profile of agents that assumes limited empathy. One assesses liberty as non-domination taking into account general experience with arbitrary power. Price would not claim that both slaves suffer the same vulnerability to arbitrary power. Price would simply say that both slaves suffer a sufficient degree of vulnerability to arbitrary power to render them unfree.

How would Price have justified this approach? He could have argued that his chief justification for liberty as non-domination, which lies in the likelihood of interference, is not undermined by pointing to a particular case of a slave with a non-interfering master. First, that master's disposition might change. Secondly, the slave may obtain at some point a different master. Thirdly, if the master is truly angelic, and there is no possibility of coming under a different master, Price might refer to his suggestion that liberty is consistent with being governed by 'men on whose superior wisdom and goodness we might absolutely depend'.[41] Recall that liberty as non-domination is a component of a broader conception of liberty that ultimately requires self-government. Under enlightened rule, significant self-government might be achieved in the private sphere, that is, in spheres other than those involving political rule. Of course, the master of a slave is operating in the private sphere, but an angelic master might stimulate and enable a slave to exercise substantial moral liberty. Price could state that while liberty may be significantly enjoyed when one is subject to angelic rulers, this opportunity is extremely rare. Such rare circumstances do not undercut the general helpfulness of a conception of liberty that emphases the risk of serious interference where there is substantial arbitrary power.

---

[41] See text to above n 15.

Price, then, did not assert the distinctiveness of liberty as non-domination through contrasting it with liberty as non-interference. His primary concern was interference damage. His argument suggests that liberty as non-domination targets the very situations that liberty as non-interference would target if the risks of arbitrary power are appreciated. Liberty as non-interference is diminished by justified or unjustified interference, but adherents of liberty as non-interference would be particularly troubled by unjustified interference. In the rare circumstance where liberty as non-interference suggests no loss to liberty because rulers are utterly dependable, liberty as non-domination would not be applied.

The main way Priceian liberty diverges from liberty as non-interference is that Priceian liberty as non-domination derives its principal justification from the assumption of likely and serious unjustified interference where there is substantial arbitrary power. The value thereby provides an emphatic affirmation of this assumption. Adherents of liberty as non-interference can adopt this assumption, but it is an assumption external to their justification for this conception of liberty. Liberty as non-interference is premised on the more modest assumption that it is worth drawing attention to interference. Whether Priceian liberty as non-domination's emphatic affirmation of the assumption of likely interference where there is arbitrary power can be attractive is considered in Section IV.

B. Second Challenge

The second challenge to Pettit's liberty as non-domination questions how well it tracks the damage caused by arbitrary power. Its claimed advantage is its sensitivity to such damage. There is interference and power damage.

In relation to interference damage, chapter four argued that liberty as non-interference is superior. This value is actually diminished by interference. Price's approach, however, suggests a way that liberty as non-domination can be defended. While liberty as non-domination is not diminished by interference, Price's justification for targeting significant arbitrary power is that this will track serious unjustified interference. In other words, Priceian liberty as non-domination provides a salutary pointer to where a serious risk of interference lies. This way of defending liberty as non-domination is not available under Pettit's interpretation, since that focuses on the distinctiveness of liberty as non-domination, in comparison to liberty as non-interference: that distinctiveness is highlighted in circumstances where there is arbitrary power but unlikely interference.

In relation to power damage, tracking this is supposed to be the strength of Pettit's liberty as non-domination. Chapter four argued, however, that liberty as non-interference will better target the constraint to be deferential. The other forms of power damage were, first, loss of status and, secondly, uncertainty leading to fear and inability to plan. These are better treated separately rather than assuming that they are sufficiently covered through a focus on liberty as non-domination or as non-interference. An example is 'democratic status': the recognition of citizens' capacity to reason on political matters achieved by conferral of the right to vote or otherwise share in political power.

That the other forms of power damage are better treated separately is a problem for Pettit's approach. Pettit recommends liberty as non-domination as a sole consequentialist target largely for normative reasons, although he also claims that this is the historical approach.[42] Pettit contrasts this monistic approach with the approach adopted with liberty as non-interference, where left-of-centre liberals typically take into account a range of other values, values that are controversial.

Liberty as non-domination was not, however, Price's single target.[43] First, his ultimate conception of liberty involves self-government. In this way, Price included considerations such as democratic status.[44] Chapter three pointed to independence as a separate value to liberty, and this chapter pointed to security.[45] Price also said that liberty is not the only essential value that a constitution should promote: 'Wisdom, union, dispatch, secrecy, and vigour are likewise requisite'.[46]

Indeed, Price did not claim that liberty necessarily tracks power damage well. He expressed concern that people may be complacent in the face of arbitrary power.[47] His emphatic warnings about the likelihood of interference are intended to make people more fearful. He generally referred to power damage in the context of interference occurring.

In summary, the second challenge to liberty as non-domination considered in the last chapter does not seem applicable to Price's interpretation, at least in relation to power damage. Price did not claim that liberty tracks this well. He did not emphasise power damage in the absence of interference. Chapter four also supported a pluralistic approach to capture values diminished not only by power damage but other factors. This also fits well with Price. In relation to interference damage, with which I began this subsection, I mentioned that Price would argue that liberty as non-domination tracks this well since arbitrary power is likely to be abused. The attractiveness of this assumption of likely abuse is explored in the next section.

IV. The Assumption of Likely Interference

The previous section commenced the case for Priceian liberty as non-domination by arguing that certain criticisms of Pettit's interpretation of liberty

---

[42] Pettit, *Republicanism* 80–1. See ch 4, s II.

[43] On Pettit, see ibid 80.

[44] See below ch 6, s IVB.

[45] See ch 3, s IIIB and above s IIB.

[46] Price, 'Additional Observations' 79.

[47] In Price, 'Observations' [1776] 26, Price expressed concern that, for instance, due to an 'accidental mildness in the administration' of a despotic regime, people may be misled into thinking they still enjoy liberty. And at 30: 'Sleep in a state, as Montesquieu says, is always followed by slavery'. See also Price, 'Additional Observations' 95–7.

as non-domination do not apply to Price. This section mounts a positive case for Pricean liberty as non-domination. This subsection points to affinities between Shklar's liberalism of fear and Pricean liberty as non-domination. Shklar is helpful in indicating how Price's central assumption of likely interference where there is arbitrary power can be helpfully drawn upon today.

The assumption of likely interference where there is arbitrary power was referred to in chapter four.[48] Kramer seems to adopt such an assumption in explaining why adherents of liberty as non-interference are often likely to target the arbitrary power that republicans are concerned about. I claimed that Kramer's reference to likely abuse where there is arbitrary power was best interpreted as suggesting that adherents of liberty as non-interference would do well to heed the warnings of historical republicans about arbitrary power in relevantly similar circumstances. This fits well with Shklar's 'liberalism of fear'. While Kramer is suggesting that liberals should target the same arbitrary power as historical republicans, such as autocratic power, Shklar argues that contemporary liberals may not fully appreciate the danger of arbitrary power; hence, the value in being reminded of the warnings issued by historical writers.

Shklar's preferred interpretation of liberalism, which she described as the liberalism of fear, has one overriding aim: to secure the political conditions necessary for the exercise of personal freedom.[49] Adults should be able to make as many effective decisions without fear or favour about as many aspects of their lives as is compatible with the like freedom of every other adult. This requires freedom from the abuse of power, and it is the state that enjoys the greatest power over individuals. The abuse of power she had primarily in mind was cruelty, by which she meant the deliberate infliction of physical harm.

The liberalism of fear takes the most serious evil as the abuse of state power, and it recommends limited government and a dispersion of power. Shklar said it draws on what Ralph Emerson described as the 'party of memory'. This involves, Shklar said, an attentiveness to the past.[50] This strand of liberalism originated in the cruelties of the religious wars and, more recently, it recalls the violence witnessed since 1914.[51] She thought that with the US as an exceptionally privileged liberal society, there was neglect of past and present political experience of cruelty in societies that lack freedom.[52]

---

[48] See ch 4, s IVB.

[49] Shklar, 'The Liberalism of Fear'. For some introductory material on Shklar, see B Yack, 'Liberalism without Illusions: An Introduction to Judith Shklar's Political Thought' in B Yack (ed), *Liberalism without Illusions: Essays on Liberal Theory and the Political Vision of Judith N Shklar* (Chicago, University of Chicago Press, 1996) 1–13.

[50] Shklar, 'The Liberalism of Fear' 26 referring to RW Emerson, 'The Conservative' [1841] in *Essays and Lectures* (New York, Library of America, 1983) 171–89. Emerson referred at 172 to a party of conservatism and of innovation, involving an opposition between, for instance, memory and hope.

[51] Shklar, 'The Liberalism of Fear' 23, 27.

[52] ibid 35–6.

There are clearly some affinities with Priceian liberty. Price's ultimate value was personal freedom (or individual self-government).[53] Religious freedom was a crucial element of that. Price focused on arbitrary state power and urged attention to its abuse. He referred, for instance, to the 'constant experience of the world'.[54] Where there is actual slavery, people are treated as beasts, with their necks bent to the yoke.[55] Price was not just alluding to the Atlantic slave trade, but to the condition of, for instance, Russians, Turks and Spaniards.[56] When discussing the power that states, tribes or clans exercise over each other, he said that humanity has been driven by contempt for others, leading to plunder and massacre.[57] He referred to the behaviour of the Romans, clans of Indians, and tribes of Arabs. His approach fits with Shklar's 'party of memory'. He said, 'The smallest attention to the history of past ages and the present state of mankind' would make the reader sensible to the importance of liberty.[58] Where there is liberty, there is a fruitful field; otherwise a frightful waste. He referred to the miserable position of contemporary, in contrast to ancient, Greece.

Price too was concerned about complacency towards arbitrary power, and he viewed the probability of serious interference as sufficiently high to justify minimising exposure to such power. While Shklar is explicit about the deliberate causing of physical harm being the primary evil, for Price it was certainly a significant evil. He mentioned that civil government is an institution for defending natural equality 'against the encroachments of violence and tyranny'.[59] Shklar was also concerned about harm extending beyond physical coercion, as is evident from her description of the risks from the accumulation of private wealth. Price's concerns also extended beyond physical coercion. He opposed, for instance, religious discrimination in holding civil and military offices.[60] Both writers, though, also recognised power damage. Shklar referred to lifting 'the burden of fear and favour'.[61] Price referred to power damage at least in the context of subjects of arbitrary power experiencing actual interference.

---

[53] See above s II.

[54] See quote to above n 15.

[55] See text to above n 17.

[56] See, eg, R Price, 'A Discourse on the Love of Our Country' [1789] in *Political Writings*, ed, DO Thomas (Cambridge, Cambridge University Press, 1991) 176–96, 179. See also A Page, '"A Species of Slavery": Richard Price's Rational Dissent and Antislavery, Slavery & Abolition' (2011) 32 *Slavery & Abolition* 53–73, 55.

[57] Price, 'Discourse' 179.

[58] ibid 184.

[59] Price, 'Additional Observations' 88.

[60] P Miller, *Defining the Common Good: Empire, Religion, and Philosophy in Eighteenth-Century Britain* (Cambridge, Cambridge University Press, 1994) ch 5. For the broader context, also see J Cannon, *Parliamentary Reform 1640–1832* (Cambridge, Cambridge University Press, 1973), say, at 125 on the Test and Corporation Acts. See also Price, 'Discourse' 191.

[61] Shklar, 'The Liberalism of Fear' 31.

Shklar contrasted the liberalism of fear with two other liberal strands. First, there is a liberalism of natural rights, represented by Locke, that looks to the fulfilment of an ideal pre-established normative order.[62] Secondly, there is a liberalism of personal development, represented by John Stuart Mill, which sees freedom as essential for personal development. Both these strands form part of a liberalism of hope. Neither of them, Shklar said, had a strongly developed historical memory.

Both the natural-rights and the personal-development strand of the liberalism of hope are also found in Price.[63] However, the liberalism of fear is closest to Priceian liberty as non-domination. Shklar's liberalism of fear suggests that it may be worthwhile in a contemporary context for a political theory to warn about complacency towards arbitrary power. Shklar did not claim that the likelihood of interference where there is significant arbitrary power is an assumption of universal validity. Her approach is evocative rather than recommending a mechanical application of this assumption. Through reminding us of a political tradition born out of experience with the abuse of arbitrary power, Shklar is urging us to recognise the danger of arbitrary power and how liberal institutions and ideas can be understood as a response to this danger.

Returning to Price, he had in mind regimes that were entirely undemocratic or, say, through a limited franchise, fell well short of democratic standards. He was suggesting that those regimes are very likely at some point to seriously abuse their power. His contention of the likely abuse of arbitrary power needs to be taken in the context of what he was challenging. Price, for instance, had in mind decision-makers who face significant temptations to abuse their power.

Perhaps the main criticism of the liberalism of fear, though, is that it reflects 'Cold War liberalism', where the dangers of empowering a state are exaggerated by generalising from atrocities committed in Nazi Germany and Stalinist Russia.[64] With Cold War liberalism, the spectre of extreme violence is used to argue in quite different circumstances for a minimalist state. Shklar was herself a Jewish émigré from Latvia who fled Nazism as a child with her family.

However, while fear of arbitrary state power could lead to endorsement of a minimalist state, both Price and Shklar envisaged a state that constrains the accumulation of private wealth. Shklar claimed that the liberalism of fear does not ignore the power of corporate business enterprises.[65] That private property

---

[62] ibid 26–7.

[63] On natural rights, see, eg, Price, 'Discourse' and also DO Thomas, *The Honest Mind: The Thought and Work of Richard Price* (Oxford, Clarendon Press, 1977) ch VI. The personal development strand is evident in Price's emphasis on moral liberty. See, eg, Price, 'Observations' [1776] 21.

[64] K Forrester, 'Hope and Memory in the Thought of Judith Shklar' (2011) 8 *Modern Intellectual History* 591–620, 593. See also S Moyn, 'Before – and Beyond – the Liberalism of Fear' in S Ashenden and A Hess (eds), *Between Utopia and Realism: The Political Thought of Judith N. Shklar* (Philadelphia, Penn, University of Pennsylvania Press, 2019) 24–46.

[65] Shklar, 'The Liberalism of Fear' 31. See also A Gutmann, 'How Limited Is Liberal Government?' in B Yack (ed), *Liberalism without Illusions: Essays on Political Theory and the Political Vision of Judith Shklar* (Chicago, University of Chicago Press, 1996) 64–81.

helpfully disperses power does not justify protecting the accumulation of private wealth in a way which leads to a substantial power to harm, such as through hiring and firing or through controlling prices. More generally, Shklar mentions, freedom requires the limitation of forms of social inequality that expose people to oppressive practices.[66]

In contrast, Price's focus was on the public sphere. Indeed, chapter three argued that a focus on an arbitrary power to interfere (found also in Pettit's but not Skinner's approach) does not capture subordination resulting from a dependency upon eagerly sought rewards.[67] Nevertheless, Price stated that most free states find a way to prevent too great an inequality in the distribution of property. He referred to the Hebrew principle of redistributing land every 50 years.[68] This could promote independence: he preferred a society of independent yeomen. He thought economic inequality would lead to political inequality, with a wealthy elite seeking to subvert a free government.[69] Given the context in which he was writing, he should not be associated today with supporting a minimalist state.[70]

So far, I have employed Shklar to indicate how Price's assumption of likely interference can have contemporary appeal. If it does, it raises the question of whether Pettit and Skinner fail to target the primary evil of arbitrary power. In fact, Shklar suggests a trenchant way of pursuing this criticism. Shklar claimed that the abstraction found in the work of contemporary moral and legal liberal theorists, with its focus on conceptual analysis, can lead to the misrepresentation and trivialisation of liberal practices such as the rule of law.[71] Conceptual analysis, she said, can inspire, bloodless and overly formal characterisations of liberal politics. Such characterisations can overlook the importance of liberal practices in reducing what would otherwise be a significant likelihood of interference.

Pettit and Skinner cannot be accused of providing purely conceptual analysis outside the party of memory. Nevertheless, chapter three suggested that Skinner's interest in achieving a sharp contrast between two conceptions of liberty – that of non-domination and non-interference – may have led to misrepresentation of what some historical writers saw as the main value of being secure from arbitrary power. The same query can be raised about Pettit's approach. Pettit and Skinner illustrate the contrasting conceptions by pointing to the hypothetical of a slave who lacks liberty as non-domination but enjoys substantial liberty as non-interference. Here, we have power, but not interference, damage. A focus, then, on conceptual

---

[66] Shklar, 'The Liberalism of Fear' 28.

[67] See above ch 3, s IIIB.

[68] R Price, 'Observations on the Importance of the American Revolution' [1785] in *Political Writings*, ed, DO Thomas (Cambridge, Cambridge University Press, 1991) 116–51, 144.

[69] ibid 145.

[70] On his approach to the poor, see Thomas, *The Honest Mind* 116–17.

[71] See J Shklar, *Legalism: Law, Morals, and Political Trials*, 2nd edn (Harvard, Harvard University Press, 1986) x–xi and J Shklar, 'Political Theory and the Rule of Law' [1987] in S Hoffmann (ed), *Political Thought and Political Thinkers* (Chicago, University of Chicago Press, 1998) 21–37, discussed in Yack, 'Liberalism without Illusions' 5–6.

analysis, and an attempt to indicate the practical importance of that conceptual analysis, seems to lead to a focus on power rather than on interference damage.

From the perspective suggested by Priceian liberty as non-domination and Shklar's liberalism of fear, Pettit and Skinner have highlighted the secondary evil of power damage. This raises the question of whether Pettit and Skinner thereby downplay or, to use Shklar's stronger term, 'trivialise' arbitrary power. Indeed, by avoiding the assumption of likely interference, they risk not only downplaying interference but also power damage. Chapter four argued that power damage may correspond to perceptions of the likelihood of interference, and those perceptions are likely to be influenced by the occurrence of actual interference and the actual probability of further interference.[72] Price referred to power damage in the context of actual unjustified interference.[73]

Shklar's liberalism of fear points, then, to how the assumption of likely interference can be defended and also employed to question Pettit's and Skinner's interpretation. However, Shklar was not simply advocating the recollection of historical writers who stressed interference damage where there is arbitrary power, so that we may be prompted to think more about present dangers. Instead, she was arguing about how to interpret a tradition that has shaped existing institutions and ideas. What that could suggest is that Price's warning about arbitrary power would be especially cogent if it were understood as part of a political tradition that has influenced existing institutions and continues to be salient today. My discussion has in fact pointed to significant affinities between Priceian liberty as non-domination and the liberalism of fear.

Pettit's approach, by contrast, places Price in a tradition that contrasts with liberalism. Pettit identifies liberalism with indifference towards arbitrary power where it is unlikely to be abused.[74] It might be thought that this resonates with Shklar's concern that contemporary liberalism can be complacent about arbitrary power. However, Shklar was pointing to the risk of severe interference. Pettit, on the other hand, highlights the risk of power damage. Furthermore, Shklar was expressing disagreement with some strands within liberalism. Pettit, by contrast, is attempting to characterise liberalism as a whole. With Price supporting both the liberalism of hope and the liberalism of fear, Shklar would have understood him as a liberal. Priceian liberty as non-domination does seem to fit within the liberalism of fear.

Rather than seeing Price as the last major figure in a line of thinkers who sought freedom from arbitrary power, his concern about arbitrary power can be understood as one that was not decisively rejected by liberalism. The critics identified by Pettit and Skinner as rejecting liberty as non-domination did not, in fact, target this value. They did prefer a probabilistic approach to security where

---

[72] Ch 4, s VB and C.
[73] See, eg, text to above n 17.
[74] See ch 2, s II.

assumptions about the likelihood of interference are not incorporated within the value. However, this did not preclude the assumption that arbitrary power is likely to be abused. That assumption was later affirmed by Bentham himself and other liberals that Pettit and Skinner would identify with liberty as non-interference.[75] Furthermore, liberty as non-domination was affirmed by important liberals.[76] With liberalism understood to have shaped existing institutions, Price is fairly invocable in understanding those institutions. Those institutions include the common law, which is referred to in the next section.

V. Applying Priceian Liberty as Non-Domination

Shklar and Price appeal to recollection of the abuse of power. It is in keeping with that appeal that this penultimate section recollects a recent instance of such abuse. The primary purpose, though, of this recollection is to further illuminate Price's interpretation of liberty as non-domination. It does so by applying it to a concrete case.

The case gave rise to a proceeding for judicial review in Australia, in which judges employed what can be described as a qualified form of liberty as non-domination. This was a common-law right to liberty. Australia does not have a national bill of rights that is justiciable by courts. Instead, courts rely significantly on common-law liberties to favour interpretations of legislation that constrain arbitrary power. This judicial practice can be described as common-law constitutionalism.[77] It is demonstrated in the case of *Haneef*.[78] I will first provide some background to the case and mention some points made by the judges that seem especially pertinent to how arbitrary power should be approached. I then consider what perspective upon liberty is suggested by Price's interpretation of liberty as non-domination.

The incidents leading to this case occurred in 2007, a national election year. The legislation at issue was enacted in the shadow of the terrorist attacks in the US on 11 September 2001. Governments around the world acquired additional powers that they claimed would help in preventing further attacks. The Australian Parliament, for instance, conferred additional powers on the executive through criminalising conduct, enabling control and preventative detention orders, and expanding powers to detain and question terrorist suspects.[79] While the powers

---

[75] See ch 2, s VIIA.

[76] See ch 3, s IVC.

[77] For a broad definition of constitutionalism, see ch 1, s IV.

[78] *Haneef v Minister for Immigration and Citizenship* (2007) 177 Federal Court Reports 40 (Federal Court of Australia).

[79] See *A Human Rights Guide to Australia's Counter-Terrorism Laws* (2008); available from www. humanrights.gov.au/human-rights-guide-australias-counter-terrorism-laws.

were less than those the government sought, they were nevertheless substantial. Some of these powers were applied to Mohammed Haneef.

Haneef was a young Indian doctor who practised in England in 2004 and 2005.[80] He met there two of his second cousins, Sabeel and Kafeel Ahmed. He and Sabeel worked as doctors at a Liverpool hospital and stayed in the same boarding house. Haneef also visited Kafeel on a few occasions at Cambridge University. When Haneef left England, he gave his mobile phone, including a SIM card with some credit on it, to Sabeel.

Haneef came to Australia in September 2006 to practise medicine at a Queensland hospital. On 29 June 2007, Kafeel drove a car laden with explosives into Glasgow Airport. There was initially some suspicion that Sabeel may have had some warning about the attack which he did not communicate to police. UK police told the Australian Federal Police that Haneef had an association with the two brothers and that he had left a mobile phone with them.

Using their additional powers, the Australian Federal Police detained Haneef without charge from 2 July for 12 days. On 14 July, he was charged with intentionally providing to a terrorist organisation resources, in the form of a SIM card, while being reckless as to whether the organisation was a terrorist organisation.[81] The police used some of the very broadly worded anti-terrorism legislation introduced after 2001.[82] The terrorist organisation was defined in the charge as consisting at least of his second cousins in England.

The magistrate Jacqui Payne granted Haneef bail despite the charge attracting a presumption against bail. She stated that the case against Haneef appeared weak: there was no evidence to suggest Haneef had any direct association with a terrorist organisation, or that the SIM card he had given to Sabeel had been used in a terrorist attack.[83] Other factors relevant to bail would have been the chance that Haneef would abscond or would pose a danger to the community. These factors favoured Haneef.

Within a few hours of the magistrate's decision, the Minister for Immigration, Kevin Andrews, cancelled Haneef's visa on character grounds. The Minister stated that Haneef had been in correspondence via online chat rooms with his second cousins, including correspondence relating to the birth of Haneef's daughter.[84] This correspondence indicated an association with his second cousins. The cousins were suspected of involvement in terrorist activity.

[80] *Haneef v Minister for Immigration* [97].

[81] ibid [113].

[82] *Security Legislation Amendment (Terrorism) Act 2002* (Cth): this amended the Criminal Code 1995 (Cth), including s 102.7: Providing support to a terrorist organisation.

[83] MJ Clarke, *Report of the Inquiry into the Case of Dr Mohammed Haneef* vol 1 (Canberra, Attorney-General's Department, 2008) 146–7.

[84] *Haneef v Minister for Immigration* [104].

A consequence of revoking Haneef's visa was placing him in immigration detention. The Minister relied upon section 501(3)(b) of the *Migration Act 1958* (Cth). Some provisions of section 501 follow, with emphasis added:

(3)   **The Minister may:**

...

    (b)   **cancel a visa** that has been granted to a person; **if:**

    (c)   the Minister reasonably suspects that **the person does not pass the character test**; and

    (d)   the Minister is satisfied that the refusal or cancellation is in the national interest.

    ...

(6)   For the purposes of this section, **a person does not pass the character test if:**

    (a)   the person has a substantial criminal record ...; or

    (b)   **the person** has or **has had an association** with someone else, or **with a group** or organisation, whom **the Minister reasonably suspects has been** or is **involved in criminal conduct;** or

    (c)   having regard to either or both of the following:

        (i)   the person's past and present criminal conduct;

        (ii)   the person's past and present general conduct;

    the person is not of good character ...

Haneef sought judicial review of the Minister's decision in the Federal Court. Haneef was successful at first instance and in the Full Federal Court. I will refer to some points relevant to liberty as non-domination that are made in the judgments.

While the Minister in his decision referred to Haneef having 'an association' with his second cousins, Haneef's counsel argued that the 'association' had to reflect adversely on his character. Counsel for the Minister, on the other hand, argued that the Minister's decision was based on a correct interpretation of the section, for the section covered an innocent association with someone the Minister suspects of criminal conduct. Justice Spender mentioned to counsel that he himself had had associations with criminals through representing them in court. He asked whether he would pass the character test.[85] Counsel replied that he would not meet the character test, but the test would not apply to him, for the judge was an Australian citizen.

In the course of rejecting the Minister's interpretation, Justice Spender affirmed the importance of the rule of law in constraining the government even on national security matters. He quoted Justice Jackson in a 1949 US Supreme Court case:

The framers of the Constitution knew, and we should not forget today, that there is no more effective practical guaranty against arbitrary and unreasonable government than to require that the principles of law which officials would impose upon a minority must be imposed generally. Conversely, nothing opens the door to arbitrary action so

[85] ibid [221].

effectively as to allow those officials to pick and choose only a few to whom they will apply legislation and thus to escape the political retribution that might be visited upon them if larger numbers were affected. Courts can take no better measure to assure that laws will be just than to require that laws be equal in operation.[86]

No comfort, then, was to be obtained through a literal interpretation of 'association' by observing that the legislation only applied to aliens. Justice Spender held that the association must reflect adversely on character.

The Minister appealed. In the course of the appeal, counsel for the Minister mentioned that while it was regrettable that entirely innocent people could be covered by his favoured interpretation of the legislation, this was the price that had to be paid to ensure the safety of the Australian community.[87] The Full Federal Court unanimously dismissed the appeal. It referred approvingly to the British constitutional theorist TRS Allan:

> Liberty is not merely what remains when the meaning of statutes and the scope of executive powers have been settled authoritatively by the courts. The traditional civil and political liberties, like liberty of the person and freedom of speech, have independent and intrinsic weight: their importance justifies an interpretation of both common law and statute which serves to protect them from unwise and ill-considered interference or restriction. The common law, then, has its own set of constitutional rights, even if these are not formally entrenched against legislative repeal.[88]

The Court applied the common-law right of liberty to support a narrow construction of 'association' so that it must involve 'some sympathy with, or support for, or involvement in, the criminal conduct of the person, group or organisation'.[89]

This case demonstrated common-law constitutionalism at work. Chapter two described the common-law conception of liberty as a qualified form of liberty as non-domination: it is not diminished by arbitrary power in general, but only arbitrary power that diminishes common-law rights.[90] As a non-domination conception, the judges did not need to discuss what damage would be caused if the Minister acquired the arbitrary power he was seeking. It was sufficient to note that such an arbitrary power would violate the liberty provided by the common law.

What perspective is suggested by Price's interpretation of liberty as non-domination? This value suggests that the main reason why liberty should be understood as diminished as soon as there is vulnerability to arbitrary power is because of the significant likelihood of serious interference. Price's paramount

---

[86] ibid [55] referring to *Railway Express Agency Inc v New York* 336 US 106 (1949).

[87] *Minister for Immigration and Citizenship v Haneef* (2007) 163 Federal Court Reports 414, [122] (Full Court of the Federal Court of Australia).

[88] TRS Allan, 'The Common Law as Constitution: Fundamental Rights and First Principles' in C Saunders (ed), *Courts of Final Jurisdiction: The Mason Court in Australia* (Sydney, Federation Press, 1996) 146–66, 148 referred to incorrectly as 'The Common Law of the Constitution …' in *Minister for Immigration v Haneef* [113].

[89] *Minister for Immigration v Haneef* [130].

[90] See ch 2, s VIIA.

concern with unjustified interference seems consistent with the approach endorsed by the judges. Turning to the quotations extracted above, Justice Jackson refers to opening 'the door to arbitrary action', and Allan refers to protection from 'unwise and ill-considered interference'.

These quotations do not indicate how likely interference will be, but they do seem to point to interference rather than power damage. Price's warnings about arbitrary state power were in the context of the general power the state enjoys over citizens who lack the protection of the franchise, so this is quite different from the limited power of a minister to ultimately deport non-citizens. Nevertheless, Price's warning can prompt us to take seriously the possibility that the significant arbitrary power that would be conferred through the Minister's interpretation of the character test would likely be exploited by a range of state officials connected to migration and law enforcement.

In considering how applicable Price's warning is, one could turn to Price's explanation for why those with arbitrary power are likely to abuse it. Price referred to an appetite for domination. Price mentioned people's 'love of domination, selfishness, and depravity' and said that 'nothing intoxicates the human mind so much as power'.[91] In this case, one might well wonder whether the Minister's decision should be seen in the light of the government pursuing a posture of toughness on terrorism, a posture viewed as enjoying significant public support.[92] A desire for re-election may have been paramount, in which Haneef was expendable.

At the same time, though, Price's explanation for the abuse of power in terms of the fallen nature of humanity may have more limited appeal today than to the audience Price was addressing.[93] There could be concern that it overstates the likelihood of power being abused. On the other hand, it might also understate the likelihood of abuse. A focus on depravity, for instance, can lead to overlooking incentives or, indeed, pressure, to abuse power. Kevin Andrews was a minister in a government, not a sole agent.[94] There is no need for us to limit ourselves to Price's portrayal of human nature; it is the general warning about likely interference where there is vulnerability to arbitrary power that is the main message to take from his approach to liberty as non-domination. It is a warning emanating from what is arguably a strand of liberalism. This makes it especially relevant to the common law, since liberalism is generally understood as the main ideology relevant to interpreting the common law.[95]

---

[91] See text to above n 15.

[92] M Head, 'The Haneef Inquiry: Some Unanswered Questions' (2009) 2 *Journal of the Australasian Law Teachers Association* 99–112, 103 suggests that the government 'seized upon the British attacks to try to launch a terrorism scare campaign in the final months of the 2007 election campaign'.

[93] For a link between the fallen nature of humanity and liberty as non-domination, see G Maddox, 'The Limits of Neo-Roman Liberty' (2002) 23 *History of Political Thought* 418–31, 421.

[94] See Head, 'The Haneef Inquiry' 107.

[95] For one prominent approach linking common-law interpretation to liberalism, see R Dworkin, *Law's Empire* (Cambridge, Mass., Belknap Press, 1986).

A warning about the risk of interference where there is substantial arbitrary state power cannot, though, furnish a complete perspective on an issue. To give one example, one might wonder what impact a contrary decision by the Federal Court could have had on the legitimacy of government in the eyes of some Muslims in Australia. It might have reinforced a sense that there is significant prejudice against them in Australia, that they are generally seen as potential terrorists, for instance. One adverse impact of this could be on cooperation with ASIO. This could reduce the likelihood of planned terrorist operations being thwarted. Admittedly, this is a speculative consideration. It is merely intended to point to the possibility that probabilistic considerations can be relevant, and those considerations cannot be assessed through Priceian liberty as non-domination. Price did not, however, offer liberty as non-domination as a sole guide. Underlying Priceian liberty as non-domination is a concern to achieve security from unjustified interference. It is consistent with Price's approach to directly take into account probabilistic considerations.

A heightened sense of suffering prejudice could have other adverse consequences, such as affecting the self-esteem of Muslims in Australia. This sense of lacking status cannot be reduced merely to a perception of being vulnerable to arbitrary power with its consequent increased likelihood of being interfered with. Price's pluralistic approach is consistent with considering status separately, not merely as a function of liberty.

The attempt here is only to give a sense of what approach might be suggested by Priceian's approach. By focusing in the first place on the likelihood of serious interference, it points to substantial harm that could have arisen from a contrary Federal Court decision. It can, though, also take other considerations into account, including direct consideration of the probability of unjustified interference and damage to status. However, its emphasis is on interference damage. Indeed, the case points to why this may be advantageous. The case highlights how substantial values may be invoked in support of arbitrary power. Here it was national security. Counsel for the Minister claimed that the deportation of innocents might be the price that needs to be paid to assure national security. In these cases, to persuasively challenge arbitrary power may require pointing to the substantial interference damage that this power can cause, together with other damage.

VI. Conclusion

Pettit, Skinner and Price share the position that the slave even of a non-interfering master is as unfree as a slave of an interfering master. Liberty as non-domination is diminished by mere vulnerability to arbitrary power. However, for Pettit and Skinner, this points to power damage. By contrast, for Price, this points to the precarious position of all slaves in terms of their exposure to likely and severe interference. Price, then, would dispute the likelihood of having a non-interfering master and that situation enduring. He was highlighting interference damage. The very likelihood of interference, though, brings with it power damage.

I captured this difference between their interpretations of liberty as non-domination by describing Price's interpretation not only as non-negative, but also having a negative-liberty dimension. It has a strong affinity with liberty as non-interference, especially in its moralized form. Just as adherents of liberty as non-interference are concerned to minimise the prospect of unjustified interference, so too was Price: security from unjustified interference was the immediate goal underlying liberty as non-domination. The distinctive quality of Priceian liberty as non-domination lay in its incorporation of the assumption of likely unjustified interference where there is arbitrary power. For adherents of liberty as non-interference, this assumption can only be external to their conception of liberty.

It is not altogether surprising, then, that the criticisms made of Pettit's liberty as non-domination in the last chapter, in defence of liberty as non-interference, are largely inapplicable to Price. Chapter four's first challenge to liberty as non-domination was to the distinctiveness of its implications. It was argued that achieving a sharp separation, so that the slave of a non-interfering master is as unfree as the slave of an interfering master, leads to difficulties since the probability of interference is relevant in measuring arbitrary power. When Pettit speaks of slaves with non-interfering and interfering masters suffering the same lack of liberty as non-domination, he is assuming those masters possess the same arbitrary power.

Priceian liberty as non-domination, by contrast, is not a continuous function where the variable is arbitrary power. Instead, it is partly discontinuous. Once arbitrary power reaches a certain level, based on a general profile of agents which assumes limited virtue or empathy, those vulnerable are simply unfree. They may, though, suffer more or less oppression.

Chapter four's second challenge to Pettit's liberty as non-domination was to its ability to track interference and power damage. In relation to power damage, this challenge is inapplicable, since Price did not claim that arbitrary power in the absence of interference necessarily leads to power damage; instead, he warned of complacency. In relation to interference damage, Pettit does not claim that liberty as non-domination does well. Indeed, Pettit's central hypothetical of a slave with a non-interfering master relies on a disjunction between arbitrary power and the probability of interference. This is not the case with Price. His central image is that of slaves suffering brutal interference. He did not, of course, have in mind a mere hypothetical. Part of his hope for American independence was, he mentioned in his *Observations*, that this would lead to the end of the slave trade.[96]

---

[96] Price, 'Observations' [1776] 56 fn 4. See also Page, 'A Species of Slavery' 55.

The contemporary attractiveness of his assumption of likely serious interference where there is substantial arbitrary power was explored through Shklar's liberalism of fear. The assumption is to be applied with judgement, taking into account the particular circumstances. Indeed, Shklar's work raises the question of whether Pettit and Skinner might trivialise arbitrary power by focusing instead on power damage in the absence of interference.

However, Shklar did not merely point to historical writing that warned about the risk of serious interference where there is substantial arbitrary power. She was referring to a strand of writing that forms part of a political tradition that has shaped, and continues to shape, political institutions. It was suggested that Priceian liberty as non-domination seems to fit within the liberalism of fear.

Both Shklar and Price were primarily concerned about the abuse of state power. The last section discussed the *Haneef* case. Here, disturbing arguments were made on behalf of the Minister to defend an interpretation of the law that would vest in him substantial arbitrary power, in the name of national security. Those arguments were resoundingly rejected, and here we saw a qualified conception of liberty as non-domination at work, with judges applying a common-law right to liberty. The case points to how substantial values, such as national security, can be urged in favour of compromising liberty as non-domination, and how in this context, it seems helpful to stress interference damage and separately consider other forms of damage. That stress, and the capacity to consider other forms of damage, is achieved by Price's approach to liberty as non-domination.

PART II

Positive Liberty

6

Positive-Liberty Dimensions in the Republican Revival

I. Introduction

The two mains strands of the republican revival are based on non-positive and positive liberty. Positive liberty is identified with citizens exercising normative reason while participating in politics. In short, liberty is identified with virtuous political participation. Non-positive liberty, by contrast, includes here two conceptions of liberty. First, it includes negative liberty, which I treat as synonymous with liberty as non-interference: it involves the absence of external constraints. Secondly, it includes liberty as non-domination. This involves the absence of vulnerability to arbitrary power: I have also described this as non-negative. Pettit's work challenged the established distinction between negative and positive liberty that had been employed in classifying interpretations of the republican tradition.

Part I of the book focused substantially on the distinction between liberty as non-domination and liberty as non-interference. This part of the book turns its attention to the place of positive liberty in the work of historical writers and the contemporary revivers of republicanism. This chapter looks backwards to non-positive-liberty republicanism, by focusing on affinities to positive liberty found in the accounts of its most prominent writers, Pettit and Skinner. This chapter also looks forward to positive-liberty republicanism by providing background for the next chapter's discussion of Michelman, the most prominent constitutional theorist to attempt to draw on a positive conception of republican liberty.

Both strands of the revival look at similar historical writers. Pettit and Skinner consider the Italian–Atlantic strand of the republican tradition. Pettit contrasts this with a Continental strand of the tradition, which did endorse positive liberty, and which he describes as populist or communitarian.[1] Michelman, on the other hand, drew on scholarship suggesting that the Italian–Atlantic tradition contained a negative- and a positive-liberty strand. While he suggested that the

---

[1] P Pettit, *Republicanism: A Theory of Freedom and Government* (Oxford, Clarendon Press, 1997) 30; P Pettit, *On the People's Terms: A Republican Theory and Model of Democracy* (New York, Cambridge University Press, 2012) 11–18.

negative-liberty strand had greater influence in eighteenth-century America, he mostly explored the positive-liberty strand.[2]

A difficulty with the negative–positive dichotomy, however, is that it is too crude to understand historical writers associated with republicanism and also contemporary republican revivers. Liberty as non-domination is one conception that does not fit with at least the most prominent understanding of the distinction, which is Berlin's. However, the concern of this chapter is not with conceptions that fall outside Berlin's understanding of the negative–positive distinction. Rather, the concern is with some broader understandings of positive liberty that Berlin accommodated within his understanding of positive liberty, but which fall outside the particular interpretation of positive liberty found in the republican revival. These broader understandings are neglected in the republican revival.

To give an example, the misleading narrative that Pettit provides of the eclipse of republican by liberal liberty, which was exposed in chapter two, partly follows from a failure to recognise that while Priceian liberty was not positive in the republican sense of being identified with virtuous political participation, it nevertheless had affinities with positive liberty through its identification of liberty with a right of political participation. It was this feature which primarily troubled the critics of Price whom Pettit mentions. To give a second example, chapter three argued that while Skinner's overall account of liberty does refer to self-government in a way that is close to Price's approach, self-government ultimately drops from view in his analytical conception of republican liberty. This also seems to distort his narrative of the eclipse of republican by liberal liberty in a similar way to Pettit's.

In previous chapters, I described conceptions of liberty that identify liberty with a right of political participation as having a 'positive-liberty dimension'. I distinguished this from positive liberty on the basis that in the republican revival, positive liberty is identified with political participation because political participation assists citizens to be self-governing in two ways. First, they share in collective self-government. Secondly, they enhance their own capacity for individual self-government, which requires individuals to exercise normative reason.

This chapter follows this understanding of positive liberty. I propose a classification of conceptions of liberty that follows the negative–positive distinction, as that is understood by Pettit and Skinner. I identify positive liberty with virtuous political participation. However, my proposed classification also recognises a variety of positive-liberty dimensions that an account of liberty may possess. While the crudity of the negative–positive divide has been observed in the literature,[3] there has been no attempt to apply this observation, at least in a systematic way, to some of the republican revivers and their interpretations of some of the historical writers. While such an application might appear to be a dry exercise

---

[2] F Michelman, 'The Supreme Court, 1985 Term – Foreword: Traces of Self-Government' (1986) 100 *Harvard Law Review* 4–77, C Sunstein, 'Beyond the Republican Revival' (1988) 97 *Yale Law Journal* 1539–90.

[3] See, eg, G MacCallum, 'Negative and Positive Freedom' (1967) 76 *Philosophical Review* 312–34.

in classification, the exercise is revealing. To simply regard certain conceptions as straightforwardly negative or positive has a procrustean effect. It substantially clouds understanding of the accounts of liberty found in historical writers associated with republicanism and in the contemporary revivers themselves. It also hides from view a rich variety of positive-liberty dimensions, some of which may merit normative consideration.

To outline how this chapter proceeds, Section II lays the foundation for the classification I propose. Subsection A indicates how Pettit and Skinner draw the negative–positive distinction. The rest of Section II briefly explores the major writers who inform their understanding of the distinction. They are Benjamin Constant, Isaiah Berlin, Gerald MacCallum and Charles Taylor.

Section IIIA provides my classification of conceptions of liberty. This classification is clarified in subsections B and C by applying it to Pettit's and Skinner's interpretations of republican liberty. Their interpretations are illuminated at the same time: their interpretations have some positive-liberty dimensions.

Section IV applies the classification to two historical writers, Harrington and Price, whom Pettit and Skinner significantly rely upon. This section discloses positive-liberty dimensions in Harrington's and Price's writing more systematically than was done in chapters two and three.

The concluding section makes some observations about the significance of the positive-liberty dimensions noted. I suggest that at least in understanding the non-positive-liberty republican strand, positive-liberty dimensions are important. How useful this chapter is for understanding positive-liberty republicanism awaits demonstration in the next chapter. I note here, though, that the way the negative–positive distinction is drawn in this chapter is consistent with Michelman's understanding. Harrington is also the main historical writer that Michelman discusses.

II. Negative and Positive Liberty in Nineteenth- and Twentieth-Century Political Thought

A. Pettit and Skinner

This section informs the classification presented in Section III. This subsection considers how Pettit and Skinner understand the negative–positive distinction. The following subsections explore some writers who have shaped their understanding of this distinction.

Pettit commences in chapter 1 of *Republicanism* with Berlin's distinction between negative and positive liberty. Pettit follows Berlin in suggesting that negative freedom consists in the absence of external obstacles to individual choice. He also refers to Berlin's positive liberty making contact with Constant's ancient liberty, and also being associated with the fulfilment obtained in the Athenian polis as that is depicted, for instance, by Arendt. Positive liberty 'involves the presence, and usually the exercise of the facilities that foster self-mastery and self-fulfilment: in particular, the presence and exercise of those participatory and voting facilities whereby the individual can unite with others in the formation of a common, popular will'.[4] In suggesting that positive liberty usually requires the exercise of capacities, Pettit refers to Taylor's contrast between opportunity and exercise conceptions of liberty. Taylor made the contrast to suggest that negative and positive liberty are truly distinct conceptions of liberty.

Pettit mentions that an historical narrative goes along with the philosophical dichotomy:

> Under that story, the concerns of those who speak of liberty in premodern times are almost always concerns with democratic membership and participation and the fulfil-ment that such belonging allegedly brings; they are concerns of the kind that would have been perfectly fulfilled for the citizens of classical Athens, for example, at least as Athens appears in the soft, nostalgic focus of the counter-Enlightenment … [he cites Arendt and Alasdair MacIntyre]. The concerns of moderns, on the other hand, are seen as the product of a changing, more individualistic society that spurns the ideal of public participation in favour of the ideal of a private sphere of activity in which each individual can get their own way. If democratic participation is supported within this philosophy of liberty, this is not because it is a good in itself, but rather because it serves a useful purpose in the protection of the individual.[5]

Skinner also treats Berlin's discussion of negative and positive liberty as the most significant modern discussion, and he too adopts Taylor's distinction between opportunity and exercise conceptions. Negative liberty is identified with opportunities for action. Positive liberty connects liberty with the performance of actions of a determinate type; it is especially concerned with self-realisation.[6] The version of positive liberty he mostly draws attention to is one where self-realisation is achieved through political participation. He describes this approach to self-realisation as Aristotelian, with twentieth-century supporters being Arendt, Taylor and MacIntyre.[7]

A subtle difference between Pettit's and Skinner's understanding of the negative–positive divide is that Pettit associates positive liberty with conceptions that require a capacity and *usually* the exercise of that capacity, while Skinner states that positive liberty *is* an exercise concept. Skinner regards internal constraints

---

[4] Pettit, *Republicanism* 18, references omitted.
[5] ibid 19. The citations are to H Arendt, *The Human Condition* [1958], with an introduction by Margaret Canovan, 2nd edn (Chicago, University of Chicago Press, 1998) and to A MacIntyre, *After Virtue* (London, Duckworth, 1987).
[6] Q Skinner, *Liberty before Liberalism* (Cambridge, Cambridge University Press, 1998) 114 fn 22.
[7] See, eg, Q Skinner, 'The Paradoxes of Political Liberty' in S McMurrin (ed), *The Tanner Lectures on Human Values*, vol VII (Cambridge, Cambridge University Press, 1986) 225–50, 249.

(such as psychological constraints) as ones that diminish negative liberty – they reduce the range of available options. He suggests that one can be free from internal constraints without achieving self-realisation or self-perfection.[8] For Pettit, however, internal constraints diminish positive liberty.[9] What is common to both writers, though, is that negative liberty involves the absence of at least external constraints. They also identify positive liberty with the exercise of certain capacities, where the exercise of those capacities leads to self-realisation.

The remaining subsections briefly discuss the main writers Pettit and Skinner rely on in drawing their analytical distinction between negative and positive liberty. They are principally Berlin and Taylor. However, with Berlin drawing partly upon Constant, it is helpful to begin with Constant. Also, with Taylor responding to MacCallum, I refer to MacCallum as well.[10] Discussing these writers not only enhances appreciation of how Pettit and Skinner understand the distinction. It also points to a diversity of conceptions of liberty, which is helpful in constructing the classification provided in Section III. On the other hand, my discussion is largely descriptive; those familiar with these writers can skip to Section III. While Pettit and Skinner also refer in their accounts of negative and positive liberty to Arendt and MacIntyre, I will not refer to them here. Arendt and MacIntyre are mostly used to indicate the benefits of political participation, in the form of self-realisation and a sense of belonging, that can be identified with positive liberty. They are not used to construct an analytical distinction between negative and positive liberty.

B. Constant

As Pettit indicates, Constant's discussion of liberty informs the contemporary understanding of the negative–positive distinction. Pettit identifies Constant's modern liberty with Berlin's negative liberty, and Constant's ancient liberty with the most prominent variety of Berlin's positive liberty.[11] In connecting ancient liberty to the Athenian polis, Constant provided an early articulation of the association between republicanism and positive liberty, which Berlin was to later reinforce.[12] Pettit also places Constant, in his preference for modern liberty, in the

---

[8] Q Skinner, 'A Third Concept of Liberty' (2002) *Proceedings of the British Academy* 237–65, 239.

[9] Pettit, *Republicanism* 17–18.

[10] Constant and MacCallum are referred to by Pettit and Skinner. In relation to MacCallum, see, eg, ibid 25 and Q Skinner, 'The Republican Ideal of Political Liberty' in G Bock, Q Skinner and M Viroli (eds), *Machiavelli and Republicanism* (Cambridge, Cambridge University Press, 1990) 293–309, 297.

[11] Pettit, *Republicanism* 18.

[12] P Pettit, 'Liberalism and Republicanism' (1993) 28 (Special Issue on Australia's Republican Question) *Australian Journal of Political Science* 162–89, 164, P Pettit, 'Keeping Republican Freedom Simple: On a Difference with Quentin Skinner' (2002) 30 *Political Theory* 339–56, 339.

liberal camp.[13] It will become apparent, though, that Constant's modern liberty does not equate with Berlin's interpretation of negative liberty.

In his famous 1819 lecture, Constant said that the liberty of the ancients consisted in directly participating in government.[14] By contrast, the liberty of the moderns is associated with representative democracy and with rights such as freedom of speech and of association and freedom from arbitrary arrest. One under-lying concern for Constant was the excesses of the French Revolution. Maximilien Robespierre, the most prominent figure of the Terror (1793–4), described it as 'the despotism of liberty', which aimed to establish a republic whose soul is virtue and equality.[15] In his most famous speech, Robespierre, echoing Cicero, said, 'We seek an order of things in which all the base and cruel passions are enchained, all the beneficent and generous passions awakened by the laws; where ambition becomes the desire to merit glory and to serve our country'.[16]

Constant suggested the revolutionaries were steeped in the cult of antiquity, a cult made respectable by writers such as Jean-Jacques Rousseau.[17] The Greek and Roman ideals of courage, patriotism and civic virtue were invoked at the expense of individual liberty. Constant mentioned that ancient institutions inconsistent with individual liberty, such as ostracism and the Roman censors, who had strong powers to act without a hearing against people thought to be a threat to Rome's well-being, were favourably referred to in defending the republic even after the Terror.[18]

Constant identified ancient liberty with the political participation available in direct democracies, where the people themselves can make decisions, for instance, about war and peace, vote on new laws, and call magistrates to account.[19] Even in Athens, where there was greater individual liberty than in other Greek republics or the Roman republic, Constant claimed that there was little recognition of the importance of liberty understood as freedom from state authority.[20] Citizens in ancient republics were subjected to the constant control of the political authority and of the community as a whole. Citizens had heavy military duties. Constant argued that the trade-off between the liberty to participate directly in politics and

---

[13] Pettit, *Republicanism* 50. Ch 3, s IVC, however, argued that Constant does not support the claim that liberalism is identified with liberty as non-interference. Instead, Constant identified liberty with certain rights that provide security against arbitrary power. Pettit had earlier stated that Constant had some republican traits: Pettit, 'Liberalism and Republicanism' 163.

[14] B Constant, 'The Liberty of the Ancients Compared with That of the Moderns' [1819] in *Political writings* trans & ed, B, Fontana (Cambridge, Cambridge University Press, 1988) 307–28, 310–11. For earlier contrasts between ancient and modern liberty, see S Holmes, *Benjamin Constant and the Making of Modern Liberalism* (New Haven, Yale University Press, 1984) 28–31.

[15] M Robespierre, 'On the Principles of Moral Policy That Ought to Guide the National Convention in the Internal Administration of the Republic' [1794] in R Bienvenu (ed), *The Ninth of Thermidor: The Fall of Robespierre* (New York, Oxford University Press, 1968) 32–49, 35, 39.

[16] ibid 33. See also P McPhee, *Robespierre: A Revolutionary Life* (New Haven, Conn., Yale University Press, 2012) 185.

[17] Constant, 'Liberty, Ancient and Modern' 319–20.

[18] ibid 321.

[19] ibid 311.

[20] ibid 316.

individual liberty that occurred in the polis is unattractive for the modern citizen. Indeed, the scale of modern states makes ancient liberty impossible. The aim of moderns is the enjoyment of security in private pleasures. The political liberty achieved through representative government is valued especially as a guarantee of individual liberty.[21] As Stephen Holmes has observed, Constant's description of the revolutionaries as steeped in the cult of antiquity enabled them to be understood as anachronistic rather than progressive.[22]

Holmes, however, notes that Constant was not only haunted by the Terror. With the restoration of the monarchy imposed by European powers after the defeats of Napoleon in 1814 and 1815, Constant was anxious to combat the ultraroyalists, who sought a return to the ancient regime, with absolutist rather than constitutional monarchy and a restoration of the position of the Church and nobility. Constant was concerned that a withdrawal by citizens from active politics facilitates tyranny.[23] There was a need, Constant felt, for citizens to exercise constant surveillance over their representatives. What could motivate such participation, given that the aim of moderns is the enjoyment of security in private pleasures?[24] He responded: 'It is not to happiness alone, it is to self-development that our destiny calls us; and political liberty is the most powerful, the most effective means of self-development that heaven has given us.'[25] The legislator must encourage the people to participate in politics.[26] Constant's modern liberty, then, incorporated a right of participation, and this right was partly defended through the claim that an active political life is a superior conception of the good.

C. Berlin

In 'Two Concepts of Liberty' (1958), Berlin described Constant as 'the most eloquent of all defenders of freedom and privacy'.[27] Berlin mentioned that no one expressed more clearly than Constant the conflict between negative liberty, as a zone of non-interference, and positive liberty, identified with a share in political power.[28] The question of what opportunities are available to citizens is obscured, Berlin claimed, by identifying liberty with the exercise of participatory rights in government.

---

[21] ibid 317.
[22] Holmes, *Benjamin Constant* 49.
[23] ibid 18–20.
[24] Constant, 'Liberty, Ancient and Modern' 317.
[25] ibid 327.
[26] ibid 328.
[27] I Berlin, 'Two Concepts of Liberty' [1958] in *Four Essays on Liberty* (Oxford, Oxford University Press, 1969) 118–72, 126.
[28] ibid 163. An echo of some criticisms Constant made of ancient liberty is found in some of Berlin's criticisms of Arendt. See K Hiruta, 'The Meaning and Value of Freedom: Berlin contra Arendt' (2014) 19 *The European Legacy* 854–68, 863.

It is, however, clear that Constant's modern liberty does not fit neatly within Berlin's understanding of negative liberty as a zone of non-interference. Constant's modern liberty also requires a share in political power.[29] In any case, there is more to Berlin's positive liberty than an identification between liberty and political participation. Berlin also associated positive liberty with a monistic approach to normative questions. This approach assumes that there can only be one correct answer to moral questions. It contrasts with the view that there are many incommensurable values, making it inevitable that choices will promote some values at the expense of others; there may be a range of reasonable responses to moral questions. The monistic approach also assumes that we have an essential nature that we should seek to fulfil. By contrast, the pluralistic approach Berlin favoured emphasises our diversity.

Berlin associated monistic assumptions with conceptions of liberty that require the exercise of certain capacities. They require agents to achieve their true nature through overcoming internal obstacles. That true nature generally involves the agent exercising reason. Immanuel Kant, for instance, identified liberty with rational self-direction by the individual. Kant suggested that when this idea was applied not merely to a person's inner life but to social relations, it suggested governance by rational law. People could then understand that even in their social relations, they are governed by reason: 'A rational (or free) state would be a state governed by such laws as all rational men would freely accept.'[30]

Berlin was concerned that the monistic approach, in less liberal hands, had led to ideas that furnished a basis for totalitarian ideologies such as fascism and communism.[31] Berlin referred to Rousseau's idea of liberty as rational self-direction. In his doctrine of the general will, Rousseau moved from the conventional and, Berlin insisted, correct view of the self, where this points to the actual desires that individuals have, to the unfortunate view of the self that points to the desires a citizen ought to have. Berlin linked this, through Kant's German disciples such as Johann Fichte, to a nationalism that provided an intellectual forefather of Fascism. Berlin claimed that for Fichte, the individual achieves freedom through submersion in a larger group, which requires renunciation of his or her desires and beliefs as an individual.[32] It can follow from this approach, Berlin thought, that once the authorities have determined the 'rational answer', those who disagree can be coerced with no loss to liberty being recognised. Rational constraints do not, under this interpretation, diminish liberty. Far better, thought Berlin, to recognise that all constraints imposed upon individuals that reduce their options diminish their liberty.

---

[29] See also Holmes, *Benjamin Constant* 44.

[30] Berlin, 'Two Concepts of Liberty' 145.

[31] C Galipeau, *Isaiah Berlin's Liberalism* (Oxford, Clarendon Press, 1994) ch 6.

[32] For an elaboration by Berlin on Rousseau and Fichte, in lectures delivered before 'Two Concepts of Liberty', see I Berlin, *Freedom and Its Betrayal: Six Enemies of Human Liberty*, ed, H Hardy, 2nd edn (Princeton, NJ, Princeton University Press, 2014).

Berlin associated positive liberty, then, with several conceptions of liberty. First, there is Constant's ancient liberty, which is achieved through participation in collective decision-making. Secondly, there is liberty as rational self-direction. Thirdly, there are conceptions of liberty where rational constraints do not diminish liberty. These are distinct conceptions. For instance, while Constant viewed political participation as an effective means of self-development, he did not define ancient liberty as requiring rational self-direction.

D. MacCallum and Taylor

MacCallum argued that the fact that Berlin's positive liberty contained several conceptions of liberty pointed to the unhelpfulness of the negative–positive divide. He instead suggested that there was one basic concept of freedom, which is in the form of an agent being constrained, or not constrained, from doing or becoming something.[33] The different interpretations of liberty concern what is free, what counts as a constraint, and what it is free to do or become. Within this triadic form, there are many conceptions of liberty, and it is misleading, MacCallum suggested, to divide these into negative and positive liberty.[34]

On the other hand, Taylor argued that MacCallum's single concept of liberty included only opportunity, but not exercise, conceptions of liberty. Taylor claimed it was helpful to conceive of a family of negative and positive conceptions of liberty.[35] He suggested that positive liberty is always an exercise conception: it requires agents to shape their own lives.[36] This requires qualities such as self-awareness, moral discrimination and self-control.[37] By contrast, negative liberty can be an opportunity conception: it can consist in the absence of certain constraints upon the range of available opportunities.[38]

Taylor favoured the positive conception. He suggested that rather than positive liberty being dangerous because it can be used to describe coercion as liberty-promoting, it is best to strongly argue for an interpretation of positive liberty that views self-realisation as something that can only be worked out independently by each individual.[39] This idea of self-realisation, Taylor argued, also provided the best justification for negative liberties. In its absence, negative liberty is difficult to support and is also difficult to apply, for judgements need to be made about the significance of different types of constraints.[40] Those judgements cannot be

---

[33] MacCallum, 'Negative and Positive Freedom' 314.

[34] ibid 322.

[35] C Taylor, 'What's Wrong with Negative Liberty' in A Ryan (ed), *The Idea of Freedom: Essays in Honour of Isaiah Berlin* (Oxford, Oxford University Press, 1979) 175–93, 175–7.

[36] ibid 177.

[37] ibid 179.

[38] ibid 177.

[39] ibid 180–1.

[40] ibid 183.

made in the absence of some view of human purposes. Taylor was not, though, suggesting that self-realisation is our single purpose: there are a diversity of goods that are valuable.[41]

While Taylor is in the positive-liberty camp, his use of opportunity and exercise conceptions in discussing negative and positive liberty has attracted Pettit and Skinner. Indeed, while not adopting positive liberty, Pettit seems to recognise some force to Taylor's defence of positive liberty. This will become apparent in Section IIIB. The classification that I will provide in the next section will refer as well to Constant and Berlin.

III. A Classification of Conceptions of Liberty and its Application to Pettit and Skinner

A. A Classification

This classification attempts to be faithful to the way republican revivers distinguish negative and positive liberty. While I have discussed Pettit and Skinner in this chapter, the classification also accords with Michelman's understanding. I build here, though, upon Pettit and Skinner.

For Pettit and Skinner, negative liberty involves the absence of certain constraints upon available options. For positive liberty, Pettit and Skinner combine some of Berlin's and Taylor's ideas: first, we are only truly free when we pursue our essential nature; secondly, our essential nature lies in exercising normative reason in directing ourselves; thirdly, the privileged locus for exercising positive liberty lies in determining and pursuing the public good with others. By combining these ideas into a single conception of liberty, their interpretation of positive liberty is a narrow one; I describe it as a full-blown positive conception of liberty. With full-blown positive liberty, the active political life, where citizens exercise normative reason in pursuit of the public good, is the best conception of the good for at least most of the citizenry.

Given the narrowness of this definition of positive liberty, it is also important to recognise accounts of liberty that are commonly understood as involving positive liberty or at least having associations with positive liberty. I describe such accounts as having positive-liberty dimensions, and I identify some of them in the rest of this subsection.

Some of these dimensions arise from what I will describe as a broad conception of positive liberty, where positive liberty is identified with *self-determination using normative reason.* This broad conception of liberty can be exercised in what I will

---

[41] C Taylor, 'The Diversity of Goods' in A Sen and B Williams (eds), *Utilitarianism and Beyond* (Cambridge, Cambridge University Press, 1982) 129–44.

describe as the personal, private and governmental spheres. The *personal* sphere focuses upon internal states or psychological attributes of the individual. Berlin referred to Kant's identification of liberty with rational self-direction by the individual. This is an example of personal positive liberty. The *governmental* sphere relates to state legislation and policy, and the *private* sphere covers all activities outside the governmental sphere.

I follow Pettit in viewing the internal constraints that can diminish personal liberty as only diminishing positive but not negative liberty. Therefore, only positive liberty can be enjoyed in the personal sphere. However, negative and positive liberty can be enjoyed in the private and governmental spheres. Negative liberty involves the absence of external constraints upon activities in the private or governmental spheres. Governmental-sphere negative liberty, for instance, would be diminished by constraints upon political participation aimed at changing government policy. Governmental-sphere positive liberty, on the other hand, involves the exercise of normative reason within this sphere. When the exercise of normative reason in the governmental sphere is privileged as the best conception of the good, such that one is only free when leading a virtuous and active political life, there is full-blown positive liberty.

The broad conception of positive liberty (involving the exercise of normative reason) can also be analysed by recognising that it involves *deliberation and enactment*. Taking personal liberty as an example, positive liberty requires deliberating on what is right, and then having the willingness to enact, to the extent possible, the outcomes of that deliberation. The extent to which such enactment is possible will depend partly on the extent of negative liberty in the private and governmental spheres.

The broad conception of positive liberty does not, however, exhaust all positive-liberty dimensions that an account of liberty may possess. For example, Berlin associated positive liberty with having a share in political power, while negative liberty involves the absence of constraints in general. Thus, Constant's modern liberty, which explicitly requires the opportunity to participate in politics, has a governmental-sphere positive-liberty dimension even though it does not require the exercise of normative reason.

Another example of a positive-liberty dimension that Constant's modern liberty furnishes lies in Constant's claim that political participation provides the most effective way of achieving self-realisation. This idea is associated with full-blown positive liberty. However, Constant did not incorporate this claim within his definition of modern liberty. Thus, this claim does not lead to Constant's modern liberty being full-blown positive liberty, but it does give his modern liberty a further positive-liberty dimension. Constant's ancient liberty is also not full-blown positive liberty. While he recognised that the demonstration of virtue in politics was an ancient value, he did not indicate that citizens only enjoyed ancient liberty when engaged in virtuous participation.

Another distinction that will prove helpful is between *public and non-public* conceptions of liberty. A public conception is what the state should adhere to.

A non-public conception is one which individuals may or should adhere to, but not the state. However, the non-public conception may be helpful in explaining the value of the public conception. The earlier subsection on Berlin referred to those arguments in 'Two Concepts of Liberty' most relevant to understanding how Pettit and Skinner draw the negative–positive distinction. However, in a 1988 interview, Berlin spoke of 'basic liberty', which involves a capacity for free choice and the exercise of free will.[42] This is basic to negative and positive liberty. Berlin viewed humans as a species able to fashion for itself a plurality of divergent natures.[43] Self-creation through choice-making, John Gray suggested, explains the value of negative liberty for Berlin. The capacity for choice that Berlin had in mind is more modest than the capacity for *rational* choice associated with autonomy. On the other hand, Galipeau points out that Berlin did not reject autonomy: Berlin's approach is consistent with regarding autonomy as helpful in making full use of the negative liberties one possesses.[44] Berlin's concern was that state constraints aimed at lessening internal constraints in an agent should not be simply understood as liberation. Instead, all constraints imposed by the state should be recognised as involving some diminution of liberty. It can be said that in Berlin's account, basic liberty and autonomy could be favoured as non-public conceptions of liberty. However, it is the public conception of liberty that is of greatest interest to republican revivers.

In summary, this classification identifies positive liberty with virtuous political participation: this is full-blown positive liberty. Accounts that endorse other conceptions of positive liberty, where those other conceptions furnish the goal the state should directly aim at, or which have some significant links to this goal, have positive-liberty dimensions. These dimensions may arise from endorsing what I described as a broad conception of liberty, where agents must govern themselves in accordance with normative reason. An account may also have a positive-liberty dimension when the public conception of liberty is non-rationalistic in the sense that liberty is not connected to the exercise of normative reason. Instead, liberty may be connected to the opportunity to participate in politics (as in Constant's ancient and modern liberty) or to the exercise of that opportunity. The value of my proposed classification will hopefully become clearer in the following subsections, where it is applied to Pettit and then Skinner.

B. Pettit's Liberty as Non-Domination

While Pettit distinguishes his approach from positive liberty, this subsection will show that his account nevertheless has three positive-liberty dimensions. The first

---

[42] Galipeau, *Isaiah Berlin's Liberalism* 86.

[43] J Gray, *Isaiah Berlin* (Princeton, NJ, Princeton University Press, 1996) 14–16, referring to Berlin, 'Two Concepts of Liberty' 169.

[44] Galipeau, *Isaiah Berlin's Liberalism* 95.

positive-liberty dimension arises from Pettit explaining the value of liberty as non-domination by referring to conceptions of liberty that require the agent to possess certain psychological and intellectual attributes. Pettit agreed with Berlin that were the state to embrace the ambition of improving people's psychology in the respects required by conceptions of liberty tied to psychological or intrapersonal factors, the state 'might well degenerate into an intrusive and oppressive agency'.[45] However, Pettit accepted that the value of more modest conceptions of liberty, such as liberty as non-domination and liberty as non-interference, when adopted as political ideals, lies in their promotion of more ambitious conceptions of liberty, such as autonomy.[46]

One can distinguish more or less stringent interpretations of autonomy. I will describe weak autonomy as involving a capacity to recognise one's self-interest and act accordingly. Strong autonomy involves a capacity to reach sound normative judgements and act accordingly. For example, Pettit endorses a conception of liberty that requires the psychological qualities necessary for agents to be morally responsible for their behaviour.[47] I describe extra-strong autonomy, on the other hand, as requiring the *exercise* of the capacity to follow one's sound normative judgements. This is equivalent to what I described as the broad conception of positive liberty. Nevertheless, Pettit's strong autonomy, through requiring the capacity to reach normative judgements and act accordingly, has an affinity with positive liberty. It requires certain psychological qualities. By recommending strong autonomy as a persuasive justification for liberty as non-domination, Pettit's account has a personal-sphere positive-liberty dimension.

The second positive-liberty dimension in Pettit's account can be discussed briefly. Liberty as non-domination shares an attribute Berlin associated with positive liberty. This is where liberty is undiminished by rational constraints. Pettit's liberty as non-domination is actually undiminished by any constraint; it is only diminished by vulnerability to arbitrary power. In circumstances where the perpetrator of interference lacks an arbitrary power of interference, there is no diminution of liberty. Chapter four mentioned that a person imprisoned after a trial that did not involve exposure to arbitrary power retains their liberty as non-domination.[48]

The third positive-liberty dimension in Pettit's account lies in the close relationship between liberty and a right of political participation. *Republicanism*, as clarified by later work, suggested that the state must be forced to track the

---

[45] P Pettit, *A Theory of Freedom: From the Psychology to the Politics of Agency* (Cambridge, Polity, 2001) 127.

[46] P Pettit, 'On *Republicanism*: Reply to Carter, Christman and Dagger' (2000) 9(3) *The Good Society* 54–7, 57, Pettit, *Republicanism* 81–2.

[47] Pettit, *A Theory of Freedom*.

[48] See ch 4, s VA.

common interests of citizens, according to citizens' own judgements of their interests.[49] This suggests that the avoidance of state arbitrary power necessarily requires a democratic process. The necessity for a democratic process seems to be affirmed in *On the People's Terms*. Pettit here defines liberty as non-domination in terms of being able to control decisions.[50]

On the other hand, the following quotation suggests some equivocation over whether there is a necessary relationship between democracy and liberty as non-domination. Pettit said:

> ... if the people governed by a state ... control the laws imposed ... then they may not suffer domination at the hands of their rulers. A state that was suitably controlled would be legitimate in the required sense of not exercising domination over its people. It would practise interference ... but it would only interfere with them on their terms, not at its own will or pleasure.[51]

The first sentence says they *may* not suffer domination, while the second sentence suggests they *would* not suffer domination.

Lovett interprets Pettit as suggesting a necessary relationship.[52] By contrast, liberty as non-interference is associated with denying any such necessary relationship. I will suggest, though, that the contrast is not so sharp. With both conceptions, the curtailment of democracy necessarily diminishes an aspect of liberty, but it does not necessarily diminish overall liberty. Take, for example, a decision to restrict the franchise. This necessarily reduces liberty as non-interference, for it strips from some people the option of voting. The reason that, overall, liberty as non-interference does not have a necessary relationship with democracy is because one would also need to assess what impact the restriction of the franchise has upon other liberties.

The decision to restrict the franchise also diminishes liberty as non-domination, for it exposes the disenfranchised to the form of public domination constituted by losing some power over the state. However, the relationship between that measure and overall liberty is, once again, a contingent one. Two hypotheticals illustrate this.

First, suppose that a consequence of restricting the franchise is that parliament passes legislation substantially reducing the arbitrary power the executive had previously enjoyed. That would seem to lessen the executive's domination of the people. Perhaps this possibility could be precluded by denying that the executive can possess significant arbitrary power where there is a democratic parliament.

---

[49] Pettit, *Republicanism* 55. Pettit, *A Theory of Freedom* 156 refers to 'avowable interests', which are based on actual preferences and those preferences that are 'conscious or can be brought to consciousness without great effort'.

[50] Pettit, *On the People's Terms* 153, 167.

[51] ibid 153.

[52] F Lovett, 'Republicanism and Democracy Revisited' in Y Elazar and G Rousselière (eds), *Republicanism and the Future of Democracy* (Cambridge, Cambridge University Press, 2019) 117–29, 124–5.

It might be claimed that since the people can take away that arbitrary power, the people ultimately control that power. However, this claim is unconvincing. That claim suggests that as long as there is a democratically elected parliament, liberty as non-domination cannot be used to challenge substantial arbitrary power in the hands of the executive. This is inconsistent with Pettit favouring in a democratic system constitutional measures that facilitate the contestation of executive decisions in order to reduce public domination.[53]

My second hypothetical is where the new, less democratic parliament passes legislation that substantially reduces private domination, that is, the arbitrary power that citizens possess with respect to each other.[54] In this way too, it is possible that non-democratic measures can lead to an overall increase in liberty as non-domination.

In defending liberty as non-interference, Berlin claimed that the question of what opportunities are available to citizens is obscured by identifying liberty with the exercise of participatory rights in government. I have just denied a necessary relationship between democracy and overall liberty as non-domination. Nevertheless, with Pettit's approach, the major focus when considering the state is on the arbitrary power it possesses by virtue of how democratic it is. Freedom is absent where there is arbitrary power that is not controlled by the people as a whole. His account thereby has affinities with accounts that establish a necessary connection between liberty and democracy. While Pettit associates positive liberty with populist conceptions of liberty, and contrasts these with liberty as non-domination, his own conception is at least somewhat populist. This gives his approach a governmental-sphere positive-liberty dimension.

In conclusion, while Pettit distinguishes liberty as non-domination from positive liberty, his own account has three significant positive-liberty dimensions: he suggests the value of liberty as non-domination lies ultimately in its promotion of autonomy; liberty as non-domination is not diminished by constraints; and liberty as non-domination is somewhat populist. This last dimension is perhaps the most striking, given that Pettit contrasts liberty as non-domination with populist conceptions of liberty.

C. Skinner's Republican Liberty

Since the late 1970s, Skinner has provided three formulations of republican liberty, as chapter three explained.[55] The first involved liberty as non-interference, but with an emphasis on what duties citizens need to perform to safeguard themselves against interference by their own state or a foreign state. The second formulation is

---

[53] See ch 4, s VIC.

[54] See P Pettit, 'The Determinacy of Republican Policy: A Reply to McMahon' (2006) 34 *Philosophy and Public Affairs* 275–83. See also above ch 4, s VIA.

[55] See ch 3, s II.

diminished by dependency upon an arbitrary power to interfere or offer benefits, and also by any form of interference. Skinner conceptualised that dependency as imposing the constraint of having to be deferential in order to reduce the risk of interference. This constraint diminished negative liberty, but not liberal liberty as non-interference. However, with his third formulation, Skinner accepted Pettit's position that the dependency upon arbitrary power that diminishes republican liberty cannot be reduced to constraints. He thereby endorsed liberty as non-domination: I have defined this conception as diminished by arbitrary power but not by constraints.[56] On the other hand, Skinner maintained that republican liberty is also diminished by interference. Skinner's third formulation combines liberty as non-domination and liberty as non-interference, with an emphasis upon the former. I too will focus on the non-domination component. This subsection will identify some important positive-liberty dimensions to his three formulations of liberty.

While Skinner's first formulation is not diminished by dependency on arbitrary power, and is therefore not my central focus, it is worth exploring partly because this involves some discussion of neutrality towards conceptions of the good, an issue that looms large in the negative–positive divide. Negative and full-blown positive liberty divide on whether a neutral or perfectionist state should be preferred. A perfectionist state promotes one or more controversial conceptions of the good, that is, conceptions that reasonable people may disagree with. By contrast, a neutral state does not privilege any controversial conception of the good from amongst the diversity of conceptions that are compatible with the requirements of justice.[57] Conceptions compatible with justice would exclude those that seriously impair the chance of others pursuing their conception of the good.

Skinner distinguished his first formulation from positive liberty.[58] Republican liberty's emphasis on civic duties was not justified on the ground that an active political life is the best conception of the good. Instead, political and military participation may safeguard the negative liberties necessary for people to pursue diverse conceptions of the good. Skinner's conception is clearly not positive. On the other hand, the importance of political participation in maintaining liberty can suggest that the state should actively promote participation. Even if the justification for a state policy strongly promoting such participation is not based on an active political life being the best conception of the good, the effect of the policy is not neutral. Consider a hypothetical where a state adopts Machiavelli's view that Christianity saps citizens' willingness to participate in politics and thereby renders the state more vulnerable to external and internal threats. Suppose this state therefore discriminates against Christianity. This might seem to be a non-neutral policy with respect to religion even if the justification seems neutral.[59]

---

[56] See, eg, ch 3, s IIC.

[57] S Wall, 'Neutralism for Perfectionists: The Case of Restricted State Neutrality' (2010) 120 *Ethics* 232–56, 238–9.

[58] Skinner, 'The Republican Ideal of Political Liberty'.

[59] For a different example, see A Patten, 'Liberal Neutrality: A Reinterpretation and Defense' (2012) 20 *Journal of Political Philosophy* 249–72, 255–6.

A governmental-sphere positive-liberty dimension appears, then, in Skinner's first formulation.

I will discuss together his second and third formulations of liberty when considering particular positive-liberty dimensions. These formulations are diminished by dependency on arbitrary power. They fit much better with state neutrality towards conceptions of the good than the first formulation. They do not highlight the importance of citizen participation in politics so clearly, which is not to deny that they are consistent with an account that regards political participation as essential to avoiding arbitrary power. Nevertheless, these formulations suggest a conception of the good involving a life without dependency. While Skinner refers to republican freedom as constituting a conception of the good, he does not relate this to state neutrality.[60] His contrast with positive liberty suggests that he understands a life not involving dependency as a neutral state goal.[61]

Skinner's second and third formulations also do not have the positive-liberty dimension of being moralized in the sense that liberty is undiminished by justified constraints. Skinner's second conception of republican liberty is diminished by constraints either resulting from the imposition of arbitrary power or otherwise. Skinner indicated that he shared Berlin's concern about conceptions of liberty that were undiminished by constraints that were deemed to be justified. Thus, he argued that Pettit's non-domination conception unfortunately encountered the paradox found with positive liberty where 'the act of obeying the law to which you have given your consent is "entirely consistent with freedom"'.[62]

Skinner's third formulation includes liberty as non-domination, and he views this as the primary focus of republicans. Since this is undiminished by constraints, his third formulation seems to have a positive-liberty dimension. On the other hand, his third formulation also involves liberty as non-interference. In considering citizens imprisoned for violating laws they have given their consent to, Skinner says they retain 'their underlying status as free-men, although they have obviously been deprived of one of their civil liberties'.[63] In this way, he seeks to indicate that in the primary sense of liberty as a status, prisoners retain their liberty. However, it can still be recognised that one of their liberties has been removed. This recognition depends, I suggest, on liberty as non-interference. With Skinner accommodating liberty as non-interference within republican liberty, the positive-liberty dimension resulting from liberty as non-domination being undiminished by constraints is much weaker than it is for Pettit's interpretation of republican liberty.

---

[60] Q Skinner, 'On the Slogans of Republican Political Theory' (2010) 9 *European Journal of Political Theory* 95–102, 98.

[61] Interestingly, Pettit describes liberty as non-domination as 'shared-value neutralism' on the basis that it is an ecumenical value: P Pettit, 'Reworking Sandel's Republicanism' in A Allen and M Regan (eds), *Debating Democracy's Discontent: Essays on American Politics, Law, and Public Philosophy* (Oxford, Oxford University Press, 1998) 40–59, 55.

[62] Skinner, *Liberty before Liberalism* 83 fn 54 quoting Pettit, *Republicanism* 66.

[63] Q Skinner, 'Freedom as the Absence of Arbitrary Power' in C Laborde and J Maynor (eds), *Republicanism and Political Theory* (Malden, MA, Blackwell, 2008) 83–101, 88.

Another positive-liberty dimension in Skinner lies in the close relationship between liberty and a right of political participation. Lovett points to the passage in *Liberty before Liberalism* (Skinner's second formulation) where Skinner mentions that to the extent to which a state is not governed by all its citizens, it 'will be moved to act by a will other than its own, and will to that degree be deprived of its liberty'.[64] This, Lovett, argues, supports his claim that Skinner too sees a necessary relationship between democracy and liberty as non-domination.

On the other hand, as indicated, interference does diminish republican liberty under Skinner's second and third formulations. Thus, while the absence of democracy means that the state is necessarily unfree, the extent of freedom individual citizens enjoy will not only be a function of whether they enjoy the franchise but also the extent of state interference they are exposed to. Nevertheless, Skinner's focus on public domination, reflected in the passage Lovett draws attention to, suggests a sufficiently close relationship between liberty and democracy to impart a governmental-sphere positive-liberty dimension to his conception.

Finally, Skinner's second formulation has a personal-sphere positive-liberty dimension. This is not present in Skinner's *conception* of republican liberty. This is defined as diminished by dependency upon arbitrary power and also by interference. However, he did embed this conception within a wider account, which draws an analogy between individual self-government and civil liberty. Just as an individual is unfree unless governed by his or her own will, a state is unfree unless governed by the will of its people. However, this only imparts a weak positive-liberty dimension to his account. The connection he drew was merely an analogy.

D. Concluding Comments

The application of the proposed classification to Pettit and Skinner has hopefully illuminated the classification and also those writers. While my classification follows the way the negative–positive distinction is understood by Pettit and Skinner, it also points to how accounts of liberty can have positive-liberty dimensions. Such dimensions exist not just in Constant's ancient but also his modern liberty. Pettit's and Skinner's favoured interpretations of republican liberty also have some significant positive-liberty dimensions, dimensions largely unacknowledged in their accounts.

The following diagram attempts to capture some of the distinctions I made. The main one it excludes is the public–non-public distinction. Examples are given in the boxes that can be populated. That only one box can be populated in the case of positive liberty points to the narrowness of the definition employed here. The classification is aimed at illuminating writers identified with the republican tradition.

---

[64] Lovett, 'Republicanism and Democracy Revisited' referring to Skinner, *Liberty before Liberalism* 27.

Figure 6.1 A Classification of Liberty

	Personal	Private sphere	Governmental sphere
Negative liberty		Absence of external constraints on participation in private sphere.	Absence of external constraints on political participation.
Positive liberty dimensions	Exercise of normative reason and willingness to act accordingly: Kantian autonomy. Capacity to exercise normative reason: Pettit's fitness to be held responsible notion of autonomy.	Exercise of normative reason in acting within the private sphere.	Exercise of normative reason in governmental sphere. Opportunity to participate through voting: Constant's modern liberty, Pettit's & Skinner's liberty as non-domination. Privileging of an active, virtuous political life, but detached from conception of liberty: Constant's modern liberty. Emphasis on citizen participation for protection: Skinner's first formulation.
Positive liberty			Exercise of normative reason when acting in governmental sphere such that in the absence of this, one is unfree.

IV. Positive-Liberty Dimensions in Historical Writing

A. Harrington

The previous section demonstrated that even with Pettit's and Skinner's interpretations of liberty as non-domination, there are some positive-liberty dimensions. This section looks at two major historical writers that feature prominently in the republican revival: Harrington and Price. I discuss Harrington in this subsection and Price in the next. It will become apparent that attempts to place these writers squarely in the non-positive- or positive-liberty camp are procrustean.

Harrington features prominently in the non-positive- and positive-liberty republican revival. Harrington is the historical writer that Michelman focuses on, and he is also a writer substantially discussed by Skinner and often referred to by Pettit.[65] Chapter three suggested that Harringtonian liberty is diminished by dependency upon an arbitrary power to interfere or confer benefits. Harringtonian liberty is at least strongly suggestive of liberty as non-domination. In this subsection, I point to positive-liberty dimensions in Harrington's account. At the same time, I note that he did not endorse full-blown positive liberty. This is contrary to Pocock's interpretation of Harrington, which furnishes a basis for Michelman's interpretation of republican liberty.[66]

---

[65] In relation to Skinner, see above ch 3, s IIIC. For Pettit, see his *Republicanism*.

[66] JGA Pocock, *The Machiavellian Moment: Florentine Political Thought and the Atlantic Republican Tradition* [1975], with a new introduction by Richard Whatmore (Princeton, NJ, Princeton University Press, 2016) 394, Michelman, 'Traces of Self-Government'.

Harrington articulated a personal positive conception of liberty. He described the 'soul of man' as 'the mistress of two potent rivals, the one reason, the other passion'.[67] Where passion rules, there is 'vice and the bondage of sin'. He also made an analogy between personal positive liberty and the liberty of the state. He said, 'if the liberty of a man consist in the empire of his reason, the absence whereof would betray him unto the bondage of his passions; then the liberty of a commonwealth consisteth in the empire of her laws, the absence whereof would betray her unto the lusts of tyrants'.[68]

Harrington was not endorsing here full-blown positive liberty. Instead, the liberty most relevant to the state appears to consist in the rule of law, which is contrasted with being vulnerable to the arbitrary power of tyrants. Those committed to understanding republican liberty ultimately in terms of liberty as non-domination do not view Harrington's personal positive conception of liberty as having a substantive role in understanding his public conception of liberty. Section IIIC mentioned that Skinner does point to an analogy between personal liberty and the liberty of the state in his overall account of liberty. Personal liberty, however, is not part of his ultimate conception of republican liberty. Lovett, an exponent of liberty as non-domination, takes a similar approach, with his inter-pretation of Harrington. He says:

> Since the metaphorical trope contrasting the freedom of the soul with the bondage of sin was ubiquitous ever since St Paul's Letter to the Romans, it would be a mistake to read this passage as suggesting any real philosophical commitment on Harrington's part to a positive conception of moral liberty. In any case, it serves no more than an analogical function in his main argument.[69]

Their approaches to Harrington are thereby inconsistent, say, with Mark Goldie's claim that a Christian reformist vision was integral to Harrington's construction of the just polity.[70] Goldie claims that for Harrington, only a free republic, as opposed to an absolute or constitutional monarchy, could achieve the structures necessary for liberty of conscience to be safeguarded. In a free republic, there would be a state Council of Religion, which would establish a national religion, where the clergy would be subject to election by the people. The Council would help instruct in 'a right application of reason unto Scripture'.[71] The Council would also be responsible for ensuring liberty of conscience. Other churches would be allowed, if they were neither 'Popish, Jewish, nor idolatrous'.[72]

---

[67] J Harrington, 'The Commonwealth of Oceana' [1656] in *The Commonwealth of Oceana and A System of Politics*, ed, JGA Pocock (Cambridge, Cambridge University Press, 1992) 1–266, 19.

[68] ibid 19–20.

[69] F Lovett, 'Harrington's Empire of Law' (2012) 60 *Political Studies* 59–75, 74 fn 20.

[70] M Goldie, 'The Civil Religion of James Harrington' in A Pagden (ed), *The Languages of Political Theory in Early-Modern Europe* (Cambridge, Cambridge University Press, 1987) 197–222.

[71] Harrington, 'The Commonwealth of Oceana' 127.

[72] ibid 81. See also at 127.

For Harrington, a national church, with the clergy being subject to popular election, was the way to achieve liberty of conscience, which was the most important liberty the state should promote.[73] There does seem a personal positive-liberty dimension in Harrington. A life involving personal positive liberty is the only appropriate conception of the good. Being able to associate with a church is also fundamental, so there is in Harrington's account a private-sphere positive-liberty dimension as well.

While Harrington did not endorse full-blown positive liberty, this does not rule out Pocock's claim that the dominant purpose of Harrington's political system was to enable citizens to demonstrate virtue through political participation.[74] If Pocock's claim is true, Harrington's conception of liberty would have a strong governmental-sphere positive liberty dimension. It would closely connect his conception to values identified with full-blown positive liberty. I will, however, suggest that Pocock's claim lacks support.

Harrington argued that a government that comes closest to the work of God unites those who enjoy the goods of the mind, such as wisdom and courage, and those who enjoy the goods of fortune, such as wealth.[75] He urged those with any piety to raise themselves 'out of the mire of private interest to the contemplation of virtue' in pursuing the right form of government.[76] The right form of government would include a senate that would be drawn from an elite recognised as particularly wise. The senate would identify and debate policy options. This elite, however, should not be trusted to promote the public interest over their own interests. Therefore, the choice between policy options must lie with the people directly or, if they are too numerous, with their elected representatives.[77] While the people will be most strongly motivated by their private interests, the public interest is most likely to be furthered when the entire community is included in decision-making. Citizens will have an informed view of what lies in their interests because they will benefit from the policy deliberation undertaken by the senate.

Harrington did not think it safe to rely on virtue in politics. Instead, constitutional arrangements must enable the public good to be achieved despite the dominance of self-interest.[78] The fundamental principle of his Commonwealth was akin to the situation where in sharing a cake, the arrangement is that one girl divides the cake, and then the other girl chooses the piece she desires.[79]

[73] See also R Beiner, 'Civil Religion and Anticlericalism in James Harrington' (2014) 13 *European Journal of Political Theory* 388–407, 392–8.

[74] Pocock, *Machiavellian Moment* 394.

[75] Harrington, 'The Commonwealth of Oceana' 10–11.

[76] ibid 19.

[77] ibid 24.

[78] See, eg, R Hammersley, 'Rethinking the Political Thought of James Harrington: Royalism, Republicanism and Democracy' (2013) 39 *History of European Ideas* 354–70, 364, G Remer, 'James Harrington's New Deliberative Rhetoric: Reflection of an Anticlassical Republicanism' (1995) 16 *History of Political Thought* 532–57, 554.

[79] Harrington, 'The Commonwealth of Oceana' 22–4.

This arrangement ensures an equitable result through the decision-making procedure. He said, 'for as man is sinful, but yet the world is perfect, so may the citizen be sinful and yet the commonwealth be perfect'.[80]

Harrington is suggesting that citizens should demonstrate the virtue necessary to contemplate and pursue the ideal constitution, yet that ideal constitution will itself require little virtue from citizens. On the other hand, in *A System of Politics*, a late work summarising his theory in aphoristic form, Harrington said:

> The more the soul or faculties of a man (in the manner of their being infused into the body of a multitude) are refined or made incapable of passion, the more perfect is the form of government.
>
> Not the refined spirit of a man, or of some men, is a good form of government; but a good form of government is the refined spirit of a nation.[81]

Unfortunately, this passage leaves unclear precisely how virtue contributes to a good constitution. Perhaps just as the creation of an ideal constitution requires civic virtue, its maintenance does as well. In any case, it does not appear from Harrington's account that the dominant role of the ideal constitution is to provide an avenue for citizens to achieve self-realisation through virtuous political participation. Harrington's account does not have the strong governmental-sphere positive-liberty dimension that comes from connecting closely with full-blown positive liberty.[82]

It does, though, have a different governmental-sphere positive-liberty dimension. Harrington said:

> The man that cannot live upon his own must be a servant; but he that can live upon his own may be a freeman.
>
> Where a people cannot live upon their own, the government is either monarchy or aristocracy; where a people can live upon their own, the government may be a democracy ...
>
> As the form of a man is the image of God, so the form of a government is the image of man.[83]

These aphorisms suggest that popular government achieves more than rational law. Popular government is befitting people capable of independence. It seems that popular government confers on citizens what I describe as 'democratic status', that is, the status derived from having a right to participate in government at least to the

[80] ibid 218.

[81] J Harrington, 'A System of Politics' [1770] in *The Commonwealth of Oceana and A System of Politics*, ed, JGA Pocock (Cambridge, Cambridge University Press, 1992) 267–93, 273. (Ch IV aphorisms 11 and 12.)

[82] The interpretation provided here is consistent with V Sullivan, 'The Civic Humanist Portrait of Machiavelli's English Successors' (1994) 15 *History of Political Thought* 73–96. See, eg, at 86–7, and V Sullivan, *Machiavelli, Hobbes, and the Formation of a Liberal Republicanism in England* (Cambridge, Cambridge University Press, 2004) ch 4.

[83] Harrington, 'A System of Politics' 269, 270, 273. (Ch 1 aphorisms 13 and 14, ch 4 aphorism 4.)

extent of voting for representatives. The democratic status that Harrington envisaged recognises that citizens at least enjoy what Section IIIB described as a weak form of autonomy: that necessary to pursue self-interest on political matters. This contrasts with extra-strong autonomy, where people pursue the common interest. The democratic status that Harrington envisages confers a weak governmental-sphere positive-liberty dimension upon his conception of liberty.

Thus, Harringtonian liberty has personal and private-sphere positive-liberty dimensions and a weak governmental-sphere positive-liberty dimension. These dimensions are not properly acknowledged in the non-positive-liberty strand. It will appear from the next chapter that in the positive-liberty strand, they are overstated in favour of full-blown positive liberty. Michelman was influenced by Pocock's interpretation.

B. Price

Chapter two suggested that Priceian liberty is diminished by arbitrary power, and Price's main justification for this was that arbitrary power leads, in all likelihood, to unjustified interference. That chapter also pointed to Price incorporating within his definition of liberty the requirement of sharing in political power. This is a governmental-sphere positive-liberty dimension. I will begin here with positive-liberty dimensions relating to the personal and private spheres before turning to the governmental sphere.

Beginning, then, with the personal sphere, Price's conception of moral liberty involved the power to act according to one's conscience. This is personal positive liberty. It is a power that must be exercised – to act wickedly indicates that one's judgement has been overpowered by one's passions.[84] Price said:

> … every man's will, if perfectly free from restraint, would carry him invariably to rectitude and virtue and that no one who acts wickedly acts as he likes, but is conscious of a tyranny within him overpowering his judgment and carrying him into a conduct for which he condemns and hates himself.[85]

His conception of moral liberty reflects the value he placed upon people's capacity to reason. As a Puritan, Price believed that people have a duty to act up to the hopes and dignity of reasonable and immortal beings.[86] People have the capacity as well as the duty to pursue the truth on moral and scientific questions.[87]

---

[84] R Price, 'Additional Observations on the Nature and Value of Civil Liberty, and the War with America' [1777] in *Political Writings*, ed, DO Thomas (Cambridge, Cambridge University Press, 1991) 76–100, 81.

[85] ibid.

[86] R Price, *Review of the Principal Questions in Morals* [1758], ed, D Raphael (Oxford, Clarendon Press, 1948) 150. See also DO Thomas, *The Honest Mind: The Thought and Work of Richard Price* (Oxford, Clarendon Press, 1977) 80.

[87] Thomas, *The Honest Mind* 12, 99.

Price linked moral to civil liberty. His *Additional Observations* said that only with free governments do citizens have the scope to be directed by their own conscience.[88] Furthermore, by securing property rights, people are 'encouraged and incited to industry'. With rights to freedom of thought, speech and religion, people are also encouraged to investigate a range of issues, and this will lead them to be guided by truth and reason rather than by error and superstition. The hope, then, is that citizens exercise at least private-sphere positive liberty. While Price's first justification for civil liberty was to avoid unjustified interference, the ultimate justification lies in the opportunity and stimulus that creates to exercise moral liberty. Price lists moral liberty as his first conception of liberty. A life involving moral liberty appears as the only appropriate conception of the good.[89] There is at least a personal- and private-sphere positive-liberty dimension to his conception of liberty.

Governmental-sphere positive-liberty dimensions are also present. The range of issues that civil liberty encourages citizens to pursue is not limited to the private sphere. Indeed, moral liberty can require citizens to participate in politics, especially when liberty is at risk. In a sermon, Price exhorted his congregation to speak out on public issues:

> He that expects to be a citizen of the heavenly Jerusalem ought to be the best citizen of this world.
>
> …
>
> If the demon of corruption is poisoning the springs of legislation and converting the securities of public liberty into instruments of slavery, let us point out to them the shocking mischief, and endeavour to recover them to a sense of their danger.[90]

Civil liberty also confers status upon citizens. Referring to such enfranchised citizens, Price said:

> Conscious of being their own governors, bound to obey no laws except such as they are given their consent to, and subject to no control from the arbitrary will of any of their fellow-citizens, they possess an elevation and force of mind that makes them great and happy.[91]

The reference to only being bound by laws they consent to suggests that part of the status achieved through civil liberty lies in having a share in political power. It would seem that Price was suggesting that an entitlement to participate in government is an official acknowledgement by the state and the community that citizens

---

[88] Price, 'Additional Observations' 84–5.

[89] See also L Hickman, *Eighteenth-Century Dissent and Cambridge Platonism: Reconceiving the Philosophy of Religion* (Abingdon, Routledge, 2017) ch 5.

[90] R Price, 'A Fast Sermon' [1781] in *Political Writings*, ed, DO Thomas (Cambridge, Cambridge University Press, 1991) 101–15, 111, 112–13.

[91] Price, 'Additional Observations' 84–5.

can responsibly exercise political power. By treating citizens in this respectful manner, by conferring what can be described as democratic status upon them, citizens' sense of confidence in their own capacities is enhanced and, presumably, their willingness to exercise their rational capacities in the private and governmental spheres.

The previous subsection suggested that Harrington recognised democratic status in the form of weak autonomy: it is the capacity to determine on political matters what lies in one's self-interest. By contrast, Price referred to the elevation of mind that comes from a right to participate in collective decision-making. For Price, democratic status is conferred where institutional arrangements suggest recognition of the capacity and willingness of citizens to exercise normative reason (strong autonomy) on political matters. Obtaining status from the opportunity to participate in politics derives from two ideas: first, the positive-liberty idea that our dignity is essentially tied to our capacity to reason and, secondly, that the governmental sphere provides an important avenue through which this capacity can be exercised. Price's inclusion of democratic status as an advantage of liberty gives his approach a governmental-sphere positive-liberty dimension.

A further governmental-sphere positive-liberty dimension lies in Price identifying civil liberty with the franchise. Indeed, he claimed that the extent of liberty was proportional to people's share in government.[92] This close link between liberty and democracy was the main feature of Priceian liberty that his critics were troubled by.[93]

While there are significant positive-liberty dimensions to Price's account, Price did not endorse full-blown positive liberty. Price suggested that in the hypothetical situation of being governed by men 'on whose superior wisdom and goodness we might absolutely depend', liberty would require us to put ourselves under their direction.[94] We should be prepared, then, to surrender the opportunity to exercise positive liberty in the governmental sphere if dependable, wise rulers are available. His main point was that no such rulers will be found. However, it also appears that governance by good laws is more valuable than self-determination on political matters.

In summary, Priceian liberty has a personal- and private-sphere positive-liberty dimension due to the way Price values security for its role in achieving personal and private-sphere positive liberty. It also has governmental-sphere positive-liberty dimensions, including its tight identification between liberty with democracy and its inclusion of democratic status as an advantage of liberty.

---

[92] R Price, 'Observations on the Nature of Civil Liberty, the Principles of Government, and the Justice and Policy of the War with America' [1776] in *Political Writings*, ed, DO Thomas (Cambridge, Cambridge University Press, 1991) 20–75, 26.

[93] Ch 2, ss IV and V.

[94] This is more fully extracted in ch 5, s IIA.

V. Conclusion

This chapter followed the distinction that the non-positive-liberty republican revivers make between negative and positive liberty. With positive liberty (or full-blown positive liberty), the exercise of moral capacities through participation in collective decision-making is privileged as a conception of the good by suggesting that it is in this way that freedom as self-realisation is achieved. Negative liberty, by contrast, focuses on interference; it suggests neutrality towards conceptions of the good.

Pettit's liberty as non-domination, Skinner's formulations of republican liberty, and the conceptions of liberty favoured by Harrington and Price do not endorse full-blown positive liberty. Nevertheless, these conceptions have features commonly associated with positive liberty. Indeed, a variety of positive-liberty dimensions were highlighted. They include drawing certain connections between liberty and the individual exercising normative reason, and between liberty and a right of political participation, and liberty being undiminished by constraints.

It might be suggested that the sheer variety of positive-liberty dimensions that were highlighted could justify Pettit and Skinner overlooking them: while neglecting them might give a misleading impression of individual writers, in seeking commonalities across diverse writers, some abstraction from their actual ideas is justified. Such an approach, however, is costly. Chapters two and three demonstrated how the neglect of the positive-liberty dimension of connecting liberty as non-domination to political participation distorted Pettit's and Skinner's narrative of the eclipse of republican liberty, which colours their contrast between liberty as non-domination and liberty as non-interference. This chapter highlighted some additional ways in which a neglect of positive-liberty dimensions distorts understanding of the historical writers. For example, the exercise of normative reason is critical in Harrington's and Price's accounts of liberty. With Harrington, there is the importance of religious liberty in designing a constitution. With Price, it seems that the ultimate rationale for promoting liberty as non-domination is to promote moral liberty.

A neglect of positive-liberty dimensions even clouds understanding of Pettit's and Skinner's own interpretations of republican liberty. For instance, Pettit's interpretation of liberty as non-domination involves a tight connection to democracy. This places an interesting complexion on the distance that Pettit achieves between liberty as non-domination and positive liberty. He connects positive liberty to populist conceptions of liberty. Another cost to overlooking positive-liberty dimensions is that this removes a ground for challenging the positive-liberty strand of the republican revival. This is convincingly challenged not by overlooking affinities with positive liberty, but by distinguishing them from full-blown positive liberty.

Recognising positive-liberty dimensions may also be helpful in considering values worthy of current application. Those dimensions might explain why liberty as non-domination or as non-interference is worth supporting. Those dimensions might also merit direct application. The next chapter suggests that Price's moral liberty may be more attractive than Michelman's contemporary adaptation of republican liberty. Part III draws on democratic status in defending constitutional juries.

7

Michelman's Republicanism

I. Introduction

The two most prominent scholars to have employed republican positive liberty for contemporary guidance on constitutional matters have been Michelman and Sunstein.[1] Together with other scholars, they drew on a substantial literature that found republican themes in eighteenth-century America. This literature burgeoned especially from the late 1960s to 1980s.[2] Michelman is the constitutional scholar who provided the most searching examination of republican positive liberty. He examined Harrington's conception of liberty and considered why republican positive liberty should command our attention. He pointed to provocative and imaginative ways in which republican positive liberty illuminates judicial review based on a bill of rights. Michelman took on the challenging task of employing a radically democratic idea to justify an institution that has prompted significant anxiety in terms of its democratic credentials. That radically democratic idea is that citizens are not free unless they actively participate in politics.

With the republican revival having been supported by some of the US's most prominent constitutional scholars, it naturally received significant attention, but also substantial criticism. Some argued that republicanism has such distasteful associations, with its exclusion of minorities, women and the unpropertied, that reviving it is problematic.[3] Others suggested that unattractive features of

---

[1] F Michelman, 'The Supreme Court, 1985 Term – Foreword: Traces of Self-Government' (1986) 100 *Harvard Law Review* 4–77, F Michelman, 'Law's Republic' (1988) 97 *Yale Law Journal* 1493–1537. For further references, see ch 1, s II. Since Sunstein will not be discussed, I mention here that he suggests some themes that 'are united by the republican conception of individual autonomy as involving selection rather than implementation of ends, and the republican conception of political freedom, which prizes collective self-determination'. The themes involve deliberation aimed at the public good and political participation. These are valued not only for their role in achieving decisions that promote the public good, but also because the educational effects of participation are valuable for the participants themselves. See C Sunstein, 'Beyond the Republican Revival' (1988) 97 *Yale Law Journal* 1539–90, 1548 and C Sunstein, *The Partial Constitution* (Cambridge, Mass., Harvard University Press, 1993) 133–4. For other scholars that have sought to revive republican positive liberty, see above ch 1, s II.

[2] See D Rodgers, 'Republicanism: The Career of a Concept' (1992) 79 *Journal of American History* 11–38.

[3] D Bell and P Bansal, 'The Republican Revival and Racial Politics' (1988) 97 *Yale Law Journal* 1609–21.

traditional republicanism remain in contemporary republicanism.[4] A quite different critique was that republican revivers drew so heavily on liberalism that the republican flavour of their analysis was weak.[5] Some regretted that the republican emphasis on citizen participation lacked sufficient presence in the revivers' work, with the revivers focusing unduly on the courts.[6] Others welcomed the fact that the revivers' republicanism was diluted by substantial reliance upon liberal values and ideas. They regretted, though, the way that republican revivers nevertheless contrasted their approach with liberalism and interest-group pluralism. This contrast is achieved by excluding significant strands of liberalism and treating a descriptive theory of interest-group pluralism as a normative theory.[7]

This chapter's critique, though, looks more closely at the conception of liberty Michelman proposed and how he applied it. It thereby provides a fresh look at his approach. It points to difficulties with his interpretation of traditional republicanism, his adaptation of republican liberty for contemporary guidance, his interpretation of liberal negative liberty, and the connections he drew between liberty and judicial review. However, Michelman's vision of those involved in constitutional review being virtually representative of the people is arresting, and it is a vision that will be pursued in the next part of the book. Michelman's work also provides an illuminating contrast to the non-positive-liberty strand of the republican revival considered in Part I. That strand contrasts its interpretation of liberty with republican positive liberty.

This chapter will focus on two of Michelman's articles. 'Traces of Self-Government' is his most substantial exploration of republican liberty and its implications. However, his discussion in 'Law's Republic' of *Bowers v Hardwick*, a Supreme Court decision that refused to extend a right of privacy to homosexual conduct, will also be examined.[8] In these articles, Michelman argued that his interpretation of republican positive liberty provides an attractive way to defend judicial activism and to interpret particular rights.

Indicating how this chapter proceeds, Section II questions some of Michelman's historical claims about republicanism. Michelman relies especially on Harrington, but also refers to Price. Section III examines the reasons Michelman

---

[4] S Gey, 'The Unfortunate Revival of Civic Republicanism' (1993) 141 *University of Pennsylvania Law Review* 801–98.

[5] R Fallon, 'What Is Republicanism, and Is It Worth Reviving?' (1989) 102 *Harvard Law Review* 1695–1735, 1734; P Brest, 'Further Beyond the Republican Revival: Towards Radical Republicanism' (1988) 97 *Yale Law Journal* 1623–31.

[6] K Abrams, 'Law's Republicanism' (1988) 97 *Yale Law Journal* 1591–1608, 1592.

[7] For concern about the distinction between republicanism and liberalism, see H Hartog, 'Imposing Constitutional Traditions' (1987) 29 *William and Mary Law Review* 75–82 (responding to Horwitz) and Fallon, 'What Is Republicanism, and Is It Worth Reviving?' (responding to Tushnet). For criticism of Sunstein's depiction of pluralism (and also Michelman's liberalism), see R Epstein, 'Modern Republicanism – or Flight from Substance' (1988) 97 *Yale Law Journal* 1633–50. Sunstein's depiction is also criticised in J Macey, 'The Missing Element in the Republican Revival' 97 *Yale Law Journal* 1673–84.

[8] 478 US 186 (1986). This was overturned in *Lawrence v Texas* 539 US 558 (2003).

offers for the contemporary appeal of republican liberty. In the process, Michelman adapts what he understands to be the historical interpretation to give it contemporary appeal. I question the contrast he draws with negative liberal liberty.

Section IV examines the implications for judicial review that Michelman finds in republican liberty. Those implications relate to the legitimacy of judicial review and the interpretation of constitutional rights. Section V considers whether some of Michelman's deviations from the two historical writers considered (Harrington and Price) has come at a normative cost. As in Part I of the book, I suggest here that Priceian liberty has attractions. Section VI concludes.

II. The Republican Tradition and Positive Liberty

A. Michelman's Account

Michelman's most substantial discussion of traditional republicanism is in 'Traces of Self-Government'. This subsection explains his discussion, and the next subsection raises some doubts about its historical soundness.

As with Pettit and Skinner, the fundamental distinction Michelman highlights is between negative and positive liberty. Negative liberty involves 'the absence of coercive social constraint against doing, or being, or becoming as one will'.[9] Positive liberty involves 'actions and self-direction according to reasons ... one gives to oneself'. Michelman said that Kant captured well the positive conception of liberty underlying traditional republicanism. Kant suggested that we are free when we are self-governing. We achieve this when we direct 'our actions in accordance with law-like reasons that we adopt for ourselves, as proper to ourselves, upon conscious, critical reflection on our identities (or natures) and social situations'.[10] While Kant is generally described as a liberal, Michelman mentioned that he was directly linked to republicanism through Rousseau. While Kant did not follow Rousseau's suggestion that freedom requires participation in the determination of common affairs, Kant's approach is at least suggestive, Michelman said, of the republican approach to liberty. To 'all who conceive of individuals as in some degree socially situated or constituted', Kantian freedom requires that norms be formed through public dialogue.[11]

In terms of the republican lineage of these ideas, Michelman relies on Pocock's interpretation of republicanism, together with his own reading of Harrington.[12] Pocock suggested that prominent Italian Renaissance humanists were inspired by

---

[9] Michelman, 'Traces of Self-Government' 25.
[10] ibid 26, referring to C Taylor, 'Kant's Theory of Freedom' in *Philosophy and the Human Sciences: Philosophical Papers*, vol 2 (Cambridge, Cambridge University Press, 1985) 318–37.
[11] Michelman, 'Traces of Self-Government' 27.
[12] ibid 36 fn 175.

Aristotle's depiction of the Athenian polis.[13] Pocock's interpretation of Aristotle was itself influenced by Arendt. For Pocock, republican liberty was achieved when citizens realise their true nature, and this is best achieved through political participation. While citizens may bring their private interests to the process, it is envisaged that they ultimately pursue with others the common good.

Michelman then points to Harrington as the pivotal figure in the Atlantic branch of republicanism that would find its way to America.[14] Following Pocock, Michelman suggests that Harrington favoured a political system that enables citizens to actively determine and pursue the common good because such active participation was essential to individual self-realisation: we have 'an inbuilt vocation for citizenship'.[15] Admittedly, Harrington's ideal constitution seems to limit the capacity for citizens to exercise virtue in politics. These limitations, however, should be understood as adaptations Harrington thought necessary to accommodate a set of empirical conditions.[16] The first empirical condition was the ever-present hazard of corruption: a 'frail citizen is all too likely to confuse particular with common interest'. Secondly, individuals differed in their talents and callings for government. Harrington therefore proposed that the people's role was to vote upon options presented to them by a senate consisting of the wise. If the people were too numerous to assemble, their representatives could vote upon policy options presented by the senate.

While seventeenth-century republicanism was based on positive liberty, Michelman stated that eighteenth-century British republicanism was largely based on negative liberty. It did not include the complaint that modern government denied its citizens the experience of ruling and being ruled.[17] Instead, the complaint was that parliamentarians were being corrupted through accepting positions and benefits offered by the Crown. The 'republican themes – common good, civic virtue, participation, independence, corruption, and balance ... were now being used in the service of self-protection against the government'.[18]

Michelman claimed that this negative-liberty strand of republicanism was also dominant in eighteenth-century America, and it fitted well with the doctrine of virtual representation. This doctrine asserts that one can be represented in a political regime through the participation of another who is one's likeness.[19] Michelman referred here to Edmund Burke's theory of the representation of interests. With the community divided into some broad interests, such as a mercantile or agricultural interest, parliamentarians sharing one of those interests would virtually represent disenfranchised people who also share that interest. Virtual representatives bring

[13] ibid 38. Reference to Pocock's approach was made in ch 1, s II.
[14] ibid 39.
[15] ibid 46.
[16] ibid 44–6.
[17] ibid 48.
[18] ibid 50.
[19] ibid 51.

an understanding of the interests of those they represent, but their obligation is to act deliberatively in the common interest.

Opponents of American independence suggested that members of the British Parliament did represent the American colonists since they shared the colonists' interests. Nevertheless, the response of supporters of independence was often not to deny the validity of virtual representation as a doctrine. Instead, they argued that British parliamentarians did not share the American colonists' interests.[20] Michelman mentioned that virtual representation illustrates how republican notions of the common good, civic virtue, deliberation and independence are severable from the republican value of self-government.[21]

Apart from this negative-liberty strand of republicanism, which Michelman refers to as 'deliberative democracy', the other main contestant in current interpretive debate over the framing of the US Constitution is 'incipient pluralist theory'.[22] While republican representatives seek the common good, pluralist representatives attempt to advance the interests they represent.

Nevertheless, Michelman mentions that a positive-liberty strain of republicanism may also have crossed the Atlantic. He refers, for instance, to scholarship discussing the influence of Price on American radicalism.[23] He also mentions there is scholarship that supports a Harringtonian interpretation of the constitutional scheme, designed to engage the civic virtue and accommodate the self-government of the people at large.[24]

B. Positive-Liberty Dimensions in the Historical Writers

I will mostly focus here on two matters: first, Michelman's understanding of the negative–positive divide and, secondly, his interpretation of Harrington and his reference to Price. Turning to the negative–positive divide, Michelman defines this in the context of the republican tradition in largely the same way as Pettit and Skinner. This is hardly surprising, since Pettit and Skinner were distinguishing the positive-liberty strand of the republican revival from their own interpretation. Michelman identifies republican positive liberty with several ideas: collective self-determination, an active and virtuous political life being the best conception of the good, and individuals exercising normative reason. This contrasts with negative liberty, involving the absence of restraints. With negative liberty, political participation is valued primarily for its role in achieving protection against unjustified governmental interference.

---

[20] ibid 52–3.

[21] ibid 51.

[22] ibid 54–5.

[23] ibid 48 fn 248 referring to S Lynd, *Intellectual Origins of American Radicalism* (Cambridge, Mass., Harvard University Press, 1968) 55–6.

[24] Michelman, 'Traces of Self-Government' 55 referring to D Epstein, *The Political Theory of the Federalist* (1984).

With Harrington being the central figure Michelman relies on in articulating positive-liberty republicanism, I begin with him. Chapter six suggested that there is little textual support in favour of Harrington's underlying ideal being full-blown positive liberty.[25] Instead, there are positive-liberty dimensions in his account. Harrington connected public liberty (the liberty the state should aim at) with personal positive liberty. Just as an individual is only free when governed by his or her reason, a state is only free when it is governed by rational law. Apart from this personal positive-liberty dimension to Harringtonian liberty, there is also a governmental-sphere positive-liberty dimension. Harrington valued a free state, where citizens can select representatives, partly because such a state recognises citizens' rationality on political matters, at least where rationality refers to a capacity to identify self-interest. The ideal constitution only requires of citizens that they consult self-interest when voting on options presented by the Senate. While the Senate is entrusted to identify worthwhile options, it is not entrusted to decide between them since it may well favour self-interest over the public interest.

Michelman also refers to the possibility of a positive-liberty strain of republicanism in America. He refers to Price as possibly influential.[26] Chapter six indicated that Pricean liberty, while having stronger positive-liberty dimensions than Harrington's conception, still cannot be equated with full-blown positive liberty. While Price incorporated a right of political participation in his conception of liberty, this was largely for protective reasons rather than because he privileged the exercise of normative reason in the governmental sphere. With neither Harrington nor Price endorsing full-blown positive liberty, at least the English foundation for the claimed positive-liberty strand of republicanism in American revolutionary thought looks shaky.[27] In any case, Michelman's discussion of the contemporary appeal of republicanism indicates less than a full embrace of positive liberty, as the next section shows.

III. The Contemporary Appeal of Positive Liberty

A. Michelman's Account

Michelman suggested that while positive liberty has maintained a grip on the American people, it has been prized for different reasons from those offered by historical writers. Positive liberty is not prized because it is only by engaging

---

[25] Above ch 6, s IVA. See also, eg, V Sullivan, 'The Civic Humanist Portrait of Machiavelli's English Successors' (1994) 15 *History of Political Thought* 73–96.

[26] See text to above n 23. In fact, Lynd did not claim that Price endorsed full-blown positive liberty. In the passage Michelman cites, Lynd referred to the implications of a natural right of self-determination for whether rights are inalienable. See also Lynd, *Intellectual Origins of American Radicalism* 57–8.

[27] See also A Gibson, 'Ancients, Moderns and Americans: The Republicanism–Liberalism Debate Revisited' (2013) 21 *History of Political Thought* 261–307, 287.

in virtuous political participation that people fulfil their potential. This reason runs against the modern liberal temper, which views as oppressive the idea that citizenship (or any other specific form of life) is the essence of the human subject.[28] Positive liberty is also not valued for its connection to practical reason, where practical reason is associated with an objectivist understanding of the common good, a common good revealed by republican deliberation.[29] This approach may lead to an intolerant attitude towards those who adhere to views that do not prevail through deliberation.

Instead, Michelman says, positive liberty provides a way of rebelling against the modern ethical dilemma described by Richard Bernstein as the Cartesian Anxiety.[30] The Cartesian Anxiety involves 'the sense of being caught between objectivism ("the belief that there are some fixed, permanent constraints to which we can appeal and which are secure and stable") and relativism (the "message ... that there are no ... constraints except those that we ... accept")'.[31] As indicated, the concern with objectivism is that it leads to domination. Objectivism can lead to privileging a particular understanding of rationality by claiming for it an unwarranted universality. On the other hand, Michelman says, relativism leads to moral chaos, with no role for practical reason, that is, for normative reasoning aimed at choosing ends. Instead, there is only technical rationality, which involves the selection of efficient means to achieve a given end.

Michelman suggests that relativism or, to use his preferred term, 'decisionism', with its denial of a connection between moral choice and rational deliberation, is modernity's common sense. It 'dwells comfortably with the doctrine of negative liberty: that freedom depends strictly on the protection of individual subjectivity against social oppression'.[32] It is hostile to the positive libertarian idea that ethical situation – inclusion in a social process of deliberation about how to live – is a condition of freedom.[33] Positive liberty affirms the possibility of reason being necessary to choose moral ends. Such reasoning involves deliberating on ends with fellow citizens in their diversity and on an equal basis, where citizens seek to justify to each other their normative positions and, through this process, reach a sounder understanding of what is publicly justifiable.[34]

Michelman recommends an interpretation of positive liberty that rejects 'all predeterminations of human essence and social role'.[35] Positive liberty becomes

[28] Michelman, 'Traces of Self-Government' 22.
[29] ibid 23.
[30] ibid 24 referring to R Bernstein, *Beyond Objectivism and Relativism: Science, Hermeneutics, and Praxis* (Oxford, Basil Blackwell, 1983).
[31] Michelman, 'Traces of Self-Government' 24 fn 110 referring to Bernstein, *Beyond Objectivism and Relativism* 18–19.
[32] Michelman, 'Traces of Self-Government' 25–6.
[33] ibid 26.
[34] ibid 26–7, including fn 129.
[35] ibid 31.

identified, then, with 'individual subjectivity'. On the other hand, positive liberty implies 'a social process of normative deliberation, based in commonality'.[36] He describes this as 'ethical situation'. He suggests certain themes that capture this tension between individual subjectivity and ethical situation.[37] They are themes of dialogue (understood as participatory and exploratory), history (our individual and collective pasts raise issues of identity and integrity, but should not foreclose individual and collective futures), responsibility (this protests against abdicating personal responsibility by referring to a distant force, such as law or the state), and identity (reflecting the tug of demands raised by ethical situation and individual subjectivity).

B. A Comparison with Negative Liberty

While I have focused on some of his philosophical claims, his discussion is broader. For instance, he applied the themes underlying ethical situations to a Supreme Court decision.[38] My concerns, though, are first with how Michelman's philosophical claims explaining the appeal of positive liberty relate to his historical understanding of republican positive liberty. Secondly, I examine his contrast between republican positive liberty and liberal negative liberty.

Turning to the first concern, Michelman's explanation for the contemporary appeal of positive liberty in fact rejects what he and also the non-positive-liberty republican revivers regard as a central element of positive liberty under the republican tradition. That central element lies in the idea that we achieve fulfilment or self-realisation through political participation, such that it can be said that it is only through such participation that we achieve liberty. Michelman rejects this idea, for it is inconsistent with the liberal temper.

This rejection of a central element of republican positive liberty raises the question of whether the philosophical ideas Michelman does regard as having contemporary appeal are compatible with negative liberty. Michelman argues that they are not compatible. In other words, negative-liberty adherents cannot comfortably endorse citizens deliberating and acting together in pursuit of the public good as a model of sound normative reasoning. Michelman claims that relativism dwells comfortably with negative liberty, for the latter supports individual subjectivity against social oppression.

---

[36] ibid.

[37] ibid 33.

[38] *Goldman v Weinberger* (1986) 475 US 503 (US Supreme Court). For another application of these themes, this time to a republican theory of judicial deliberation, see E Ghosh, 'Republicanism, Community Values and Social Psychology: A Response to Braithwaite's Model of Judicial Deliberation' (1998) 20 *Sydney Law Review* 5–41.

However, Michelman does not establish a clear link between relativism and supporting individual subjectivity. Perhaps stronger support for linking relativism to negative liberty can be found by pointing to Berlin. There is controversy over whether Berlin skirted close to relativism in rejecting monism (where there is a single right answer to moral questions) and favouring pluralism (where there are many incommensurable values). Berlin also identified negative liberty with value pluralism and positive liberty with monism.[39] On the other hand, given the doubt as to whether relativists can provide consistent and sincere support for particular values, relativism may not dwell comfortably with negative liberty.[40]

Adherents of negative liberty can accept that there are more or less sound understandings of the common interest. They can also view the model of citizens conscientiously deliberating together in pursuit of the public good as an attractive process for determining what lies in the common interest. Favouring this model is also consistent with recognising that the conclusions citizens reach are provisional, relying on fallible judgements. A recognition of the fallible character of judgement, and respect for the autonomy of individuals, may also be sufficient to avoid Michelman's link between objectivism and oppression.[41]

Michelman is on stronger ground in claiming that negative liberty rejects the proposition that ethical situation – inclusion in a social process of deliberation about how to live – is a condition of freedom. Negative liberty is associated with opportunities, and one opportunity is inclusion in a social process of deliberation. However, negative liberty does not require the exercise of that opportunity. It would seem that the main difference between negative liberty and Michelman's adaptation of positive liberty lies in whether social deliberation should be viewed as necessary to achieve liberty.

IV. Constitutional Implications of Republican Liberty

A. Governmental-Sphere Positive Liberty

A fuller understanding of Michelman's interpretation of positive liberty is obtained by examining his application of this value to judicial review based on

---

[39] See A Gutmann, 'How Limited Is Liberal Government?' in B Yack (ed), *Liberalism without Illusions: Essays on Political Theory and the Political Vision of Judith Shklar* (Chicago, University of Chicago Press, 1996) 64–81, 65–7; J Cherniss and H Henry, 'Isaiah Berlin' in E Zalta (ed), *The Stanford Encyclopedia of Philosophy*: https://plato.stanford.edu/archives/sum2018/entries/berlin/ s 4.4: 'Value pluralism after Berlin'.

[40] See, eg, E Westacott, 'Cognitive Relativism' in J Fieser and B Dowden (eds), *Internet Encyclopedia of Philosophy*: www.iep.utm.edu/cog-rel/.

[41] For an argument that deliberative democracy requires the claim of moral objectivity if it is to be distinguished from public choice theory, see D Estlund, 'Who's Afraid of Deliberative Democracy? On the Strategic/Deliberative Dichotomy in Recent Constitutional Jurisprudence' (1993) 71 *Texas Law Review* 1437–77.

the US Bill of Rights. This subsection explores Michelman's argument that positive liberty cautions against overstating the loss to democracy where judges overrule the elected branches of government. Concern about this loss to democracy is often described as 'the counter-majoritarian difficulty'. Subsection B uses the case of *Bowers v Hardwick*, which Michelman discussed in 'Law's Republic', to explore his claim that positive liberty can provide a sounder justification for judicial decisions than negative liberty. Subsection C examines Michelman's claim in 'Traces of Self-Government' that activist judicial review may be valued as representing to the people the ideal of self-government.

Turning to this subsection's concern, Michelman argued that the counter-majoritarian difficulty appears overly acute if freedom is understood negatively. Negative liberty consists in doing and commanding as one wills. Negative liberty suggests that whatever decision-making power is taken by the courts leads to a corresponding diminution in the people's freedom to participate in politics; it leads to the imposition of constraints upon the people's power to enact their preferences.[42] Michelman continues:

> But if freedom consists of socially situated self-direction – that is, self-direction by norms cognizant of fellowship with equally self-directing others – then the relation between one agent's freedom and another's is additive: one realizes one's own only by confirming that of others. This seems to hold no less for a judge than for any other agent.[43]

Michelman is suggesting, then, that the reduction in the option of being able to directly influence collective decisions on rights through the elected branches resulting from courts, say, striking down legislation may not diminish positive liberty at all. Chapter six distinguished between deliberative and enactive components of positive liberty.[44] Using that terminology, Michelman is suggesting that positive liberty is not simply about the opportunity to enact one's preferences. Positive liberty also has a deliberative component: it involves the exercise of normative reason. If judicial decisions can improve the normative understanding of citizens, this gain is relevant to liberty.

Furthermore, the loss to one's opportunity to enact one's preferences takes on a different hue when one applies positive liberty. Michelman mentions that for a citizen of Geneva, it was perhaps imaginable that positive liberty could be realised for everyone through direct-democratic self-government. However, for US citizens, 'national politics are not imaginably the arena of self-government'.[45] Legislation a court might strike down is not legislation made by the citizens themselves. Michelman stated that while we should be wary of court-fetishism, we should also be wary of government-fetishism.

---

[42] Michelman, 'Traces of Self-Government' 74–5.
[43] ibid 75.
[44] Ch 6, s IIIA.
[45] Michelman, 'Traces of Self-Government' 75.

Michelman, then, is suggesting contrasting implications when applying positive and negative liberty. It seems that positive liberty may be more receptive to
judicial review than negative liberty: a Supreme Court decision constraining
Congress may not diminish positive liberty at all, but it must diminish negative
liberty. On the other hand, both approaches can suggest that the loss to liberty
involved in citizens losing some enactive power with respect to legislation may
not be very substantial. Negative liberty is associated especially with a concern for
outcomes. The lost option of exercising political influence on a particular issue
may be offset if the decision leads to a welcome reduction in interference with
important rights. In their different ways, both approaches seem to draw attention
towards the impact of judicial review decisions on the options citizens enjoy not
just in the governmental sphere, but in other spheres as well.

B. Intimate- and Civil-Sphere Positive Liberty

In 'Law's Republic', Michelman affirmed that the governmental sphere, which
covers 'formal channels of electoral and legislative politics' such as legislatures
and the councils of major cities, offers limited opportunities for exercising positive liberty.[46] He suggested reconceptualising the public sphere, where diverse
citizens deliberate together, as extending beyond the governmental sphere
to what can be described as the civil sphere. This sphere includes 'town meetings and local government agencies; civic and voluntary organizations; social
and recreational clubs, schools ..., managements, directorates and leadership
groups of organizations of all kinds; workplaces ...; public events and street life'.[47]
In the civil sphere, citizens come closest to exercising positive liberty on matters
of common concern. He suggested that citizenship consists not just in formal
participation in affairs of state, but also in having a 'distinct and audible voice ...
in public and social life at large'.[48] Indeed, understandings reached in the civil
sphere feed into the governmental sphere.

Michelman thereby departs from the understanding of the public sphere
found in the historical works discussed, for instance, in the previous chapter.
The public sphere was there identified with the formal governmental sphere. By
expanding the public sphere, he redefines the private sphere. With the historical writers, forms of association such as the workplace exist in the private
sphere. Under Michelman's approach, the private sphere is limited to what will
be described here as the intimate sphere: this includes interactions within associations such as the family. Differences between Michelman's and the historical
understanding of the public and private spheres are indicated in the diagram
below. With Michelman dealing here with spheres in which positive liberty can

[46] Michelman, 'Law's Republic' 1531.
[47] ibid.
[48] ibid.

be exercised, I refer here, for the sake of completeness, to the personal sphere as well. The last chapter describes this as concerned largely with the individual's psychological attributes.

Figure 7.1 Michelman's expanded public sphere

Personal sphere	Social sphere (positive liberty diminished by internal & external constraints)		
(positive liberty diminished by internal constraints)	Traditional private sphere		Traditional governmental sphere
	Intimate sphere	Civil sphere	
	Michelman's private sphere	Michelman's public sphere	

Michelman, then, is contrasting the governmental sphere, where people individually have minimal influence, with a civil sphere, where people can have a significant influence upon others, including in ways that feed into the governmental sphere. Michelman does not, however, point to limitations upon relying on the civil sphere for the exercise of positive liberty. Focusing here on participation in associations, Nancy Rosenblum has argued that such participation cultivates the disposition to cooperate.[49] However, she said that while the disposition to cooperate is a vital element of personal development, it is morally neutral in the sense that '[c]ooperation enables the worst as well as the best social actions'.[50] Michelman's model of citizens engaging with diverse others and thereby enlarging their moral horizons as they pursue together matters of collective concern may apply to a limited number of associations. Citizens' enactive power within their associations may also vary considerably. Some associations may have undemocratic structures. Even if democratic, the power of the association in relation to the larger community in which it resides may be small.[51] I am not, however, denying the potential significance of the civil sphere in enabling the exercise of positive liberty. The remainder of this subsection illuminates Michelman's approach to the civil sphere by exploring his discussion of *Bowers v Hardwick*.

In previous decisions, the Supreme Court had found that a constitutional right to privacy was violated, for instance, by laws banning contraception.

---

[49] N Rosenblum, *Membership and Morals: The Personal Uses of Pluralism in America* (Princeton, NJ, Princeton University Press, 1998) 59.

[50] ibid.

[51] See, eg, R Dahl and E Tufte, *Size and Democracy* (Stanford, Stanford University Press, 1973) on a trade-off between individual and collective influence depending on the size of the collective body.

However, in *Bowers v Hardwick*, the Supreme Court refused to expand this right so that it would be compromised by anti-sodomy legislation.[52] Michelman encapsulated the Court's justification for this refusal in the following way:

> It is not for the Court to 'impose' its members' 'own choice of values' on the people by 'announc[ing] … a fundamental right to engage in homosexual sodomy,' contrary to both the formally legislated will of the Georgia majority and … 'the Nation's history and tradition' as manifested in state legislation widely in force when both the Ninth and Fourteenth Amendments were ratified.[53]

Michelman referred, though, to arguments suggesting that privacy would, in fact, be a poor basis upon which to invalidate laws penalising homosexual sex. The concern is that privacy is associated with conduct which deserves protection from state interference simply because it is private: it does not impact adversely on others. However, as a Note in *Harvard Law Review* said:

> The … [public–private dichotomy] is especially ill-suited to the affirmation of gay rights, because it assumes that homosexuality is merely a form of conduct that can take place in the privacy of the bedroom at a specified time, rather than a continuous aspect of personality or personhood that usually requires expression across the public/private spectrum. As Professor Tribe has argued, '[F]reedom to have impact on others – to make the 'statement' implicit in a public identity – is central to any adequate conception of the self.' Such public manifestations may be necessary not only as personal expressions of gay identity, but also as means for heightening public awareness of homosexuality and thus perhaps broadening public acceptance of gay lifestyles … Withholding social recognition from the public aspects of gay personhood … is inherently unequal not only in its substantive restriction of gay liberties, but also in its imputation of stigma: homosexuality, like obscenity, may be tolerated only if quarantined.[54]

While the Note argued that gay rights are best protected by invoking equality through the fourteenth amendment, which provides for 'equal protection of the laws', Michelman followed Laurence Tribe's claim that privacy can be relied on if the public dimensions of conduct are fully acknowledged.[55] In other words, the factors that the Note suggested should be taken into account when considering gay rights can be incorporated within an understanding of privacy.

Michelman characterised the approach to privacy criticised in the Note as salient in US constitutional thought.[56] With this, 'privacy stands for an attitude of hostility towards public life and a need for refuge from and protection against arbitrary power'. Michelman contrasts this with a republican approach. The republican approach considers the impact of a right to privacy upon people's

---

[52] 478 US 186 (1986).

[53] Michelman, 'Law's Republic' 1497.

[54] Note: 'The Constitutional Status of Sexual Orientation: Homosexuality as a Suspect Classification' (1985) 98 *Harvard Law Review* 1285–1309, 1290–1. I have quoted the Note more fully than occurs in Michelman, 'Law's Republic' 1534.

[55] See L Tribe, *American Constitutional Law* (Mineola, NY, Foundation Press, 1978) 887–9.

[56] Michelman, 'Law's Republic' 1534.

'admission to full and effective participation in the various arenas of public life'.[57] It stresses the importance of the public expression of lifestyles and ideas – through this, citizens engage in dialogue with others, enlarge their moral perspectives, and shape their own identities. A right to privacy here would not only benefit homosexuals but also heterosexuals through expanding their moral horizons. To use the distinction I made earlier, the small loss to citizens' enactive power in the governmental sphere that would have resulted from the Supreme Court invaliding anti-sodomy legislation would have been offset by gains in enactive power outside the governmental sphere and in the deliberative component of positive liberty.

I turn now to considering Michelman's approach, especially against his criterion of consistency with the 'liberal temper'. The liberal temper views as oppressive the idea that citizenship (or any other specific form of life) is the essence of the human subject.[58] It is first helpful to articulate the approach suggested by liberal negative liberty. Michelman does not explicitly link liberal negative liberty with the approach to privacy criticised in the Note. If one were to apply negative liberty, one would identify constraints produced by an anti-sodomy statute that significantly diminish people's capacity to pursue their conceptions of the good. Most obviously, anti-sodomy statutes proscribe certain sexual conduct, so the intimate sphere is implicated. Even where the practice is not to enforce anti-sodomy statutes, the possibility of such prosecution remains. Furthermore, anti-sodomy statutes might reinforce social constraints. They might, for instance, support discrimination against homosexuals in the civil sphere. Such legislation conveys and could reinforce community disapproval of homosexuality, thereby damaging, for instance, their opportunity to publicly identify as homosexual. Negative liberty would, then, draw attention to the constraints upon 'gay lifestyles' referred to in the Note as a constraint additional to the one that applies to the intimate sphere.

Nevertheless, from a liberal perspective, Michelman's highlighting of social deliberation seems problematic. This can be illustrated through adopting some additional empirical assumptions. Assume that the lack of enforcement of anti-sodomy statutes means that the law does not impose significant constraints upon the intimate sphere. Assume further that the failure to invalidate anti-sodomy laws prompted greater political mobilisation in the community than the contrary decision would have achieved. It seems that the decision did prompt significant mobilisation and discussion. William Eskridge has mentioned that as a result of the decision, 'many gay lawyers came out of the closet, and gaylegal activism was reenergized overnight. American culture itself – from movies and television to newspapers and magazines to the new electronic media – seemed gay-crazy all of a sudden'.[59] The assumption I am making is that the decision created greater

---

[57] ibid 1533.

[58] This is referred to in above s IIIA.

[59] W Eskridge, *Gaylaw: Challenging the Apartheid of the Closet* (Cambridge, Mass., Harvard University Press, 1999) 167–8. The possibility of victims of oppression being energised to exercise their rational capacities was referred to in J Stephen, *Liberty, Equality, Fraternity* [1874], ed, R White (Cambridge, Cambridge University Press, 1967) 81.

political discussion and engagement than if the contrary decision had been made. With this assumption, it is conceivable that the actual decision promoted positive liberty at least in the short term.

It is less conceivable that the actual decision could be defended with negative liberty. One would have to suggest that the gaylegal activism and overall cultural reaction to the decision might have reduced social constraints upon the public expression of gay identity to a greater extent than if the opposite decision had been reached. The focus, however, would not be on whether the decision led to greater social normative deliberation where this is valued for its role in enabling citizens to lead more moral lives. Social deliberation is valuable, but the danger in defining liberty in these terms is that it can render liberty entirely consistent with constraints rather than drawing attention to constraints. It can suggest applauding *Bowers v Hardwick* for enhancing liberty through enriching social deliberation rather than focusing upon the impact of the decision on the constraints people face. This is a consequence of republican liberty privileging a life of social deliberation. Michelman states that he favours an interpretation of positive liberty that rejects all predeterminations of human essence and social role. However, he does privilege a life involving social normative deliberation.

Interestingly, Robert Goodin questions the privileging of social deliberation found in deliberative democratic theory.[60] He favours conceptualising democratic deliberation as something that occurs within each individual's head, and not exclusively or even primarily in an interpersonal setting. Deliberation on political matters can be achieved through reading, for instance, rather than discussion in social contexts. The more general point is that there may be diverse ways of achieving a moral life. Privileging social normative deliberation can appear, from a liberal perspective, to be arbitrary.

C. Representing Positive Liberty

The final connection that Michelman draws between positive liberty and judicial review is that judicial review can represent positive liberty to the community. Michelman pursued this connection in 'Traces of Self-Government'. Michelman suggested here that the US Supreme Court could be valued for representing positive liberty to the community. I will first outline Michelman's argument and then discuss it.

Michelman argued that while the US Constitution did not embrace the ideal of self-government, this ideal maintains a hold on the American people. This raises the question of whether traces of self-government can still be found in the American political system. Michelman mentions four approaches. The first echoes

---

[60] R Goodin, *Reflective Democracy* (Oxford, Oxford University Press, 2003).

the republican vision of an engaged citizenry.[61] It envisions the people at large engaged more or less regularly in politics.

By contrast, the other approaches recognise that virtue is too limited to support a highly engaged citizenry. With the second approach, articulated by Sunstein, self-government is practised by the people's representatives. James Madison, a constitutional framer, had suggested that the constitutional solution to insufficient virtue in the citizenry at large was to adopt representative government – representatives should be selected who have the motivation and capacity to deliberate and thereby discern the public good.[62]

A third approach was provided by Bruce Ackerman. He suggested that while there is insufficient virtue in the people to sustain political engagement aimed at the public good, people are sometimes genuinely aroused on political issues they regard as fundamental.[63] One such constitutional moment occurred in the 1930s, when persistent popular endorsement of the welfare state in the face of the Supreme Court blocking welfare legislation led to the Court abandoning its resistance. However, while Ackerman sees judicial review as a means of ensuring that the Congress and the government do not abuse the will of the people as expressed in constitutional moments, Michelman notes that the judiciary enjoys substantial discretion in interpreting these constitutional moments. It is unclear, then, to what extent the people are involved in self-government during Ackerman's moments of constitutional politics.[64]

A fourth approach was provided by Ronald Dworkin. Dworkin suggested that Americans value judicial review partly because judges, in attempting to articulate principles which best cohere with the country's political order, confirm the principled character of the community.[65] However, Michelman says, Dworkin did not explain how judges confirm the principled character of the American association by striving to reach their own principled opinions. Michelman suggests that the answer lies in virtual representation. If judges are sufficiently similar to the people, the people can identify with the judges. Michelman says, 'Unable as a nation to practice our own self-government (in the full, positive sense), we – or at any rate we of 'the reasoning class' – can at least identify with the judiciary's as we idealistically construct it.'[66] The reference to 'the reasoning class' comes from John Ely: Ely was referring to the 'upper-middle, professional class from which most lawyers

---

[61] Michelman, 'Traces of Self-Government' 57.

[62] ibid 58, referring to C Sunstein, 'Interest Groups in American Public Law' (1985) 38 *Stanford Law Review* 29–87.

[63] Michelman, 'Traces of Self-Government' 61, referring to B Ackerman, 'The Storrs Lectures: Discovering the Constitution' (1984) 93 *Yale Law Journal* 1013–72.

[64] Michelman, 'Traces of Self-Government' 65.

[65] ibid 73, referring to R Dworkin, *Law's Empire* (Cambridge, Mass., Belknap Press, 1986) 264.

[66] Michelman, 'Traces of Self-Government' 74. The note attached to 'the reasoning class' is omitted. It refers to J Ely, *Democracy and Distrust: A Theory of Judicial Review* (Cambridge, Mass., Harvard University Press, 1980) 59, including fn **.

and judges' are drawn. Michelman continues: 'The judge ... represents by his own self-government our missing self-government, by his own practical reason our missing dialogue. What he thereby confirms is possibility. Could that be what we value?'[67]

Michelman admitted that it was surprising to locate the ideal of self-government in the elite form of decision-making constituted by a superior court engaged in judicial review: it 'sounds like a pathology of court-fetishism'.[68] The judges may enjoy positive liberty, but what about the citizens? Michelman refers at this point to the claims I discussed in Section IVA. Those claims suggest that court decisions can promote positive liberty. First, court decisions can enhance citizens' understanding of public issues.[69] Secondly, constraining legislators is different from constraining citizens. National politics is not a promising arena for citizens in general to exercise positive liberty.

These two claims can be supplemented by Michelman's argument in 'Law's Republic' that the promising arena for the exercise of positive liberty for most citizens lies in the civil sphere. Supreme Court decisions, Michelman suggests, can enhance positive liberty in this sphere. While Michelman does not put it this way, these claims can assist by suggesting that in appreciating judicial review symbolically from the perspective of positive liberty, we can recognise that its symbolic value is not undercut by judicial review having a significant practical outcome that lessens positive liberty. Instead, judicial review can enhance positive liberty.

One difficulty with Michelman's argument is that the symbolic value of judicial review, with judges providing a model of reasoning based on a conscientious search for what is right, can also be appreciated with negative liberty. Negative liberty suggests such deliberation by decision-makers may be valued not as a trace of the governmental-sphere positive liberty denied to ordinary citizens, but because such deliberation may lead to decisions that reduce unjustified state interference. Indeed, Dworkin suggested that the model of judicial deliberation based on principle rather than power can institute a culture that influences public officials, particularly those who have gone to law school, in other branches of government.[70]

Positive liberty's distinctive perspective upon this model of judicial deliberation lies in connecting this model to citizens governing themselves. In attempting this connection, Michelman appeals to the idea of judges as virtual representatives. The significance of being able to identify with judges as our virtual representatives is that it reduces the sense of distance between decision-makers and ourselves. We may be able to appreciate their reasoning as the reasoning we would ourselves engage in if we were in their position. How, though, does this relate to us governing ourselves? Perhaps we could point out that at the collective level, the power of

---

[67] Michelman, 'Traces of Self-Government' 73.
[68] ibid 74.
[69] ibid 74–5.
[70] R Dworkin, 'The Forum of Principle' (1981) 56 *New York University Law Review* 469–518, 517–18.

self-government should be consistent with others enjoying the same power. While that might suggest being a direct participant in decision-making, the next best alternative may be being governed by representatives who reflect our own reason and that of other citizens. While this may be the best we can hope for, the puzzle remains: from the perspective of positive liberty, the very ideal of self-government suggests that we should recognise the distance between being a direct participant in decision-making and decision-making by others, even if we can identify with them. Interestingly, Michelman himself associated negative-liberty republicanism with deliberative democracy and with virtual representation.

Of course, Michelman, is only suggesting that we might value judicial decision-making on the basis that it represents our *missing* self-government; not that it makes us self-governing. In that way, virtual representatives could indeed represent our missing self-government. However, the extent to which this representation is prized must be substantially limited by positive liberty standing against virtual representation. Positive liberty requires citizens to govern themselves.

Interestingly, Michelman himself provided a decade later in *Brennan and Democracy* a quite different understanding of the relationship between positive liberty and judicial review. He recognised that identifying with the laws of a community is different from it being reasonable for you to 'regard yourself as a law-maker to yourself'.[71] He emphasised that even if you feel that you did the lawmaking, 'Feeling is not doing, and for you to "identify" sympathetically with the doer of an act is not for you to have done the act'. He claimed, instead, that judicial review links to positive liberty through enhancing the legitimacy of the overall political system. He suggested that positive liberty could be exercised through willingly abiding by laws even if you disagree with them.[72] One follows the law not primarily due to its coercive power but because one recognises a moral obligation to do so. Here, positive liberty involves being governed by one's own reason. This is a Kantian, rather than republican, interpretation of positive liberty; it is detached from political participation.

In conclusion, the symbolic significance of conscientious deliberation by virtual representatives is, at best, ambivalent when considering Michelman's republican positive liberty. Michelman himself associated conscientious deliberation by virtual representatives with negative-liberty republicanism. Negative liberty fits better with this model of decision-making.

V. Returning to the Historical Writers

Part I of the book, after critiquing Pettit's and Skinner's historical and normative claims about republican liberty, suggested that it was worthwhile to return to one

---

[71] F Michelman, *Brennan and Democracy* (Princeton, NJ, Princeton University Press, 1999) 32.
[72] ibid 55.

of the historical writers, Price, to see if a more attractive interpretation of liberty as non-domination appears there. This chapter questioned Michelman's historical claims about Harrington and Price, and then questioned the normative attractiveness of Michelman's adaptation of republican liberty. I will now consider whether there are normative advantages in some of the positive-liberty dimensions found in the historical writers Michelman refers to. I begin with Harrington, but will mostly discuss Price.

Recall that Michelman endorses a conception of liberty that is identified with the exercise of normative reason, and normative reason is best enhanced through social interaction with diverse others. By contrast, Harrington recommended constitutional arrangements that do not require citizens to demonstrate virtue. The democratic status that Harrington's constitution confers upon citizens lies in a recognition that citizens can promote their self-interest. I will not, though, urge Harrington's approach. Indeed, I argue in Part III that there should be consideration of constitutional arrangements that do rely upon the exercise of virtue.

I turn, then, to Price. While Price stated that 'most men make no other use of their reason than to justify whatever their interest or their inclinations determine them to do', he valued all citizens having a share in government partly because it reflected their dignity, which lay in their capacity to act virtuously.[73] The democratic status that Price had in mind is one that confers a greater dignity upon citizens than what Harrington envisaged. The status that Price had in mind seems fairly uncontroversial today. Chapter five referred to its importance in considering judicial review, with Waldron's argument that this institution compromises citizens' status by suggesting mistrust in their capacity to reach sound views on rights. Michelman, of course, would disagree that citizens' status would be compromised, pointing to the distance between legislation and citizens, but his approach is consistent with recognising that a democratic system can suggest a level of respect for citizens' capacity to responsibly exercise the political power democracy confers. He points to limitations to citizens' ability to exercise positive liberty in the governmental sphere, given the scale of US democracy, but he does not dismiss the importance of the governmental sphere for citizens.

Another significant positive-liberty dimension in Price is identifying liberty with the franchise. Price's incorporation of a right of participation within his definition of liberty can be valued today as a warning that where people are excluded from the franchise, they suffer a significant likelihood of unjustified interference. Chapter five, however, suggested a more general warning from Priceian liberty as non-domination, which lies in the risk of interference where there is arbitrary power. It is beyond the confines of the discussion in the present chapter to consider how helpful a contemporary warning about the franchise is likely to be. In relation

---

[73] R Price, 'Additional Observations on the Nature and Value of Civil Liberty, and the War with America' [1777] in *Political Writings*, ed, DO Thomas (Cambridge, Cambridge University Press, 1991) 76–100, 90, 84–5.

to Michelman, as indicated, he does not dismiss the importance of the governmental sphere. Michelman's approach is consistent with recognising the importance of the franchise in protecting citizens' rights in general.

It is with the third positive-liberty dimension in Price that an important contrast opens up with Michelman's approach. This dimension consists in moral liberty, which involves the exercise of sound moral judgement by individuals. Price privileges a moral life. By contrast, Michelman privileges a particular way of achieving a moral life: this involves social interaction with diverse others in which normative reflection is prompted. Section IVB argued that this privileging seems arbitrary. Price's moral liberty does not privilege social deliberation. It accommodates a greater diversity of conceptions of the good than Michelman's approach.

On the other hand, Price's moral liberty does not achieve the neutrality associated with negative liberal liberty. Price privileged a life lived in accordance with correct normative judgements. This can seem ominous from a liberal perspective: people are unfree unless they reach 'correct' moral positions. However, self-government is the central idea behind Price's understanding of moral liberty: the agent's actions must be the outcome of the agent's own will. Indeed, Price did not suggest that the state should directly aim at moral liberty. Instead, Price's conception of civil liberty is a non-domination conception.[74] Liberty as non-domination is achieved when citizens enjoy a right of political participation and also civil rights, such as religious freedom and security of property.[75] Liberty as non-domination provides the security from oppression that enables and encourages citizens to develop and exercise their moral liberty.[76]

This might suggest that liberty as non-domination is Price's public conception of liberty, while moral liberty is his non-public conception of liberty. In the last chapter, I suggested that autonomy can be understood as a non-public conception when considering Berlin's and Pettit's approaches.[77] They view autonomy as providing an attractive justification for their favoured public conceptions of liberty.

However, this approach would not be consistent with Price, for Price's moral liberty provides the ultimate justification for liberty as non-domination.[78] Moral liberty is not merely a value that *may* be employed to justify liberty as non-domination. It seems best, then, to view Price's moral liberty as a public conception of liberty. This is consistent with recognising that the state should not seek to directly promote this value. Liberty as non-domination should be the first goal of the state, largely because this provides security from unjustified interference.[79]

[74] See ch 5, s IIA.
[75] Price, 'Additional Observations' 82.
[76] See ch 5, s IIA and ch 6, s IVB.
[77] See ch 6, s IIIA and B.
[78] See ch 6, s IVB.
[79] See ch 5, s IIB.

That security from unjustified interference serves the ultimate value of moral liberty.

In considering contemporary strands of liberalism, chapter five described Priceian liberty as non-domination as fitting well with Shklar's liberalism of fear, while Price's moral liberty suggested Shklar's liberalism of personal development.[80] The liberalism of personal development is identified with John Stuart Mill.[81] Its aim is to enhance citizens' knowledge and moral capacities. This strand of liberalism can also be described as a perfectionist strand. Perfectionist theories recognise that the state can be justified in promoting controversial conceptions of the good, rather than seeking neutrality.[82] The most prominent contemporary versions require a weak version of autonomy.[83] Steven Wall's version requires people to engage in sufficient reflection so that their choices and commitments reflect their own understanding of what is valuable.[84] By contrast, Price's moral liberty requires sound moral judgement and a life lived accordingly. It involves a narrower conception of the good; it is a more stringent ideal.

Whether there should instead be a preference, say, for Wall's perfectionism or an anti-perfectionist form of liberalism cannot be considered here. My more modest ambition in this chapter on Michelman, at least so far as it relates to Price, is to suggest that not only has Michelman overlooked positive-liberty dimensions in historical writers he draws upon, but that those dimensions may have normative advantages over his own interpretation. One such dimension is moral liberty. Michelman's ethical situation, where citizens engage with diverse others in the civil sphere and thereby enlarge their moral horizons, can deepen understanding of an attractive conception of the good. His ethical situation can sensitise us to claims such as those made by Hardwick, which are strengthened when one conceives of privacy as extending beyond intimate or private conduct to freedom to have an impact on others in a way that has a normative dimension. However, privileging ethical situation as *the* conception of the good is questionable. Priceian moral liberty conforms better to liberal tolerance towards conceptions of the good than Michelman's approach, and this may well be a normative advantage.

Perhaps clearer still, in terms of normative attractiveness, is the Priceian positive-liberty dimension of democratic status, discussed earlier in this section.

---

[80] See ch 5, s IV.

[81] J Shklar, 'The Liberalism of Fear' in N Rosenblum (ed), *Liberalism and the Moral Life* (Cambridge, Mass., Harvard University Press, 1989) 21–38, 27.

[82] For an argument linking Price with perfectionism, see L Hickman, *Eighteenth-Century Dissent and Cambridge Platonism: Reconceiving the Philosophy of Religion* (Abingdon, Routledge, 2017) ch 5. See also above ch 6, s IIIA.

[83] On autonomy being a controversial conception of the good, see S Wall, *Liberalism, Perfectionism and Restraint* (Cambridge, Cambridge University Press, 1998) ch 7.

[84] ibid ch 6. This version of weak autonomy is still stronger than the weak version I articulated in ch 6, s IIIB. That would be satisfied if agents simply consult self-interest without attempting to engage in normative deliberation. I contrasted this with a strong version of autonomy, which requires agents to be able to reach reasonable judgements on what is normatively required. For another perfectionist theory, see J Raz, *The Morality of Freedom* (Oxford, Clarendon, 1986).

This seems relatively uncontroversial. I employ democratic status in Part III in defending constitutional juries.

VI. Conclusion

Michelman provides a provocative and imaginative approach to justifying judicial review. He took on the significant challenge of addressing the counter-majoritarian difficulty by drawing upon the most democratically demanding of values, a value I have described as full-blown positive liberty. This value demands of citizens virtuous participation in decision-making if they are to count as free. Michelman suggested a historical pedigree for this value that connects America's constitutional tradition to the English republican tradition. Michelman pointed especially to Harrington but also to Price.

Chapter six, however, argued that these historical writers are best described as providing accounts that do not endorse full-blown positive liberty but, instead, have positive-liberty dimensions. Furthermore, in emphasising the contemporary appeal of republican liberty, Michelman distanced himself from full-blown positive liberty. I suggested that the reason he presents for positive liberty having contemporary appeal are in fact consistent with negative liberty. Negative liberty is consistent with rejecting relativism. On the other hand, while Michelman rejects the idea that a virtuous and active political life is the best conception of the good, he does privilege a life of social normative engagement. Michelman's approach does seem to violate the liberal temper that Michelman endorses.

While Michelman's discussion of *Bowers v Hardwick* illustrates a republican interpretation of rights, that discussion also supports his defence of judicial activism. That defence is assisted by demonstrating that Supreme Court decisions can promote positive liberty in the civil sphere. Positive liberty also assists in avoiding too much weight being placed on the loss of democratic opportunity that citizens might suffer when the Supreme Court invalidates legislation. These considerations together are helpful for Michelman in suggesting that the Supreme Court can symbolically promote positive liberty to the community. I argued, however, that the model of conscientious deliberation aimed at discerning the public good, which Michelman idealistically associates with the Supreme Court, can better be appreciated with negative liberty.

Finally, Michelman's deviation from at least one of the positive-liberty dimensions found in Price has also come, I argued, at a normative cost. Price's approach can be understood as a perfectionist theory based on moral liberty; this theory fits better with the liberal temper that Michelman endorses than his preferred conception of republican liberty.

Michelman's work does, however, contain helpful insights. He not only provided a provocative approach to judicial review. He also explored deeply the implications of republican positive liberty. Exploring his approach gives a better understanding of this value, and it is this value that the non-positive-liberty strand partly defines itself against. Michelman's ethical situation, where citizens engage with diverse others in the civil sphere and thereby enlarge their moral horizons, is an attractive one if it is not privileged as the best conception of the good. Michelman's view of constitutional review being conducted by virtual representatives is suggestive, and will be pursued in the next two chapters. One way that full-blown positive liberty is valuable is that it places at centre-stage the model of diverse citizens engaging with each other to determine matters of collective concern. This may be valuable even if that model of decision-making is ultimately prized for reasons other than those identified with republican positive liberty.[85]

---

[85] This is similar to Pettit prizing Rousseau's ideal of a deliberative assembly despite rejecting Rousseau's wider theory: P Pettit, *On the People's Terms: A Republican Theory and Model of Democracy* (New York, Cambridge University Press, 2012) 15.

PART III

Sortition

8

A Citizens' Court: Foundations

I. Introduction

The aspect of constitutionalism that has generated the greatest concern, in terms of its consistency with democratic values, is strong-form judicial review based on a bill of rights (hereafter 'strong-form judicial review'). With strong-form judicial review, judicial interpretations of rights, which can lead to legislative provisions being declared invalid, cannot be abrogated through ordinary legislation. This form of judicial review has been supported by republican revivers employing two conceptions of liberty. One is liberty as non-domination, which is diminished by arbitrary power. Pettit suggests that this is an attractive value to support constitutionalism, including judicial review. Judicial review is an institution that might, along with elected institutions, lessen arbitrary power.[1]

The other conception is positive liberty: this is associated with citizens achieving their moral potential and achieving self-rule through deciding together collective rules that best promote the public good. Michelman suggested that judicial review may promote opportunities for citizens to actively participate not just in formal governmental institutions at the federal and state level, but also in other forums including local government, workplaces and voluntary associations.[2] He also claimed that the judiciary could represent positive liberty to the community if judges are perceived as virtual representatives, that is, representing through resemblance rather than election. Michelman said, 'The judge ... represents by his own self-government our missing self-government, by his own practical reason our missing dialogue.'[3]

While chapter seven indicated difficulties with valuing deliberation by virtual representatives on the basis of positive liberty, Michelman's idea of furthering

---

[1] P Pettit, *Republicanism: A Theory of Freedom and Government* (Oxford, Clarendon Press, 1997) 181; P Pettit, 'Minority Claims under Two Conceptions of Democracy' in D Ivison, P Patton and W Sanders (eds), *Political Theory and the Rights of Indigenous Peoples* (Cambridge, Cambridge University Press, 2000) 199–215, 208. *Cf* P Pettit, *A Theory of Freedom: From the Psychology to the Politics of Agency* (Cambridge, Polity, 2001) 172; P Pettit, *On the People's Terms: A Republican Theory and Model of Democracy* (New York, Cambridge University Press, 2012) 284–5.

[2] F Michelman, 'Law's Republic' (1988) 97 *Yale Law Journal* 1493–1537, 1531.

[3] F Michelman, 'The Supreme Court, 1985 Term – Foreword: Traces of Self-Government' (1986) 100 *Harvard Law Review* 4–77, 73.

democratic legitimacy through virtual representatives engaged in constitutional review is an intriguing one. This part of the book will argue that the republican institution of sortition indicates how virtual representation in constitutional review might be achieved. The virtual representatives would sit on constitutional juries. Constitutional juries, it will be argued, provide a promising way of achieving democratic legitimacy in constitutional review. In other words, constitutional juries hold promise in addressing the counter-majoritarian difficulty.

Bernard Manin argues that sortition played a significant role in prominent republics, such as in ancient Athens and Renaissance Florence. By contrast, in liberal representative democracies, sortition was not substantially employed.[4] My proposal of constitutional juries derives, then, from an attempt to draw on the republican tradition to illuminate the counter-majoritarian difficulty. I look beyond conceptions of liberty to the republican institution of sortition. Sortition is also found in the common-law tradition, with juries. Indeed, Horacio Spector links jury nullification to constitutional juries.[5] Jury nullification occurs when juries refuse to apply a law they regard as illegitimate. A limitation of relying upon the common-law tradition alone, however, is that juries are officially limited to determining facts and applying the law to the facts they determine. Jury nullification is an exceptional power.[6] By contrast, I will draw on the Athenian People's Court as a republican institution. With this Court, juries enjoyed the official power to invalidate legislation and administrative actions.

This chapter provides the historical, normative and empirical foundation for chapter nine's construction and defence of constitutional juries. The historical foundation lies in connecting constitutional juries with ideas and practices associated with republicanism (Section II). The normative foundation lies in exploring some values relevant to evaluating institutional arrangements (Section III). The empirical foundation lies in discussion of deliberative polls (Section IV).

II. The Republican Tradition and Constitutional Juries

A. The Athenian Polis and the People's Court

I begin, then, with some republican ideas and institutions relevant to constitutional juries. This subsection considers the use of sortition. As already indicated, Manin identifies sortition with the republican tradition and refers to ancient Athens and Renaissance Florence. While I will focus on Athens, it is worth referring initially

---

[4] B Manin, *The Principles of Representative Government* (Cambridge, Cambridge University Press, 1997) 79.

[5] H Spector, 'The Right to a Constitutional Jury' (2009) III *Legisprudence* 111–123, 117.

[6] J Goldsworthy, *The Sovereignty of Parliament: History and Philosophy* (Oxford, Clarendon Press, 1999) 268.

to the use of sortition in the Florentine republic. Sortition was officially established in Florence by a 1328 ordinance and contributed to the most egalitarian period where, between 1494 and 1512, perhaps 20 per cent of adult males were members of the Great Council.[7] The Great Council employed sortition and election for important offices.

However, sortition was most extensively used in Athens, and its People's Court is of particular interest here. The remainder of this subsection will focus on Athens. In Athens, women, slaves and metics were excluded from citizenship. The guidance Athens offers lies in its inclusion of citizens in decision-making. It is, of course, for us to consider whether any contemporary proposal with historical affinities to an Athenian institution depends for its feasibility on restricting citizenship.[8] It is difficult to see why any such restriction would be necessary for contemporary constitutional juries.

In considering Athenian democracy, one can distinguish the 'radical' democracy of the fifth century, specifically 462–411 and 410–404BC, from the 'moderate' democracy of the fourth century. During both periods, the Assembly provided an opportunity for all citizens to make proposals and vote upon them. In the fifth century, citizens could pass laws and also decrees. Decrees could, for instance, be about foreign policy or individual situations.[9] However, a trend in the fourth century was to limit the Assembly to passing decrees. Law-making shifted to the *nomothetai* (legislators).[10] The *nomothetai* were selected by lot from those who had sworn an oath to decide matters in accordance with law and justice. Legislative proposals were considered by a jury of 500 or more citizens assembled for a day.[11] Fourth-century democracy was moderate in the sense that it involved institutions that lessened the powers exercised through direct democracy in the Assembly. On the other hand, the Assembly retained, for instance, the initiative in legislation: its decrees empowered *nomothetai* to consider proposals.[12]

In the fourth century, sortition was predominantly used in selecting magistracies, which generally employed boards of 10 and which undertook administrative tasks.[13] The most important magistracy, the Council, though, had 500 members. Furthermore, some magistracies requiring military or financial expertise were purely elective. Terms were generally limited to a year.

---

[7] J Najemy, *Corporatism and Consensus in Florentine Electoral Politics, 1280–1400* (Chapel Hill, University of North Carolina Press, 1982) 102; D Wootton, 'Introduction' in N Machiavelli, *The Prince*, trans and ed, D Wootton (Indiana, Hackett Publishing, 1995) xi–xliv, xiv–xv.

[8] On connections between active citizenship and restrictions to citizenship, see M Hansen, *The Athenian Democracy in the Age of Demosthenes: Structure, Principles and Ideology*, trans, JA Crook (Oxford, Basil Blackwell, 1991) 316–18.

[9] ibid 152.

[10] ibid 150–1.

[11] ibid 163, 169.

[12] ibid 152–3.

[13] ibid 229–35.

Of particular interest here, however, are certain trials conducted by the People's Court. Like the *nomothetai*, the Court employed juries of around 500.[14] One role of the juries was to hear complaints that a person had initiated an unconstitutional proposal in the Assembly. The procedure was called the *graphe paranomon*.[15] The proposal being scrutinised might be to pass a decree or legislation. A broad interpretation was taken of an unconstitutional proposal: damaging the public interest was relevant in determining constitutionality.[16] The People's Court could hear a complaint that a proposal was unconstitutional even if the decree or legislation the subject of the proposal had been passed by the Assembly. If the complaint was upheld, the initiator of the proposal was generally fined and any Assembly decision passing the proposal was quashed.[17]

Four features of the trials suggest that they functioned as a deliberative check on the Assembly. First, the jurors were at least 30 years old, while the qualifying age for the Assembly was 20. Mogens Hansen suggests that this qualifying age of 30, which also applied to the *nomothetai* and to magistrates, would have excluded around one-third of citizens, and it can be understood as aimed at ensuring that only those with greater experience and sounder judgement could serve on these bodies.[18] Secondly, jurors were required to take an oath that they would vote in accordance with law or their sense of justice in cases not covered by law.[19] Hansen emphasises the solemnity of the oath: those who broke it were understood to be subject to divine punishment. Those participating in Assembly decisions did not take an oath. Thirdly, the trials involved an adversarial proceeding set down for a day. By contrast, Assembly decisions could be passed with minimal debate. Finally, the People's Court relied on secret ballot, while Assembly votes were by show of hands.[20] Secret ballot reduced the chance of corruption or outside pressure.

While the *graphe paranomon* was employed in the fifth century to challenge proposals leading to legislation and decrees, I mentioned that in the fourth century, legislation shifted to the *nomothetai*. However, a new procedure enabling complaints 'for having proposed and carried an unsuitable law' enabled the People's Court to also check the *nomothetai*: this procedure was called the *graphe nomon me epitedeion theinai*.[21] There is dispute over the relative importance of legal arguments, which were largely confined to claiming that an incorrect legal procedure had been followed, and policy arguments, which claimed that the proposal went

---

[14] ibid 181. For reference to other secondary literature, see, eg, K Werhan, 'Popular Constitutionalism, Ancient and Modern' (2012) 46 *UC Davis Law Review* 65–131, 96–9.

[15] Hansen, *The Athenian Democracy* 205ff.

[16] ibid 206.

[17] Manin, *Representative Government* 21.

[18] Hansen, *The Athenian Democracy* 88–90, 181.

[19] ibid 182–3.

[20] Manin, *Representative Government* 21.

[21] Hansen, *The Athenian Democracy* 212.

against the city's interests.[22] It suffices to note here that both arguments were considered by the Court.

The People's Court can also be understood as providing a deliberative check upon the *nomothetai*, although both institutions employed juries. It set aside a day to consider particular legislation, while *nomothetai* may have passed several pieces of legislation in a single day.[23] The People's Court also voted by secret ballot while the *nomothetai* voted by show of hands.[24]

B. The People's Court and the Judicial Branch

This subsection establishes that the People's Court employed constitutional juries, that is, juries that serve a function similar to modern judicial review. In this way, contemporary constitutional juries would enjoy a strong republican connection. The connection between the People's Court and contemporary constitutional juries is explored through considering some claims made by Adriaan Lanni.

Lanni raises doubts about the strength of the connection between the People's Court and constitutional juries by suggesting that the People's Court has more in common with bicameralism than modern judicial review. She does not deny there is also an affinity between the People's Court and judicial review, so the doubts she raises do not exclude a republican connection between this Court and contemporary constitutional juries. However, the purpose of this subsection is not merely to establish a relatively strong connection between the People's Court and contemporary constitutional juries in order to support the claim that such juries can be described as republican. A discussion of Lanni's arguments also draws attention to some features of judicial review. This is helpful since I suggest constitutional juries as an alternative to judicial review. In chapter nine, I compare judicial review with constitutional juries, and I also justify my placement of sortition in an institution that sits within the judicial rather than the legislative branch of government.

Lanni refers to two features of the People's Court to support her claim that this Court has a stronger affinity with modern bicameralism than judicial review – she has the US system especially in mind. The first feature of the People's Court is that it not only considered legal but also policy arguments. The second feature is that it could uphold proposed decrees that had never been passed by the Assembly thereby giving them the force of law. I will address these features in turn, focusing especially on the first one.

In considering the first feature (that the People's Court considered policy arguments), there is, indeed, a sharp distinction between the People's Court and the US

---

[22] A Lanni, 'Judicial Review and the Athenian "Constitution"' (2010) 56 *Entretiens sur l'Antiquité Classique* 235–63, 238.

[23] Hansen, *The Athenian Democracy* 212.

[24] While Hansen does not mention this when contrasting the two bodies, he mentions in ibid 169 that the *nomothetai* voted by a show of hands.

Supreme Court: the latter can only invalidate legislation on the ground of inconsistency with constitutional law, not the public interest.[25] However, we need to consider whether the Supreme Court draws the line between law and policy in a similar way to the People's Court.

Lanni points to uncertainty over whether legal argument heard by the People's Court tended to be quite narrow, focusing on procedural illegality and direct conflict with a provision of a standing law, or whether there were broader values relied on that derived from statutes. Lanni suggests an intermediate position. Legal arguments were narrow in that they focused upon the *procedural* value of safeguarding popular decision-making in the Assembly and courts. However, they were broad in the sense that these arguments drew upon democratic *principles* rather than a direct conflict with a statutory provision.[26]

Lanni draws a parallel with US judicial review, noting Ely's process theory.[27] Ely attempted to avoid the counter-majoritarian difficulty by suggesting that the Constitution left substantive values almost entirely to the political process and focused instead on procedural fairness in individual disputes and ensuring broad participation in the political process.[28] With respect to those excluded from the political process, Ely favoured strict scrutiny of government action that burdens 'discrete and insular minorities'.[29] Lanni acknowledges that this strict scrutiny with respect to discrete and insular minorities extends substantially beyond the process rights referred to in the Athenian cases she covers. Nevertheless, she maintains a parallel between legal arguments in the Athenian People's Court and the US Supreme Court. Thus, the main distinction between the two institutions lies in the People's Court having recourse not only to legal but also general policy arguments.

However, I would suggest that in considering US judicial review, what is most relevant is whether Ely's process theory can in fact explain Supreme Court decisions. Lawrence Tribe, for instance, argued that the strict scrutiny of discrete and insular minorities that Ely brought within his procedural model could only occur once discrete and insular minorities were identified through applying a substantive theory of justice.[30] Ely did not, in any case, seek to defend all progressive decisions made from the late 1950s. Most prominently, he excluded *Roe v Wade*, which found a right to an abortion.[31]

It is also worth noting theories of judicial review that adopt a more capacious understanding of the legal arguments that are made, and can appropriately be

---

[25] J Goldsworthy, 'Legislative Intentions, Legislative Supremacy, and Legal Positivism' (2005) 42 *San Diego Law Review* 493–518, 506–7.

[26] Lanni, 'Judicial Review and the Athenian "Constitution"' 244.

[27] ibid 260.

[28] J Ely, *Democracy and Distrust: A Theory of Judicial Review* (Cambridge, Mass., Harvard University Press, 1980) 87.

[29] ibid ch 6.

[30] L Tribe, 'The Puzzling Persistence of Process-Based Constitutional Theories' (1980) 89 *Yale Law Journal* 1063–80, 1072–7. Lanni does refer to Tribe in Lanni, 'Judicial Review and the Athenian "Constitution"' 260 fn 101.

[31] 410 US 113 (1973). See Ely, *Democracy and Distrust* ch 1.

made, by the US Supreme Court. Christopher Eisgruber, for instance, argues that the Supreme Court should be understood as a representative institution in which judges, selected by institutions that are themselves representative by virtue of the electoral process, apply their moral judgements to cases.[32] He suggests that legal argument is in fact capacious enough to target the main moral considerations that are raised by an issue, and that judges decide on the basis of their moral judgement. With this understanding, the Supreme Court does and should take into account some of the policy arguments that Lanni identifies with the People's Court and which she uses to suggest that this Court has more in common with a modern legislative rather than judicial branch of government. I am not suggesting, though, that all policy considerations the People's Court could take into account are of a kind that the Supreme Court has taken into account. Rather, the point is that Lanni's contrast between the People's Court and the Supreme Court, based on the former taking into account policy arguments, unlike the latter, may be overdrawn.

In considering Lanni's suggestion of a greater affinity between the People's Court and an upper house rather than a court, she draws attention to two features of the People's Court.[33] First, the People's Court considered policy arguments. This is, of course, a commonality with legislatures. However, Lanni suggests that the People's Court had to find that legislation is contrary to law for it to be ruled invalid. There is no such requirement, of course, for a legislature in rejecting a bill. This is a significant difference.

The second feature of the People's Court that Lanni draws attention to is its power to not only invalidate proposed decrees but also approve them so that they have the force of law. This seems an exercise of executive power, and this power is not associated with judicial review. By contrast, the US Senate's role in confirming appointments of judges, ambassadors, ministers and other offices is similar to a power to confirm proposed executive actions.[34] On this point, the People's Court is closer to the Senate than to the Supreme Court. Nevertheless, it is unclear why this point should be given such weight as to suggest that, overall, the People's Court has greater affinity with an upper house than a court engaged in judicial review. Indeed, my proposal of constitutional juries is placed in the Australian context, and the Australian Senate does not have a role in confirming executive appointments.[35]

It is not clear that the People's Court has a greater affinity with a modern upper house than with a court engaged in judicial review. Indeed, Lanni recognises affinities between the People's Court and judicial review. She mentions that review by

---

[32] See C Eisgruber, 'Constitutional Self-Government and Judicial Review: A Reply to Five Critics' (2002) 37 *University of San Francisco Law Review* 115–90, 163–7, comparing the US Supreme Court with the UK House of Lords.

[33] Lanni, 'Judicial Review and the Athenian "Constitution"' 258–9.

[34] US Constitution art II, s 2, cl 2.

[35] See, eg, M Spry, 'Executive and High Court Appointments' in G Lindell and B Bennet (eds), *Parliament: The Vision in Hindsight* (Sydney, Federation Press, 2001) 419–53.

the People's Court was only triggered by a complaint by a citizen and the complaint had to indicate the laws that the statute under review allegedly contradicted.[36] Lanni further states that 'the Athenian procedures are particularly striking because they offer an alternative model of "democratic" judicial review'.[37] Lanni clearly recognises affinities between the Athenian People's Court and judicial review even if she thinks there are greater affinities with a legislative upper house. She ultimately describes the People's Court as a hybrid institution. That description can be endorsed. What has been doubted is her suggestion that the People's Court is closer in its function to the Senate than to the Supreme Court.

My interest in this subsection was not to suggest a precise parallel between the Athenian People's Court and constitutional juries placed in a contemporary setting. Instead, I suggest that the two share a sufficient affinity to support the claim that constitutional juries have a republican inspiration. A proposal for constitutional juries can be understood as following from an attempt to consider practices associated with republicanism that may offer attractive contemporary guidance. Referring to the capacious character of legal argument that can be found with contemporary judicial review also establishes a point of comparison with constitutional juries. It would be wrong, for instance, to claim that this comparison yields a sharp contrast based on courts making technical decisions versus juries making moral decisions.

C. Sortition, the Mixed Constitution, and Judicial Review

This subsection shifts from a republican institution (the People's Court) to some republican ideas that can support constitutional juries. I first refer to the republican association between sortition and democracy and the republican idea of a mixed constitution. I then turn to the implications of these republican ideas for judicial review and constitutional juries.

Beginning with sortition, Manin notes that Athenians gave sortition a substantial role, probably due to a belief that sortition leads to a greater degree of equality than elections.[38] I will focus here, though, on Aristotle's discussion of sortition and how he placed this in the context of a mixed constitution. Aristotle was highly influential for writers who drew on ideas and experiences from ancient Athens and Rome.

Aristotle referred to sortition as a democratic practice while elections were oligarchic.[39] He associated democratic rule with rule by the poor in their interests,

---

[36] Lanni notes, however, that Mogens Hansen instead claimed that legal and policy arguments were alternative grounds for invalidation. See Lanni, 'Judicial Review and the Athenian "Constitution"' 238–9.

[37] ibid 259.

[38] Manin, *Representative Government* 39–40.

[39] Aristotle, *The Politics*, trans, T Sinclair, revised, T Saunders (Penguin, 1992) bk IV, ch ix 1294b.

while oligarchic rule was rule by a wealthy elite pursing its interests. The ideal types of government were aristocracy (rule by a virtuous elite) and *politeia* (rule by citizens who are able to buy the necessary military equipment so that they can serve in the city's army).[40] The common constitutions, though, were oligarchy (rule by the wealthy few) and democracy (where day labourers and the poor were included as citizens). Aristotle viewed Athens as a democracy.

A mixed constitution combines elements of oligarchy and democracy.[41] Aristotle suggested that a mixed constitution, in comparison to oligarchy and democracy, was more likely to have laws that promote the common good and to enjoy the stability that comes when a regime is supported by the wealthy and the poor.[42] Aristotle also suggested that a mixed constitution could involve election and sortition.[43] If a mixed constitution was substantially egalitarian rather than elitist, it could still be described as a *politeia* rather than a democracy.[44] It would seem, then, that a mixed constitution can be an ideal constitution as well.

The idea of the mixed constitution, which can helpfully combine egalitarian and elitist elements, is linked to the republican tradition. Also linked to the tradition is the association of sortition with democracy and election with aristocracy. Manin suggests that these associations were established in Renaissance Florence largely through experience with these forms of selection.[45] Sortition led to ordinary citizens, in contrast to a wealthy elite, having a greater chance of becoming decision-makers.

In the remainder of this subsection, I first turn to the association of sortition with democracy to suggest a limitation to Bickel's understanding of the counter-majoritarian difficulty. Secondly, I indicate how the association of sortition with democracy and the idea of the mixed constitution have been employed to illuminate contemporary democracies that have judicial review. This situates my proposal for constitutional juries in the contemporary literature.

I turn, then, to how the counter-majoritarian difficulty is understood. While I use the term 'counter-majoritarian difficulty' as a shorthand expression for concern about the democratic legitimacy of judicial review; this term was coined by Bickel and he had a particular understanding of what underlay it.[46] Bickel had the US Supreme Court in mind. He understood the difficulty as lying in judges having greater freedom than politicians to make decisions inconsistent with the majority's preferences, since judges are not constrained by an interest in re-election. In suggesting that courts engaged in judicial review are therefore undemocratic

---

[40] See, eg, M Hansen, 'The Mixed Constitution versus the Separation of Powers: Monarchical and Aristocratic Aspects of Modern Democracy' (2010) 31 *History of Political Thought* 509–31, 518.

[41] Aristotle, *The Politics* bk IV, ch ix.

[42] ibid bk IV, ch viii 1293b and ch ix 1294a for reference to good laws being part of the goodness of states, and to the willingness of all classes to maintain the constitution.

[43] See Hansen, 'The Mixed Constitution versus the Separation of Powers' 520.

[44] Hansen, *The Athenian Democracy* 67.

[45] Manin, *Representative Government* 57–63.

[46] See A Bickel, *The Least Dangerous Branch: The Supreme Court at the Bar of Politics* [1962], with a new forward by H Wellington, 2nd edn (New Haven, Yale University Press, 1986) 16–23.

institutions, democracy is equated with a system where majority preferences, via the electoral system, at least loosely constrain decision-making.

From an Aristotelian perspective, Bickel had a narrow conception of democracy, for he overlooked sortition.[47] Some Athenian institutions drawing on sortition gave decision-makers substantial freedom to depart from majority preferences. For example, jurors on the Athenian People's Court voted by secret ballot. What made sortition democratic, it seems, was that it appeared to give ordinary citizens greater influence over decisions than the system of election.

Aristotle was not, of course, reflecting on modern electoral politics, with its distinctive attributes such as political parties. The broad message to take from Aristotle's approach is that democracy should not be exclusively identified with a system that somewhat constrains decision-makers through the electoral system to follow majority preferences. Sortition might increase the chance of decisions that reflect the interests of ordinary citizens. When considering the democratic credentials of judicial review, the point of reference need not be limited to elected branches of government.

Indeed, there have been attempts to apply the association of sortition with democracy and the idea of the mixed constitution to contemporary democracies, including those with judicial review. While Manin did not address judicial review, it is worth beginning with his influential discussion. He presented sortition as a republican device and related it to modern representative democracies. He argued that the absence of sortition from liberal representative democracies, despite knowledge of ancient republics, suggests a conscious rejection of this democratic method.[48] Liberal representative democracies can be described, he argued, as mixed constitutions. One aristocratic feature of elections is that they invariably lead to the selection of elites: elections favour those possessing uncommon and positively valued characteristics.[49] This aristocratic feature, however, is balanced, ideally, by ordinary citizens' capacity to define what constitutes an elite and who belongs to it.[50] Manin recognised the skewing effect of wealth and the difficulty in eliminating this. Nevertheless, he seemed satisfied with modern democracies; at least, he did not examine whether contemporary political systems were optimal in the absence of sortition.

Manin's point about the elitism of liberal democracies, with their rejection of sortition, has been employed by constitutional scholars to lessen the contrast

---

[47] Bickel's narrow conception of democracy is also recognised in C Zurn, *Deliberative Democracy and the Institutions of Judicial Review* (New York, Cambridge University Press, 2006) ch 1. It will become apparent in s IIIA that Dworkin and Waldron were not limited in evaluating the counter-majoritarian objection to Bickel's conception.

[48] Manin, *Representative Government* 91–3.

[49] ibid 140.

[50] ibid 157–60.

in democratic credentials between electoral democracy and judicial review. For example, Eisgruber, while recognising that judicial review is more elitist than electoral democracy, argued that opponents of judicial review cannot simply equate democracy with election. They must instead defend the claim of legislative supremacy based on a pragmatic assessment of how well legislatures serve democratic values.[51]

Spector followed Manin in using sortition to highlight the elitism of representative democracy.[52] Spector made his reference to sortition concrete through considering constitutional juries. He suggested in a brief discussion that the main objections to constitutional juries could be answered. He did not, though, use constitutional juries to highlight the elitism of judicial review. Instead, he suggested that the possibility of constitutional juries highlights the lack of substantive political equality achieved through electoral democracy. In its avoidance of substantive political equality, representative democracy is similar to judicial review. This, Spector argued, made it difficult to argue that judicial review is inconsistent with commitments underlying representative democracy.

Keith Werhan, on the other hand, compared US judicial review with the Athenian People's Court.[53] While Manin, Eisgruber and Spector used sortition to highlight the elitism of electoral democracy, Werhan used sortition to highlight the elitism of judicial review: he suggested that the Athenian model was consciously rejected. He endorsed that rejection: the Athenian judicial system suffered significant defects, such as lack of predictability and the possibility of injustice, as symbolised by Socrates' trial.

Discussion of sortition in the context of judicial review was, then, largely aimed at supporting judicial review. However, in 2009, Spector proposed that complainants in constitutional cases should have the option of choosing between a judge or jury trial.[54] He drew on the common-law practice of jury nullification and defences of it to suggest that 'the idea of a constitutional jury is very close to actual historical and present-day practice'.[55] Spector maintained that the elitism of electoral democracy is such that the extent to which judicial review violates equal political liberty should not be overstated.[56] Nevertheless, he suggested that constitutional juries would fully realise the ideal of equal political liberty. Citizens would have an equal chance of participating in constitutional decisions without the biases and distortions that affect systems with elected representatives and appointed

---

[51] C Eisgruber, *Constitutional Self-Government* (Cambridge, Mass., Harvard University Press, 2001) 51–2.

[52] See H Spector, 'Judicial Review, Rights, and Democracy' (2003) 22 *Law and Philosophy* 285–334, 331–3.

[53] Werhan, 'Popular Constitutionalism, Ancient and Modern'.

[54] See Spector, 'The Right to a Constitutional Jury' 116–20. For an earlier suggestion of constitutional juries, see D Held, *Models of Democracy*, 3rd edn (Cambridge, Polity, 2006) 279 fn 9. This footnote appears from the 1st edn (1987) 286.

[55] Spector, 'The Right to a Constitutional Jury' 117.

[56] ibid 119.

judges. He argued that constitutional juries are likely to be more impartial than a constitutional court and could give reasoned responses.

While Spector proposed constitutional juries as an additional option for complainants and remained largely supportive of judicial review, I suggested, in 2010, constitutional juries as an alternative to judicial review.[57] I argued that if such juries are feasible, they raise a new concern about the legitimacy of judicial review. In a more recent article, Spector suggested that constitutional juries should not adjudicate on matters dealing with minority rights.[58] By contrast, I had suggested that constitutional juries could interpret a broad bill of rights including social welfare rights and a catch-all provision capturing substantial injustice.

This and the next chapter expand on my 2010 article. That expansion partly lies in connecting my proposal more clearly to its motivation, which lay in thinking about the constitutional implications of the republican tradition. The next chapter also refers to Spector's 2009 article, which I had overlooked, and discusses criticisms of constitutional juries made by Christopher Zurn.[59] Some elements of my proposal have also been revised.

In summary, the previous two subsections linked the idea of constitutional juries to Athenian practice, with its People's Court. This subsection considered some republican ideas. I argued that the republican association of, first, democracy with sortition and, secondly, aristocracy with election suggest that Bickel's understanding of the counter-majoritarian difficulty is rather narrow. These republican associations together with the idea of the mixed constitution have in fact been applied to modern democracies to support and challenge judicial review. One challenge lies in proposing constitutional juries.

III. Assessing Institutional Arrangements

A. Outcome and Process Considerations

This section considers what values should be employed in assessing institutional arrangements including constitutional juries. It begins, in this subsection, with the distinction between outcome and process considerations. The next subsection

---

[57] E Ghosh, 'Deliberative Democracy and the Countermajoritarian Difficulty: Considering Constitutional Juries' (2010) 30 *Oxford Journal of Legal Studies* 327–59. The association of sortition with democracy has been used in other ways to challenge judicial review. John McCormick is critical of Pettit's support for judicial review, arguing that it provides an unfortunate aristocratic dimension to the US political system. The US could instead have an institution inspired by the Roman tribunes of the plebeians, involving sortition: J McCormick, *Machiavellian Democracy* (New York, Cambridge University Press, 2011) 153, 183.

[58] H Spector, 'The Theory of Constitutional Review' in M Jovanović (ed), *Constitutional Review and Democracy* (The Hague, Eleven International Publishing, 2015) 17–37, 36–7.

[59] C Zurn, 'Judicial Review, Constitutional Juries and Civic Constitutional Fora: Rights, Democracy and Law' (2011) 58 *Theoria* 63–94.

distinguishes between values more or less attached to particular institutional forms. Subsection C refers to the ideal of deliberative democracy.

I turn first to outcome and process considerations relevant to evaluating decision-making processes.[60] The outcome consideration focuses on decisions made. It is principally concerned about the moral soundness of those decisions, but it is also concerned with indirect empirical consequences of a decision. Those are consequences other than the distribution of benefits and burdens, for instance, that results directly from decisions. Process considerations can be divided into process-instrumental factors, which rely on empirical consequences of a process other than the decisions it produces, and process-intrinsic considerations.

These considerations can be illustrated by applying them to some ideas and practices mentioned in this chapter – the mixed constitution, sortition in Florence and judicial review – and also to interpretations of liberty explored in this book. Both outcome and process considerations are found in the republican tradition and in debate about the counter-majoritarian difficulty.

Beginning with the mixed constitution, Aristotle supported this partly because of the likely outcome of good laws and also for process-related reasons. One such reason was popular legitimacy. Acceptance of a process by the people and a wealthy elite was helpful in achieving stability and commitment to the regime. This is a process-instrumental consideration to the extent that popular accept-ance is a consequence of a decision-making process that, for instance, empowers different sections of the community. However, popular acceptance is also likely to result from the justice of the decisions generated by the process. This is an outcome consideration: it is one of the indirect consequences of particular decisions. The relationship between outcome and process considerations can be one of mutual influence.

A process-intrinsic consideration is where a decision-making process is supported because it is fair. Take, for instance, the 1328 ordinance establishing sortition in Florence. This ordinance's stated rationale referred to the fair distri-bution of the honours of political office to those worthy and aspiring to political office.[61] This rationale suggests that it is only fair that the honour of political office should be awarded to those who most deserve it.

Outcome and process considerations are also relevant to the conceptions of liberty discussed earlier in the book. Part I compared liberty as non-interference with liberty as non-domination. Liberty as non-interference depends upon the probability of not being interfered with, and its adherents are likely to be especially concerned about unjustified interference. Pricean liberty as non-domination is also motivated by a concern with unjustified interference: it suggests that such interference is highly likely where there is substantial arbitrary power. Thus,

---

[60] J Waldron, 'The Core of the Case against Judicial Review' (2006) 115 *Yale Law Journal* 1346–1406 refers to outcome- and process-related reasons.

[61] Najemy, *Corporatism and Consensus in Florentine Electoral Politics* 102.

a concern underlying both values is avoiding unfavourable outcomes. Both values, though, can recognise that the decision-making process can itself create options that are valuable for reasons other than improving decisions. Liberty as non-interference is diminished by the removal of participatory options. Priceian liberty as non-domination is diminished by a discretionary power to remove participatory options, for such power renders such options precarious.

Pettit's interpretation of liberty as non-domination, on the other hand, is justified by reference to the damage caused by a decision-making process that creates vulnerability to arbitrary power, in the form of feelings of uncertainty, having to engage in strategic conduct to lessen the chance of interference, and suffering the humiliation of lower social status.[62] With Pettit stressing that these forms of damage can occur in the absence of decisions involving unjustified interference, Pettit is pointing here to process-instrumental concerns.

Part II of the book discussed positive-liberty dimensions that may be found in accounts of liberty. A positive-liberty dimension found in Price, which I described as democratic status, involves a process-intrinsic consideration. For Price, it was intrinsically valuable for citizens to have the opportunity to participate in government since this opportunity appropriately reflected their rational capacities, the capacities that bring people closest to God.

Outcome and process considerations are also evident in, say, debate between Dworkin and Waldron over judicial review. The main outcome consideration is whether judicial review leads to just decisions. Dworkin argued that the majoritarian pressures registered through the electoral process can lead to the oppression of minorities, and judges' relative insulation from those pressures and their focus on rights-based arguments render them well-suited to provide some protection against such oppression.[63] Waldron, on the other hand, doubted that the quality of decisions produced by the political system is likely to be superior where there is judicial review. He suggested that supporters of judicial review can have an overly negative view of legislators and ordinary citizens, viewing legislators as simply interested in re-election and ordinary citizens as ignorant and self-interested.[64] Instead, legislators should be understood as substantially motivated by the public good, and their diversity, in contrast to judges, gives them an advantage in determining what is just.[65] Furthermore, legislators are likely to engage directly with the moral issues, while legal reasoning, with its emphasis on textual interpretation and following precedent, can distract from those issues.[66]

Some of the arguments of Dworkin and Waldron closely combine outcome and process considerations. This is evident in Dworkin's response to the claim that judicial review is problematic because it diminishes the opportunity and

---

[62] Pettit, *Republicanism* 86–7.

[63] R Dworkin, *Taking Rights Seriously* (London, Duckworth, 1977) 85.

[64] J Waldron, *Law and Disagreement* (New York, Oxford University Press, 1999) 227–31.

[65] ibid ch 3.

[66] Waldron, 'The Core of the Case against Judicial Review' 1383–4.

incentive for citizens to participate on issues of rights that are justiciable by courts.[67] Dworkin had in mind what he describes as the civic republican concern that, in the absence of political participation, citizens cannot develop their sense of moral responsibility. He had, then, in mind the positive-liberty interpretation of the republican tradition. Dworkin's response to this concern was that judicial review itself prompts political and popular discussion of rights. He claimed that an awareness that a proposal raises constitutional questions that will ultimately be heard by the Supreme Court prompts a focus in debate in legislatures and in the community upon individual rights. Furthermore, Supreme Court decisions can themselves prompt a national debate about rights. Dworkin's claim about anticipatory debate seems a process-instrumental claim, while debate after Supreme Court decisions seems an outcome-related claim. Waldron, however, challenged Dworkin's response to the civic republican concern about judicial review by retorting that civic republicans are interested in active citizenship, and that requires citizens to share in power, not just to deliberate on issues.[68] In any case, as Waldron recognised, the justification for judicial review that generally is most heavily relied on is the outcome consideration that Supreme Court decisions have promoted justice.[69]

Waldron himself, though, relies heavily on a process-intrinsic consideration. His principal argument against judicial review is that it conveys a message of mistrust in the autonomy of citizens: they cannot be trusted to respect the rights of minorities.[70] Of course, with citizens acting through their representatives, the argument must be that citizens lack sufficient commitment to minorities to ensure that their representatives are suitably constrained to also demonstrate that respect. This message of mistrust perhaps offends most seriously against a process-intrinsic consideration, which is that it is intrinsically wrong to have a decision-making process that disrespects citizens' capacity to engage in moral deliberation. Dworkin, on the other hand, believed that the franchise provides a sufficient symbolic affirmation of citizens' equal standing.[71] His anxiety about majoritarian tyranny suggests he would have regarded Waldron as having an overly rosy view of the autonomy citizens demonstrate on political matters.

To sum up, outcome and process considerations are found in writing associated with the republican tradition and also in debate over the counter-majoritarian difficulty. The distinction between these considerations is helpful in analysing arguments employed in assessing institutional arrangements. I will argue in the next chapter that these considerations may well be promoted by constitutional juries.

---

[67] R Dworkin, *Freedom's Law: The Moral Reading of the American Constitution* (Cambridge, Mass., Harvard University Press, 1996) 342–7.

[68] Waldron, *Law and Disagreement* 290–1.

[69] ibid 286.

[70] ibid 221–3.

[71] R Dworkin, *Sovereign Virtue: The Theory and Practice of Equality* (Cambridge, Mass., Harvard University Press, 2000) ch 4.

B. Attached Conceptions of Liberty

There is a further distinction worth making partly because it clarifies the approach that should be taken in evaluating institutional arrangements and also because it throws light on the conceptions of liberty that have been discussed in this book and their relationship to sortition. This is a distinction between values that are more or less attached to a decision-making process. The strongest form of attachment is where there is a necessary connection to a decision-making process.

This attached–detached distinction tracks on to positive and negative liberty. For example, the main feature that rendered Priceian liberty positive, from the critical perspective of Lind, for instance, was that it did not merely require the absence of constraints but positively required a broad franchise. Price's critics were concerned that Priceian liberty thereby circumvented an analysis of the costs and benefits of broadening the franchise.[72] Full-blown positive liberty is also an attached conception. Its connection to virtuous participation in decision-making ties liberty to institutional forms that promote such participation. A form of direct democracy that creates the opportunity and incentive for citizens to deliberate extensively with each other before collectively deciding matters would seem the ideal. Representative democracy would be a second-best solution.

The remainder of this subsection explores liberty as non-domination because it poses a particular challenge to sortition. Liberty as non-domination is attached to what Jane Mansbridge describes as the sanctions model of representation.[73] This model assumes that the interests of the people and their representatives may not align. It relies on sanctions to discipline representatives and thereby constrain the arbitrary power they would otherwise enjoy. With electoral democracy, for instance, a sanction for representatives lies in not being re-elected.

By contrast, Mansbridge's selection model relies on obtaining representatives whose interests align with the people for reasons other than the possibility of sanctions. In holding up the ideal of US Supreme Court judges being virtual representatives, Michelman was clearly relying on the selection model. So too is Eisgruber: he emphasises judges' democratic credentials by claiming that the selection process, involving Presidential nomination and Senate confirmation, ensures that judges' values conform to the mainstream.[74]

With liberty as non-domination being attached to the sanctions model, it may seem puzzling that Pettit can claim that liberty as non-domination looks favourably at measures such as judicial review.[75] (Recall that by 'judicial review', I generally have in mind review based on a bill of rights.) Pettit suggests that judicial review

---

[72] See ch 2, ss IV–VI.

[73] J Mansbridge, 'A "Selection Model" of Political Representation' (2009) 17 *Journal of Political Philosophy* 369–98.

[74] Eisgruber, *Constitutional Self-Government* 65–6.

[75] See above n 1.

promises an impartial forum for considering minority interests. It can thereby diminish parliament's arbitrary power over minorities. Chapter four argued that in considering the dispersion of power, probabilistic considerations are highly relevant.[76] Pettit does seem to be relying on an assessment that there is a significant probability that judicial review will lead to outcomes that protect minority interests against unjustified incursions. He does not point, for instance, to the arbitrary power that is conferred upon tenured judges by judicial review. It would seem that while liberty as non-domination can approve of a selection model of representation, it is likely to only do so as a means of reducing the arbitrary power enjoyed by a body employing the sanctions model of representation. The selection model itself is inimical to liberty as non-domination.

Sortition also relies on the selection model of representation, especially where it leads to juries deciding through secret ballot.[77] While Pettit does not acknowledge that courts enjoy arbitrary power, he does claim that a body selected through sortition is linked with a certain sort of domination, for it can form a will of its own and exercise that under few constraints.[78] With liberty as non-domination favouring the sanctions over the selection model, one can echo the caution about attached conceptions of liberty sounded by Price's critics. Noting that institution X is desirable because it favours a conception of liberty when that conception of liberty is attached to institution X can hardly be conclusive. That attached conception can highlight relevant considerations, but ultimately all advantages and disadvantages of institution X should be taken into account.

The approach I am recommending here is consistent with what I proposed in chapter five. I suggested there that Price's non-domination conception of liberty should be applied from within a pluralistic framework. I suggested it be understood as a way of emphasising the danger of arbitrary power, but it may not always be an appropriate value to pursue. Applying that point here, while Pettit explicitly addresses sortition, Price did not contemplate sortition. He was envisaging decision-makers who have interests clearly distinct from the people. Priceian liberty as non-domination suggests, though, that complacency would not be in order where the selection model is alleged to apply well to a particular institution. One would need to investigate whether distinct and substantial interests can arise for representatives. If they can, Priceian liberty as non-domination warns about a significant likelihood that arbitrary power will be abused. However, if this line of investigation fails to unearth particular dangers, an assumption of likely abuse of power may be unwarranted. The constitutional juries that I will propose in the next chapter would have limited powers. One limitation lies in the Senate being able to abrogate jury decisions. It is also unclear what distinct interests could arise

---

[76] Ch 4, s VIC.
[77] For one sanction that could otherwise apply, see Pettit, *Republicanism* 223–4.
[78] Pettit, *On the People's Terms* 204–5.

for a jury sitting on a single matter. Liberty as non-domination should not stand in the way of constitutional juries.

C. Deliberative Democracy

In exploring normative approaches to evaluating institutional arrangements, it is also worth referring briefly to the theory of deliberative democracy: this is the dominant contemporary normative democratic theory.[79] Chapter seven noted that Michelman tied negative republican liberty to deliberative democracy.[80] With negative republican liberty, citizens' commitment to the common good and to participation are valued largely for their role in achieving protection from government rather than for their role in enabling citizens to broaden their moral horizons and achieve self-government.

However, the substantial literature on deliberative democracy since then has not been especially tied to negative-liberty republicanism. Thus, deliberative democracy need not be understood simply as a means of constraining the state. Instead, deliberative democracy provides a general test for the legitimacy of institutions. The deliberative component to the deliberative democratic ideal involves participants seeking the common good through a respectful exchange of views. The democratic component lies in those potentially affected by a decision being able to participate in a way consistent with their equality.

Beyond this broad conception of the deliberative democratic ideal, however, lies disagreement, for instance, on how political equality is to be achieved and what counts as a deliberative contribution to decision-making.[81] The justification for the ideal is also controversial. However, in articulating outcome and process considerations as relevant to evaluating institutions, I am committed to the claim that a crucial justification for deliberative democratic procedures must be outcome-related: those procedures should promote the making of decisions that reflect the common good.[82] A process-intrinsic justification for an inclusive and deliberative process is that this process treats citizens with respect by recognising their capacity to reach reasonable views on the common good.

The deliberative democratic approach does not articulate a precise idea of what the common good is when thinking about policy questions. Academic

---

[79] See, eg, J Mansbridge et al, 'The Place of Self-Interest and the Role of Power in Deliberative Democracy' (2010) 18 *Journal of Political Philosophy* 64–100. I applied a deliberative-democratic approach in Ghosh, 'Deliberative Democracy and the Countermajoritarian Difficulty' and considered an empirical dimension of it in E Ghosh, 'Deliberative Constitutionalism: An Empirical Dimension' in J King et al (eds), *Cambridge Handbook on Deliberative Constitutionalism* (Cambridge, Cambridge University Press, 2018) 220–32.

[80] See ch 7, s IIA.

[81] See, eg, Mansbridge et al, 'The Place of Self-Interest and the Role of Power in Deliberative Democracy' 66–9.

[82] This claim is defended in D Estlund, 'Who's Afraid of Deliberative Democracy? On the Strategic/ Deliberative Dichotomy in Recent Constitutional Jurisprudence' (1993) 71 *Texas Law Review* 1437–77.

discussion of values relevant to assessing what the public good requires can enrich understanding of relevant considerations. However, the deliberative democratic approach suggests that the best way of reaching an understanding of the common good, ultimately, is through decision-making procedures that are inclusive and deliberative. In this process, a multiplicity of values are likely to come into play.

This approach to the common good is consistent with the approach taken in the previous two subsections. Subsection A merely suggested that in evaluating institutional arrangements, outcome and process considerations are relevant. These considerations feature in arguments of writers associated with the republican political tradition and are also invoked in debate about the counter-majoritarian difficulty. Subsection B suggested that attached conceptions can be valuable in drawing our attention to certain considerations, but ultimately a pluralistic approach is desirable. Deliberative democratic theory, of course, is attached to democracy. Nevertheless, the ideal of deliberative and inclusive decision-making is sufficiently abstract to enable the generation of diverse institutional recommendations. Constitutional juries, I will suggest, could deepen the inclusive and deliberative quality of political systems.

IV. Deliberative Polls and the Counter-Majoritarian Difficulty

A. Deliberative Polls

While the last section explored some normative approaches to evaluating institutional arrangements, this section considers some empirical material relevant to constitutional juries. There has been substantial experimentation with bodies involving sortition in the last few decades.[83] The deliberative polls devised by James Fishkin have had the highest ambition in attempting to obtain statistically representative groups for deliberation.[84] I will focus upon them here.

With deliberative polls, several hundred citizens are brought together to deliberate on particular issues. Fishkin indicated that the deliberative polls were Athenian in inspiration. The idea was at least partly prompted by the question of whether the politics of face-to-face societies could be adapted to mass societies.[85] This question had been posed by Peter Laslett.[86] He saw ancient Athens as a face-to-face society.

---

[83] See, eg, J Gastil and P Levine (eds), *The Deliberative Democracy Handbook: Strategies for Effective Civic Engagement in the 21st Century* (San Francisco, CA, Jossey-Bass, 2005).

[84] J Mansbridge, 'Deliberative Polling as the Gold Standard' (2010) 19 *The Good Society* 55–62.

[85] J Fishkin and P Laslett, 'Introduction' in J Fishkin and P Laslett (eds), *Debating Deliberative Democracy* (Malden, MA, Blackwell, 2003) 1–6, 1.

[86] P Laslett, 'The Face to Face Society' in P Laslett (ed), *Philosophy, Politics and Society* (Oxford, Basil Blackwell & Mott, 1957) 157–71. Fishkin refers to 'polis envy' rather than Laslett himself.

He doubted that we could adapt that idea. He was, in effect, suggesting that we abandon 'polis envy'. Fishkin, however, suggested that the participants in deliberative polls would approach the conditions of face-to-face societies.[87]

It seems, though, that Athens did not have a face-to-face society. Laslett envisaged that in the People's Assembly, communal business could be decided through a meeting of the whole; he suggested an Athenian citizenry as low as 1,000. However, Hansen has more recently suggested around 30,000 citizens, with around 6,000 attending Assembly meetings.[88] Fishkin has subsequently acknowledged a lack of face-to-face discussion not only in the Assembly but also in Athenian bodies selected by sortition.[89] Voting occurred after hearing arguments from both sides; the processes did not incorporate any formal opportunity for citizens to deliberate with each other before voting. Fishkin, however, noted that a further Athenian connection for deliberative polls lay in the People's Court providing the closest historical parallel.[90] Indeed, there are parallels. The People's Court, with its large juries, could aspire to representativeness and could consider matters of broad public interest.

Fishkin combined this republican inspiration with the modern practice of opinion polling. Deliberative polls usually commence with a telephone survey of a statistically representative sample of the population.[91] The sample is then invited to participate in a weekend discussion concerned with the same issues canvassed by the survey.[92] Inducements include free accommodation, meals and travel and an honorarium. On the weekend, there is small-group discussion assisted by a moderator and plenary sessions in which questions decided upon in the small-group discussion can be put to experts taking contrasting positions on the issue under consideration. At the end of the weekend, the participants are again surveyed. Over 100 deliberative polls in 28 countries have been conducted between 1994 and 2018.[93]

---

[87] J Fishkin, *Democracy and Deliberation: New Directions for Democratic Reform* (New Haven, Yale University Press, 1991) 90–3.

[88] Hansen, *The Athenian Democracy* 92, 130. See also at 60.

[89] J Fishkin, *When the People Speak: Deliberative Democracy and Public Consultation* (Oxford, Oxford University Press, 2009) 12.

[90] Fishkin, *Democracy and Deliberation* 87.

[91] One exception is the deliberative poll in Mongolia on constitutional proposals, where face-to-face polling occurred on randomly selected individuals from randomly selected households: J Fishkin, 'Random Assemblies for Lawmaking? Prospects and Limits' (2018) 46 *Politics & Society* 359–79, 369, J Fishkin and G Zandanshatar, 'Deliberative Polling for Constitutional Change in Mongolia: An Unprecedented Experiment' (20 September 2017) *Constitutionnet Newsletter*: http://constitutionnet. org/news/deliberative-polling-constitutional-change-mongolia-unprecedented-experiment.

[92] There are also online polls, but the face-to-face polls seem likely to prompt greater deliberation: Fishkin, *When the People Speak* 170–1. For the first face-to-face poll, see R Luskin, J Fishkin and R Jowell, 'Considered Opinions: Deliberative Polling in Britain' (2002) 32 *British Journal of Political Science* 455–87.

[93] Center for Deliberative Democracy, *What Is Deliberative Polling?* from http://cdd.stanford.edu/ what-is-deliberative-polling/.

Fishkin has reported that those participating in the weekend discussions are attitudinally representative of the larger sample which participates in the telephone survey. In other words, the responses in the initial telephone survey to questions about the issues the focus of the deliberative poll are similar between those who do and those who do not go on to participate in the weekend discussion. Participants in the weekend discussion, Fishkin reports, are generally a bit older, better educated and more interested and knowledgeable about those issues than non-participants, but not by much.[94]

The polls often result in significant shifts in opinion.[95] Two examples will suffice. In a poll concerned with which party to vote for in the 1997 British election, support for the Conservatives and for Labour each decreased by 8 per cent and support for the Liberal Democrats increased by 20 per cent.[96] In a 2001 poll concerned with reconciliation between indigenous and non-indigenous Australians, there was over a 20 per cent increase in support for certain positions sympathetic to indigenous Australians, including an apology to the 'stolen generation', who were removed from their families.[97] The polls also typically produce gains in knowledge.[98] Indeed, the changes in opinion seem information-driven: those who gain the most knowledge are most likely to change their opinions. In summary, it seems that participants are fairly representative of the community. Furthermore, they are likely to express more rational opinions, in the sense of being better informed, in the final rather than the initial survey.

I mentioned earlier that Fishkin pointed to the Athenian People's Court as offering the closest historical parallel for deliberative polls. I refer here to two differences between them. One is that the Court made decisions while the polls issue opinions. Deliberative poll opinions might be an official input into decisions.[99] To give an example relevant to constitutionalism, in 2017, Mongolia passed legislation requiring a deliberative poll before a constitutional amendment could be considered by the legislature.[100] The conclusions of the poll that was subsequently conducted appear to have impacted upon the proposals being considered by the legislature.[101] Nevertheless, while the poll opinions may sometimes be influential,

---

[94] J Fishkin and R Luskin, 'Experimenting with a Democratic Ideal: Deliberative Polling and Public Opinion' (2005) 40 *Acta Politica* 284–98, 290. See also Fishkin, *When the People Speak* 118–19.

[95] Fishkin and Luskin, 'Experimenting with a Democratic Ideal' 290.

[96] Fishkin, *When the People Speak* 137–8.

[97] In relation to an apology, support increased from 46 to 68 per cent. See *Australia Deliberates: Reconciliation – Where from Here? Final Report*, Issues Deliberation Australia (Glenelg, South Australia, 2001) 55.

[98] Fishkin and Luskin, 'Experimenting with a Democratic Ideal' 291.

[99] Fishkin, 'Random Assemblies for Lawmaking?' 366.

[100] ibid 369.

[101] Fishkin and Zandanshatar, 'Deliberative Polling for Constitutional Change in Mongolia'. Other bodies chosen through sortition but not modelled on deliberative polls have also been involved in proposing constitutional change. In 2005, in British Columbia, a Citizens' Assembly met for a year and its favoured proposal for electoral reform was submitted to a referendum. See M Warren and H Pearce (eds), *Designing Deliberative Democracy: The British Columbia Citizens' Assembly* (Cambridge, Cambridge University Press, 2008).

they are only opinions. Fishkin is, in fact, critical of the decision-making power of the People's Court: the Court could make oppressive decisions, as symbolised by Socrates' trial.[102]

A second difference is that the juries in the Athenian People's Court voted through secret ballot straight after hearing the arguments from the parties or their representatives. By contrast, the deliberative polls feature not only plenary but also small-group sessions. Participants, it seems, view the small-group discussions as the most valuable part of the experience.[103] Experimental studies, however, have suggested that group discussion on factual questions can lead to worse decisions by a group than relying upon the statistical mean opinion of the group formed before group discussion.[104] Polarisation may occur. Here, the initial majority opinion prevails after social deliberation, but in a more extreme form. Those initially with minority views shift to what appears early in the deliberations to be the majority view, while those in the initial majority take more extreme positions. The concern is that the initial balance of opinion in the group strongly influences outcomes, independent of the force of the best arguments. Fishkin, though, has not found in deliberative polls a systematic tendency towards polarisation in the small groups. This may be due to the provision of balanced written material beforehand, anonymity in completing the final survey, and the use of moderators.[105]

It can nevertheless be said that it is unclear whether the structure of deliberative polls is optimal. Precisely what role the different components of the process have in achieving better opinions is uncertain: the questionnaires have generally been provided only at the beginning and end of the process.[106] Some polls have canvassed so many issues in the short time allocated to onsite deliberation that it seems questionable that those polls elicited highly rational opinions.[107] The polls

---

[102] Fishkin, *Democracy and Deliberation* 89.

[103] Fishkin, *When the People Speak* 120.

[104] C Sunstein, 'Group Judgments: Statistical Means, Deliberation, and Information Markets' (2005) 80 *New York University Law Review* 962–1049, 982. See also T Mendelberg, 'The Deliberative Citizen: Theory and Evidence' in M Delli Carpini, L Huddy and R Shapiro (eds), *Political Decision-Making, Deliberation and Participation* (Bingley, Emerald, 2002) 151–93.

[105] Sunstein, 'Group Judgments' 1011. See also B Ackerman and J Fishkin, *Deliberation Day* (New Haven, Yale University Press, 2004) 61–5. For research on ordinary juries used in legal proceedings, which employ procedures markedly different from those employed in deliberative polls, see W Abbott and J Batt (eds), *A Handbook of Jury Research* (Philadelphia, Pa, American Law Institute-American Bar Association Committee on Continuing Professional Education, 1999).

[106] Disaggregating the components has been attempted in some polls, though. See K Hansen, *Deliberative Democracy and Opinion Formation* (Odense, University Press of Southern Denmark, 2004) 196, C Farrar et al, 'Disaggregating Deliberation's Effects: An Experiment within a Deliberative Poll' (2010) 40 *British Journal of Political Science* 333–47.

[107] See, eg, the first deliberative poll, conducted in 1994 in Britain: R Luskin, J Fishkin and R Jowell, 'Considered Opinions: Deliberative Polling in Britain' (2002) 32 *British Journal of Political Science* 455–87, 468–9, 484. For some criticism of the polls, see R Gibson and S Mishkin, 'Australia Deliberates? The Role of the Media in Deliberative Polling' in J Warhurst and M Mackerras (eds), *Constitutional Politics: The Republic Referendum and the Future* (St Lucia, Qld., University of Queensland Press, 2002) 163–75; P Sturgis, C Roberts and N Allum, 'A Different Take on the Deliberative Poll: Information, Deliberation, and Attitude Constraint' (2005) 69 *Public Opinion Quarterly* 30–65, and D Merkle, 'The Polls – Review: The National Issues Convention Deliberative Poll' (1996) 60 *Public Opinion Quarterly* 588–619.

do, however, seem structured in a way likely to produce more rational opinions by a fairly representative sample of the community.

B. Implications for the Counter-Majoritarian Difficulty

One implication deliberative polls have for the counter-majoritarian difficulty is that they cast doubt upon the autonomy citizens exercise while voting. We can distinguish weak autonomy, where citizens vote in an informed way to achieve their self-interest, narrowly conceived, from strong autonomy, where citizens cast an informed vote in pursuit of the public interest.[108] The counter-majoritarian difficulty is greater where citizens exercise strong autonomy. First, the outcome-related justification for leaving issues of justice to legislatures unconstrained by judicial review is strengthened. While there is some looseness in the constraints imposed by majority opinion upon elected representatives – elections generally only provide a choice between policy packages and between a small number of candidates – it seems likely that a strongly autonomous citizenry would place substantial pressure upon legislators to promote just outcomes. Secondly, the process-intrinsic consideration of dignity is impaired to a greater extent by judicial review when citizens exercise strong autonomy in politics: it can then be argued that judicial review unfairly disparages citizens by implying that they do not exercise strong autonomy.[109] This was Waldron's argument. He urged academics to perceive popular disagreement in the way they view disagreement amongst themselves, that is, as disagreement amongst intelligent, morally conscientious individuals.[110]

It appears, though, that a significant number of citizens lack the information to exercise strong and even weak autonomy. The most substantial evidence has been gathered in the US, with comparative studies suggesting that other Western countries may not differ very substantially.[111] US polls have indicated that generally half the people admit either to having no idea where the Republican and Democratic parties stand on the issues of the day, or they get it wrong, placing the Republican Party to the left of the Democrats.[112] For example, with the 2000 Presidential

---

[108] The definitions of weak and strong autonomy here differ from those used in ch 6, s IIIB. Those definitions pointed to possession, rather than the exercise, of capacities.

[109] See above s IIIA.

[110] Waldron, *Law and Disagreement* 227–31.

[111] For reference to one cross-cultural study see J Mondak and D Canache, 'Knowledge Variables in Cross-National Social Inquiry' (2004) 85 *Social Science Quarterly* 539–58. *Cf* P Sturgis, N Allum and P Smith, 'The Measurement of Political Knowledge in Surveys' (2008) 72 *Public Opinion Quarterly* 90–102. There are, of course, national surveys as well. See, eg, I McAllister, 'Civic Education and Political Knowledge in Australia' (1998) 33 *Australian Journal of Political Science* 7–23, 11ff, *Whereas the People: Civics and Citizenship Education*, Report of the Civics Expert Group, (Canberra, Australian Government Publishing Service, 1994) 140 and, for Britain, R Andersen, A Heath and R Sinnott, 'Political Knowledge and Electoral Choice' (2002) 12 *Journal of Elections, Public Opinion & Parties* 11–27.

[112] Referred to in Luskin, Fishkin and Jowell, 'Considered Opinions' 457.

election between George W Bush and Al Gore, prominent issues in the campaign included the environment and abortion. Poll results on whether Gore was more supportive than Bush on environmental regulation and on abortion rights were worse than if the answers were randomly generated.[113] Across a broader range of political knowledge questions, the results also suggest low levels of political knowledge. Ilya Somin estimates that the percentage of those who appear to lack basic political knowledge relevant to understanding politics (as opposed to information, say, on home states of political candidates) is around 34 per cent.[114]

Some hope, however, that citizens can rely upon heuristic devices. In other words, while many citizens do not themselves have sufficient knowledge about politics, they can rely on shortcuts to ensure that their voting behaviour is similar to what it would have been if they had that knowledge. They may rely, for instance, on cues from respected opinion leaders.[115] Alternatively, errors of voters may cancel each other out.[116] Politicians would then face the same electoral constraints they would face if citizens generally exercised strong autonomy. In that case, the outcome-related argument against judicial review would be unaffected by the non-deliberative character of much voting.

Conventional surveys, however, have raised doubts about the possibility that election results are unaffected by deficits in deliberation by the electorate.[117] The significance of deliberative polls here is that they support these doubts. The 1997 deliberative poll in Britain mentioned in the last subsection demonstrated a significant shift in support for political parties once voters engaged in greater deliberation.

Indeed, the Australian poll on reconciliation referred to earlier reinforces liberal concern about majoritarian tyranny that motivates supporters of judicial review.[118] This poll indicated that the absence of deliberation can prejudice minority groups. Policies involving indifference or hostility towards the rights of minorities may appeal to a sufficient section of a non-deliberative public to be electorally rewarding.

Not only do deliberative polls support other evidence that a significant number of voters lack sufficient knowledge to exercise strong and even weak autonomy. That conclusion is rendered more palatable by findings from deliberative polls. Highlighting voter ignorance can seem condescending; it also sits well with anti-democratic thought or elite democratic theory.[119] However, the deliberative polls

---

[113] See I Somin, 'Political Ignorance and the Countermajoritarian Difficulty: A New Perspective on the Central Obsession of Constitutional Theory' (2004) 89 *Iowa Law Review* 1287–1371, 1306–9.

[114] ibid 1312.

[115] See ibid 1320.

[116] ibid 1323.

[117] See, eg, S Althaus, 'Information Effects in Collective Preferences' (1998) 92 *American Political Science Review* 545–8. In relation to the 2001 British election, see Andersen, Heath and Sinnott, 'Political Knowledge and Electoral Choice'.

[118] See text to above n 97. Other examples are also discussed in Fishkin, *When the People Speak* 161–9.

[119] See, eg, Held, *Models of Democracy* ch 5 on elite democratic theory.

indicate that when citizens are given the opportunity and incentive to deliberate on political questions, there is a willingness and capacity to do so. Citizens often lack a significant incentive to become politically well-informed. Given the near-impossibility of a citizen's vote affecting election results, citizens might often achieve more good in the lives of themselves and others if they devote themselves to other matters.[120] Following politics is more likely to be motivated by an interest in politics, and citizens' interests are, of course, diverse.

The last paragraph's reference to citizens being willing to deliberate when given appropriate opportunities and incentives does suggest faith in citizens' rationality. However, it should also be noted that a majority of those polled do not generally volunteer. Take, for example, the deliberative poll on reconciliation. Of the 1,220 who were interviewed for around 20 minutes by phone, only 334 attended the weekend discussion, despite follow-up phone calls to persuade the more reticent and to assist those otherwise unable to attend. Around 73 per cent, then, did not attend.[121] This finding too could be employed to support judicial review. One response to the low level of political knowledge in the electorate is to suggest measures to engage the citizenry as a whole in political discussion rather than relying on judicial review.[122] The deliberative poll experience sounds a cautionary note about the achievement of such a participatory society.

Altogether, there are findings from deliberative polls that seem supportive of judicial review. First, they confirm that lack of deliberation can affect election results and can lead to positions less sympathetic to minority groups. Secondly, they render more palatable findings of political ignorance: acceptance of such findings does not imply a disrespectful attitude towards citizens. Thirdly, the level of participation in deliberative polls suggests some caution in assuming that a participatory society can be achieved. If significant political ignorance is intractable, that again seems to support judicial review.

On the other hand, the findings are also helpful in questioning whether judicial review itself could be replaced by the use of juries engaged in constitutional review. Deliberative polls cast encouraging light on how representative and competent juries would be when dealing with policy questions. If the constitutional jury idea is attractive, it suggests a different counter-majoritarian concern. Judicial review would involve unwarranted elitism not based on the claim that the electoral system is less elitist and judicial review does not contribute significantly to the protection

---

[120] I Somin, *Democracy and Political Ignorance: Why Smaller Government Is Smarter* (Stanford, Stanford University Press, 2013) ch 3.

[121] *Australia Deliberates* 39. See Luskin, Fishkin and Jowell, 'Considered Opinions' 463 for a similar result with the first deliberative poll. On the other hand, the Mongolian deliberative poll dealing with proposals for constitutional amendment did not use telephone polls but face-to-face interviews of randomly selected household members, where those households were themselves randomly selected. Of those interviewed, 85 per cent attended the weekend deliberation (669 of 785): Fishkin, 'Random Assemblies for Lawmaking?' 369. Perhaps the potential to have a real impact encouraged participation.

[122] See, eg, B Barber, *Strong Democracy: Participatory Politics for a New Age*, 20th anniversary edn (Berkeley, Calif., University of California Press, 2003) 158–60.

of rights. Rather, the unwarranted elitism would lie in the possibility that a genuinely democratic body could engage instead in constitutional review.

V. Conclusion

This chapter has drawn attention to the republican device of sortition as a way of pursuing Michelman's idea of constitutional review being conducted by virtual representatives, an idea he connects to republican positive liberty. I turned to the Athenian People's Court to suggest how Michelman's idea might be realised: this court employed what can be described as constitutional juries. While this court took into account broad policy considerations, courts engaged in modern judicial review also take into account policy considerations. Not only does the republican tradition, through its origins in Athenian political practice and thought, provide the idea of constitutional juries, but Aristotle's links between sortition and democracy, and election and oligarchy, links later confirmed through Renaissance Florentine experience, are suggestive. These links suggest, for instance, that the counter-majoritarian difficulty need not be understood simply in terms of courts having greater freedom to depart from majority preferences.

Aristotle also referred to a mixed constitution combining democratic and oligarchic elements. The idea of a mixed constitution has been applied to modern democracies, with consideration of the implications of their exclusion of sortition from a substantial role. Sortition's absence from the US political system has been used by constitutional scholars to highlight the elitism of both electoral democracy and judicial review in a way that has been largely supportive of judicial review. However, the association of democracy with sortition has also led to the suggestion that constitutional juries could provide a more egalitarian approach to constitutional review than relying upon judges.

To assess such a proposal, it is helpful to identify relevant considerations. I distinguished outcome from process considerations. Both are found in arguments associated with the republican tradition as well as in contemporary discussion of judicial review. I then suggested that while conceptions of liberty can inform evaluation, caution needs to be exercised in applying conceptions that are attached to particular institutional forms. One such conception is liberty as non-domination, which is attached to electoral representation in contrast to sortition. I affirmed a pluralistic approach to the values that are relevant in evaluating institutions. This approach is, I suggest, also consistent with a deliberative democratic approach.

Turning to empirical evidence, some findings from deliberative polls can support judicial review. For instance, the significant information-driven shifts in opinion that occur with deliberative polls cast doubt on the deliberation underlying elections. On the other hand, promising findings about achieving representativeness through voluntary means and encouraging deliberation suggest that consideration of constitutional juries may be warranted.

9

A Citizens' Court: The Proposal

I. Introduction

The last chapter explored sortition as a republican device and its association with democracy. It mentioned that this association has been used to highlight the elitism of electoral democracy in order to defend judicial review. However, the association can also highlight the elitism of judicial review. Indeed, the example of the Athenian People's Court raises the question of whether constitutional juries may be attractive. Evidence from deliberative polls gives some cause for optimism that fairly representative groups can be formed without coercion and that they can engage in reasoned decision-making on policy questions. I suggested that if constitutional juries are attractive, a new counter-majoritarian difficulty would emerge. The unwarranted elitism of judicial review would lie in the possibility that a genuinely democratic body could engage instead in constitutional review and make sound decisions.

This chapter argues that constitutional juries may well be attractive. Demonstrating this is assisted by a concrete proposal and evaluation of it. This chapter proposes a Citizens' Court, which employs large juries. It is placed in the Australian context. Australia does not have a national justiciable bill of rights and this, perhaps, could lead to greater openness to alternative ways of protecting rights. On the other hand, the proposal made here is unlikely to be adopted any time soon. The proposal's immediate purpose is to throw light on the counter-majoritarian difficulty.

Section II sketches the proposal, and Sections III to V defend it. Section III mentions some advantages in placing sortition in the judicial rather than legislative branch of government. Section IV compares my proposal to strong-form judicial review. Section V considers Chris Zurn's critique of constitutional juries. Section VI concludes with some implications of my proposal for the counter-majoritarian difficulty. Constitutional juries may provide an exciting way to reconcile democracy with an aspect of constitutionalism – constitutional review. Constitutional juries may deepen democracy and also provide better protection for constitutional rights.

II. The Proposal

In situating my proposal in the Australian context, it should first be noted that the Constitution includes only a few express individual rights, and the High Court has only found a few implied rights.[1] While there is no national justiciable bill of rights, there is legislation requiring what can be described as 'political rights review'. This imposes an obligation upon the executive and parliament to scrutinise bills against a wide set of rights contained in international human rights instruments Australia has ratified.[2]

My proposal's relevance, though, is not limited to Australia. I rely on findings from deliberative polls conducted in several countries, including Britain and the US. Different perceptions of highest courts can also have a bearing upon the comparison between such courts and constitutional juries. For example, a sense that appointments to the highest court are influenced by partisan considerations would be stronger in the US than in Australia, partly influenced by the substantial power the Supreme Court has due to its bill of rights and the politically charged character of some of its decisions, with finding a right to an abortion being the most prominent one in the last 50 years. Different systems of judicial appointment can also have some bearing on this. In the US, the public confirmation hearings in the Senate can reinforce a sense of partisanship. In Australia, the government can simply appoint High Court judges. In some other common-law countries, including Britain, judicial appointments commissions have been introduced, which may lessen but, it would seem, not remove executive influence over appointments.[3] There are, of course, other variables. In Britain, for instance, there is ultimate recourse to the European Court of Human Rights. Nevertheless, British courts must only consider Strasbourg jurisprudence; they are not bound by it.[4] A Court employing large juries could provide a distinctive perspective on Convention and other rights.

I will now sketch the proposal. I explain some of its features, especially relating to the juries, by comparing them with the Athenian People's Court, deliberative polls, and Spector's proposal for constitutional juries. I will also refer to the process the Court could follow.

My proposed Citizens' Court would employ juries of around 200. I would suggest that the non-coercive process found with deliberative polls be tried. As with deliberative polls, there would be a modest reward for participation and, if

---

[1] G Williams and D Hume, *Human Rights under the Australian Constitution*, 2nd edn (Melbourne, Oxford University Press, 2013) ch 4.

[2] See T Campbell and S Morris, 'Human Rights for Democracies: A Provisional Assessment of the Australian *Human Rights (Parliamentary Scrutiny) Act 2011*' (2015) 34 *University of Queensland Law Journal* 7–27.

[3] P Russell, 'Conclusion' in K Malleson and P Russell (eds), *Appointing Judges in an Age of Judicial Power: Critical Perspectives from around the World* (Toronto, University of Toronto Press, 2006) 420–35. Perhaps the perception of political appointments is weaker in the UK than in Australia. On the UK, see KD Ewing, 'A Theory of Democratic Adjudication: Towards a Representative, Accountable and Independent Judiciary' (2000) 38 *Alberta Law Review* 708–33, 729.

[4] Human Rights Act 1998, s 2.

necessary, stratification to achieve a representative group in terms of gender, age, socio-economic status and locality.[5] It may also be possible, depending upon the issue under consideration, to assess attitudinal representativeness. As with deliberative polls, jurors would receive free accommodation and travel for the on-site deliberation, child-care (if necessary) and an honorarium.

Avoiding compelled participation on the juries might enhance the level of deliberation. With deliberative polls, the group participating in the weekend deliberation is slightly better educated, older and more knowledgeable than the group participating in the telephone poll. Interestingly, the requirement that jurors on the Athenian People's Court be over 30 might have reflected a desire for a body of more mature and knowledge citizens than those participating in the Assembly. If the Citizens' Court achieves this simply as a function of willingness to participate, it may not be necessary to correct this through stratification.

Avoiding compulsion does, however, constrain the commitment that can be sought from jurors; the larger the commitment, the less representative the juries would be. Deliberative polls require a commitment for a weekend. Written material is provided before the weekend of deliberation, but that seems to prompt less deliberation than what occurs on the weekend.[6] Compulsion is an aspect of criminal juries, and criminal trials can last weeks. Especially where a two-day trial in the Citizens' Court would be insufficient, compulsion may be necessary. As the next paragraph indicates, representativeness is a weighty criterion.

My proposal follows the Athenian People's Court and deliberative polls in having substantial juries and a secret ballot. Such substantial juries, together with drawing people from around the country, would be expensive. It might also be thought that in small juries, such as common-law juries of 12 or Spector's proposed constitutional juries of 36 to 72, jurors enjoy greater participatory opportunities and a greater incentive to deliberate, since each vote counts for more.[7] The principal advantage of large juries, though, is that a plausible claim can be made that they are representative of the community. I would suggest that the juries would only be able to find a violation of rights if a majority of 60 per cent is obtained. This supermajoritarian requirement, together with the size of the juries, can enhance confidence that decisions made by the Citizens' Court might well reflect what the community's deliberative view on the matter would be. At the same time,

[5] R Luskin, J Fishkin and R Jowell, 'Considered Opinions: Deliberative Polling in Britain' (2002) 32 *British Journal of Political Science* 455–87, 462.

[6] J Fishkin, *When the People Speak: Deliberative Democracy and Public Consultation* (Oxford, Oxford University Press, 2009) 120.

[7] N Crosby and D Nethercut, 'Citizens Juries: Creating a Trustworthy Voice of the People' in J Gastil and P Levine (eds), *The Deliberative Democracy Handbook: Strategies for Effective Civic Engagement in the 21st Century* (San Francisco, CA, Jossey-Bass, 2005) 111–19, 113. See also H Spector, 'The Right to a Constitutional Jury' (2009) III *Legisprudence* 111–123, 118 and above ch 8, s IIC.

the supermajority required is not so stringent as to induce too many false negatives (where the court wrongly fails to find a contravention of a right). Partly to safeguard against false positives (wrong findings of a rights contravention), I will recommend that the Senate should have the power to abrogate Citizens' Court decisions.

To invalidate decisions of a democratically elected legislature, the body must enjoy substantial legitimacy. Having a body that can make a plausible claim to being representative of the community is likely to be helpful in furthering the process consideration of popular legitimacy. In terms of outcomes, I mentioned the concern that jurors on larger juries may have less incentive to deliberate, since their individual responsibility is less. However, the Citizens' Court would, like deliberative polls, employ small-group discussion as well: this is likely to prompt deeper individual engagement with the issues. At the same time, the large juries increase the chance of including people with diverse perspectives.

I propose that the Court would be entrusted with a bill of rights that includes the standard civil and political rights, but also social welfare rights, which are less commonly justiciable.[8] I would suggest that there also be a catch-all phrase to capture serious contraventions of the public interest. I will not, however, discuss the content of the proposed bill of rights: the general idea of constitutional juries is of greater interest. In relation to social rights, I merely direct the reader to Cécile Fabre's defence of their inclusion.[9] While Fabre defends a judicial role in interpreting social rights, Section III will claim that constitutional juries may have an advantage over judges in interpreting such rights. In relation to a provision referring to serious contraventions of the public interest, the juries are thereby not constrained by a particular formulation of liberal rights. There is a similarity here with the duties suggested by the oath taken by those on the Athenian People's Court: to vote in accordance with law or their sense of justice in cases not covered by law.[10]

I turn now to the procedure that could be employed. The initial step would lie in applications to the Court by parties claiming a contravention of the bill of rights. The government would then file a defence, and the applicants, a reply. Perhaps twice a year, applications, taking into account the defence and reply, would be

---

[8] Social welfare rights are also referred to as 'social rights', 'social and economic rights' or 'positive rights'. They include, for instance, a right to shelter and a right to minimum subsistence. See M Tushnet, 'Social Welfare Rights and the Forms of Judicial Review' (2004) 82 *Texas Law Review* 1895–1919, 1895 fn 2; M Tushnet, *Weak Courts, Strong Rights: Judicial Review and Social Welfare Rights in Comparative Constitutional Law* (Princeton, Princeton University Press, 2008).

[9] C Fabre, *Social Rights under the Constitution: Government and the Decent Life* (Oxford, Clarendon Press, 2000).

[10] M Hansen, *The Athenian Democracy in the Age of Demosthenes: Structure, Principles and Ideology*, trans, JA Crook (Oxford, Basil Blackwell, 1991) 182–3. This was referred to above in IIA.

ranked in a process aimed at ensuring that a case-selection jury can make an informed selection of the cases to be heard within the following year. To increase the chance that case-selection juries are presented with a diversity of perspectives on how to rank applications, there should be some diversity on the advisory panel that would write recommendations on what cases should be selected. The two main parties represented in the Senate are the Labor Party and the Liberal Party: they are left- and right-of centre parties. With the Senate being elected through proportional representation, there are also minority parties and independents. A Senate Committee including minority party representation could provide lists of preferred candidates for the four-member advisory panel. From these lists, advisors for a particular panel could be selected by sortition, constrained to ensure that the panels consist of advisors supported by at least three parties, two of whom are currently not in government.[11]

The case-selection trials would be presided over by a Federal Court judge assisted by two other Federal Court judges. The judges themselves would be subject to a confidential nomination process involving the aforementioned Senate Committee. For the sake of diversity, the three judges on each trial should be supported by different parties, at least one of which is not in government. Having an odd number of judges could tilt each panel in a right- or left-wing direction, but at least achieving some diversity on each panel should encourage greater moderation.[12] The judges would not be publicly identified by the Court in terms of which party they were nominated by. The judges would be responsible for ensuring that the case-selection jurors are presented with material that summarises the views expressed by the members of the case-selection advisory panel in a fair and accessible way. Members of the case-selection advisory panel would be available for questioning in plenary sessions at the trial. Small-group discussion would also occur. The judges would be able to offer guidance to the jury before it selects a small number of cases to be heard.

Once a matter is selected for a hearing, there would be preliminary hearings aimed at defining the issues in the trial and ensuring that the parties' arguments are sufficiently accessible so that they can be adequately considered over a weekend, if this is possible. The preliminary hearings would be presided over by three judges, selected again to achieve some diversity. Those preliminary hearings would also resolve factual controversies so the focus in the jury hearing would be on

---

[11] Where there is an absence of minority parties, independents could be selected to achieve the diversity sought on the Senate Committee. In 'Deliberative Democracy and the Countermajoritarian Difficulty: Considering Constitutional Juries' (2010) 30 *Oxford Journal of Legal Studies* 327–59, 346–7, I suggested there that the panellists must be Federal Court judges. That might overly restrict the diversity on the panels.

[12] C Sunstein, 'Group Judgments: Statistical Means, Deliberation, and Information Markets' (2005) 80 *New York University Law Review* 962–1049, 987–8.

normative matters. The determination of preliminary matters would be subject to appeal to a jury of 12 with a supermajoritarian requirement of nine for an appeal to be upheld. This appellate jury could provide a short statement of reasons after consulting with the instructing judge. The rationale for this appellate mechanism is to achieve some popular control over the preliminary determinations. The appellate jury could come from the larger case-deciding jury with some stratification to enhance representativeness. The supermajoritarian requirement would ensure that appeals do not occur too readily. The appeals would be against decisions by three judges, not a single judge.

Turning to the main hearing, the case-deciding jury could make declarations and orders if, as mentioned earlier, a majority of 60 per cent is reached. It could declare invalid legislation or executive action, declare how a statutory provision should be interpreted in order to avoid conflict with the bill of rights, or issue orders to the executive branch of government. The jury would also issue a short statement of reasons. This statement could be derived once the majority jurors vote on one or more possible rationales for their decision.

However, the Senate, with a majority of 60 per cent, would have the power to abrogate the Citizens' Court declaration or orders. It is extremely unlikely that a governing party or coalition would alone be able to achieve such a supermajority.[13] Support, say, from minority parties and independents may permit such a supermajority in the absence of support from the main party in opposition. If parliament attempts to circumvent this requirement for a supermajority by, for instance, passing legislation similar to that declared invalid, a majority amongst, ideally, the three judges involved in the trial that declared the legislation invalid could issue further declarations or orders to enforce the jury's declarations or orders. No other court would have this power. The bill of rights employed by the Citizens' Court would not be justiciable by other courts. The Citizens' Court could, however, co-exist with the existing political rights review.[14]

The power of abrogation by a supermajority in the Senate constrains the power of the Citizens' Court, which seems appropriate for a new institution that would lack the popular legitimacy of the elected branches of government. The Citizens' Court would also engage in a limited number of interventions. I sum up some features of the proposal in the diagram below.

---

[13] See S Bach, *Platypus and Parliament: The Australian Senate in Theory and Practice* (Canberra, Department of the Senate, 2003) 50, 158–9. For the type of minority parties represented, see Z Ghazarian, 'The Changing Type of Minor Party Elected to Parliament: The Case of the Australian Senate from 1949 to 2010' (2012) 47 *Australian Journal of Political Science* 441–54.

[14] See above n 2.

Figure 9.1 A Citizens' Court

Selection of cases

- Applications filed in court, followed by defence and reply
- Case-selection advisory panel makes recommendations
- Case-selection jury makes final selection

Determination of selected cases

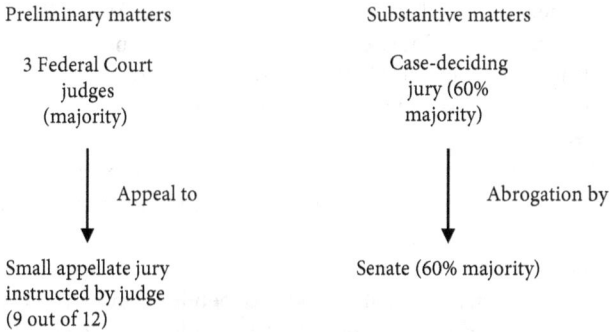

Preliminary matters	Substantive matters
3 Federal Court judges (majority)	Case-deciding jury (60% majority)
↓ Appeal to	↓ Abrogation by
Small appellate jury instructed by judge (9 out of 12)	Senate (60% majority)

III. A Comparison with Sortition in Parliament

This section explains some advantages in placing sortition in the judicial branch of government. In the last chapter, I challenged Lanni's suggestion that the Athenian People's Court has a greater affinity to bicameralism than to the Supreme Court.[15] However, a body involving sortition could be placed in the legislative branch. That would, in fact, have republican credentials, given the *nomothetai*. In fact, there have been proposals in the UK and the US to employ sortition in one of two houses of parliament.[16] My proposal, however, is more modest. I envisage juries sitting for

---

[15] See ch 8, s IIB.

[16] For the UK, see K Sutherland, *A People's Parliament: A (Revised) Blueprint for a Very English Revolution* (Exeter, Imprint Academic, 2008) (focusing on the House of Commons and referring to republicanism including Harrington) and A Barnett and P Carty, *The Athenian Option: Radical Reform for the House of Lords* [1998] (Exeter, Imprint Academic, 2008). For the US, see E Callenbach and M Phillips, *A Citizen Legislature* [1985] (Exeter, Imprint Academic, 2008) (focusing on the House of Representatives) and K O'Leary, *Saving Democracy: A Plan for Real Representation in America* (Stanford, Calif, Stanford University Press, 2006) for assemblies to supplement Congress. *Cf* J Fishkin, 'Random Assemblies for Lawmaking? Prospects and Limits' (2018) 46 *Politics & Society* 359–79. Perhaps the most radical proposal for sortition is in J Burnheim, *Is Democracy Possible? The Alternative to Electoral Politics* (Cambridge, Polity Press, 1985). For a more modest proposal, see B Barber, *Strong Democracy: Participatory Politics for a New Age*, 20th anniversary edn (Berkeley, Calif, University of California Press, 2003) ch 10.

a weekend. The juries would not exercise general review over all bills but would only hear a small number of cases a year. The limited commitment from each juror should enable a more representative group of citizens. It also involves jurors in a setting not so far removed from deliberative polls, for which there is experimental evidence.[17]

On the other hand, individuals selected by lot could have quite limited terms in parliament. Barnett and Carty have suggested that the UK House of Lords could largely consist of individuals selected by lot, with them being allocated to juries of around 70 members, each of which would focus on a particular bill.[18] One task would be to review that bill for conformity with basic constitutional values.[19] The jurors would meet perhaps over a year at certain times. While Barnett and Carty suggest that the reformed House of Lords would complement rather than compete with elected politicians in the House of Commons, my proposal presents, I will suggest, a lesser challenge to the elected branches of government.[20] My proposal may therefore be more politically feasible: the support of governments will be necessary for the implementation and continuation of an institution involving sortition. It is also appropriate for a relatively untested institution to have a subordinate status to electoral representation.

One way my proposal presents a lesser challenge to the elected branches is that it involves concrete constitutional review: it depends upon parties claiming that in a particular case, their rights have been violated. With the passage of time between legislation being enacted and the review occurring, the political agenda may have moved on to other issues, thereby possibly reducing the extent to which the executive's political priorities are challenged by any invalidation of the legislation. With its reliance upon parties bringing a case claiming their rights have been violated, concrete review has greater affinity with the judicial than the legislative branch.[21] This contrasts with abstract constitutional review.[22] Abstract *judicial* review tends to be initiated by a specified parliamentary minority and enables the constitutional court to declare a statute invalid before it commences.

The second way that my proposal offers a lesser challenge to the electoral branch is that the proposal can be conceptualised as extending the jury system from the criminal to the constitutional arena. Placing sortition in the judicial

---

[17] For this, and some other criticisms of using sortition in parliament, see Fishkin, 'Random Assemblies for Lawmaking?' 364–6.

[18] Barnett and Carty, *Athenian Option* 40.

[19] ibid 37.

[20] ibid 24.

[21] For a proposal to introduce abstract review in Australia, see G Winterton, 'An Australian Rights Council' (2001) 24 *University of New South Wales Law Journal* 792–9.

[22] See W Sadurski, *Rights before Courts: A Study of Constitutional Courts in Postcommunist States of Central and Eastern Europe* (Dordrecht, Springer, 2005) chs 2 and 3.

branch suggests that the jurors have a different role from legislators. The suggestion that constitutional juries could be conceptualised as an extension of a common-law practice might seem, however, at odds with chapter eight's point that the common-law practice is quite different in that jury nullification has an exceptional character.[23] However, while I tease out republican connections in these chapters, there is no intention to exclude other connections from being considered or highlighted.

Finally, I note the possibility of placing in the executive branch a body selected by sortition and having a role similar to constitutional review. In my 2010 articulation of a proposal for a Citizens' Court, I suggested that an incremental step towards constitutional juries would be to vest in a body selected by sortition the power to make delegated legislation that overrides parliamentary legislation inconsistent with certain rights.[24] Such a step should not require an amendment to the Australian Constitution, but would also not enjoy the legitimacy derived from constitutional entrenchment. As a delegated law-making body, it would also not be perceived as easily as an extension of common-law juries. On the other hand, it would clearly be subordinate to Parliament, and it may therefore mount a lesser challenge to electoral democracy than employing sortition within parliament. My focus in this chapter, though, is on constitutional juries.

IV. A Comparison with Strong-Form Judicial Review

I will now defend my proposal by arguing that it may well be superior to the High Court exercising strong-form judicial review.[25] With this, parliament cannot through ordinary legislation abrogate judicial interpretations of rights even though those interpretations might lead to legislative provisions being declared invalid. Instead, a supermajority in parliament may be required, or the agreement of State Parliaments, or a referendum. These types of requirements are associated with constitutional amendment, but I am defining strong-form judicial review as involving any requirement more stringent than an ordinary parliamentary majority. Since I suggest a supermajoritarian requirement for the Senate to abrogate Citizens' Court decisions, this Court would exercise strong-form constitutional review.

In comparing these institutions, I consider outcome- and process-related values. The last chapter mentioned that doubts about the democratic legitimacy of

---

[23] See ch 8, s I.

[24] Ghosh, 'Deliberative Democracy and the Countermajoritarian Difficulty' 357.

[25] For a comparison with weak-form judicial review, see ibid 353–5.

judicial review rest on concern that judicial review diminishes these values.[26] This subsection argues that those values may be better promoted by a Citizens' Court than by judicial review. Furthermore, a Citizens' Court could enhance the political system as a whole.

I start with process considerations. The last chapter mentioned Michelman's attempt to reconcile constitutional review with positive liberty.[27] Michelman suggested that judges, as virtual representatives, could represent positive liberty to the community. The first puzzle this raises is how those involved in constitutional review could be plausibly perceived as virtual representatives. This puzzle could be solved if jurors substituted for judges.

The second puzzle is how virtual representatives can represent positive liberty to the community. With full-blown positive liberty, citizens are only free when pursuing the common good. Chapter seven suggested that with an integral aspect of positive liberty lying in self-government, virtual representation can only have a limited capacity to symbolically promote positive liberty.[28] Thus, having constitutional juries would not solve this second puzzle.

However, Priceian liberty indicates how constitutional juries can symbolically connect to positive liberty. A positive-liberty dimension in Price lies in valuing the franchise for its affirmation of the potential of citizens to exercise positive liberty on political matters. This affirmation confers upon citizens what I have described as democratic status.[29] The provision of the opportunity to select between parties and candidates in an election does, indeed, suggest some faith in the autonomy of citizens. On the other hand, it need not express much faith: it may instead be justified on the basis that the popular legitimacy of a regime is dependent upon the franchise. The Citizens' Court would supplement the democratic status conferred by the franchise. By empowering citizens themselves to decide challenges to government policy on important questions of justice, the Citizens' Court conveys greater confidence in the autonomy that citizens can exercise. If such confidence in ordinary citizens is justified, the Court furthers the process-intrinsic consideration of dignity.

Price also suggested that democratic status could stimulate citizens to exercise their rational capacities: this is a process-instrumental rather than process-intrinsic argument for democracy. Along these lines, one might argue that the greater confidence in citizens expressed by the Citizens' Court could enhance citizens' sense of efficacy and their attention to politics. This effect, however, may be quite weak,

---

[26] See ch 8, s IIIA.
[27] See ch 8, s I.
[28] See ch 7, s IVC.
[29] See ch 6, s IVB.

with the possible exception of that tiny proportion of the population who would have sat on constitutional juries.[30]

Another significant process consideration is popular procedural legitimacy, understood here in terms of popular attitudes towards institutions where those attitudes derive largely from the process adopted rather than from the decisions made. Judges are drawn from an elite group within the legal profession and political appointments by one party may dominate benches. By contrast, large juries would have a strong claim to being representative of the people, a powerful source of legitimacy.[31] Indeed, the openness of the political system to representative deliberative opinion achieved through the Citizens' Court may enhance the legitimacy of the political system as a whole. Popular attitudes towards institutions, however, may depend upon a range of contingencies. The cultural preconditions for popular legitimacy are also difficult to assess. It may be that constitutional juries should only be proposed as an institution ripe for adoption if the use of mini-publics (small representative groups of citizens) becomes more widespread, better known and better accepted. There has been substantial interest in and practice with mini-publics, which goes beyond deliberative polls. Deliberative polls are more expensive than using smaller groups, say, in the form of planning cells, citizens' juries, and so on, which may involve between 12 and 25 participants.[32] Perhaps through experimentation with diverse types of mini-publics, some greater legitimacy might attach to them.

A process-related consideration against the Citizens' Court is cost. This is addressed here by a cap of a small number of hearings each year. Case-selection juries can be guided to choose a small number of cases, with some flexibility where such juries make a strong recommendation that some additional matters be heard. Undoubtedly, judicial review could consider a larger number of matters, due to its lesser cost. However, the disadvantage of the Citizens' Court deciding fewer matters should not be overstated. It is first worth noting that while the juries will only hear a small number of cases, case-selection advisory panels would express opinions about many applications. With the panels enjoying some diversity and having members likely to command some respect, their opinions, especially to the extent that there is substantial agreement, could signal to politicians and citizens that certain applications merit attention, regardless of whether they are ultimately heard by a case-deciding jury. Secondly, while judicial review can handle a larger volume of cases, many cases can involve matters which are finely balanced. The

---

[30] R Luskin and J Fishkin, 'Deliberation and "Better Citizens"' (Research paper, 2002) available from http://cdd.stanford.edu/research/.

[31] For empirical support for Australians' receptiveness to randomly selected citizens having constitutional functions, see R Levy, 'Breaking the Constitutional Deadlock: Lessons from Deliberative Experiments in Constitutional Change' (2010) 34 *Melbourne University Law Review* 805–38.

[32] See, eg, J Gastil and P Levine (eds), *The Deliberative Democracy Handbook: Strategies for Effective Civic Engagement in the 21st Century* (San Francisco, CA, Jossey-Bass, 2005).

case-selection process for the Citizens' Court may exclude such matters with little loss to justice. The Court would hear those matters it views as most significant. Thirdly, with constitutional juries, a broader bill of rights may be possible, including social welfare rights and a catch-all provision, since the juries would enjoy some democratic legitimacy. In this way, they may hear significant matters that would not be heard through judicial review.

Turning now to the outcome consideration, I will focus here on the quality of the decisions made. Chapter eight indicated that with deliberative polls, fairly representative groups of citizens are prepared to spend time deliberating on policy questions, they gain knowledge through the process and are open to revising their views in light of that knowledge.[33] The comparative competence of jurors versus judges will be discussed by applying factors relevant to sound decision-making: diversity, analytical skills, extent of reflection, empathy, and capacity and willingness to act on understandings of justice reached.

The first factor is diversity. Interacting directly with fellow decision-makers with different perspectives can heighten deliberation. It can prompt consideration of other perspectives and interests. The assumption here is that decisions are more likely to be correct if they take into account a wider range of relevant considerations.

The juries are very likely to be more diverse in their perspectives than High Court benches. There is not only the matter of diversity with respect to gender and social background.[34] Partisan appointments can impact more strongly upon the diversity of perspective on benches. Given that High Court judges in Australia can exercise significant power, including invalidating or restrictively interpreting the government's legislation even in the absence of a bill of rights, it is hardly surprising that Australian governments use their power of appointment to promote judges who 'are known to be in general sympathy with … [their] own aims and perspectives'.[35]

The second factor is analytical skills. This favours judges. Analytical skills increase in importance, however, with the complexity and volume of material to be digested. For a Citizens' Court to reach a good standard of reasoning, the jurors

---

[33] See ch 8, s IVA.

[34] With respect to gender, see R Davis and G Williams, 'Reform of the Judicial Appointments Process: Gender and the Bench of the High Court of Australia' (2003) 27 *Melbourne University Law Review* 819–63.

[35] M Spry, 'Executive and High Court Appointments' in G Lindell and B Bennet (eds), *Parliament: The Vision in Hindsight* (Sydney, Federation Press, 2001) 419–53, 448 referring to Gareth Evans, 'The Politics of Justice: An Agenda for Reform', *Victorian Fabian Pamphlet* no 33 (Melbourne, 1981). Gareth Evans became Attorney-General in 1983. This is not to deny that judges sometimes decide contrary to the ideological leaning of the government that selected them nor to deny the complexity of the relationship between general political ideology and particular cases. See also P Donegan, 'The Role of the Commonwealth Attorney-General in Appointing Judges to the High Court of Australia' (2003) 29 *Melbourne Journal of Politics* 40–55.

would need accessible information. The preliminary processes should achieve this, enabling jurors to focus on the trade-offs between competing values that bill-of-rights cases generally entail.

An impression of great complexity in interpreting rights can be conveyed by case-law. However, this complexity is partly based on attempts to reconcile decisions with precedent and authoritative texts. There is a strong tradition of legal reasoning that seeks authority for decisions through interpretations of a substantial body of legal material. At least outside the context of judicial decision-making, that technicality and complexity is unnecessary for reaching sound moral decisions. Waldron, in fact, argues that legal reasoning can detract from reaching sound moral decisions.[36] Even within the context of judicial decision-making, the extent to which judges should emphasise coherence with a wide body of material is controversial.[37] A Citizens' Court is likely to focus on the competing values relevant to a case. To the extent that the Court considers its past decisions, those decisions would involve a short statement of reasons, not lengthy judgments.

Turning to the third factor, which is the degree of reflection before making a decision, judges would have some advantages over jurors. Judges have a greater chance of influencing results, for only a few sit together on a case. They also have a larger reputational interest at stake, due to their greater exposure to scrutiny. Writing a judgment is likely to prompt more deliberation than merely voting in favour or against the applicant and endorsing an underlying principle together with a short statement of justification. On the other hand, judges devote a significant amount of the time spent in drafting judgments on demonstrating that their decisions are authorised by previous cases and authoritative texts, in contrast to engaging in substantial and open discussion of the competing policy considerations. Jurors are likely to focus on the competing policy considerations.

The fourth factor is a capacity to empathise with others. This facilitates taking proper account of the perspectives and interests of others. This capacity is unlikely to correlate neatly with analytical skills. Indeed, a government with an ideology that reflects a lack of empathy for certain groups in the community may seek judges with a similar bent.[38]

Finally, there is the willingness of decision-makers to decide in accordance with their conscientious view of what justice requires. The counter-majoritarian concern can lead judges to doubt their moral authority to invalidate acts by the other branches of government. Indeed, governments may prefer judges inclined

---

[36] J Waldron, 'The Core of the Case against Judicial Review' (2006) 115 *Yale Law Journal* 1346–1406, 1383–4 (referred to above in ch 8, s IIIA).

[37] J Raz, 'The Relevance of Coherence' (1992) 72 *Boston University Law Review* 273–321; *cf* R Dworkin, *Justice in Robes* (Cambridge, Mass, Belknap Press, 2006) ch 2.

[38] See, eg, Y Hasson et al, 'Are Liberals and Conservatives Equally Motivated to Feel Empathy toward Others?' (2018) 44(10) *Personality and Social Psychology Bulletin* 1449–59 on the relationship between empathy and ideology.

towards deference.[39] Judges may also be concerned that the stock of popular goodwill towards courts could be depleted if their decisions are resented by the public or government. Judges are likely to be especially reluctant to interpret social welfare rights, for their interpretation may appear to pose a greater challenge to the government's priorities. In this way, civil and political rights may be privileged over social welfare rights. Undue deference towards the government is, however, unlikely to be demonstrated by a Citizens' Court. The government cannot stack this court with members who favour deference towards the elected branches. While there could be concern that jurors may be overly deferential towards the expert opinions they are presented with, jurors would receive conflicting expert opinions, necessitating a choice between them.

To sum up, this subsection first argued that a Citizens' Court may better promote process values than strong-form judicial review, although hearing each matter would be more costly. The Court has the potential to enjoy greater popular procedural legitimacy. I then argued that a Citizens' Court may well make sounder decisions even though judges are likely to have sharper analytical skills than average jurors. Jurors would have the advantage of greater diversity and greater independence from the government. If a Citizens' Court makes sounder decisions, the process-intrinsic consideration of appropriately recognising citizens' autonomy would also be promoted.

While the direct comparison here was between the Citizens' Court and the High Court, this discussion was premised on the view that relying on the political process alone to protect rights may not be optimal. The last chapter referred to some findings from deliberative polls which support concerns by supporters of judicial review about the political process. In the present chapter, I suggested that the Citizens' Court could reinforce the process-intrinsic consideration of democratic status, in comparison to the current political system. In suggesting that the Citizens' Court may well promote outcome considerations better than the High Court, the suggestion is, as well, that a Citizens' Court can improve the outcomes of the political process overall. It can enhance the inclusive and deliberative quality of the political process through providing an additional forum through which issues can be ventilated and considered. The breadth of the bill of rights possible with a Citizens' Court might also be helpful in opening the political system to inclusive and deliberative public opinion. While the decisions of the Citizens' Court would be subject to parliamentary abrogation, those decisions could be highly influential due to the popular legitimacy the court would hopefully enjoy.

---

[39] There is a perception that this occurred in Australia especially under the conservative government lead by John Howard. See J Pierce, *Inside the Mason Court Revolution: The High Court of Australia Transformed* (Durham, NC, Carolina Academic Press, 2006) 279–84.

V. Zurn's Critique

Zurn provided the most substantial critique of my first presentation of a proposal for constitutional juries and also of Spector's proposal for constitutional juries.[40] He saw similar problems with both proposals. His thoughtful critique has prompted some revisions and clarifications, which will be referred to below. The main part of this subsection, though, is a defence against his criticisms. The literature also contains general criticisms of providing mini-publics with decision-making power, but I will focus on Zurn's specific critique of constitutional juries.[41]

Zurn takes a deliberative democratic approach inspired by Jurgen Habermas. With this approach, autonomy is the central value, and this value is best promoted through deliberative democratic processes that are safeguarded through constitutional rules, rules that protect citizens' private and public autonomy.[42] Those constitutional rules must be ones that citizens can understand that they are the authors of. Zurn suggests that there is likely to be disagreement over whether constitutional rules have been violated, and it is therefore important that the function of constitutional review should be institutionalised.[43]

He suggests three desiderata for institutionalizing constitutional review. The first one is structural independence from the parties involved in the dispute: 'the referees responsible for policing the rules of the game should not themselves have ... any special alignment with any of the competing parties'.[44] The second is legal integrity. He says that constitutions are, in part, law, and this gives rise to a desire for legal integrity, that is, 'the systematic coherence of the entire corpus of a nation's law'.[45] Zurn especially has the nation's constitutional law in mind. He suggests that decisions should be consistent with past decisions and should set out rules and principles that provide guidance for other litigants. The third desideratum is democratic sensitivity.[46] Institutions must be open to the various opinions and perspectives of those potentially affected by their decisions. While constitutional lawmaking is a power that belongs to the people, some degree of constitutional legislation is inevitable with constitutional review; hence, the importance of this desideratum.

---

[40] C Zurn, 'Judicial Review, Constitutional Juries and Civic Constitutional Fora: Rights, Democracy and Law' (2011) 58 *Theoria* 63–94, Another critique is in J Colón-Ríos, 'The Counter-Majoritarian Difficulty and the Road Not Taken: Democratizing Amendment Rules' (2012) 25 *Canadian Journal of Law and Jurisprudence* 53–78.

[41] See, eg, C Lafont, 'Deliberation, Participation, and Democratic Legitimacy: Should Deliberative Mini-Publics Shape Public Policy?' (2015) 23 *Journal of Political Philosophy* 40–63, C Lafont, *Democracy without Shortcuts: A Participatory Conception of Deliberative Democracy* (Oxford, Oxford University Press, 2020).

[42] Zurn, 'Judicial Review, Constitutional Juries and Civic Constitutional Fora' 70.

[43] ibid 71–2.

[44] ibid 72.

[45] ibid 73.

[46] ibid 74.

Zurn's desiderata cover important considerations, and I will focus on his application of them. Zurn begins with judicial review. He says it performs well against the desiderata of independence and legal integrity. However, it does poorly on democratic sensitivity. He nevertheless supports judicial review and seeks to ameliorate its lack of democratic sensitivity through proposing a more democratic constitutional amendment process. Mentioning his proposal here will be helpful in understanding his critique of constitutional juries.

The first and fourth steps of his proposed constitutional amendment process draw on procedures followed in citizen-initiated referendums: the first step involves collecting sufficient signatures from citizens in favour of an initiative, and the fourth and concluding step is a referendum.[47] The two intermediate steps aim to render the process more deliberative. With the second step, three 'deliberative democratic assemblies' spaced over a significant time span would occur, and only if all three approve of an initiative would it be certified.[48] Those assemblies would be modelled on deliberative polls. The third step is a Deliberation Day, where all interested citizens participate in modified deliberative polls held in their locality to evaluate the certified initiatives.[49] This Deliberation Day would occur on a national holiday, with citizens receiving US$150 if they participate. It would occur soon before the referendum.

Against this background, Zurn's criticisms of constitutional juries can be explored. Zurn argues that my proposal does reasonably well on independence, but the effectiveness of constitutional juries is crucially compromised in three ways. First, the Citizens' Court is only concerned with individual rights violations by the executive, rather than with legislation.[50] This is, however, a misunderstanding: the Court would have the power to declare legislation invalid.[51]

Secondly, he mentions that the Citizens' Court would avoid hard cases. I had stated that a cap of hearing a few cases a year may be appropriate. I refer now to a 'small number'. I envisage that the number would be significantly less than is feasible with judicial review. In addressing concern that a cap could exclude many deserving cases that would be heard if judicial review were available, I mentioned that many judicial review cases involve finely balanced matters. In these cases, the loss to justice in not hearing them may not be large. Zurn, though, is disturbed that there may be an absence of constitutional oversight for such cases. He mentions campaign finance laws, where their validity involves weighing, for instance, free speech against political equality. It is, however, unusual to defend judicial review

---

[47] See C Zurn, *Deliberative Democracy and the Institutions of Judicial Review* (New York, Cambridge University Press, 2006) 336. The process could also commence with a referral from a legislature.

[48] ibid 338.

[49] Zurn is employing here an idea developed in B Ackerman and J Fishkin, *Deliberation Day* (New Haven, Yale University Press, 2004).

[50] Zurn, 'Judicial Review, Constitutional Juries and Civic Constitutional Fora' 81.

[51] Ghosh, 'Deliberative Democracy and the Countermajoritarian Difficulty' 328.

on the ground that it deals with finely balanced cases. The usual defence appeals to scenarios where clearly unjust laws are made, so that their invalidation by courts can be generally accepted as promoting justice.

Thirdly, he is concerned that Parliament, with a 60 per cent majority, could override Citizens' Court decisions or even prevent review by this Court. Zurn is writing from a US perspective. My proposal, situated in the Australian context, drew upon features of the Australian political landscape and some reasoning that was not articulated. While I had not specified this in my article, this chapter indicates that I have the Senate in mind. To obtain a 60 per cent majority for abrogating Citizens' Court decisions, a governing party or coalition would almost certainly need support from a range of minority parties and independents in the absence of support from the main opposition party.[52] I did not suggest a higher supermajority such as two-thirds because the governing party would then need the support of the main opposition party or coalition. I was concerned that opposition parties can oppose government initiatives for tactical rather than genuine policy reasons: opposition might be useful in conveying a negative impression of the government and in garnering additional support. Of course, minority parties and independents are also influenced by tactical considerations, but their calculations may be different from the main opposition party. The greater the supermajority, the greater the demands upon the Citizens' Court, in terms of its legitimacy, in comparison to Parliament.

The question of what power of abrogation parliaments should enjoy has been substantially ventilated in the context of some Commonwealth countries introducing weak-form judicial review. Weak-form judicial review may involve courts having a power to invalidate or restrictively interpret legislation; its essential feature is that parliament can abrogate judicial decisions through ordinary legislation. In fact, a still weaker form of judicial review is the only one to have found favour in Australia in recent decades, with its introduction in Victoria and the Australian Capital Territory: apart from engaging in strained interpretation of legislation to render it compatible with rights, courts can only declare parliamentary legislation incompatible with rights, a declaration that does not affect legal validity.[53]

Arguments for weak-form judicial review have rested upon it effecting a more appropriate balance between parliaments and courts than strong-form judicial review.[54] An aim of weak-form judicial review is to improve outcomes not through giving courts what will often, in effect, be the final word, but giving courts significant influence. Conferring this weaker power on courts can be defended on the basis that it appropriately recognises that courts too are fallible institutions, with limited legitimacy and power compared with parliaments.

---

[52] On the composition of the Senate, see Bach, *Platypus and Parliament* 50, 158–9.

[53] S Gardbaum, *The New Commonwealth Model of Constitutionalism: Theory and Practice* (Cambridge, Cambridge University Press, 2013) ch 8.

[54] ibid ch 9.

These considerations are also relevant to my proposed Citizens' Court even though it involves strong-form review. From Zurn's perspective, my proposal might appear as weak-form constitutional review since it involves an easier abrogation process than for US judicial review. The US Supreme Court's decisions cannot be abrogated in the absence of constitutional amendment.[55] In any case, the parliamentary power of abrogation I propose fits, I suggest, with the fallibility of the Citizens' Court and its likely limited legitimacy. The hope is that the Court would enjoy sufficient popular procedural legitimacy to lead to political costs where its decisions are abrogated.

To sum-up so far, while Zurn suggests my proposal performs well against the first desideratum of independence, he mentions three ways in which the effectiveness of constitutional juries is crucially compromised. I have addressed these three ways. However, it appears that Zurn's deeper concern is that constitutional juries should not have significant power. His other criticisms of constitutional juries need to be considered.

I turn, then, to his second desideratum, which is legal integrity. Zurn's reference to achieving the 'systematic coherence of the entire corpus of the nation's law' might seem to resonate with the high ambition of Dworkin's ideal judge.[56] In Joseph Raz's terminology, it is an aspiration for global rather than local coherence, an aspiration Raz disagrees with.[57] In any case, Zurn claims that juries would fail to reach even a minimal level of coherence. He says the juries will be relatively if not entirely unconstrained by concern to achieve coherence with past juries' decisions or to follow judicially developed substantive or methodological doctrine.[58] He refers to my statement that a 'Citizens' Court is likely to feel freer in openly departing from earlier decisions, and the open-ended nature of the bill of rights will also lead to less emphasis on textual interpretation'.[59]

My statement, however, was in a paragraph concerned with whether bill-of-rights cases might be too complex for jurors. I suggested that an impression of great complexity can be conveyed by the case law, but that complexity may not be necessary to achieve morally sound decisions on rights. I mentioned Waldron's criticism of legal reasoning as involving discussion of precedent and an emphasis on textual interpretation that can distract from achieving sound moral outcomes. Those features of legal reasoning, Waldron suggests, can be a symptom of judges seeking authority for their decisions in the absence of the democratic legitimacy that legislatures enjoy.[60] My point was that the difficulties with legal reasoning

---

[55] See Art V of the US Constitution: constitutional amendment requires a two-thirds majority in each house of Congress and ratification by three-quarters of state legislatures.

[56] See text to above n 45, R Dworkin, *Law's Empire* (Cambridge, Mass., Belknap Press, 1986).

[57] Raz, 'The Relevance of Coherence' 315.

[58] Zurn, 'Judicial Review, Constitutional Juries and Civic Constitutional Fora' 83–4.

[59] ibid 83 referring to Ghosh, 'Deliberative Democracy and the Countermajoritarian Difficulty' 351.

[60] Waldron, 'The Core of the Case against Judicial Review' 1383–4.

that Waldron refers to seem less applicable to constitutional juries. Juries would be freer to openly depart from earlier decisions. Such departures would not be disguised to the extent that occurs in legal judgments, especially those following a formalist style of reasoning, a style more prevalent in Australia than in the US.[61] With formalism, explicit rejection of a past decision can be avoided through somewhat strained attempts at distinguishing that past decision.

A lesser emphasis on textual interpretation might also follow from the less technical approach that might be expected with juries. This might be reinforced by juries not having to engage in strained interpretations of rights when there is a catch-all provision aimed at capturing cases involving a serious contravention of the public interest. Such a catch-all provision is not intrinsic to constitutional juries, so that particular feature need not be emphasised here. What is most pertinent here is that I was not suggesting that constitutional juries would necessarily attach no weight to past decisions or the language in which rights are expressed. In relation to past decisions, my assumption would be that the rationality that both Zurn and I expect from mini-publics would also extend to balancing the competing values that might be at stake in following or refusing to follow a past decision the current jury disagrees with. In relation to textual interpretation of rights and of legislation that is under challenge, the juries would be guided by judges and the legal advocates for the parties.

Zurn also says that it would be objectionable if the Court could consider challenges to parliamentary legislation and if it could articulate principles. The court would then be making constitutional legislation. That power, Zurn says, properly belongs to the people. He recognises that judges inevitably legislate to some extent when interpreting constitutional provisions, and it is partly for this reason that he wishes to democratise the amendment process.[62] It would seem, however, that Zurn is concerned that juries would be bolder than judges.

Part of Zurn's concern may be prompted by a view that juries would be entirely unconstrained by past decisions and judicially developed doctrine. I have already suggested that this possibility seems inconsistent with the rationality Zurn and I expect from mini-publics. Furthermore, the extent to which the interpretive method constrains judges is one that the Critical Legal Studies movement has queried.[63] The greater constraint might lie in judges' sense of their limited democratic legitimacy, understood either normatively or sociologically (in terms

[61] On Australia, see L Zines, 'Legalism, Realism and Judicial Rhetoric in Constitutional Law' (2002) 5 *Constitutional Law and Policy Review* 21–30.

[62] Zurn, 'Judicial Review, Constitutional Juries and Civic Constitutional Fora' 86.

[63] See, eg, A Altman, 'Legal Realism, Critical Legal Studies, and Dworkin' (1986) 15 *Philosophy & Public Affairs* 205–35. To the extent that Zurn's concern is with predictability, the extent to which adherence to rule-based precedential approach promotes predictability is questioned, albeit in a different context, in O Raban, 'The Fallacy of Legal Certainty: Why Vague Legal Standards May Be Better for Capitalism and Liberalism' (2010) 19 *Public Interest Law Journal* 175–90.

of elite and popular attitudes). Let us assume here that constitutional juries do make bolder decisions, that is, decisions that are more likely to challenge the other branches of government. That power would be constrained by the Senate being able to abrogate Citizens' Court decisions. This denies to the 'constitutional legislation' of the Citizens' Court the entrenched status that would accord to constitutional legislation by the people themselves. While Zurn is uncomfortable with this parliamentary power of abrogation, this power actually lessens a significant concern Zurn has with the proposal.

The Citizens' Court, then, is consistent with Zurn's view that full democratic legitimacy with respect to constitutional legislation is only obtainable through approval by the people themselves once they have had the opportunity and incentive to deliberate substantially on any proposal. Zurn hopes that his amendment process can provide a significant check upon outcomes of judicial review that are inconsistent with what a deliberative public would approve. However, I have questioned elsewhere how effective a check it would be.[64] A more general concern about constitutional amendment processes is that proposals to abrogate judicial review outcomes would need to compete with all other constitutional proposals for inclusion in a limited agenda.[65]

Zurn's final criticism is that there will be leakage, so that rather than the Citizens' Court being the institution to engage in review based on a bill of rights, constitutional elaboration would be carried out by the ordinary courts in Australia. He assumes there would otherwise be an institutional vacuum. This assumption, however, seems to be based on the incorrect belief that there would be a bill of rights justiciable by ordinary courts and the Citizens' Court would not deal with challenges to legislation.

To conclude, perhaps Zurn's most fundamental objection to constitutional juries lies in their power of constitutional legislation. However, the parliamentary power of abrogation I have recommended significantly constrains this power. Zurn's heavy reliance on the gold-plated legitimacy conferred upon constitutional amendments achieved through his favoured process may have made him less amenable to proposals involving the democratisation of constitutional review.

VI. Conclusion

While the previous chapter laid some of the historical, normative and empirical groundwork for constitutional juries as a republican proposal, this chapter

---

[64] Ghosh, 'Deliberative Democracy and the Countermajoritarian Difficulty' 344.

[65] For an alternative proposal relating to citizen-initiated referendums, albeit one that would only replicate the jurisdiction of state legislatures, see Fishkin, 'Random Assemblies for Lawmaking?' 373. I make brief reference to a constitutional amendment process in E Ghosh, 'The Australian Constitution and Expressive Reform' (2012) 24 (Special issue on The Commonwealth of Australia) *Giornale di Storia Costituzionale (Journal of Constitutional History)* 95–116, 112–13. These proposals involve sortition.

articulated a particular form that constitutional juries could take. Large juries could be involved in selecting cases and deciding them. I argued, based on outcome and process considerations, that constitutional juries may be superior to judicial review and may enhance a political system without judicial review. I suggested there were advantages in including sortition within the judicial branch, and I addressed the main critique that has been made of constitutional juries.

My proposal aims to cast worthwhile light on the counter-majoritarian difficulty, which has been the most prominent concern within the literature on constitutionalism. If constitutional juries may well be attractive, this would raise a new counter-majoritarian concern: it would suggest that a more democratic way to promote rights may be available.

Apart from raising a new counter-majoritarian difficulty, considering the proposal can cast fresh light on this difficulty more generally. As the last chapter indicated, the case for judicial review is assisted by a negative view of electoral politics, which includes a negative view of the autonomy exercised by voters.[66] The case against judicial review, on the other hand, is assisted by a positive view of electoral politics. Opponents of judicial review can tap into anxiety of the politically well-informed class not to adopt an arrogant attitude towards the electorate in general. They can also tap into anxiety that a dim view of voter rationality fits well with anti-democratic thought.

By contrast, the argument that a significant number of voters exercise fairly low autonomy in elections is combined here with support for the radically democratic mechanism of sortition. This support is based on a positive appraisal of citizens' potential autonomy when provided with different opportunities and incentives. A negative view of voter rationality can be associated with support for elitist institutions. To the extent that it is this association that can discourage acceptance of empirical findings of low voter rationality, the argument for a new counter-majoritarian concern made here can influence attitudes towards the traditional counter-majoritarian concern. That is so regardless of whether constitutional juries are ultimately regarded as potentially attractive.

On the other hand, it would seem unfortunate if the only impact of these chapters is to encourage acceptance of findings about low voter rationality and thereby provide stronger support for elitist institutions. The implications of this chapter are not all favourable to judicial review even if I have failed to persuasively argue that constitutional juries may well be attractive. The proposal can still throw into sharper relief the elitist character of judicial decision-making. This would certainly be the case if constitutional juries are rejected simply because the political obstacles to their introduction will be too large, or they are unattractive for some other reason that does not reflect poorly on the rationality that the jurors would be likely to demonstrate. Of course, if constitutional juries are rejected on the basis that

---

[66] See ch 8, s IIIA.

they would be incompetent, this contrasting model would not throw a negative light upon the elitism of judicial review.

I have not attempted to draw out all implications that can be generated from considering constitutional juries. One implication I have drawn out elsewhere is for a strand of legal reasoning that justifies constitutional decisions based on community values. I have argued that the idea of constitutional juries helps us to understand how such community values should be interpreted.[67] The central implication to draw from considering constitutional juries, though, lies in throwing light on the legitimacy of judicial review. The more general point is that constitutional juries may provide a way to reconcile democracy with an aspect of constitutionalism – constitutional review. Constitutional juries may deepen democracy and also provide better protection for constitutional rights. They have been presented in the last two chapters as a republican device. The pursuit of constitutional juries provides a new way of exploring implications of the republican tradition.

---

[67] E Ghosh, 'Judicial Reference to Community Values – a Pointer Towards Constitutional Juries?' in T Bustamante and B Fernandes (eds), *Democratizing Constitutional Law: Perspectives on Legal Theory and the Legitimacy of Constitutionalism* (Switzerland, Springer, 2016) 247–71.

10

Conclusion

The revival of the republican political tradition over the last few decades has been an exciting development. With Pettit's and Skinner's non-positive-liberty strand, there is the promise of restoring an old and forgotten value – liberty as non-domination – which was eclipsed towards the end of the eighteenth century by liberty as non-interference. Liberty as non-domination, they claim, lies at the core of a tradition tracing back to ancient Rome, a tradition which attempted to articulate ideals that were relatively democratic for the time. This value challenges the mere existence of arbitrary power, even if that power is unlikely to be abused. Pettit has suggested that it was a radical value in eighteenth-century England when it was combined with the suggestion that everyone should enjoy liberty. Indeed, he suggests that liberty as non-interference, which was to become central to liberalism, may well have eclipsed liberty as non-domination because more conservative writers sought to draw attention to a less radical ideal. Today, though, Pettit claims, liberty as non-domination is a challenging yet attainable ideal.

Skinner endorses much of this, although overall he is more cautious. He does not claim that republican liberty was eclipsed by liberty as non-interference because it was too radical. However, he agrees that republican liberty is a demanding value. The value recognises how mere vulnerability to arbitrary power damages status and prompts humiliating behaviour such as having to be deferential towards those with arbitrary power. These forms of damage are not recognised through liberty as non-interference.

Pettit and Skinner place their claims about liberty and the republican and liberal traditions in the broader context of the aims of political philosophy and intellectual history. Beginning first with Pettit, in *Republicanism*, he suggested that a task of the political philosopher is to examine languages in which politics is conducted partly in order to clarify those languages, including their underlying assumptions, but also to discover new terms in which to frame political debate.[1] Pettit suggested that individual philosophers can only expect their voices to be heard in a small circle, and if they reach other audiences, that will be because others are saying related things – they are part of a conversational cascade.[2] That limited expectation is helpful in avoiding a disillusionment with politics that can

---

[1] P Pettit, *Republicanism: A Theory of Freedom and Government* (Oxford, Clarendon Press, 1997) 2.
[2] ibid 3.

lead to despair about the role of normative discussion in politics, with politics being viewed as merely the exercise of power in which political arguments only serve to rationalise positions reached for other reasons.

Turning secondly to Skinner, in *Liberty before Liberalism*, he suggested that when he started his postgraduate study in the 1960s, a canon of leading texts was the only proper object of research in the history of political thought.[3] Instead of viewing texts as addressing a set of perennial questions, he became part of a group of scholars seeking to situate texts in their historical context, answering to specific controversies at the time. A senior figure in this movement was Pocock, who encouraged a wide-ranging investigation of the changing political languages in which societies talk to themselves.[4] A recognition that those texts were addressing particular concerns does not, however, preclude the possibility that they can illuminate theories and concepts that we use.[5]

While Pettit urged limited expectations in relation to the influence of political philosophy, quite remarkably, his work did cross into practical politics, with its adoption by the Spanish Prime Minister Zapatero. Upon achieving leadership of the socialist party in 2000, Zapatero was looking for a philosophical basis to express the commitments he had articulated in favour of democracy, liberty and solidarity. This involved looking for a language that distinguished his position from the older generation of socialists, and was also distinct from the language of the 'Third Way', taken from sociologist Anthony Giddens and which was employed by Tony Blair's British Labour Party.[6] Pettit's republicanism provided Zapatero with a fresh language in which to express his convictions, and he drew on this in his public addresses, leading to Pettit's philosophy being discussed in the popular media as well.[7]

That it made this cross-over into practical politics attests to the impressive qualities of Pettit's work. The idea that there is something wrong with the subordination involved where one is vulnerable to power – a circumstance where one may have to be deferential, where one cannot look the other in the eye – is an idea with widespread appeal. It is a circumstance that most of us can identify with at some point; it can arise without being interfered with. Pettit took this appealing idea and wove it into a captivating narrative in which one political tradition eclipsed another. Furthermore, he then explained comprehensively how this ideal can shape our approach to how political authority is structured and what broad policies governments should follow. Skinner's elegant and authoritative discussion

---

[3] Q Skinner, *Liberty before Liberalism* (Cambridge, Cambridge University Press, 1998) 101.

[4] ibid 105, referring, for instance, to JGA Pocock, *Virtue, Commerce, and History: Essays on Political Thought and History, Chiefly in the Eighteenth Century* (Cambridge, Cambridge University Press, 1985).

[5] Skinner, *Liberty before Liberalism* 109–10. See also above ch 3, s V.

[6] J Martí and P Pettit, *A Political Philosophy in Public Life: Civic Republicanism in Zapatero's Spain* (Princeton, Princeton University Press, 2010) 8–10.

[7] ibid 15–17, 26–30.

of republicanism supported this interpretation of the revival and, indeed, paved its way with his initial challenge to positive-liberty republicanism.

The positive-liberty republican revival has also involved the excavation of an old value, in this case, a value associated with that ancient exemplar of democracy, Athens. This value involves the challenging claim that we are only free when we lead an active and virtuous political life. I also described this as full-blown positive liberty. This conception of liberty formed the basis for Pocock's highly influential interpretation of the tradition, a tradition that extended into the late eighteenth century. His *The Machiavellian Moment* thereby suggested that positive liberty cannot be dismissed as merely an ancient value that disappeared along with the city-state.

In a similar vein, Michelman suggested that the ideal of positive liberty contin-ues to exert a hold over the American imagination, although for different reasons from those that justified the original ideal. The original reasons are inconsistent with the liberal temper, with its openness to a wide range of conceptions of the good. Instead, in an age where politics is often understood as involving merely the pursuit of self-interest, the ancient ideal enables us to recover a model of norma-tive reasoning. Michelman then took on the formidable challenge of justifying activism by the US Supreme Court on the basis of the most demanding of demo-cratic values.

A reason for the substantial attention that the republican revival has received is that the revivers do not merely present an analytical conception of liberty for contemporary guidance. Instead, this value is woven into a narrative involving the eclipse of one political tradition by another. It is a narrative that challenges our understanding of the dominant tradition of liberalism and, more generally, our understanding of Western political thought.

This book, though, points to some different narratives. I will highlight one here. This concerns the way in which ideas holding contemporary appeal appear to have exerted an influence over the interpretation of the historical writers relied upon. In the case of the non-positive-liberty republican revival, an interest in the conceptual differences between liberty as non-domination, on the one hand, and liberty as non-interference and full-blown positive liberty, on the other hand, appears to have influenced the interpretation of the historical writers. The contrast with liberty as non-interference suggests a focus, in understanding liberty as non-domination, on power damage where interference is unlikely. The contrast with positive liberty may have contributed to overlooking in the historical writing ideas with associations to positive liberty but which do not amount to full-blown posi-tive liberty.

Achieving these contrasts with liberty as non-interference and positive liberty may have contributed, to give an example, to Pettit's erroneous narrative of why Priceian liberty as non-domination was eclipsed in late eighteenth-century England. Pettit draws attention to this value being diminished by arbitrary power rather than by interference as its radical quality. I argued, however, that the charge of radicalism levelled at Price by this contemporaries was not directed at his interpretation of liberty as non-domination. Instead, it was directed at his identification of liberty with a broad franchise, an identification that gave his conception of liberty a positive-liberty dimension.

In the case of the positive-liberty republican revival, a contemporary concern with alienation and disengagement from politics has perhaps led to a fascination with an ideal that suggested that political participation aimed at contributing to the public good is an individual good as well: it forms an especially valuable, perhaps the most valuable, conception of the good. This ideal of full-blown positive liberty provided a lens for Pocock through which to view thinkers, such as Harrington, whose work actually demonstrates only positive-liberty dimensions. Pocock's interpretation was adopted by Michelman in his exploration of the constitutional implications of the republican tradition.

While excavating the past partly with an eye to contemporary implications can distort historical interpretation, this book did not suggest that such excavation should not be undertaken. The appeal of stories that connect the past to the present is too great for any such message to be heeded. Instead, I too engaged in acts of excavation.

First, I provided a significantly different interpretation of Priceian liberty as non-domination. I connected this with Shklar's liberalism of fear. Shklar provided her own narrative, in which writing preoccupied with the evil of cruelty and the danger of arbitrary power forms part of an important strand of a political tradition that has shaped, and continues to shape, existing institutions. This strand of liberalism, Shklar thought, has been somewhat overlooked, at least in the US. I suggested that Priceian liberty as non-domination fits reasonably well within the liberalism of fear. In Price, there is certainly a preoccupation with the risk of oppression where there is arbitrary power. Rather than placing Price as one of the last figures in a tradition that was eclipsed by liberalism, Price can instead be viewed as a writer in an enduring tradition.

From the perspective of Priceian liberty as non-domination, Pettit's and Skinner's focus on power damage downplays the greater evil of interference damage. However, Price did not propose liberty as non-domination as a comprehensive political ideal. Instead, this value must be considered within a pluralistic framework. It cannot carry the ambition of Pettit's interpretation of liberty as non-domination, with its claim of providing us with a single goal that can unify our commitments.

I argued, though, that Pettit's interpretation has normative limitations. While Pettit contrasts the value with liberty as non-interference, the value relies significantly on probabilistic considerations that liberty as non-interference takes into account. Therefore, the implications of these conceptions on, say, the dispersion of power achieved through judicial review do not diverge as substantially as one might have supposed. While liberty as non-domination is offered as a single goal, its application is also more complex than one might have expected. Pettit's and Skinner's interpretations also fail to successfully capture the damage caused by vulnerability to arbitrary power even though a strength of liberty as non-domination is supposedly its ability to capture such damage. Furthermore, Pettit's approach excludes other values and considerations that provide significant support for the policies that Pettit would favour. Partly through examining the Haneef case and its application of a common-law (or constitutional) right of liberty, which I described as a qualified form of liberty as non-domination, I pointed to the importance of consulting a rich array of considerations, including the danger of likely unjustified interference and also the status damage that is neither captured by liberty as non-domination nor liberty as non-interference. Priceian liberty as non-domination highlights the danger of unjustified interference and is consistent with taking other considerations into account.

My second act of excavation lay in recovering positive-liberty dimensions especially to Priceian liberty. These connect to Shklar's liberalism of hope and to a perfectionist strand of liberalism based on strong autonomy. I suggested that this at least fits better with liberal tolerance towards conceptions of the good than Michelman's preferred approach. Michelman privileges social deliberation. This is apparent in his approach to *Bowers v Hardwick*. Price, on the other hand, privileges a life lived according to sound moral principles, where those principles are arrived at freely by the individual. While Price's ideal of strong autonomy is a controversial one, there is another positive-liberty dimension in Price that is likely to attract greater support. This is democratic status: the status of being recognised as someone capable of exercising political power responsibly. I applied this in defending my proposal for constitutional juries.

My third act of excavation, indeed, recovered sortition for the purpose of constitutional guidance. The republican association between sortition and democracy received its most powerful recent articulation in Manin's *Principles of Representative Government*. Within liberalism, democracy is equated with electoral democracy. Manin, however, focused on the republican association of sortition with democracy, and election with aristocracy. He suggested we understand liberal representative democracies as involving a conscious rejection of the republican identification of democracy with sortition.

I pursued some implications for judicial review that follow from identifying democracy with sortition. I pointed to Bickel's understanding of the counter-majoritarian difficulty. For Bickel, the concern with the democratic legitimacy of judges thwarting the will of the elected branches of government lay in judges not being as tightly constrained to follow the preferences of the people. I suggested, though, that the Athenian People's Court and the republican association of democracy with sortition raise the question of whether, if constitutional juries were adopted, democracy might actually be promoted as well as constitutionalism.

I sketched and defended a proposal for constitutional juries, which I placed in the Australian context, where there is no national justiciable bill of rights and where there might be greater openness to unconventional approaches to protecting constitutional rights. On the other hand, while there has been substantial experimentation with mini-publics, including deliberative polls, it seems unlikely that an extension of juries from the criminal to the constitutional arena will occur any time soon. I suggested, nevertheless, that in exploring the legitimacy of judicial review, it seem important to explore alternatives. Such exploration can provide a distinctive perspective upon existing institutions and conventional alternatives.

Of course, my acts of excavation raise the question of whether my interest in demonstrating their contemporary appeal has led to distortion of the historical material. That is, of course, for others to judge, as is the soundness of the other historical, conceptual and normative claims made in this book. My hope is that I have at least contributed helpfully to a literature that seeks to explore historical ideas and practices partly with the aim of enriching our conversations about the political ideals and constitutional arrangements we should support.

BIBLIOGRAPHY

Abbott, W and Batt, J (eds), *A Handbook of Jury Research*. (Philadelphia, Pa, American Law Institute-American Bar Association Committee on Continuing Professional Education, 1999).

Abrams, K, 'Law's Republicanism' (1988) 97 *Yale Law Journal* 1591–1608.

Ackerman, B, 'The Storrs Lectures: Discovering the Constitution' (1984) 93 *Yale Law Journal* 1013–72.

Ackerman, B, *We the People*, vol 1: Foundations (Cambridge, Mass., Belknap Press of Harvard University Press, 1991).

Ackerman, B and Fishkin, J, *Deliberation Day* (New Haven, Yale University Press, 2004).

Allan, TRS, 'The Common Law as Constitution: Fundamental Rights and First Principles' in C Saunders (ed), *Courts of Final Jurisdiction: The Mason Court in Australia* (Sydney, Federation Press, 1996) 146–66.

Althaus, S, 'Information Effects in Collective Preferences' (1998) 92 *American Political Science Review* 545–58.

Altman, A, 'Legal Realism, Critical Legal Studies, and Dworkin' (1986) 15 *Philosophy & Public Affairs* 205–35.

Andersen, R, Heath, A and Sinnott, R, 'Political Knowledge and Electoral Choice' (2002) 12 *Journal of Elections, Public Opinion & Parties* 11–27.

Ando, C, '"A Dwelling Beyond Violence": On the Uses and Disadvantages of History for Contemporary Republicans' (2010) 31 *History of Political Thought* 183–217.

Arendt, H, *The Human Condition* [1958], with an introduction by Margaret Canovan, 2nd edn (Chicago, University of Chicago Press, 1998).

Aristotle, *The Politics*, trans, T Sinclair, revised by T Saunders (Penguin, 1992).

Austin, J, *The Province of Jurisprudence Determined* (London, John Murray, 1832).

Australia Deliberates: Reconciliation – Where from Here? Final Report, Issues Deliberation Australia, (Glenelg, South Australia, 2001).

Bach, S, *Platypus and Parliament: The Australian Senate in Theory and Practice* (Canberra, Department of the Senate, 2003).

Barber, B, *Strong Democracy: Participatory Politics for a New Age*, 20th anniversary edn (Berkeley, Calif., University of California Press, 2003).

Barnett, A and Carty, P, *The Athenian Option: Radical Reform for the House of Lords* [1998] (Exeter, Imprint Academic, 2008).

Beiner, R, 'Civil Religion and Anticlericalism in James Harrington' (2014) 13 *European Journal of Political Theory* 388–407.

Belchem, J, 'Republicanism, Popular Constitutionalism and the Radical Platform in Early Nineteenth-Century England' (1981) 6 *Social History* 1–32.

Bell, D and Bansal, P, 'The Republican Revival and Racial Politics' (1988) 97 *Yale Law Journal* 1609–21.

Bellamy, R, 'Democracy as Public Law: The Case of Constitutional Rights' (2013) 14 *German Law Journal* 1017–37.

Bentham, J, *Constitutional Code*, eds, F Rosen and JH Burns, vol 1 (Oxford, Clarendon Press, 1983).

Bentham, J, 'A Fragment on Government' [1776] in *A Comment on the Commentaries and a Fragment on Government*, eds, JH Burns and HLA Hart (London, University of London Athlone Press, 1977) 393–551.

Bentham, J, *The Theory of Legislation* [1840], ed, C Ogden (London, Morrison & Gibbs, 1931).

Berlin, I, *Freedom and Its Betrayal: Six Enemies of Human Liberty*, ed, H Hardy, 2nd edn (Princeton, NJ, Princeton University Press, 2014).

Berlin, I, 'Two Concepts of Liberty' [1958] in *Four Essays on Liberty* (Oxford, Oxford University Press, 1969) 118–72.

Bernstein, R, *Beyond Objectivism and Relativism: Science, Hermeneutics, and Praxis* (Oxford, Basil Blackwell, 1983).

Bickel, A, *The Least Dangerous Branch: The Supreme Court at the Bar of Politics* [1962], with a new forward by H Wellington, 2nd edn (New Haven, Yale University Press, 1986).

Braithwaite, J and Pettit, P, *Not Just Deserts: A Republican Theory of Criminal Justice* (Oxford, Clarendon Press, 1990).

Brest, P, 'Further Beyond the Republican Revival: Towards Radical Republicanism' (1988) 97 *Yale Law Journal* 1623–31.

Burke, E, 'Reflections on the Revolution in France' [1790] in *Revolutionary Writings*, ed, I Hampsher-Monk (Cambridge, Cambridge University Press, 2014) 1–250.

Burnheim, J, *Is Democracy Possible? The Alternative to Electoral Politics* (Cambridge, Polity Press, 1985).

Burns, JH, 'Bentham and the French Revolution' (1966) 16 *Transactions of the Royal Historical Society* 95–114.

Callenbach, E and Phillips, M, *A Citizen Legislature* [1985] (Exeter, Imprint Academic, 2008).

Campbell, T and Morris, S, 'Human Rights for Democracies: A Provisional Assessment of the Australian *Human Rights (Parliamentary Scrutiny) Act 2011*' (2015) 34 *University of Queensland Law Journal* 7–27.

Campos Boralevi, L, *Bentham and the Oppressed* (Berlin, W de Gruyter, 1984).

Campos Boralevi, L, 'James Harrington's "Machiavellian" Anti-Machiavellism' (2011) 37 *History of European Ideas* 113–19.

Cannon, J, *Parliamentary Reform 1640–1832* (Cambridge, Cambridge University Press, 1973).

Canovan, M, 'Two Concepts of Liberty – Eighteenth-Century Style' (1978) 2 *The Price–Priestley Newsletter* 27–43.

Canovan, M, *Hannah Arendt: A Reinterpretation of Her Political Thought* (Cambridge, Cambridge University Press, 1992).

Carter, I, *A Measure of Freedom* (Oxford, Oxford University Press, 1999).

Carter, I, 'How Are Power and Unfreedom Related?' in C Laborde and J Maynor (eds), *Republicanism and Political Theory* (Malden, MA, Blackwell, 2008) 58–82.

Carter, I and Shnayderman, R, 'The Impossibility of "Freedom as Independence"' (2019) 17 *Political Studies Review* 136–46.

Castiglione, D, 'Republicanism and Its Legacy' (2005) 4 *European Journal of Political Theory* 453–65.

Charvet, J, 'Quentin Skinner on the Idea of Freedom' (1993) 2 *Studies in Political Thought* 5–16.

Christman, J, 'Saving Positive Freedom' (2005) 33 *Political Theory* 79–88.

Clarke, MJ, *Report of the Inquiry into the Case of Dr Mohammed Haneef*, vol 1 (Canberra, Attorney-General's Department, 2008).

Colón-Ríos, J, 'The Counter-Majoritarian Difficulty and the Road Not Taken: Democratizing Amendment Rules' (2012) 25 *Canadian Journal of Law and Jurisprudence* 53–78.

Constant, B, 'The Liberty of the Ancients Compared with That of the Moderns' [1819] in *Political Writings* trans & ed, B, Fontana (Cambridge, Cambridge University Press, 1988) 307–28.

Craig, P, *Public Law and Democracy in the United Kingdom and the United States of America* (Oxford, Clarendon Press, 1990).

Crosby, N and Nethercut, D, 'Citizens Juries: Creating a Trustworthy Voice of the People' in J Gastil and P Levine (eds), *The Deliberative Democracy Handbook: Strategies for Effective Civic Engagement in the 21st Century* (San Francisco, CA, Jossey-Bass, 2005) 111–19.

Dagger, R, *Civic Virtues: Rights, Citizenship, and Republican Liberalism* (New York, Oxford University Press, 1997).

Dagger, R, '*Republicanism* Refashioned: Comments on Pettit's Theory of Freedom and Government' (2000) 9(3) *The Good Society* 50–3.

Dagger, R, 'Autonomy, Domination, and the Republican Challenge to Liberalism' in J Christman and J Anderson (eds), *Autonomy and the Challenges to Liberalism: New Essays* (Cambridge, Cambridge University Press, 2005) 177–203.

Dahl, R and Tufte, E, *Size and Democracy* (Stanford, Stanford University Press, 1973).

Davis, R and Williams, G, 'Reform of the Judicial Appointments Process: Gender and the Bench of the High Court of Australia' (2003) 27 *Melbourne University Law Review* 819–63.

de Bruin, B, 'Liberal and Republican Freedom' (2009) 17 *Journal of Political Philosophy* 418–39.

de Dijn, A, 'Republicanism and Democracy: The Tyranny of the Majority in Eighteenth-Century Political Debate' in Y Elazar and G Rousselière (eds), *Republicanism and the Future of Democracy* (Cambridge, Cambridge University Press, 2019) 59–74.

Donegan, P, 'The Role of the Commonwealth Attorney–General in Appointing Judges to the High Court of Australia' (2003) 29 *Melbourne Journal of Politics* 40–55.

Duff, RA, *Punishment, Communication, and Community* (Oxford, Oxford University Press, 2001).

Dworkin, R, *Taking Rights Seriously* (London, Duckworth, 1977).

Dworkin, R, 'The Forum of Principle' (1981) 56 *New York University Law Review* 469–518.

Dworkin, R, *Law's Empire* (Cambridge, Mass., Belknap Press, 1986).

Dworkin, R, *Freedom's Law: The Moral Reading of the American Constitution* (Cambridge, Mass., Harvard University Press, 1996).

Dworkin, R, *Sovereign Virtue: The Theory and Practice of Equality* (Cambridge, Mass., Harvard University Press, 2000).

Dworkin, R, *Justice in Robes* (Cambridge, Mass, Belknap Press, 2006).

Edge, M, 'Athens and the Spectrum of Liberty' (2009) 30 *History of Political Thought* 1–45.

Eisgruber, C, *Constitutional Self-Government* (Cambridge, Mass., Harvard University Press, 2001).

Eisgruber, C, 'Constitutional Self-Government and Judicial Review: A Reply to Five Critics' (2002) 37 *University of San Francisco Law Review* 115–90.

Elazar, Y, 'The Liberty Debates: Richard Price and His Critics on Civil Liberty, Free Government, and Democratic Participation' (PhD thesis, Princeton University, 2012).

Elazar, Y and Rousselière, G, 'Introduction' in Y Elazar and G Rousselière (eds), *Republicanism and the Future of Democracy* (Cambridge, Cambridge University Press, 2019) 1–10.

Ely, J, *Democracy and Distrust: A Theory of Judicial Review* (Cambridge, Mass., Harvard University Press, 1980).

Emerson, RW, 'The Conservative' [1841] in *Essays and Lectures* (New York, Library of America, 1983) 171–89.

Epstein, J, *Radical Expression: Political Language, Ritual, and Symbol in England, 1790–1850* (Oxford, Oxford University Press, 1994).

Epstein, R, 'Modern Republicanism – or Flight from Substance' (1988) 97 *Yale Law Journal* 1633–50.

Eskridge, W, *Gaylaw: Challenging the Apartheid of the Closet* (Cambridge, Mass., Harvard University Press, 1999).

Estlund, D, 'Who's Afraid of Deliberative Democracy? On the Strategic/Deliberative Dichotomy in Recent Constitutional Jurisprudence' (1993) 71 *Texas Law Review* 1437–77.

Ewing, KD, 'A Theory of Democratic Adjudication: Towards a Representative, Accountable and Independent Judiciary' (2000) 38 *Alberta Law Review* 708–33.

Fabre, C, *Social Rights under the Constitution: Government and the Decent Life* (Oxford, Clarendon Press, 2000).

Fallon, R, 'What Is Republicanism, and Is It Worth Reviving?' (1989) 102 *Harvard Law Review* 1695–1735.

Farrar, C et al, 'Disaggregating Deliberation's Effects: An Experiment within a Deliberative Poll' (2010) 40 *British Journal of Political Science* 333–47.

Filmer, R, 'Observations Upon Aristotles Politiques, Touching Forms of Government, Together with Directions for Obedience to Governours in Dangerous and Doubtfull Times' [1652] in *Patriarcha and Other Writings*, ed, J Sommerville (Cambridge, Cambridge University Press, 1991) 235–86.

Fishkin, J, *Democracy and Deliberation: New Directions for Democratic Reform* (New Haven, Yale University Press, 1991).

Fishkin, J, *When the People Speak: Deliberative Democracy and Public Consultation* (Oxford, Oxford University Press, 2009).

Fishkin, J, 'Random Assemblies for Lawmaking? Prospects and Limits' (2018) 46 *Politics & Society* 359–79.

Fishkin, J and Laslett, P, 'Introduction' in J Fishkin and P Laslett (eds), *Debating Deliberative Democracy* (Malden, MA, Blackwell, 2003) 1–6.

Fishkin, J and Luskin, R, 'Experimenting with a Democratic Ideal: Deliberative Polling and Public Opinion' (2005) 40 *Acta Politica* 284–98.

Forrester, K, 'Hope and Memory in the Thought of Judith Shklar' (2011) 8 *Modern Intellectual History* 591–620.

Frame, R, *Liberty's Apostle: Richard Price, His Life and Times* (Cardiff, University of Wales Press, 2015).

Friedman, B, 'The Turn to History' (1997) 72 *New York University Law Review* 928–65.

Galipeau, C, *Isaiah Berlin's Liberalism* (Oxford, Clarendon Press, 1994).

Gardbaum, S, *The New Commonwealth Model of Constitutionalism: Theory and Practice* (Cambridge, Cambridge University Press, 2013).

Garnett, M, 'The Autonomous Life: A Pure Social View' (2014) 92 *Australasian Journal of Philosophy* 143–58.

Gastil, J and Levine, P (eds), *The Deliberative Democracy Handbook: Strategies for Effective Civic Engagement in the 21st Century*. (San Francisco, CA, Jossey-Bass, 2005).

Gey, S, 'The Unfortunate Revival of Civic Republicanism' (1993) 141 *University of Pennsylvania Law Review* 801–898.

Ghazarian, Z, 'The Changing Type of Minor Party Elected to Parliament: The Case of the Australian Senate from 1949 to 2010' (2012) 47 *Australian Journal of Political Science* 441–54.

Ghosh, E, 'Republicanism, Community Values and Social Psychology: A Response to Braithwaite's Model of Judicial Deliberation' (1998) 20 *Sydney Law Review* 5–41.

Ghosh, E, 'Applying Pettit's Republican Liberty to Criminal Justice and Judicial Decision-Making: The Need for Other Values Including Desert and a Suggestion That They Be Understood Consequentially' (1999) 22 *University of New South Wales Law Journal* 122–54.

Ghosh, E, 'From Republican to Liberal Liberty' (2008) 29 *History of Political Thought* 132–67.

Ghosh, E, 'Deliberative Democracy and the Countermajoritarian Difficulty: Considering Constitutional Juries' (2010) 30 *Oxford Journal of Legal Studies* 327–59.

Ghosh, E, 'The Australian Constitution and Expressive Reform' (2012) 24 (Special issue on The Commonwealth of Australia) *Giornale di Storia Costituzionale (Journal of Constitutional History)* 95–116.

Ghosh, E, 'Judicial Reference to Community Values – a Pointer Towards Constitutional Juries?' in T Bustamante and B Fernandes (eds), *Democratizing Constitutional Law: Perspectives on Legal Theory and the Legitimacy of Constitutionalism* (Switzerland, Springer, 2016) 247–71.

Ghosh, E, 'Deliberative Constitutionalism: An Empirical Dimension' in J King et al (eds), *Cambridge Handbook on Deliberative Constitutionalism* (Cambridge, Cambridge University Press, 2018) 220–32.

Gibson, A, 'Ancients, Moderns and Americans: The Republicanism–Liberalism Debate Revisited' (2013) 21 *History of Political Thought* 261–307.

Gibson, R and Mishkin, S, 'Australia Deliberates? The Role of the Media in Deliberative Polling' in J Warhurst and M Mackerras (eds), *Constitutional Politics: The Republic Referendum and the Future* (St Lucia, Qld., University of Queensland Press, 2002) 163–175.

Goldie, M, 'The Civil Religion of James Harrington' in A Pagden (ed), *The Languages of Political Theory in Early-Modern Europe* (Cambridge, Cambridge University Press, 1987) 197–222.

Goldie, M, 'The English System of Liberty' in M Goldie and R Wokler (eds), *The Cambridge History of Eighteenth-Century Political Thought* (Cambridge, Cambridge University Press, 2006) 40–78.

Goldsworthy, J, *The Sovereignty of Parliament: History and Philosophy* (Oxford, Clarendon Press, 1999).

Goldsworthy, J, 'Legislative Intentions, Legislative Supremacy, and Legal Positivism' (2005) 42 *San Diego Law Review* 493–518.

Goodin, R, 'Folie Républicaine' (2003) 6 *Annual Review of Political Science* 55–76.

Goodin, R, *Reflective Democracy* (Oxford, Oxford University Press, 2003).

Goodwin, A, *The Friends of Liberty: The English Democratic Movement in the Age of the French Revolution* (London, Hutchinson, 1979).

Gourevitch, A, 'Labor and Republican Liberty' (2011) 18 *Constellations* 431–54.

Gourevitch, A, *From Slavery to the Cooperative Commonwealth: Labor and Republican Liberty in the Nineteenth Century* (New York, Cambridge University Press, 2015).

Gray, J, *Isaiah Berlin* (Princeton, NJ, Princeton University Press, 1996).

Guicciardini, F, *Dialogue on the Government of Florence*, ed, A Brown (Cambridge, Cambridge University Press, 1994).

Gutmann, A, 'How Limited Is Liberal Government?' in B Yack (ed), *Liberalism without Illusions: Essays on Political Theory and the Political Vision of Judith Shklar* (Chicago, University of Chicago Press, 1996) 64–81.

Hammersley, R, 'Introduction: The Historiography of Republicanism and Republican Exchanges' (2012) 38 *History of European Ideas* 323–37.

Hammersley, R, 'Rethinking the Political Thought of James Harrington: Royalism, Republicanism and Democracy' (2013) 39 *History of European Ideas* 354–70.

Hansen, K, *Deliberative Democracy and Opinion Formation* (Odense, University Press of Southern Denmark, 2004).

Hansen, M, *The Athenian Democracy in the Age of Demosthenes: Structure, Principles and Ideology*, trans, JA Crook (Oxford, Basil Blackwell, 1991).

Hansen, M, 'The Mixed Constitution versus the Separation of Powers: Monarchical and Aristocratic Aspects of Modern Democracy' (2010) 31 *History of Political Thought* 509–31.

Harling, P, 'Leigh Hunt's *Examiner* and the Language of Patriotism' (1996) 111 *English Historical Review* 1159–81.

Harrington, J, *The Commonwealth of Oceana and A System of Politics*, ed, JGA Pocock (Cambridge, Cambridge University Press, 1992).

Hartog, H, 'Imposing Constitutional Traditions' (1987) 29 *William and Mary Law Review* 75–82.

Hasson, Y et al, 'Are Liberals and Conservatives Equally Motivated to Feel Empathy toward Others?' (2018) 44(10) *Personality and Social Psychology Bulletin* 1449–59.

Hayek, FA, *The Constitution of Liberty* [1960], ed, R Hamowy (Chicago, Chicago University Press, 2011).

Head, M, 'The Haneef Inquiry: Some Unanswered Questions' (2009) 2 *Journal of the Australasian Law Teachers Association* 99–112.

Held, D, *Models of Democracy*, 3rd edn (Cambridge, Polity, 2006).

Hickman, L, *Eighteenth-Century Dissent and Cambridge Platonism: Reconceiving the Philosophy of Religion* (Abingdon, Routledge, 2017).

Hirschl, R, 'The Judicialization of Politics' in K Whittington, R Kelemen and G Caldeira (eds), *Oxford Handbook of Law and Politics* (Oxford, Oxford University Press, 2008) 119–41.

Hiruta, K, 'The Meaning and Value of Freedom: Berlin contra Arendt' (2014) 19 *The European Legacy* 854–68.

Hobbes, T, *Leviathan* [1651], ed, R Tuck (Cambridge, Cambridge University Press, 1996).

Holmes, S, *Benjamin Constant and the Making of Modern Liberalism* (New Haven, Yale University Press, 1984).

Honohan, I, *Civic Republicanism* (New York, Routledge, 2002).

Horwitz, M, 'Republicanism and Liberalism in American Constitutional Thought' (1987) 29 *William and Mary Law Review* 57–74.

Kahn, R, *The Supreme Court and Constitutional Theory: 1953–1993* (Lawrence, Kan., University Press of Kansas, 1994).

Kamugisha, A, 'Orientalism, Western Republicanism, and the Ancient *Polis*: Patricia Springborg's *Western Republicanism and the Oriental Prince* and the Canon of Political Thought' (2007) *The Philosophical Forum* 173–98.

Kelly, PJ, *Utilitarianism and Distributive Justice: Jeremy Bentham and the Civil Law* (Oxford, Clarendon Press, 1990).

Koikkalainen, P, 'Contextualist Dilemmas: Methodology of the History of Political Theory in Two Stages' (2011) 37 *History of European Ideas* 315–24.

Kramer, L, 'The Supreme Court 2000 Term Foreword: We the Court' (2001–2002) 115 *Harvard Law Review* 5–169.

Kramer, M, *The Quality of Freedom* (Oxford, Oxford University Press, 2003).

Kramer, M, 'Liberty and Domination' in C Laborde and J Maynor (eds), *Republicanism and Political Theory* (Malden, MA, Blackwell, 2008) 31–57.

Kymlicka, W, *Contemporary Political Philosophy: An Introduction*, 2nd edn (New York, Oxford University Press, 2002).

Lafont, C, 'Deliberation, Participation, and Democratic Legitimacy: Should Deliberative Mini–Publics Shape Public Policy?' (2015) 23 *Journal of Political Philosophy* 40–63.

Lafont, C, *Democracy without Shortcuts: A Participatory Conception of Deliberative Democracy* (Oxford, Oxford University Press, 2020).

Lamb, R, 'Recent Developments in the Thought of Quentin Skinner and the Ambitions of Contextualism' (2009) 3 *Journal of the Philosophy of History* 246–65.

Lanni, A, 'Judicial Review and the Athenian "Constitution"' (2010) 56 *Entretiens sur l'Antiquité Classique* 235–63.

Larmore, C, 'A Critique of Philip Pettit's Republicanism' (2001) 11 *Philosophical Issues* 229–43.

Larmore, C, 'Liberal and Republican Conceptions of Freedom' (2003) 6 *Critical Review of International Social and Political Philosophy* 96–119.

Laslett, P, 'The Face to Face Society' in P Laslett (ed), *Philosophy, Politics and Society*, ed, P Laslett (Oxford, Basil Blackwell & Mott, 1957) 157–71.

LeMahieu, DL, *The Mind of William Paley: A Philosopher and His Age* (Lincoln, University of Nebraska Press, 1976).

Levy, R, 'Breaking the Constitutional Deadlock: Lessons from Deliberative Experiments in Constitutional Change' (2010) 34 *Melbourne University Law Review* 805–38.

Lim, B, *Australia's Constitution after Whitlam* (Cambridge, Cambridge University Press, 2017).

Lind, J, *Three Letters to Dr Price* (London, T Payne, J Sewell, and P Elmsly, 1776).

List, C and Valentini, L, 'Freedom as Independence' (2016) 126 *Ethics* 1043–74.

Locke, J, *Two Treatises of Government*, ed, P Laslett, 2nd edn (Cambridge, Cambridge University Press, 1967) 285–446.

Long, D, *Bentham on Liberty: Jeremy Bentham's Idea of Liberty in Relation to His Utilitarianism* (Toronto, University of Toronto Press, 1977).

Lovett, F, *A General Theory of Domination and Justice* (New York, Oxford University Press, 2010).

Lovett, F, 'Harrington's Empire of Law' (2012) 60 *Political Studies* 59–75.

Lovett, F, 'Non–Domination' in D Schmidtz and C Pavel (eds), *The Oxford Handbook of Freedom* (Oxford, Oxford University Press, 2018) 106–20.

Lovett, F, 'Republicanism and Democracy Revisited' in Y Elazar and G Rousselière (eds), *Republicanism and the Future of Democracy* (Cambridge, Cambridge University Press, 2019) 117–29.

Luskin, R, Fishkin, J and Jowell, R, 'Considered Opinions: Deliberative Polling in Britain' (2002) 32 *British Journal of Political Science* 455–87.

Lynd, S, *Intellectual Origins of American Radicalism* (Cambridge, Mass., Harvard University Press, 1968).

MacCallum, G, 'Negative and Positive Freedom' (1967) 76 *Philosophical Review* 312–34.

Macey, J, 'The Missing Element in the Republican Revival' (1988) 97 *Yale Law Journal* 1673–84.

Machiavelli, N, *The Prince* [1532], eds, Q Skinner and R Price (Cambridge, Cambridge University Press, 1988).

MacIntyre, A, *After Virtue* (London, Duckworth, 1987).

Macleod, E, 'British Spectators of the French Revolution: The View from across the Channel' (2013) 197 *Groeniek* 377–92.

Maddox, G, 'Constitution' in T Ball, J Farr and R Hanson (eds), *Political Innovation and Conceptual Change* (Cambridge, Cambridge University Press, 1989).

Maddox, G, 'The Limits of Neo–Roman Liberty' (2002) 23 *History of Political Thought* 418–31.

Manin, B, *The Principles of Representative Government* (Cambridge, Cambridge University Press, 1997).

Mansbridge, J, 'A "Selection Model" of Political Representation' (2009) 17 *Journal of Political Philosophy* 369–98.

Mansbridge, J, 'Deliberative Polling as the Gold Standard' (2010) 19 *The Good Society* 55–62.

Mansbridge, J et al, 'The Place of Self-Interest and the Role of Power in Deliberative Democracy' (2010) 18 *Journal of Political Philosophy* 64–100.

Martí, J and Pettit, P, *A Political Philosophy in Public Life: Civic Republicanism in Zapatero's Spain* (Princeton, Princeton University Press, 2010).

Maynor, J, *Republicanism in the Modern World* (Cambridge, Polity Press, 2003).

McAllister, I, 'Civic Education and Political Knowledge in Australia' (1998) 33 *Australian Journal of Political Science* 7–23.

McCormick, J, *Machiavellian Democracy* (New York, Cambridge University Press, 2011).

McPhee, P, *Robespierre: A Revolutionary Life* (New Haven, Conn., Yale University Press, 2012).

Mendelberg, T, 'The Deliberative Citizen: Theory and Evidence' in M Delli Carpini, L Huddy and R Shapiro (eds), *Political Decision-Making, Deliberation and Participation* (Bingley, Emerald, 2002) 151–93.

Merkle, D, 'The Polls – Review: The National Issues Convention Deliberative Poll' (1996) 60 *Public Opinion Quarterly* 588–619.

Michelman, F, 'The Supreme Court, 1985 Term – Foreword: Traces of Self-Government' (1986) 100 *Harvard Law Review* 4–77.

Michelman, F, 'Law's Republic' (1988) 97 *Yale Law Journal* 1493–1537.

Michelman, F, *Brennan and Democracy* (Princeton, NJ, Princeton University Press, 1999).

Mill, J, 'Essay on Government' [1820] in *Utilitarian Logic and Politics: James Mill's 'Essay on Government', Macauley's Critique and the Ensuing Debate*, eds, J Lively and J Rees (Oxford, Clarendon Press, 1978) 53–95.

Miller, D, *Market, State, and Community: Theoretical Foundations of Market Socialism* (Oxford, Clarendon Press, 1989).

Miller, P, 'Introduction' in J Priestley, *Political Writings*, ed, P Miller (Cambridge, Cambridge University Press, 1993) xi–xxviii.

Miller, P, *Defining the Common Good: Empire, Religion, and Philosophy in Eighteenth-Century Britain* (Cambridge, Cambridge University Press, 1994).

Mondak, J and Canache, D, 'Knowledge Variables in Cross-National Social Inquiry' (2004) 85 *Social Science Quarterly* 539–58.

Montesquieu, C, *The Spirit of the Laws* [1748], trans and eds, A Cohler, B Miller and H Stone (Cambridge, Cambridge University Press, 1989).

Mouritsen, P, 'Four Models of Republican Liberty and Self-Government' in I Honohan and J Jennings (eds), *Republicanism in Theory and Practice* (London, Routledge, 2006) 17–38.

Moyn, S, 'Before – and Beyond – the Liberalism of Fear' in S Ashenden and A Hess (eds), *Between Utopia and Realism: The Political Thought of Judith N. Shklar* (Philadelphia, Penn, University of Pennsylvania Press, 2019) 24–46.

Najemy, J, *Corporatism and Consensus in Florentine Electoral Politics, 1280-1400* (Chapel Hill, University of North Carolina Press, 1982).

Nelson, E, *The Greek Tradition in Republican Thought* (Cambridge, Cambridge University Press, 2004).

Nelson, E, 'One Concept Too Many?' (2005) 33 *Political Theory* 58–78.

Note: 'The Constitutional Status of Sexual Orientation: Homosexuality as a Suspect Classification' (1985) 98 *Harvard Law Review* 1285–1309.

O'Leary, K, *Saving Democracy: A Plan for Real Representation in America* (Stanford, Calif, Stanford University Press, 2006).

Oldfield, A, *Citizenship and Community: Civic Republicanism and the Modern World* (London, Routledge, 1990).

Page, A, '"A Species of Slavery": Richard Price's Rational Dissent and Antislavery, Slavery & Abolition' (2011) 32 *Slavery & Abolition* 53–73.

Paley, W, *The Principles of Moral and Political Philosophy* [1785], forward by DL Le Mahieu (Indianapolis, Ind., Liberty Fund, 2002).

Pateman, C, *The Sexual Contract* (Cambridge, Polity, 1988).

Patten, A, 'The Republican Critique of Liberalism' (1996) 26 *British Journal of Political Science* 25–44.

Patten, A, 'Liberal Neutrality: A Reinterpretation and Defense' (2012) 20 *Journal of Political Philosophy* 249–72.

Pettit, P, 'A Definition of Negative Liberty' (1989) II *Ratio* 153–68.

Pettit, P, 'Liberalism and Republicanism' (1993) 28 (Special Issue on Australia's Republican Question) *Australian Journal of Political Science* 162–89.

Pettit, P, *Republicanism: A Theory of Freedom and Government* (Oxford, Clarendon Press, 1997).

Pettit, P, 'Reworking Sandel's Republicanism' in A Allen and M Regan (eds), *Debating Democracy's Discontent: Essays on American Politics, Law, and Public Philosophy* (Oxford, Oxford University Press, 1998) 40–59.

Pettit, P, 'Republican Freedom and Contestatory Democratization' in I Shapiro and C Hacker–Cordón (eds), *Democracy's Value* (Cambridge, Cambridge University Press, 1999) 163–90.

Pettit, P, 'Republicanism: Once More with Hindsight' in *Republicanism: A Theory of Freedom and Government*, paperback edn (Oxford, Clarendon Press, 1999) 283–305.

Pettit, P, 'Minority Claims under Two Conceptions of Democracy' in D Ivison, P Patton and W Sanders (eds), *Political Theory and the Rights of Indigenous Peoples* (Cambridge, Cambridge University Press, 2000) 199–215.

Pettit, P, 'On *Republicanism*: Reply to Carter, Christman and Dagger' (2000) 9(3) *The Good Society* 54–7.

Pettit, P, 'Republican Liberty and Its Constitutional Significance' (2000) 25 *Australian Journal of Legal Philosophy* 237–56.

Pettit, P, *A Theory of Freedom: From the Psychology to the Politics of Agency* (Cambridge, Polity, 2001).

Pettit, P, 'Keeping Republican Freedom Simple: On a Difference with Quentin Skinner' (2002) 30 *Political Theory* 339–56.

Pettit, P, 'In Reply to Bader and Vatter' in M Williams and S Macedo (eds), *Political Exclusion and Domination* (New York, New York University Press, 2005) 182–8.

Pettit, P, 'The Determinacy of Republican Policy: A Reply to McMahon' (2006) 34 *Philosophy and Public Affairs* 275–83.

Pettit, P, 'Republican Freedom: Three Axioms, Four Theorems' in C Laborde and J Maynor (eds), *Republicanism and Political Theory* (Malden, MA, Blackwell, 2008) 102–30.

Pettit, P, *On the People's Terms: A Republican Theory and Model of Democracy* (New York, Cambridge University Press, 2012).

Pettit, P, *Just Freedom: A Moral Compass for a Complex World* (New York, WW Norton & Co, 2014).

Pettit, P, 'The General Will, the Common Good, and a Democracy of Standards' in Y Elazar and G Rousselière (eds), *Republicanism and the Future of Democracy* (Cambridge, Cambridge University Press, 2019) 13–40.

Philp, M, 'English Republicanism in the 1790s' (1998) 6 *Journal of Political Philosophy* 235–62.

Pierce, J, *Inside the Mason Court Revolution: The High Court of Australia Transformed* (Durham, NC, Carolina Academic Press, 2006).

Pitkin, H, 'The Idea of a Constitution' (1987) 37 *Journal of Legal Education* 167–9.

Pocock, JGA, *Virtue, Commerce, and History: Essays on Political Thought and History, Chiefly in the Eighteenth Century* (Cambridge, Cambridge University Press, 1985).

Pocock, JGA, *The Machiavellian Moment: Florentine Political Thought and the Atlantic Republican Tradition* [1975], with a new introduction by Richard Whatmore (Princeton, NJ, Princeton University Press, 2016).

Pocock, JGA, 'Afterword' [2003] in *The Machiavellian Moment: Florentine Political Thought and the Atlantic Republican Tradition*, 2nd edn (Princeton, NJ, Princeton University Press, 2016) 553–83.

Price, R, *Review of the Principal Questions in Morals* [1758], ed, D Raphael (Oxford, Clarendon Press, 1948).

Price, R, *Political Writings*, ed, DO Thomas (Cambridge, Cambridge University Press, 1991).

Price, R, *Additional Observations on the Nature and Value of Civil Liberty, and the War with America* (London, T Cadell, 1777).

Priestley, J, 'An Essay on the First Principles of Government' [2nd ed, 1771] in *Political Writings*, ed, P Miller (Cambridge, Cambridge University Press, 1993) 1–127.

Prokhovnik, R, 'An Interview with Quentin Skinner' (2011) 10 *Contemporary Political Theory* 273–85.

Raban, O, 'The Fallacy of Legal Certainty: Why Vague Legal Standards May Be Better for Capitalism and Liberalism' (2010) 19 *Public Interest Law Journal* 175–90.

Rahe, P, 'Situating Machiavelli' in J Hankins (ed), *Renaissance Civic Humanism: Reappraisals and Reflections* (Cambridge, Cambridge University Press, 2000) 270–308.

Ratnapala, S, 'Republicanism's Debt to Liberalism: Comments on Pettit' (2000) 25 *Australian Journal of Legal Philosophy* 263–71.

Rawls, J, *A Theory of Justice* (Oxford, Oxford University Press, 1972).

Raz, J, *The Morality of Freedom* (Oxford, Clarendon, 1986).

Raz, J, 'The Relevance of Coherence' (1992) 72 *Boston University Law Review* 273–321.

Reid, J, *The Concept of Liberty in the Age of the American Revolution* (Chicago, University of Chicago Press, 1988).

Remer, G, 'James Harrington's New Deliberative Rhetoric: Reflection of an Anticlassical Republicanism' (1995) 16 *History of Political Thought* 532–57.

Robespierre, M, 'On the Principles of Moral Policy That Ought to Guide the National Convention in the Internal Administration of the Republic' [1794] in R Bienvenu (ed), *The Ninth of Thermidor: The Fall of Robespierre*, ed, R Bienvenu (New York, Oxford University Press, 1968) 32–49.

Rodgers, D, 'Republicanism: The Career of a Concept' (1992) 79 *Journal of American History* 11–38.

Rogers, M, 'Republican Confusion and Liberal Clarification' (2008) 34 *Philosophy & Social Criticism* 799–824.

Rosen, F, *Bentham, Byron, and Greece: Constitutionalism, Nationalism, and Early Liberal Political Thought* (Oxford, Clarendon Press, 1992).

Rosen, F, 'Introduction' in *An Introduction to the Principles of Morals and Legislation*, eds, JH Burns and HLA Hart (Oxford, Clarendon Press, 1996) xxxi–lxix.

Rosenblum, N, *Membership and Morals: The Personal Uses of Pluralism in America* (Princeton, NJ, Princeton University Press, 1998).

Russell, P, 'Conclusion' in K Malleson and P Russell (eds), *Appointing Judges in an Age of Judicial Power: Critical Perspectives from around the World* (Toronto, University of Toronto Press, 2006) 420–35.

Sadurski, W, Review of *Not Just Deserts: A Republican Theory of Criminal Justice* by John Braithwaite and Philip Pettit (1991) 10 *Law and Philosophy* 221–34.

Sadurski, W, *Rights before Courts: A Study of Constitutional Courts in Postcommunist States of Central and Eastern Europe* (Dordrecht, Springer, 2005).

Sandel, M, *Democracy's Discontent: America in Search of a Public Philosophy* (Cambridge, Mass., Belknap Press of Harvard University Press, 1996).

Sandel, M, 'Reply to Critics' in A Allen and M Regan (eds), *Debating Democracy's Discontent: Essays on American Politics, Law, and Public Philosophy* (Oxford, Oxford University Press, 1998) 319–35.

Shaw, CK, 'Quentin Skinner on the Proper Meaning of Republican Liberty' (2003) 23 *Politics* 46–56.

Sherry, S, 'Civic Virtue and the Feminine Voice in Constitutional Adjudication' (1986) 72 *Virginia Law Review* 543–616.

Shklar, J, *Legalism: Law, Morals, and Political Trials*, 2nd edn (Harvard, Harvard University Press, 1986).

Shklar, J, 'The Liberalism of Fear' in N Rosenblum (ed), *Liberalism and the Moral Life* (Cambridge, Mass., Harvard University Press, 1989) 21–38.

Shklar, J, 'Political Theory and the Rule of Law' [1987] in S Hoffmann (ed), *Political Thought and Political Thinkers* (Chicago, University of Chicago Press, 1998) 21–37.

Shnarydermann, R, 'Liberal vs Republican Notions of Freedom' (2012) 60 *Political Studies* 44–58.

Sidgwick, H, *The Elements of Politics*, 2nd edn (London, Macmillan, 1897).

Sidney, A, *Discourses Concerning Government* [1698], ed, T West (Indianapolis, Liberty Fund, 1996).

Skinner, Q, 'Meaning and Understanding in the History of Ideas' (1969) 8 *History and Theory* 3–53.

Skinner, Q, *Foundations of Modern Political Thought*, vol 1: The Renaissance (Cambridge, Cambridge University Press, 1978).

Skinner, Q, 'The Paradoxes of Political Liberty' in S McMurrin (ed), *The Tanner Lectures on Human Values*, vol. VII (Cambridge, Cambridge University Press, 1986) 225–50.

Skinner, Q, 'Meaning and Understanding in the History of Ideas' [1969] in J Tully (ed), *Meaning and Context: Quentin Skinner and His Critics* (Cambridge, Polity Press, 1988) 29–67.

Skinner, Q, 'A Reply to My Critics' in J Tully (ed), *Meaning and Context: Quentin Skinner and His Critics* (Cambridge, Polity Press, 1988) 231–88.

Skinner, Q, 'The Republican Ideal of Political Liberty' in G Bock, Q Skinner and M Viroli (eds), *Machiavelli and Republicanism* (Cambridge, Cambridge University Press, 1990) 293–309.

Skinner, Q, *Liberty before Liberalism* (Cambridge, Cambridge University Press, 1998).

Skinner, Q, 'Classical Liberty and the Coming of the English Civil War' in M van Gelderen and Q Skinner (eds), *Republicanism: A Shared European Heritage*, vol. II: The Values of Republicanism in Early Modern Europe (Cambridge, Cambridge University Press, 2002) 9–28.

Skinner, Q, 'The Idea of Negative Liberty: Machiavellian and Modern Perspectives' in *Visions of Politics*, vol. II: Renaissance Virtues (Cambridge, Cambridge University Press, 2002) 186–212.

Skinner, Q, 'Machiavelli on *Virtù* and the Maintenance of Liberty' in *Visions of Politics*, vol. II: Renaissance Virtues (Cambridge, Cambridge University Press, 2002) 160–85.

Skinner, Q, 'A Third Concept of Liberty' (2002) *Proceedings of the British Academy* 237–65.

Skinner, Q, 'Freedom as the Absence of Arbitrary Power' in C Laborde and J Maynor (eds), *Republicanism and Political Theory* (Malden, MA, Blackwell, 2008) 83–101.

Skinner, Q, *Hobbes and Republican Liberty* (Cambridge, Cambridge University Press, 2008).

Skinner, Q, 'On the Slogans of Republican Political Theory' (2010) 9 *European Journal of Political Theory* 95–102.

Skinner, Q, 'Freedom of Inclination: On the Republican Theory of Liberty' (2014) 21 *Juncture* 131–35.

Somin, I, 'Political Ignorance and the Countermajoritarian Difficulty: A New Perspective on the Central Obsession of Constitutional Theory' (2004) 89 *Iowa Law Review* 1287–1371.

Somin, I, *Democracy and Political Ignorance: Why Smaller Government Is Smarter* (Stanford, Stanford University Press, 2013).

Sparling, R, 'Political Corruption and the Concept of Dependence in Republican Thought' (2013) 41 *Political Theory* 618–47.

Spector, H, 'Judicial Review, Rights, and Democracy' (2003) 22 *Law and Philosophy* 285–334.

Spector, H, 'The Right to a Constitutional Jury' (2009) III *Legisprudence* 111–123.

Spector, H, 'The Theory of Constitutional Review' in M Jovanović (ed), *Constitutional Review and Democracy* (The Hague, Eleven International Publishing, 2015) 17–37.

Spitz, J–F, 'The Concept of Liberty in "A Theory of Justice" and Its Republican Version' (1994) 7 *Ratio Juris* 331–47.

Springborg, P, *Western Republicanism and the Oriental Prince* (Cambridge, Polity Press, 1992).

Springborg, P, 'Republicanism, Freedom from Domination, and the Cambridge Contextual Historians' (2001) 49 *Political Studies* 851–76.

Springborg, P, *Mary Astell: Theorist of Freedom from Domination* (Cambridge, Cambridge University Press, 2005).

Spry, M, 'Executive and High Court Appointments' in G Lindell and B Bennet (eds), *Parliament: The Vision in Hindsight* (Sydney, Federation Press, 2001) 419–53.

Stephen, J, *Liberty, Equality, Fraternity* [1874], ed, R White (Cambridge, Cambridge University Press, 1967).

Sturgis, P, Allum, N and Smith, P, 'The Measurement of Political Knowledge in Surveys' (2008) 72 *Public Opinion Quarterly* 90–102.

Sturgis, P, Roberts, C and Allum, N, 'A Different Take on the Deliberative Poll: Information, Deliberation, and Attitude Constraint' (2005) 69 *Public Opinion Quarterly* 30–65.

Sullivan, V, 'Machiavelli's Momentary "Machiavellian Moment": A Reconsideration of Pocock's Treatment of the *Discourses*' (1992) 20 *Political Theory* 309–18.

Sullivan, V, 'The Civic Humanist Portrait of Machiavelli's English Successors' (1994) 15 *History of Political Thought* 73–96.

Sullivan, V, *Machiavelli, Hobbes, and the Formation of a Liberal Republicanism in England* (Cambridge, Cambridge University Press, 2004).

Sunstein, C, 'Interest Groups in American Public Law' (1985) 38 *Stanford Law Review* 29–87.

Sunstein, C, 'Beyond the Republican Revival' (1988) 97 *Yale Law Journal* 1539–90.

Sunstein, C, *The Partial Constitution* (Cambridge, Mass., Harvard University Press, 1993).

Sunstein, C, 'Group Judgments: Statistical Means, Deliberation, and Information Markets' (2005) 80 *New York University Law Review* 962–1049.

Sutherland, K, *A People's Parliament: A (Revised) Blueprint for a Very English Revolution* (Exeter, Imprint Academic, 2008).

Swift, A, 'Response to Spitz' (1994) 7 *Ratio Juris* 349–52.

Taylor, C, 'What's Wrong with Negative Liberty' in A Ryan (ed), *The Idea of Freedom: Essays in Honour of Isaiah Berlin* (Oxford, Oxford University Press, 1979) 175–193.

Taylor, C, 'The Diversity of Goods' in A Sen and B Williams (eds), *Utilitarianism and Beyond* (Cambridge, Cambridge University Press, 1982) 129–44.

Taylor, C, 'Kant's Theory of Freedom' in *Philosophy and the Human Sciences: Philosophical Papers*, vol. 2 (Cambridge, Cambridge University Press, 1985) 318–37.

Thomas, DO, *The Honest Mind: The Thought and Work of Richard Price* (Oxford, Clarendon Press, 1977).

Tomkins, A, *Our Republican Constitution* (Oxford, Hart Publishing, 2005).

Tribe, L, *American Constitutional Law* (Mineola, NY, Foundation Press, 1978).

Tribe, L, 'The Puzzling Persistence of Process-Based Constitutional Theories' (1980) 89 *Yale Law Journal* 1063–80.

Tushnet, M, *Red, White, and Blue: A Critical Analysis of Constitutional Law* (Cambridge, Mass., Harvard University Press, 1988).

Tushnet, M, 'Social Welfare Rights and the Forms of Judicial Review' (2004) 82 *Texas Law Review* 1895–1919.

Tushnet, M, *Weak Courts, Strong Rights: Judicial Review and Social Welfare Rights in Comparative Constitutional Law* (Princeton, Princeton University Press, 2008).

Tyler, T, *Why People Obey the Law* (New Haven, Yale University Press, 1990).

van Parijs, P, *Real Freedom for All. What (If Anything) Can Justify Capitalism?* (Oxford, Clarendon Press, 1995).

van Parijs, P, 'Contestatory Democracy Versus Real Freedom for All' in I Shapiro and C Hacker-Cordón (eds), *Democracy's Value* (Cambridge, Cambridge University Press, 1999) 191–98.

van Gelderen, M and Skinner, Q (eds), *Republicanism: A Shared European Heritage*, vol. 1: Republicanism and Constitutionalism in Early Modern Europe. (Cambridge, Cambridge University Press, 2002).

Vatter, M, 'Political Ontology, Constituent Power, and Representation' (2015) 18 *Critical Review of International Social and Political Philosophy* 679–86.

Viroli, M, *Republicanism*, trans, A Shugaar (New York, Hill and Wang, 2002).

Volk, C, *Arendtian Constitutionalism: Law, Politics and the Order of Freedom* (Oxford, Hart Publishing, 2015).

Waldron, J, 'Homelessness and the Issue of Freedom' (1991–92) 39 *University of California Law Review* 295–324.

Waldron, J, *Law and Disagreement* (New York, Oxford University Press, 1999).

Waldron, J, 'The Core of the Case against Judicial Review' (2006) 115 *Yale Law Journal* 1346–1406.

Wall, S, *Liberalism, Perfectionism and Restraint* (Cambridge, Cambridge University Press, 1998).

Wall, S, 'Neutralism for Perfectionists: The Case of Restricted State Neutrality' (2010) 120 *Ethics* 232–56.

Warren, M and Pearce, H (eds), *Designing Deliberative Democracy: The British Columbia Citizens' Assembly*. (Cambridge, Cambridge University Press, 2008).

Weinstein, WL, 'The Concept of Liberty in Nineteenth Century English Political Thought' (1965) 13 *Political Studies* 145–62.

Werhan, K, 'Popular Constitutionalism, Ancient and Modern' (2012) 46 *UC Davis Law Review* 65–131.

Whereas the People: Civics and Citizenship Education, Report of the Civics Expert Group, (Canberra, Australian Government Publishing Service, 1994).

White, GE, 'Reflections on the "Republican Revival": Interdisciplinary Scholarship in the Legal Academy' (1994) 6 *Yale Journal of Law & the Humanities* 1–35.

Whittington, K, 'Constitutionalism' in K Whittington, R Kelemen and G Caldeira (eds), *Oxford Handbook of Law and Politics* (Oxford, Oxford University Press, 2008) 281–99.

Williams, G and Hume, D, *Human Rights under the Australian Constitution*, 2nd edn (Melbourne, Oxford University Press, 2013).

Winterton, G, 'An Australian Rights Council' (2001) 24 *University of New South Wales Law Journal* 792–9.

Wolin, S, 'Norm and Form: The Constitutionalizing of Democracy' in J Euben, J Wallach and J Ober (eds), *Athenian Political Thought and the Reconstruction of American Democracy* (Ithaca, NY, Cornell University Press, 1994) 29–58.

Wootton, D, 'Introduction' in N Machiavelli, *The Prince*, trans and ed, D Wootton (Indiana, Hackett Publishing, 1995) xi–xliv.

Wootton, D, Review of *Republicanism: A Shared European Heritage* edited by M van Gelderen and Q Skinner (2005) 120 *English Historical Review* 135–39.

Yack, B, 'Liberalism without Illusions: An Introduction to Judith Shklar's Political Thought' in B Yack (ed), *Liberalism without Illusions: Essays on Liberal Theory and the Political Vision of Judith N Shklar* (Chicago, University of Chicago Press, 1996) 1–13.

Zines, L, 'Legalism, Realism and Judicial Rhetoric in Constitutional Law' (2002) 5 *Constitutional Law and Policy Review* 21–30.

Zurn, C, *Deliberative Democracy and the Institutions of Judicial Review* (New York, Cambridge University Press, 2006).

Zurn, C, 'Judicial Review, Constitutional Juries and Civic Constitutional Fora: Rights, Democracy and Law' (2011) 58 *Theoria* 63–94.

INDEX

www.ingramcontent.com/pod-product-compliance
Lightning Source LLC
Chambersburg PA
CBHW050416280326
41932CB00013BA/1882